LANDSCAPES OF STRUGGLE

PITT LATIN AMERICAN SERIES

George Reid Andrews, General Editor

LANDSCAPES OF STRUGGLE

Politics, Society, and Community in El Salvador

Edited by Aldo Lauria-Santiago and Leigh Binford

University of Pittsburgh Press

Published by the University of Pittsburgh Press, Pittsburgh, Pa., 15260
Copyright © 2004, University of Pittsburgh Press
Manufactured in the United States of America
Printed on acid-free paper
10   9   8   7   6   5   4   3   2   1

LIBRARY OF CONGRESS CATALOGING-IN-PUBLICATION DATA

Landscapes of struggle : politics, society, and community in
El Salvador / edited by Aldo Lauria-Santiago and Leigh Binford.

p.   cm. — (Pitt Latin American series)
Includes bibliographical references and index.
ISBN 0-8229-4224-0 (cloth : alk. paper)
ISBN 0-8229-5838-4 (pbk. : alk. paper)
1. El Salvador—History—20th century. 2. El Salvador—
History, Local. 3. El Salvador—Social conditions—20th century.
I. Lauria-Santiago, Aldo. II. Binford, Leigh, 1948– III. Series.
F1488.L36 2004
972.8405'2—dc22

2003021182

Contents

Abbreviations

ADC   Democratic Peasant Alliance (Alianza Democrática Campesina)

ADESCO   Community Development Associations (Asociación de Desarollo Comunal)

ANTA   National Association of Agricultural Workers (Asociación Nacional de Trabjadores del Campo)

ARENA   Nationalist Republican Alliance (Alianza Republicana Nacionalista)

ATAES   Association of Agricultural Workers of El Salvador (Asociación de Trabajadores Agropecuarios de El Salvador)

ATM   Workers Association of Morazán (Asociación de Trabajadores de Morazán)

BPR   Popular Revolutionary Block (Bloque Popular Revolucionario)

CCR   Coordinator of Communities in Development of Chalatenango (Coordinadora de Comunidades en Desarrollo Chalatenango, formerly Coordinadora de Comunidades de Repoblaciones)

CEBs   Christian Base Communities (Comunidades Eclesiales de Base)

CGS   General Confederation of Unions (Confederacíon General de Sindicatos)

CNR   National Coordinator of Repopulation (Coordinadora Nacional de Repoblacíon)

CONADES   National Commission for Aid to the Displaced of El Salvador (Comisión Nacional de Asistencia a los Desplazados de El Salvador)

CORDES   Foundation for Cooperation and Community Development of El Salvador (Fundación para la Cooperación y el Desarrollo Comunal de El Salvador)

CRIPDES   Christian Committee for the Displaced (Comité Cristiano Pro Desplazados de El Salvador)

CROS   Salvadoran Committee for Union Reorganization (Comité de Reogranización Sindical Salvadoreño)

ERP   People's Revolutionary Army (Ejercito Revolucionario Popular)

FECCAS   Christian Federation of Salvadoran Peasants (Federacion Cristiana de Campesinos Salvadoreños)

FINATA   National Financial Institute for Agricultural Lands (Financiera de Tierras Agricolas)

FMLN   Farabundo Martí National Liberation Front (Frente Farabundo Marti para la Liberación Nacional)

FPL   Popular Forces of Liberation (Fuerzas Populares de la Liberación)

FRTS   Regional Federation of Workers of El Salvador (Federación Regional de Trabajadores de El Salvador)

FSM   Segundo Montes Foundation (Fundación Segundo Montes)

FUNDASAL   Salvadoran Foundation for Development and Housing (Fundación Salvadoreña de Desarrollo y Vivienda Minima)

FUNDE   National Foundation for Development (Fundacion Nacional para el Desarrollo)

FUSADES   Salvadoran Foundation for Economic and Social Development (La Fundación Salvadoreña para el Desarrollo Económico y Social)

ICR   Institute for Rural Colonization (Instituto de Colonización Rural)

ISTA   Salvadoran Institute for Agrarian Transformation (Instituto Salvadoreño de Transformación Agraria)

IWGIA   International Working Group for Indigenous Affairs

NGO   Nongovernmental Organization

NRP   National Reconstruction Plan

ONUSAL   UN Observer Mission in El Salvador

ORDEN   Democratic Nationalist Organization (Organización Democrática Nacionalista)

PCN   National Conciliation Party (Partido de Conciliacíon Nacional)

PD   Social Democratic Party (Partido Democratico)

PDC   Christian Democrat Party (Partido Demócrata Cristiano)

PDHS   Sustainable Human Development Program (Programa de Desarrollo Humano Sostenible)

PN   National Police (Policía Nacional)

PNC   National Civilian Police (Policía Nacional Civil)

PPLs   *poderes populares locales* (FMLN-organized community structures)

PRI   Institutional Revolutionary Party (Partido Revolucionario Institucional)

Pro-Patria   National Party of the Fatherland (Partido Nacional Pro-Patria)

PRUD   Salvadoran Revolutionary Party of Democratic Unification (Partido Revolucionario de Unificacíon Democrática)

PTT   Land Transfer Program (Programa de Transferencia de Tierras)

SAA   Secretariat of Agrarian Affairs

UCA   Central American University

UFT   Fraternal Union of Workers (Unión Fraternal de Trabajadores)

UN   United Nations

UNDP   UN Development Program

UNT   National Union of Workers (Unión Nacional de Trabajadores)

UPR   "United to Reconstruct" campaign *(unidos para reconstruir)*

USAID   U.S. Agency for International Development

UTC   Union of Farm Workers (Union de Trabajadores del Campo)

Aldo Lauria-Santiago and Leigh Binford

Local History, Politics, and the State in El Salvador

Most North Americans came to be aware of El Salvador in the 1980s during its revolutionary civil war and the subsequent involvement of the U.S. government. El Salvador, one of the smallest and most densely populated of the Latin American republics, was torn by intense social and military conflict during the 1980s, as were other countries in the region. The conflict resulted in a slow and contradictory movement away from authoritarian, military rule, partially as a result of Peace Accords between the government and the rebel Farabundo Martí National Liberation Front (Frente Farabundo Marti para la Liberación Nacional, FMLN) in 1992.

In the aftermath of the political settlement, the military was restructured and at least formally removed from the political system; consequently, El Salvador entered the path of "transition" to electoral democracy. Ex-guerrillas transformed the FMLN into a political party (known by the same name) and became major players in the electoral politics of the country, winning most of the nation's largest municipalities and thirty-one of the eighty-two positions in the National Assembly in national elections in 2000. However, elections and political liberalization have not resolved most of the nation's chronic prewar social and economic problems. Income is highly concentrated, and, despite postwar redistribution of 12 percent of the agricultural land, landlessness and low wages remain facts of life for most Salvadorans. During the war the United States became a magnet for many people fleeing government repression, combat, and economic dislocation; after the peace settlement, Salvadorans continued to move north, as migration and a transnational diaspora became central features of Salvadoran life, with even remote villages incorporated into migratory circuits (see David Pedersen's chapter). One of the goals of this book is to make some of the complex aspects of the Salvadoran experience before, during, and after the civil war visible to other Latin Americanists and also to encourage further studies about this country and its people.

Observers often find a paradox when trying to understand El Salvador's recent history. On the one hand El Salvador seems to be a nation without history—that is, its people, institutions, and government have only a weak and fragmented sense of their own past. Yet El Salvador often appears to be deeply, even overly, engaged with its "rootedness," with a sense that where it is now and where it has been lately are all tightly determined by its past, a past in which things are known to have occurred but remain for the more demanding observer elusively ambiguous and vague. The chapters in this book set out to navigate the terrain created by this paradox, as they explore small pieces of El Salvador's history, both recent and centuries old. The authors shed light on local experiences that address familiar themes in the study of El Salvador, but they go beyond these themes to pose new questions and research agendas.

El Salvador is Latin America's least researched nation-state, perhaps because of the perceived absence of a large, visible, and "exotic" indigenous population to attract the attention of foreign anthropologists, as occurred in southern Mexico and Guatemala. El Salvador's indigenous people and cultures have been "hidden" behind the experience of actual *mestizaje* and the myth of their past or persistent de-indianization (see Henrik Ronsbo's chapter).[1] A contributing factor has been the limited sociological and anthropological training available in the country. As of the late 1990s there existed no university degree-granting program in anthropology,[2] and training in sociology remained highly abstract and theoretical, rarely leading to in-depth fieldwork or research.

Historical studies have not fared any better than sociological and anthropological studies. The country's authoritarian legacy contributed to a weak historiographical tradition and limited programs in higher education. The first bachelor's-level degree *(licenciatura)* in history was introduced at the National University of El Salvador only in 2002. More generally, the country's elites displayed little interest in investing in academic infrastructure—which might have helped develop a stronger national dialogue and research about the country's history—for they educated their own children outside of the country.[3] Nor did the military, during its almost fifty years of rule (1932–1979), provide the basis for even a minimal research agenda into the country's history. A condition of "weak hegemony" made it clear to elites of both civilian and military stripe that achieving political hegemony through the study and postulation of a national culture and history would fail. Elite disinterest in historical work offered free rein for the urban Left, mainly in the person of the multitalented Roque Dalton (poet, historian, sociologist), who published a series of books in which he offered general but informed and critical Marxian interpretations of El Salvador's history from the conquest to the writer's present.[4]

Interest in Central America expanded in the 1980s, and outside observers generated hundreds of new studies on Nicaragua, Guatemala, Honduras, and Costa Rica; but El Salvador only fell further behind as war and repression kept away most foreign researchers, disrupted local educational institutions, and forced the emigration of many college-age youth and established academics. Scholars addressing the conflict did produce an array of publications that posed crucial questions, mostly related to the sources of political and social conflict in the country; however, the limited previous work and the practical impossibility of carrying out empirical research in the midst of a civil war affected the answers, as did the exigencies of the political situation itself. At least in the United States, much wartime social, political, and economic analysis was written by journalists, political scientists, and human rights activists and was pitched at a high level of generalization and abstraction with little attention given to local and regional differences within El Salvador.[5] Books bore such titles as *El Salvador: The Face of Revolution, Weakness and Deceit: U.S. Policy and El Salvador,* and *El Salvador: Background to the Crisis.* These analysts strove to explain the conflict to a U.S. public whose government would eventually invest $6 billion to prevent an FMLN vic-

El Salvador

Heads of State in El Salvador, 1894–Present

Head of state	Year assumed power	Head of state	Year assumed power
Rafael Antonio Gutiérrez	1894	Osmin Aguirre y Salinas	1944
Tomás Regalado	1898	Salvador Castañeda	1945
Pedro José Escalón	1903	Directorio Civil y Militar	1948
Fernando Figueroa	1907	Oscar Osorio	1950
Manuel Enrique Araujo	1911	José María Lémus	1956
Carlos Meléndez	1913	Junta	1960
Alfonso Quiñónez Molina	1914	Directorio	1961
Carlos Meléndez	1915	Julio A. Rivera	1962
Alfonso Quiñónez Molina	1918	Fidel Sanchez Hernández	1967
Jorge Menéndez	1919	Arturo Armando Molina	1972
Alfonso Quiñónez Molina	1923	Carlos Humberto Romero	1977
Pio Romero Bosque	1927	Junta Revolucionaria de Gobierno	1979
Arturo Araujo	1931	José Napoleon Duarte	1980
Military Directorate	1931	Alvaro Magaña	1982
Maximiliano Hernández Martínez	1932	José Napoleón Duarte	1984
Andres Ignacio Menéndez	1934	Alfredo Felix Cristiani	1989
Maximiliano Hernández Martínez	1935	Armando Calderón Sol	1994
Andrés Ignacio Menendez	1944	Francisco Flores Perez	1999

tory while tolerating (if not facilitating) massive human rights violations by the state institutions it financed. Given the crisis on the ground—particularly in the early 1980s when the Salvadoran military and death squads linked to it were murdering tens of thousands of unarmed and often politically unaffiliated civilians—the differences between, on the one hand, peasants and rural workers in the rugged northern areas bordering Honduras and, on the other, those residing in the highly capitalized South Coast regions of Usulután and San Miguel Departments *seemed* of minor importance. But even had investigators wished to discuss social, economic, and cultural specificities—which would undoubtedly have enriched our understanding of the conflict—they would have encountered problems arising from the dearth of previous local historical, sociological, and ethnographic research.

The 1970s and early to mid-1980s did produce a limited number of competent studies that considerably influenced our intellectual understanding of Salvadoran history and society. For instance, William Durham's *Scarcity and Survival in Central America* drew on detailed cultural ecological studies of Tenancingo, El Salvador, and Langue, Honduras, as the basis for an alternative to mainstream explanations of the 1969 "Soccer War" between El Salvador and Honduras; and Jesuit priest and sociologist Segundo Montes (murdered by the army along with five of his compatriots, their housekeeper, and her daughter on November 16, 1989) wrote a respectable book on *compadrazgo,* which analyzed the role of ritual coparenthood in the maintenance of local political power in four indigenous municipalities of the departments of Ahuachapan and Sonsonate.[6] More important than either of these, however, was Rafael Cabarrús's *Genesis de una Revolución,* published in 1983 by La Casa Chata, a small Mexican press. *Genesis* contained a nuanced analysis of economic relations and peasant mobilization in the Aguilares region on the eve of the revolution.[7] Earlier, historian Thomas P. Anderson published *Matanza,* still the most complete study of the 1932 popular rebellion and the brutal massacres that followed its suppression by government forces, and David Browning's pioneering work on land and geography contains important research leads into the post–World War II agrarian landscape that warrant close attention by researchers.[8]

To the studies just cited we would add Jenny Pearce's important study of peasant rebellion in Chalatenango, much of which was based on interviews carried out behind guerrilla lines.[9] But, on the whole, detailed local and regional historical and social scientific work awaited the end of the conflict and the arrival to El Salvador of a new generation of students and researchers with the time, resources (financial and otherwise), and institutional contacts to plan and carry out research projects, often as part of postgraduate training in U.S. universities. In many instances foreign investigators' interest in El Salvador grew out of their participation in the U.S.-Central America solidarity movement, which worked to stop U.S. intervention in the region during the 1980s.[10] These investigators eschewed the broad political science approach in order to study relations before, during, and after the conflict in particular areas of the country and by examining specific institutions; in other words, they spent considerable time "in the field" or, what might be considered the historian's equivalent, in the archives. Because their work set the stage for the research presented here, we briefly review some of the more trenchant contributions of the 1990s.[11]

Lauria-Santiago's research on the peasantry and agrarian social relations during the nineteenth and early twentieth centuries demonstrates the need to properly contextualize the political behavior of local actors with a deep examination of the history of local landowning, production, class relations, and the often-unpredictable linkages between local politics and national politics. More recently, his joint work with Jeffrey Gould has melded oral histories with archival sources and produced a more complex and nuanced interpretation of the social movements that led to the 1932 revolt.[12] Patricia Alvarenga has opened up the relationship between local peasants and communities and the policing and judicial networks of state power to careful study. She examines the role of peasants in networks of power and authority that tied them to a national state too decentralized to organize its own direct policing apparatus but sufficiently connected to local administrators, conflicts, and disputes to recognize the need for close relationships with local people. While her conclusions about the class basis of the state and the goals of local policing might be questioned, her work provides an important guide to researchers of local communities especially regarding the conflicted loyalties of peasants when confronted with the judicial system.[13]

Erik Ching's studies of local networks of power and patronage trace the continuities of political authority and factional networks in various western municipalities during the civilian and military governments of the 1920s and 1930s. Ching notes how politics at the municipal and regional levels have always been complex and open to corruption and bossism but there are also local examples of political insurgency. Ching also documents how the leaders of indigenous political factions resisted and adapted to the demands and impositions of local ladino power holders and national state policies, even after the 1932 revolt and massacre.[14]

The military and its local roots emerges as a theme in the work of Philip Williams and Knut Walter. They treat the military as a multifaceted, internally heterogeneous institution with its own interests and motivations. They view militarization and demilitarization of different aspects of state and society as relative continuums rather than absolute outcomes. They use this approach to explain El Salvador's long-standing tradition of authoritarian politics—the military's "tutelary" power over the political system and their paramilitary networks of social control. In this light, civilian-military collaboration only further institutionalized the military's power. The authors suggest that the military's penetration of rural power networks was a major contributor to social control prior to 1979, a point that should stimulate additional investigation into regions and communities elsewhere in the country.[15]

More recently, and perhaps in somber contrast with Cabarrús's work of the late 1970s, Leigh Binford wrote an ethnography of El Mozote, Morazán. This work is an ethnography of a massacre. In a careful study that brings the people and community of El Mozote to life and questions the role of anthropologists as observers of state violence, Binford discusses features of kinship relations and agricultural organization of El Mozote as well as the connections through which some residents became linked to activist catechists, revolutionary organizations, and the government's counterinsurgency plans. In the process he avoids the sweeping, unsubstantiated generalizations that marred much earlier interpretations, a point we discuss briefly here.[16]

Rodolfo Cardenal shows how studying local communities can elucidate national politics. Like Cabarrús, Cardenal focused on the important (and perhaps unique in its polarized politics) municipality of Aguilares, in which peasant frustration and stratification intersected with church activism, revolutionary organizing, and state-led repression. But while Cabarrús employs an ethnographic process tantamount to "fieldwork under fire,"[17] Cardenal uses parish archives and news records to reconstruct the relationship between church, state repression, and peasant mobilization.[18]

Elisabeth J. Wood provides evidence not only of the persistent and dynamic relationship between revolutionary forces and sectors of the peasantry but also of the peasantry's ability to understand its own reality without outside or "push" factors. By carefully integrating a micro-level analysis of places and actors with a larger comparative framework for interpreting transitions to democracy, Wood's work bridges the difficult and often vulgarized links between macro-level arguments and local-level research.[19]

Other important investigations that articulate local situations and often analyze them in national (and even international) contexts include Mark Pedalty's study of international press coverage of the war, Serena Fogaroli and Sara Stowell's little known sociological study of postwar reconstruction in Tecoluca municipality (San Vicente Department), John Hammond's sociological survey of popular education, and the work of Mandy MacDonald and Mike Gatehouse and Steve Cagan and Beth Cagan on the Colomocagua refugee camp and the Salvadoran community of Ciudad Segundo Montes, which was created following the refugees' repatriation.[20]

Landscapes of Struggle combines locally oriented investigations by some of the scholars we have mentioned (Binford, Ching, Lauria-Santiago, Wood) with offerings from a new generation of researchers (Kowalchuk, Moodie, Pedersen, Ronsbo, Silber). Along with forming part of a continuing effort to broaden our knowledge of the country and its history—especially the areas outside the capital city—we seek through this volume to stimulate dialogue and intellectual exchange among historians and other social scientists, as occurred in Mexican studies following the publication of *Everyday Forms of State Formation*.[21] No well-trained contemporary anthropologist should undertake a study of El Salvador without delving heavily into the historical literature; no contemporary historian, working primarily from archives, should hazard interpretations without at least a basic acquaintance with the results of sociological and anthropological research. The current volume pursues these historical contextualizations, bringing to bear on them critical perspectives and debates that have been part of social and historical analysis of Latin American countries during the last decades but that have often been marginalized or absent from Salvadoran historiography and sociology/

anthropology. Although the authors in this volume treat very different themes from the perspectives of different disciplines and approaches, we consider the work as a whole an interdisciplinary dialogue that will inform future studies of El Salvador as well as Central America. It is the product of an unusual international collaboration among contributors based in Latin America (El Salvador, Costa Rica, and Mexico), the United States, and Europe (Denmark). We hope it will contribute to improving El Salvador's future insofar as a deep accounting of the past and a knowledge of the present are keys to doing so, particularly for El Salvador's people.

The Autonomy of Local Politics and Actors

Because of their generalized nature, studies of El Salvador have in the past generally failed to unravel how the familiar large-scale, state-centered, national-level processes have been assembled from local, small-scale interactions and actors. This oversight applies to all aspects of the country's history, including the origins and process of the civil war, the formation of the authoritarian military state, urban and rural class relations, and many other critical themes. As a result, we not only lack insight into "local" Salvadoran places, institutions, and experiences that might have arisen from this kind of research but we also have missed opportunities to reposit and reframe the larger, national perspectives.

Until recently scholars tended to view structure and agency as mutually exclusive rather than dialectically related points of departure. They treated classes and class fractions abstractly and used structuralist approaches to frame many debates over the causes of the Salvadoran revolution, giving little or no attention to specific local/regional social relations and their contradictory historical development. Analysts *presumed* that the spread of coffee cultivation led to the eradication of communal and peasant landholdings and their replacement with large-scale private coffee estates. They *assumed* that the government's massacre of 10,000 people in the wake of the 1932 rebellion crushed the ethnic identity of the remaining indigenous population. And a common logic, which contemporary research is only now beginning to address, held that the civil war of the 1980s was *exclusively* a product of growing landlessness and land poverty resulting from a combination of rapid postwar population growth, land concentration (particularly in the formerly sparsely inhabited South Coast), and the post-1969 disappearance of the Honduran safety valve; liberation theology was generally treated as an ideological matchstick that, combined with the positive example of the Cuban Revolution (and later the Sandinista defeat of Somoza's National Guard in Nicaragua), touched off the social time bomb.

The point is not that these explanations were entirely incorrect; each certainly contains elements of truth. But taken as unassailable generalizations rather than tentative hypotheses subject to further examination through archival investigation and fieldwork in specific regions and locales, they have impeded the advance of understanding by foreclosing the investigation of many key issues, some of which are taken up in this book. To take but one example, it made little sense to take local actors seriously as long as they were represented uniformly as "peasants" or "workers" and treated categorically as the unconscious bearers of structurally based processes, as opposed to social agents consciously maneuvering to realize ends that accorded with their particular experiences and interests. By contrast, different chapters here contest the simplicity of the above-mentioned "truisms" and provide nuanced analyses of previously oversimplified local and regional social relations and historical processes (see the chapters by Aldo Lauria-Santiago, Leigh Binford, and Henrik Ronsbo).

The chapters in this book take seriously the agency of peasants, workers, and other local actors, freeing them from the common teleological arguments about the character of Salvadoran politics and society. No matter how oppressive or repressive Salvadoran society might have been, the blanketlike power of elites and state-based institutions and discourses has been overstated; understanding the agency of popular sectors requires the kind of analysis and research presented in these chapters. Furthermore, the premise of much that has previously been written about the Salvadoran poor rests on alternating but equally flat images of peasants and rural workers: heroic fighter or stoic passive victims. But it would be better to approach El Salvador's "exceptional" countryside in the light of the many years of research into local agrarian patterns in other Latin American countries.[22] Framed in this way, El Salvador's agrarian exceptionalism might become merely a position among other similar experiences, but this also enhances the importance of studying local history in order to find the true sources of the country's uniqueness.

To reiterate, privileging deteriorating material conditions in the analysis of the civil war is not necessarily wrong, but such an approach cannot account for specific cases of collaboration with the state or opposition to it without the provision of a series of mediating concepts and the historical study of actors' maneuverings on local and regional fields of power. The analyses presented in this collection uncover the complex and contradictory operations of hegemony and counter-hegemony at particular times and places in the late nineteenth and twentieth centuries, embracing, therefore, prewar, wartime, and postwar El Salvador. They deal with the formal exercise of political power, but they also explain how such exercise is simultaneously founded on and resisted through more subtle social and cultural processes that have received scant attention in writings on El Salvador, which have been overly concerned with issues of structural and political violence. Victor Hugo Acuña Ortega and Erik Ching explain how patronage and clientelism allowed the government and military to forge links with the nascent middle classes and residents of rural communities, respectively, during the first half of the twentieth century; Kati Griffith and Leslie Gates analyze post–World War II military governments' manipulation of reigning gender ideologies in order to strengthen their hegemony over the organized working classes of San Salvador; and Leigh Binford discusses the roles played by rural catechist training centers in disseminating liberation theology into remote rural areas, where it challenged conservative religious discourses in areas with limited government presence.

The Postwar Reconfiguration of El Salvador

Almost half the contributions transcend the period of conflict in order to address the postwar (post-1992) situation. As we alluded to earlier, the country underwent a monumental, unplanned transformation as a consequence of the twelve-year civil war.[23] Large areas of conflictive zones were depopulated for more than a decade as hundreds of thousands of Salvadorans fled to urban centers and displaced persons and refugee camps or left the country entirely. Those who opted to return to their places of origin (see Elisabeth J. Wood's and Vincent J. McElhinny's chapters) tended to concentrate in settlements, which they perceived as "safer" than dispersing among households in the countryside, the prewar rural standard.[24] Others settled in San Salvador (whose population more than doubled), eking out a living in the burgeoning urban "informal" economy. Approximately 20 percent of the Salvadoran population still resides outside the country—mainly in the United States—remitting over a billion dollars annually, more than three times the foreign exchange generated by the crisis-ridden coffee industry. Contrary to predictions, privatization of state enterprises and economic liberalization, which have been accompanied by growing integration of Salvadoran and U.S. economies, have not improved the material situation of the majority of people but have had disastrous impacts both on small rural farmers, who cannot compete with heavily subsidized and industrialized U.S. agriculturalists, and on urban workers, who find it hard to survive on the low wages available in assembly plants or through petty commerce and service work. Poverty and desperation, youth alienation, the ready availability of weapons, and other factors contributed to an epidemic of criminal violence that touches all regions and social classes and has resulted in an annual homicide rate higher than during all but the worst years of the civil war.[25]

Much has been published assessing post-conflict reconstruction and the "transition to democracy" in general terms, but we still do not know very much about how particular groups of people in particular places negotiated the postwar years.[26] Several of the contributors to this collection carried out field research in the mid- to late 1990s directed specifically toward discerning this. We expect that most of them will eventually publish book-length accounts of the results of their work. Until that time, this collection provides a sampling of individual and group responses to complex postwar social situations that vary greatly from one place to another. In separate contributions several authors discuss the dialectic of political mobilization and demobilization in a resettled community in northern Morazán (Vince McElhinny); among NGOs, grassroots organizations, and communities in Chalatenango (Irina Silber); and in cooperatives in western El Salvador characterized by different levels of organization (Lisa Kowalchuk). Three other contributors (Henrik Ronsbo, David Pedersen, and Ellen Moodie) apply sophisticated forms of discourse analysis (that have made important in-roads in cultural anthropology but have seldom been used by investigators in El Salvador) to cases that turn around three issues that have become increasingly important in the last fifteen years: international migration, violence, and ethnicity. Collectively, these six contributions provide a good barometer of the impact of and response to the enormous changes that have occurred during the last ten years.

Following a loose historical format, this book is divided into three thematic/chronological sections, each of which is introduced by a brief discussion that summarizes the chapters therein. The first section contains new and often revisionist historical research into some of the most important themes of the 1890–1980 period. The second section revisits the civil war and key problems of the post–civil war period, including the social bases of support for the FMLN in different regions and the formation of postwar communities and identities. The final section provides innovative ethnographic discussions of three crucial themes of contemporary El Salvador that have important historical roots: violence, migration, and identity.

Linking the Local with the National—Prewar Salvadoran History Reconsidered

The process of researching Salvadoran history almost inevitably leads to revisionist claims. In a country with perhaps the weakest historiography in Latin America and at least as many standing myths as any, the need not only to reconsider accepted notions but also to carry out extensive empirical research could not be greater. Historical studies in El Salvador since the nineteenth century have rarely ventured beyond standard accounts of political or military narrative. During the 1970s a few Salvadoran intellectuals worked against the current and tried to understand some of the more crucial political crises in the country's past but usually without formal training in historical research and with little use of primary, especially archival, sources. War, repression, limited resources, and an official culture of resistance to looking closely at the past—the result of the impunity bred by a succession of repressive regimes—and the relative international isolation of El Salvador before 1979 have all contributed to the dearth of historical studies about this country.

Academics and political actors alike have contributed to perpetuating many unsubstantiated generalizations about Salvadoran history, especially those characterizing the country as an unchanging militarized farm run by a small oligarchy. The chapters in this section aim, in a restrained and careful way, to reposit both classic and revisionist historical questions about important issues for

El Salvador in the twentieth century. By linking relevant historical questions with empirical research these chapters suggest a larger agenda for investigation that may encourage others to continue working with similar materials.

The analyses presented here examine specific social sectors and processes that are part of the historiography of most Latin American countries—indigenous peasants, rural communities, urban workers, and middle sector artisans. These analyses are especially important because they attempt to identify the agency of Salvadorans without imposing overarching a priori explanatory schemes derived from the country's national-level political history. In doing so these chapters identify some of the ways in which solidarities and conflicts have emerged in El Salvador in different historical contexts. They also address how these social sectors have interacted with and influenced the formation of the national state and the local state, as clients, allies, or opponents. This theme in particular is extremely important to understanding the origins of El Salvador's civil war of the 1980s; it also begins to raise questions about the state's impact on different people over the years—a welcome addition to traditional state-centered analyses and narratives.

One of the goals of this volume is to enable readers to draw connections between the historical themes presented in this section and the more contemporary periods addressed in the chapters that follow. Another goal is to suggest ways for social scientists who examine contemporary problems to consider both the historical ruptures and the continuities in El Salvador's past; the analyses in this section provide a historical background that goes beyond the familiar, mechanical, and sketchy renditions of the past that so often pervade any discussion of the years before 1980. The historical chapters should serve to remind all historians working on El Salvador (and the rest of Latin America for that matter) not to ignore the ways in which large, long-term explanations are built from small, local experiences, including those of seemingly marginal people. Furthermore, despite the problems posed by the lack of sources, the chapters in this section provide case studies that should stimulate further integration of historical and contemporary themes in the study of local-state relations in El Salvador. Ultimately, the goal is to help break down the artificial distinctions that are often made between "contemporary" and "historical" studies precisely because this opposition is an obstacle to understanding the country and the experiences of its people.

Aldo Lauria-Santiago's chapter identifies the potential the study of local communities has for broadening our understanding of both the construction of national history and the complex entanglements of local actors as they struggled for land, political power, communal organization, and ethnic identity. The story of the indigenous population of Dolores Izalco has one foot in the nineteenth century and the other at the doorstep of the twentieth. By looking at how indigenous residents became individual peasant landowners (for the most part) Lauria-Santiago's analysis also helps us understand the setting within which local actors fought for control of local resources and how some of these actors became local representatives and mediators of the authority of the national state even while they constituted themselves as an emerging elite.

Eric Ching's chapter reminds us that all state politics are, to some extent, local. By examining the local roots of the Martínez regime and the incipient establishment of what would become a well-institutionalized authoritarian state, Ching's work urges us to look carefully at any regime connected to local actors through repression or patronage. Ching reconstructs the formative years of military rule, and his work should encourage others to reconstruct the local bases of more recent governments for which oral histories can be gathered.

Victor Hugo Acuña Ortega's chapter also contains important lessons for contemporary studies. By examining the middle sectors in what observers have all too often characterized as a starkly polarized social structure, he reminds us not only of the existence of middle sectors but also of their persistent political importance in establishing stability and legitimacy for a political and social order. His conclusion—that the middle sectors associated with La Concordia, an artisan's organization, while politically inclined did not seem to have much of a democratic disposition—should spur further work on these provincial middle sectors and their role as the "glue" holding localities to the national state.

Kati Griffith and Leslie Gates present an even more complex portrait of labor-state relations as a context for gender-role formation. Through their meticulous and ground-breaking research, they argue that agreement about gender categories and their operation in the workplace and in the larger society created a space for negotiation and cooperation between government officials and labor leaders in the 1950s and 1960s. Their careful use of news and government sources to gain insight into gender relations and women's role in the labor force should provide many clues for researchers focusing on other aspects of gender and women's experiences in El Salvador.

Carlos Benjamín Lara Martínez's contribution links the middle and late twentieth-century periods. His analysis also crosses the divide created by the pre– and post–revolutionary war periods. By examining a community of peasants created by reformist and development projects of the authoritarian governments of the 1940s–1950s he calls attention to this obscure period of the country's social and political history. The community he investigates escapes traditional perceptions of the structure of the Salvadoran countryside. Lara Martínez's study exposes the problems internal to peasant-run reforms in the context of limited and state-controlled social transformation and may provide lessons for the postrevolutionary period. Although the larger political context has changed, rural Salvadorans face many of the same economic dilemmas they faced prior to the revolution; a principal one is their having to choose between subsistence and commercial production, even when they are able to make decisions on their own about the use of the land and other resources.

Aldo Lauria-Santiago

Land, Community, and Revolt in Late Nineteenth-Century Indian Izalco

Instances of violence in the Indian communities of late nineteenth-century El Salvador have often been cited as evidence of popular opposition to the liberal state and resistance to the privatization of Indian-held lands. One such instance occurred on the night of November 14, 1898, when simmering resentments in the Indian community of Dolores Izalco (hereinafter simply Dolores) erupted in a violent confrontation. In addition to sixteen leaders, more than eighty men were involved in the fighting, and at least twenty-seven were captured by government authorities. One of the targets of the attack was Simeón Morán, a former administrator who had been responsible for partitioning the communal lands. Morán was killed along with members of his family and supporters, but more significance has been attributed to his having had a hand chopped off during the violence. This attack entered the historiographical record in a frequently cited account of Salvadoran nineteenth-century land issues: "The relationship of cause and effect between the loss of land and the rural workers' revolt is clear: in the revolt of 1898, for example, various judges who had divided public lands were punished by the severing of their hands, which they had used to measure and distribute the land of the rural workers."[1] Interpretations such as this stem from and contribute to the perpetuation of a relatively straightforward story: Indian communities supported themselves through subsistence agriculture, they came into conflict with the agro-export elites and their repressive state, they lost their lands when the liberal state enforced the dissolution of common lands, and they then revolted over the loss of these lands. The story thus constructed explains the 1898 attack on the supposedly ladino *juez partidor* (partitioning judge) as a defensive mechanism against the wholesale and violent appropriation of community lands by outside coffee oligarchs. Without doubt the privatization of communal lands is one of the most important transformations that has affected the history of El Salvador. However, I argue that conflicts over land tenure and the privatization process in El Salvador have long been misunderstood and misinterpreted, precisely because generalized accounts of the privatization process have rarely considered the internal dynamics of Indian communities and their complex political relationships with external forces.

This chapter presents new research on the implementation and consequences of the partition and privatization of Indian communal lands in El Salvador. By providing a close account of the internal conflicts and divisions over the partitioning of lands in Dolores, one of Izalco's two indigenous communities (the other was Asunción Izalco), it examines how the 1898 revolt grew out of complex local politics in Dolores. As reconstructed here, factional divisions within this growing and complex Indian community—factionalism that resulted from its decades-long involvement with commercial agriculture and regional political alliances—to a great extent determined how this community experienced the partitioning of its lands.[2] Previous accounts have considered the attack on the *juez partidor* in Dolores to have stemmed from a confrontation between Indian peasants and the state, but I argue that the confrontation emerged instead from the fragmentation of local ethnic solidarity and organization, which split the community into feuding factions that actively enlisted external social and political forces. The alliances made by local peasant leaders with local elites and entrepreneurs and with political actors at the regional and state level, as well as their own competitive ones, determined how the conflictive process of privatization played out. In the end, the demise of Dolores as an indigenous community was not simply the result of liberal reforms enforced by the state but was also predicated on the complex maze of interests, both internal and external, that ran through Izalco's two Indian communities, Dolores and Asunción, as they faced the privatization of their long-held lands.

Ethnicity and Agrarian Society in Izalco

Izalco is one of the largest municipalities in western El Salvador. In the mid-nineteenth century it contained the largest Indian settlement in the region and was surpassed in population only by the municipalities of Ahuachapán and Santa Ana. Izalco's long tradition of combining small-scale peasant agriculture with commercial production began in the sixteenth century and extended into the twentieth, despite the increased commercialization of agrarian society in the region. By 1900 there were a few *haciendas* in Izalco, having been formed by the subdivision of two older colonial-era estates. There were also a greater number of small peasant farms and a rapidly growing number of middle-sized commercial farms. While most local families held sufficient land for both subsistence and market production, a small but growing number of Izalco peasants began to work for wages on the *haciendas* and emerging commercial farms of the Sonsonate-Ahuachapán region. In part, peasants engaged in wage labor in order to complement their subsistence and commercial production; but during the 1880s and 1890s, the expanding role of wage work also reflected the impact of a deepening disparity in access to land and irrigation among both Indian and ladino peasants in Izalco. Izalco's ladino population—an ethnic category that in El Salvador included all non-Indians, including those "former Indians" who simply started to define themselves as ladinos—had grown steadily during the preceding half-century. Between 1850 and 1870, the percentage of the population identified as ladino increased significantly, and by the 1890s the approximately 9,000 inhabitants of Izalco were divided roughly equally between Indians and ladinos.[3] The ladinization of the population and its effects on land tenure were a source of increasing tensions and conflict throughout the century.

By the 1860s commercial agriculture and trade were flourishing in the region, and Izalco's large commercial feria was attracting many merchants.[4] Agricultural entrepreneurs in Izalco had embarked on efforts to produce coffee and sugar, and by the 1890s the municipality was a dynamic and diversified agricultural center that tied both ladino and Indian peasants to local and regional networks of trade, credit, labor, and land. In regard to its major commercial crops, in 1892 Izalco produced only a modest amount of coffee, about 150 tons, most of which was cultivated by small-scale growers, both Indian and ladino.[5] However, by the early twentieth century the bulk of Izalco's coffee was produced in the *hacienda* of El Sunza, which was owned by the Araujo family. Izalco's sugar production also increased, though its development seems to have preceded that of coffee by a couple of decades. Thus, in 1892 there were twelve medium-sized sugarcane farms and dozens of smaller farms (usually dedicated to the production of aguardiente or panela for local markets) in operation by 1892.[6] Yet despite the expansion of enterprises dedicated to sugar and coffee, these crops did not displace agricultural production for local consumption, and the region remained a net exporter of grains and other basic food products well into the twentieth century. Thus, even though Izalco participated in the expansion of export and commercial agriculture, its older patterns of subsistence agriculture, seasonal wage labor, and diverse peasant participation in local and regional markets remained important features of the local economy.

The politics of nineteenth-century economic development in the region must be understood in the context of historical patterns of land tenure. Throughout the colonial period, landownership was central to the status and identity of Izalco's Indian communities. Izalco had been composed of two distinct towns, each controlled by its own Indian community. After independence these two adjacent towns were united, separated, and finally reunited in a single municipality. Still, despite the establishment of a single municipal center and urban core, the two Indian communities, Asunción and Dolores, retained distinct identities, corporate representation, and control over local resources, which included two urban barrios, agricultural land, and irrigation systems.[7] Landownership provided the basis for Izalco's economic and political autonomy, and after independence command over this resource allowed the Indian communities to control the settlement of ladinos in the region. Before the 1850s Izalco's two Indian communities were adamant about keeping ladinos off their lands and out of municipal office—a goal not always achieved. Although before mid-century Indians did retain control over all common lands, after the 1850s the ladino population, including an emerging commercial elite, expanded, and ladinos came to control most seats in the municipal government, eventually acquiring control over the 70 *caballerías* (3,150 hectares) of municipal common lands known as *ejidos*.

In 1867 the second administration of President Francisco Dueñas (1863–1871) ordered the separation of municipal and community lands throughout the nation. While providing legal recognition and protection to community-based landholdings that fell outside municipal *ejido* lands, this act also facilitated ladino encroachment onto lands in Izalco. According to the new legislation, lands that were originally allocated to a town as part of an initial colonial land grant (usually 37 *caballerías,* 1,665 hectares) would be recognized as an *ejido* and managed by the municipal corporation, which could rent the land to any town resident or settler. Any additional lands purchased by or granted to groups of peasants, usually a long-standing ladino or Indian community, would continue to be collectively owned and controlled as communal lands. For Izalco, the effect of this legislation was to place *ejido* lands under ladino control by virtue of their hold on the municipal government. Actual compliance with the 1867 legislation took a few years in Izalco, but by 1870 Dolores and Asunción had moved to clarify their holdings and distinguish them from the municipal *ejidos,* which were now controlled by ladinos. For some time the ladino-controlled municipality had claimed rights over the Indian's communal lands and charged rent to their occupants. But after litigation in 1870, the Indian communities regained undisputed control over their lands (the excess beyond 37 *caballerías* that had belonged to Asunción and Dolores, which had been Izalco's original municipalities), and Indian tenants stopped paying the *canon* (land rent) to the municipality.[8] Together, the two Indian communities held almost 150 *caballerías* (6,750 hectares) of land, and the municipality controlled another 72 *caballerías* (3,240 hectares) as *ejidos*.[9] This placed both the municipality of Izalco and its two Indian communities among the largest holders of common lands in the country. By 1879 Izalco's extensive municipal *ejidos* had all been rented, often to ladino entrepreneurs and farmers from Izalco and Sonsonate who established farms and pastures in Izalco, generating a significant income that was controlled by the ladino municipal leaders.[10] Privately owned *haciendas* and farms made up the municipality's remaining 270 *caballerías* (12,150 hectares) of land.[11]

There is significant evidence that politically and economically successful *indígenas* detached themselves from their communities.[12] Although recently "ladinoized" *indígenas* continued to rent communal lands, some began to join the ranks of a growing ladino elite. Alongside this new elite were older ladino families (such as the Barrientos, Vega, and Herrera families) who continued as some of the principal tenants of both municipal and communal lands. Their initial wealth derived from commercial farms they had developed on the town's municipal *ejidos,* but they rapidly extended their operations into other financial ventures. During the twenty years from 1880 to 1900, they also came to control the extensive small-scale transactions in plots, loans, cash advances, and coffee and grain sales in which hundreds of Indian and ladino peasants from Izalco participated.[13] The significance of their activity was recognized in 1913 by the governor of Sonsonate, who attributed Izalco's "flowering progress" to the "many and very important ladino families who have managed to dominate the Indian masses, since for many years the local authorities have been composed of ladinos."[14]

Relations between Indian peasants and the ladino entrepreneurs who regularly attempted to use their control over the municipal government to favor their families and allies often turned conflictive and litigious.[15] But tensions related to access to land also existed within the Indian communities themselves, particularly given that many Indian *comuneros* had begun to develop valuable commercial sugar and coffee farms on community lands. There is ample evidence that variations in plot sizes and in commercial activity resulted in significant differentiation among *comuneros* in both Izalco's indigenous communities.[16] Clearly, then, intracommunity competition and conflicts for control of valuable parcels did not begin with the privatization of land. As Izalco's agricultural frontier started to close as a result of expanding population and commercial production, the centuries-old limits—both physical and conceptual—on common land use were about to be tested and transformed.

The Partition of Community Lands in Dolores

In 1881 and 1882, as part of its attempt to stimulate investment in commercial agriculture and create a class of entrepreneurial peasants and farmers, the Salvadoran state abolished corporate rights to village and municipal lands. The principal motive for privatization was to encourage those farmers and peasants already involved in commercial production to expand their investments. Throughout the country, hundreds of valuable coffee and sugar farms of all sizes had been established on municipal *ejidos* and community lands, but the land remained the property of a corporate body. By the late 1870s, significant sectors of the population considered communal and municipal land tenure to be an obstacle to further agricultural development. Members of Indian communities who already engaged in commercial agriculture often supported the transition from corporate to private holdings, which would give them more secure ownership of lands that they farmed continually and that they had improved by investing in the construction of permanent structures. *Comuneros* who controlled large farms linked to commercial networks stood to gain the most from privatization. But in the context of unequal and contested access to community lands, continued guaranteed access to a subsistence plot could also benefit small landholders.

The privatization of land in Dolores was a long and conflictive process, but the numerous internal disputes and the frequent protests made to external authorities were overwhelmingly about how the laws were being implemented rather than challenges to the justice or intent of the laws themselves. The state played a contradictory and complex role in privatizing corporate holdings and in managing and mediating diverse interests. While the Salvadoran national state was sufficiently consolidated by the early 1880s to conceive, justify, and legislate a national transformation of land ownership, it did not have the technical, administrative, juridical, or police resources to actually carry out the partition nor ensure its completion. The state relied instead on local officials, including municipal and community leaders, to carry out the reform. Paradoxically, although the law privatizing communal land eliminated the legal status of communities, in practice it established a policy that resulted in adding another administrative function, that of land partition, to the communal organization of villages. The implementation of the law was therefore a contentious issue that provoked internal strife as community factions were pitted one against another, each trying to secure the best parcels of land for itself. But differences were not limited to struggles over access to land; political conflicts, often connected to broader regional and national disputes, affected privatization and exacerbated internal rivalries and animosities.

Of all the indigenous communities in western El Salvador, Dolores suffered from one of the most prolonged, tortuous, and conflictive processes of land partition and privatization. Divisions both internal and external to the community exacerbated the technical difficulties of a procedure that involved surveying hundreds of small plots, rights to which were based on ancient land titles and local custom. Near the beginning of this process, the community of Dolores became divided, probably along lines associated with political alliances and kinship rather than emerging class differences. The partitioning and titling of the community's extensive landholdings was complicated by these conflicts and by the competing interests of *comunero* factions that struggled for control over land and the process of privatization. Disputes escalated to the point of violence as the factions created and then mobilized political alliances that transcended Indian and municipal politics in Izalco. During the previous decades, various community factions had established patron-client relations with potential allies among national politicians. In part this was a legacy of Izalco's participation in the political and military alliances that had divided El Salvador since independence; in part it stemmed from the general acceptance of the national state's land policies and from the community's reliance on legal and clientelistic ties to resolve its conflicts. Because of these complications, the division of the lands of Dolores extended over five presidential administrations. And with each presidential succession came new possibilities for alliances, delays, or reversals.

Although the abolition of communal holdings was ordered in 1881, there is little documented evidence of any progress in the partition of Dolores's lands before 1885. By then the community was already suffering from internal divisions relating to the partition. That same year, after a recent change in government, at least 131 male *comuneros* from Dolores sent a complaint to the new president, General Francisco Menéndez (1885–1890).[17] The authors accused Simeón Morán, the Indian *comunero* who during the previous presidential administration had been elected by community leaders to partition community lands, of seriously abusing his position and of failing to complete his mandate. According to their complaint, Morán had embezzled money from "collections" he had made and from lands he had sold to outsiders. The petition noted the indifference of officials toward the local communities during the administration of the previous president, Doctor Rafael Zaldívar (1876–1885), including the hostility of General Hipólito Belloso, who had been governor of Sonsonate, toward these same communities. Some petitioners complained of having been jailed for denouncing abuses.

The Indian petition to President Menéndez reflected previously established political alliances. In 1885 a combination of popular revolts, factional mobilizations, and an invasion by Guatemala led to the overthrow of Zaldívar, whose regime had lasted nine years. When Guatemalan president Justo Rufino Barrios attacked El Salvador on April 1, 1885, with the aim of toppling Zaldívar's government, his massive forces took the towns of Chalchuapa and Santa Ana, located between Izalco and the Guatemalan border, with the support of five hundred Salvadoran militia men, mostly Indian peasants from El Volcán de Santa Ana, Nahuizalco, and Atiquizaya.[18] These *comuneros* were in effect allied with prominent western liberals and landowners such as General Francisco Menéndez, Rafael Meza, Rosa Pacas, and Manuel Pacas, all of whom supported the overthrow of Zaldívar. While Indian *comuneros* fought against Zaldívar, the ladino elite that controlled Izalco's municipal government supported the president's rule and formed their own alliances with other supporters from outside the region.[19] In the extensive fighting that ensued, parts of Izalco itself were attacked by General Figueroa, a Zaldívar supporter whose troops robbed and raped a number of Izalco Indians.[20]

After Menéndez replaced Zaldívar as president, the Indians of Izalco began to test the new political waters, hoping to tilt the local balance of power in their favor by consolidating their alliances with the new national coalitions. The new departmental governor, receptive of the *comuneros'* complaint against Morán, relieved him of his position and began judicial proceedings against him.[21] However, after four years as administrator, Morán had left a bitter legacy of divisions and conflict that would only deepen as the partition process proceeded.

Following Morán's removal, community leaders elected Francisco Punche to continue with the partition of their land, but his efforts did not fare well either. Soon after his election in 1886, Punche, an Indian, was threatened with arrest as a result of complaints that community members had sent to the governor.[22] In 1887 about seventy-five *comuneros* lodged an additional complaint, requesting the removal of the new Indian *partidor y administrador* (administrator and partitioner), Francisco Correa, who had succeeded Punche. They accused him of crimes similar to those that had been attributed to Morán: selling off communal lands for low prices, demanding contributions in cash and grain from *comuneros,* and embezzling community funds. These discontented *comuneros,* including some who had in fact voted for Correa, accused him of enriching himself at their expense. Correa defended himself before the governor, explaining that the community was divided, and that those who opposed him were looking for any excuse to remove him. The true reason for the complainants' opposition, he asserted, was that he would not assign them additional lands after they had sold their initial lots to outsiders. He offered substantial proof that the sale of plots to ladinos had been made according to the legal procedures of the partition, for appropriate amounts of money, and that the revenues had gone toward paying a surveyor and his assistant. He also pointed out that many of the signatures on the complaint against him were falsified, since among them was the signature of his own aide, whom he knew with certainty had not signed the petition.[23] As a result of these conflicts, by the late 1880s the community was hopelessly divided. Although it is not always possible to precisely identify who did what to whom, the repeated clashes make it clear that the problem was not simply caused by the character or personal ambitions of the various *partidores*. Instead, what emerges is a process of complex political positioning and repositioning by groups of *comuneros* in which any long-standing sense of communal solidarity fell apart.

The election of a new *partidor y administrador* in 1889 provides further evidence of the conflicts and tensions within Dolores. Like the election of administrators before the legal abolition of communities, this election was supervised by the local mayor. He found that one community faction had excluded a large number of Indians from the official list of community members.[24] The governor noted that his efforts to conciliate the two factions by electing a neutral person had failed. Because of this failure and the endemic problems in Dolores, he called on the National Assembly to reverse the law that had privatized communal lands, "since under the current law to try to partition communities is to create a threat to public order."[25] That same year the governor reported to the Ministry of the Interior that the elected administrators usually did not dedicate themselves to assigning lands but instead involved themselves in quarrelsome affairs that only delayed the partitioning and exacerbated community divisions.[26] By this time tensions were so high that armed *comuneros* were holding late-night meetings in the countryside.[27] By 1891 ten years of conflict resulted in a community that had virtually ceased to function. The selling of the assembly house that had once been used for community meetings, "because the large meetings of before are no longer held," was a clear signal that internal cohesion and solidarity were in decline.[28]

Luciano Argueta, who served as the *partidor y administrador* of Dolores from 1890 to 1895, was more circumspect than previous administrators, and before he proceeded to divide the land, he compiled a list of 266 mostly male *comuneros* who were entitled to receive titled plots.[29] The governor ordered Argueta to add many more names to the list, resulting in a total of 491 *comuneros*.[30] Despite these advances, however, the community still failed to allot the required amount of lands, even after an 1891 decree that established national guidelines and a timetable for a new partitioning and titling of communal lands. That year a change in government again provided an opportunity to resolve the issue, when General Carlos Ezeta (1891–1894), with some Indian support, overthrew Menéndez's increasingly unpopular and repressive government. By allowing communities more generous terms and greater time to partition their lands, Ezeta provided peasants with an opportunity to solve their pending land disputes without losing their claims in the legal limbo of the late 1880s. To take advantage of this decree, the community of Dolores needed to secure a new surveyor, something they failed to do within the allotted time because, so they claimed, they lacked the funds. Attempts by the Ezeta regime to gain support in the countryside, especially in the west, gave local factions the idea that they need not hurry to finish partitioning their land. By the early 1890s, a stalemate acceptable to all sides seems to have been reached.

Following another change in presidents in 1895, when General Rafael Antonio Gutiérrez (1895–1898) took office, the conflicts again heated up. The former *partidor* Simeón Morán and 150 other *comuneros* signed a petition requesting that a June 1, 1895, decree allowing the nearby Indian community of Asunción more time to partition their land be extended to cover Dolores as well.[31] Morán's faction requested and received governmental support to name a surveyor and continue with the partition.[32] As a result of this new initiative, Morán asked the recently elected governor to nullify the partition of communal lands that Argueta had carried out in an area known as Rincón del Tigre.[33] Another group submitted a counterpetition, signed by 120 *comuneros,* that accused Morán of having continued to assign lands "to his people" without authorization. This group, which claimed to represent "the majority of the *comuneros,*" demanded that Argueta (still legally the administrator) be allowed to work with a surveyor and continue to partition not only unoccupied lands but also those being litigated by Morán as well.[34]

Tensions heightened when a large group requested titles to communal land that they had previously been assigned but to which many had never received the appropriate documentation. Morán convinced a hundred of these *comuneros* to file a complaint against Argueta in which they accused him of having sold off large portions of the community's idle lands and of harassing those who had already possessed plots simply because they did not have titles.[35] This complaint was followed by a more extensive one in 1896. This time Morán and sixty *comuneros,* who asserted that they had legal title to their holdings, charged Argueta with having surreptitiously sold about 4 *caballerías* (180 hectares) of land to General Abraham Castillo Mora, a speculator and regional strongman, in such a way so that it appeared that the titleholders themselves had sold him these parcels. They also alleged that Argueta then transferred 500 *tareas* (22 hectares) of their lands to Eliseo Godines, a ladino who worked as secretary to the local judge, by registering the title under the name of Godines's aide. In addition, Argueta was accused of feigning the sale of two other plots of 1,000 and 600 *tareas* (44 and 26.4 hectares, respectively). The aggrieved *comuneros* claimed that they had been threatened with jail by Godines, "who given his position does whatever he de-sires." Given that the governor of Sonsonate who held their titles would not re-turn them, the *comuneros* sought justice at a higher level, taking their claim di-rectly to the president.[36]

In the mayor's follow-up report to the president in regard to this complaint, he reported that most of the people whose names appeared in the document pre-sented by Morán had disavowed their signatures. The two *comuneros* who ac-knowledged having "given authority to the plebe to complain to the president of the Republic," said that they were opposed to General Carlos Zepeda, a ladino speculator, and not to Argueta. Moreover, they mentioned that the president had already solved their land problem one year earlier.[37] To add to the confusion, Zepeda's name also appeared on Morán's petition. Another *comunero* who denied having signed the petition revealed that he had in fact received his lands from Morán fifteen years previously and had no complaints. The only irregularity men-tioned in the follow-up report was that one *comunero* had sold 500 *tareas* (22 hectares) when he only had rights to 200. Moreover, if *comuneros* had indeed sold 4 *caballerías* (260 hectares) to General Castillo Mora, the transaction was perforce illegal, given that parcels of this size could never have been possessed and titled in the first place.[38] Godines went far in defending his reputation, offering in evi-dence the titles to lands he had previously purchased from *comuneros* and claiming his right to expel those who laid claim to his lands. Yet at least one of those he had expelled also had his own title for some of the disputed 500 *tareas*. The mayor warned the ministry that there were certain ladinos who made a living by exploiting the presumed ignorance of the Indians, "making them believe that by presenting four lies to the executive, he is going to give them back the same lots that these very same unfortunate individuals had sold in the past, perhaps even following the dictates of their own leaders."[39]

Ten years after Morán was removed as *partidor,* complaints against him contin-ued to mount. In 1896 a *comunera* wrote to the governor, accusing Morán of hav-ing given her lands to others. She also made a broader claim against Morán when she asserted that "many people have relied on Simeón Morán to acquire titles based on time-honored possession and he is arbitrarily charging money for these transactions; . . . [he demands] so much that Linares Recinos was charged 150 pe-sos for his title, but he refused to pay and they did not put him on the list [of those who were to receive titles]. As this is a criminal abuse and fraud, I denounce him before your authority."[40]

Finally, in 1897 President Gutiérrez issued a decree conceding that part of the partition carried out by Morán was invalid. The decree allowed for the legal cer-tification of incomplete titles that had been granted before 1897 and made provisions for *comuneros* who had been excluded from the initial allotments carried out by Morán. As of August 1897, 248 *comuneros* had been granted titles based on land assignments that Morán had made years earlier. The size of their parcels ranged from 4 to 28 *manzanas* (2.8 to 19.6 hectares) and averaged about 6.7 *manzanas* (4.7 hectares).[41] Those *comuneros* who possessed untitled parcels could now legalize their holdings. The government also reversed a section of the 1891 decree according to which land that had not been titled or partitioned would revert to the state if not titled within six months. Under the 1897 decree, all unpartitioned land was ceded to the *comuneros* so that they might distribute it to the landless. This decree also allowed for some of these lands to be sold to outsiders in order to pay for expenses. As another fund-raising measure, individual *comuneros* would have to pay the governor two pesos to acquire individual titles. The decree appointed Carlos Zimmerman, a government surveyor, to survey community lands and complete the partition.[42] At long last it seemed that the community of Dolores would be able to divide its remaining lands and provide all *comuneros* with appropriate titles.

Not surprisingly, Zimmerman encountered myriad problems when he attempted to survey and distribute the community's remaining lands. Not the least was opposition from Morán. Soon after he began the survey, Zimmerman complained to the governor that Morán would not hand over the titles to the communal lands. Indeed, Morán was so intent on keeping the titles in his possession that he even hired a legal adviser to help him. To complete his survey, therefore, Zimmerman was forced to rely on lists held by the governor that identified those *comuneros* who had received land but who had no title, as well as those who had no land at all.[43] Making sense of all previous partitions, allocations, titles, and registry books was a complicated task. Zimmerman found that Morán had given land and title to 299 *comuneros*. Another 213 appeared in previous ledgers as having land but no legal title, and an additional 384 appeared as having no lands at all (even though they undoubtedly possessed lands that they had not officially received). Morán protested against the redistribution and even accused the mayor of trying to take his land and give it to others. In response, the mayor reminded the minister that Morán had been removed from office, tried, and even jailed for his irregular administration of community lands between 1881 and 1886. He also mentioned a list of illegal titles that Morán had issued and that were held by the governor; he requested that these titles not be confirmed.[44]

In addition to extensive internal problems over the partition of its lands, the community of Dolores faced numerous external problems. Difficulties with ladino entrepreneurs and neighboring peasant communities contributed to the conflicts and the eventual outbreak of violence. Anticipating that his attempt to

set boundaries would be opposed by neighboring landholders, Zimmerman pru-
dently asked the community elders of Dolores and all ex-*partidores* to accompany
him in his boundary survey. One of the most potentially violent disputes involved the border with Nahuizalco, an adjoining Indian community and municipality that had a long history of conflicts with both Dolores and Asunción. For
example, in 1893 a group of Izalco peasants were harassed by an armed "gang"
from Nahuizalco. Izalco's mayor complained to the governor and asked him to
order the mayor of Nahuizalco to end the harassment.[45] Fearing that the presence of all six hundred *comuneros* from Dolores would provoke a confrontation,
Zimmerman asked the governor to assign thirty soldiers to assist him in surveying
the border with Nahuizalco.[46] Even well after the survey, in 1899, peasants from
Nahuizalco would continue to contest Izalco's claims by invading lands along the
border and asserting that instead of honoring titles or recognizing the courts,
"they would fix everything with their machetes."[47]

In addition to the problems brought about by conflict with Nahuizalco, there
were other difficulties. Some neighboring *hacendados* (estate owners) as well as
leaders of other communities refused to participate in the survey. For example, at
first the representatives of the bordering community of El Volcán de Santa Ana
did not show up, nor did Emilio Araujo, owner of the *hacienda* of El Sunza.[48]
Araujo refused to recognize Zimmerman's right to set the boundary, and asserted
that a previous inspection ordered by the Juzgado General de Hacienda had reviewed the communal titles of Dolores when it established the existing border.[49]
All of these obstacles caused considerable delays. To make matters worse, Zimmerman died before he could complete the survey and, despite various requests
by community leaders, the government did not replace him. With Zimmerman's
death any hopes for a negotiated solution to the land disputes among the *comunero* factions of Dolores dwindled; as a result, a significant portion of its land
was left in the possession of many ladino peasants and farmers from neighboring
municipalities. As the community's internal divisions grew, it only became easier
for aggressive neighbors to seize more portions of the community's lands.

Previous to these disputes, dozens of farmers from the region had rented community land and built up valuable commercial farms. But it was not only neighboring landowners who were interested in contesting Indian interpretations of
boundary markers or survey maps; local officials, lawyers, and military officers
also attempted to take advantage of the partition of community land by both fomenting and engaging in the internal disputes. Well before 1880, the ladino presence in Dolores had been established, not only after decades of interethnic competition over land rights and local power but also as the result of Indian-ladino
collaboration in municipal government and Indian participation in commercial

agriculture. Thus, well before the partition process began, ladino peasants, farmers, and officials had established a presence in the community life of Dolores. These included some farmers and *hacendados* from the municipalities of Izalco and Sonsonate who rented community land, such as Benigno Barrientos, Domingo Arce, Wenceslao Herrera, and General Carlos Zepeda.[50] In 1889 the *partidor y administrador* of Dolores received permission from the Ministerio de Gobernación to expel these tenants from community lands. But some of them continued to press claims for the lands they occupied and in all likelihood remained in possession of their farms after the partition had been completed.[51] Typical of these men was Ruperto Machado, a local farmer who was said to be a lawyer. He represented Dolores as its scribe *(escribiente)* and benefited from Morán's questionable practices.[52] In 1885 Morán paid Machado 4,200 pesos for representing the community in legal proceedings in San Salvador, and he was later accused of having improperly granted Machado title to at least 2 *caballerías* of land as part of this deal.[53] Machado defended his rights by claiming that he had not obtained the land from Morán and that his 1880 lease of these lands had in fact constituted a sale. Like many other ladino tenants, Machado used his de facto possession of rented lands as a basis for claiming legal title. In the confusion and constant disputes over the privatization process, men like Machado and other tenants, including the mayor himself, most likely remained in control of at least portions of the lands they had been renting.[54]

General Castillo Mora was one of the few outsiders who actively and openly speculated in claims to communal lands in Dolores.[55] He "purchased" 4 *caballerías* for 4,200 pesos; and although he claimed that he had bought the land from four *comuneros,* it appears much more likely that it had been given to him by Luciano Argueta, who at the time of the acquisition was *partidor* of the community of Dolores. To avoid losing his holdings with no compensation at all, Castillo Mora had to request assistance from the national government because a group of peasants from the nearby ladino community of El Volcán de Santa Ana had invaded his property, distributed it among themselves, and had then begun to clear and plant the land. With his holdings both occupied and surrounded by hostile peasants, therefore, Castillo Mora was ironically forced to ask the government to buy his lands, which would then be "granted" to the "usurpers."[56] The government's legal adviser who reviewed this case decided that such a procedure would be unconstitutional, and suggested that Castillo Mora be advised to take his case to the courts.

Another speculator, General Carlos Zepeda, had more success in obtaining state assistance in a similar situation involving other nearby plots.[57] Zepeda was among the tenants who had attempted—and apparently succeeded—to title the community lands he had leased but for which he had not paid rent since 1880.[58]

The lands had been taken over by peasants from both Izalco and Nahuizalco. Like Castillo Mora, Zepeda probably had little chance of ever regaining control of these lands. In part to resolve the conflict, but mostly as a way of rewarding the *indígenas* of Nahuizalco, who provided important militia services to the state, in 1899 the government paid Zepeda 30,000 pesos in government bonds for 6 *caballerías* (270 hectares) of land. The documents drawn up for the sale failed to mention that Zepeda had been a tenant of Dolores, and this fact was probably unknown to both the surveyor and local government officials. The Indians themselves were perhaps unaware of the exact terms of the transaction, although they probably would not have been overly concerned that the government had effectively bribed Zepeda in order to give them legal title to their land.

The parcels in question, located at a place known as Los Cuilotales, were at first thought to be within the community of Nahuizalco. But later they were found to be occupied by residents of both Dolores and Nahuizalco, the precise boundary having been left open to local interpretation.[59] The municipalities of both Nahuizalco and Izalco had given out title to many of the peasants who had taken possession of the lands that Zepeda had leased. Other peasants, from Dolores, had received their documents in the partition carried out by Morán, who allegedly issued titles from his house, without even visiting the plots to see if previous possession had indeed been established. When the land bought from Zepeda was surveyed, some adjacent lands were found to be held by peasants who did not benefit from the government purchase and titling; other nearby plots were in fallow and unoccupied. The surveyor measured and titled a total of fifty-five plots, an effort that the *indígenas* received "with joy."[60] But when he reached the purchase size of 6 *caballerías*, he abruptly stopped, leaving unsurveyed (and hence untitled) fifty possessed plots.

In sum, the partition of the community lands of Dolores became a complex struggle involving internal and external actors in a competition that did not always follow predictable lines. But as the Indian peasants of Dolores struggled to retain some control over the process, the political alliances of their factional leaders became an important component of the struggle. The long-standing entanglements of the residents of Dolores in regional and national political struggles only made the internal process of partitioning more conflictive and unpredictable, culminating in the violent confrontation of 1898.

The 1898 Revolt and Local and National Politics

It is evident that when factional strife in Dolores exploded into violence in 1898, the long and bitter dispute for control over the privatization of community lands was preeminent among the causes. But it would be a mistake to attempt to interpret this intra-community violence (which was later perceived as a conflict between Indian peasants and ladino judges) without taking into consideration either the political alignments of the factions that faced off that year or local perceptions of the confrontation. Indeed, it was not simply a coincidence that the 1898 confrontation took place on the same night that the government of President Gutiérrez was overthrown by General Tomás Regalado. The alliances forged by factions within the community of Dolores extended far beyond the boundaries of local politics and tied the fate of both sides to the success or failure of national political alliances. The Indian factions within Dolores had much to gain from aligning themselves with and supporting national political and military leaders in their quest for executive power. Without a discussion of the links between the *comuneros* of Dolores and outside political factions and the state, the story of this village's divisive history up to the violence of 1898 would remain incomplete. It is therefore necessary to understand the connections between communities such as this one and the military men struggling for control of the national state. The factional and clientelistic basis of national politics in nineteenth-century El Salvador meant that political leaders, including military officers, had to develop power bases that combined corporate, ethnic, personalist, ideological, regional, national, and even extranational ties and alliances. Since the 1820s, Indians from Izalco had established important precedents by participating in the wars and statewide politics that characterized nation-state formation in El Salvador. These alliances ranged from support for Guatemala's frequent invasions of western El Salvador to participation in efforts to remove presidents from power. In the period just before the 1898 revolt, Indian militias from Izalco had participated in the successful overthrows of Presidents Zaldívar (1885) and Ezeta (1894).[61] In many cases military units identified with and were loyal to their place of origin and were likely to reflect the political affiliations of their home bases.[62] Often these very same militias mobilized, either independently or in alliance with other forces, as most likely occurred during the violence of 1898. The militia experience of peasants from Dolores is indicated by the fact that the leaders of the opposition to Morán signaled their attack with a trumpet.

The ability of peasants and their communities in western El Salvador either to act in autonomous uprisings or as allies of national political factions rested on a variety of factors. Because of its proximity to the Guatemalan border, the western region had always been of strategic importance, as both the Salvadoran and Guatemalan governments competed there for support. Indians were also the favored recruits for El Salvador's army and militia units, a fact that gave indigenous communities some bargaining leverage despite their often being forcibly pressed into service.[63] Indian militias, aware of their strategic importance to national factions, used this to extract favors from government authorities, giving them an advantage over other communities or even over competing groups within their own communities. Within Dolores, *comunero* support for one or another national faction did not necessarily imply adherence to the ideological or political goals of particular leaders or groups. Rather, the numerous petitions to regional and national authorities regarding internal land disputes suggests that *comunero* factions offered political and military support more with the expectation that they would receive a favorable hearing of future claims than because of any ideological commitment. This was likely the reason behind Morán's support of General Tomás Regalado, who rose to power and became the provisional president in 1898. Morán's power had been curtailed under President Gutiérrez, whose administration supported the partitioning efforts of Argueta and Zimmerman. Unfortunately for Morán, his family members, and associates, they were not allowed to enjoy the fruits of their alliance with the victorious Regalado.

Regalado was a local military officer who contended for national power. In 1894 he participated in the overthrow of President Ezeta, and he expected, though he did not receive, the presidency.[64] As was typical of presidential transitions during the nineteenth century, Regalado's revolt against President Gutiérrez incited divisive conflict not only in Izalco but throughout the country. In many towns ethnic tensions worsened as Indians and ladinos aligned with or against the new government.[65] After the fighting Regalado seized the presidency, which he usurped in hastily called and fraudulent elections, thus provoking renewed military and popular opposition to his government.[66] But for those in western El Salvador, Regalado was not simply another general vying for national power; he was also a local landowner who resided in the city of Santa Ana and who owned a *hacienda* in Izalco. When Morán and his associates aligned themselves with Regalado, they mobilized networks of political alliances that for years had tied Izalco's factions to different elite contenders for power.

Those close to the events of 1898 highlighted the political nature of the confrontation. One account, written soon after the events by a parish priest from Cojutepeque, attributed the violence to competition among national political factions. "The Indians of Izalco," he said, "numbering about 200, took advantage of the lack of a garrison . . . [and] began to break down doors and burn the archive; and there was a fight between them and a few Regalistas who were heading toward Santa Ana, which resulted in about ten or twelve dead and many wounded."[67] A few years later, the governor of the department of Sonsonate reinforced this view when he explained, in a manner typical of ladinos when referring to Indian violence, that the events were the result of outsiders who exploited

Indian ignorance. The governor's account emphasized that the attack had targeted supporters of General Regalado's bid for presidential power and, perhaps given this change in focus, the victims had now become ladino: "a mob of Indians of an opposing band headed out to cut off a large number of ladinos who were heading to San Salvador to join the forces of General Regalado as a result of the political events of that year that brought him to power; an encounter [took place] that left several people dead and wounded, demonstrating the tragic consequences of the spirit of party affiliation when inculcated in the ignorant masses, who without hesitation set out to commit criminal acts, only for individual [leaders], without following any personal ideals that could bring them any advantage."[68]

But the ladino category itself was fluid, for both outsiders and the *comuneros* of Dolores. Thus, for many of them, Morán and his faction quickly became ladinos. Just two years after the 1898 confrontation a group of *indígenas* who complained to the national government of the many abuses they had suffered at the hands of ladinos, and whose lands were the "object of their excessive greed," remembered Morán and his allies as ladinos who had been killed for taking away their lands.[69] In the minds of these *comuneros,* Indians became ladinos when they *acted* like ladinos, and thus they stripped away Morán's ethnic identity with a polarized and politicized definition of Indianness. By aligning himself in the land struggle with the faction that was perhaps more closely tied to ladino forces outside of Dolores, Morán and his supporters had broken with their Indian identity and opened themselves up to being censured and labeled as ladinos.[70] Nevertheless, the local factions cut across class and ethnic lines. Indians and ladinos, as well as community leaders and entrepreneurs, often found themselves on the same side during this confrontation, which until now has been understood as having pitted Indian peasants against ladino agents of the liberal state. For example, among those who attacked Morán was Pedro Bolaños, a community leader who initiated many of the complaints and petitions over land. Bolaños also led the opposition to the titling of plots by the mayor of Izalco and he had hidden the community's land titles. The cross-class and interethnic nature of the struggle is exemplified by the fact that siding with the Indian leader Bolaños was Calixto Vega, a ladino who was one of Izalco's more successful landowners and commercial entrepreneurs.[71]

After 1898, factional leaders continued to petition the government over the partition of community lands, but there were no significant changes. For example, in 1900 a total of fifty *comuneros* from both of Izalco's indigenous communities asked the National Assembly to resurvey the borders of their former communal lands. The petitioners did not mention the long history of intracommunity conflict and wrote as if the lands had remained intact and undivided, when in fact most plots had been held privately for years. The National Assembly forwarded the request to the president's office without any apparent result. Again in 1903 Bolaños and his supporters petitioned the recently inaugurated president, General Pedro José Escalón (1903–1907), for a new survey and partition. They denied that they were quarrelsome, or that they wanted to recover their ancient communal lands by dislodging neighboring *hacendados;* what they wanted, they claimed, was "justice." This group of Indians promised Escalón that if he supported them they would become his "faithful supporters" and stand next to him in defending liberty. The group included thirty people who identified themselves as members of the "former community of *indígenas*." This time the dossier (which did find its way into the president's office) narrated the procedures and problems of the preceding years, including Zimmerman's efforts to reestablish village boundaries.[72]

Although the pleas of local Indians to the national government to reopen the partition of lands fell on deaf ears, the mayor of Izalco reinitiated the partition by starting to title existing plots. This effort, however, still reflected the continuing divisions within the local Indian population. The mayor hoped to complete Zimmerman's work, and to do so he made use of a map and list that the surveyor had made. The material showed the plots possessed by the 303 *comuneros* titled by Morán, the land of 213 *comuneros* who had been left without title, and the possessions of 82 non-*comunero* tenants who had not paid rent since 1882; Zimmerman's material also listed the 384 individuals who had received neither land nor title.[73] In response to the mayor's actions, a group of *comuneros* led by Bolaños, and claiming to be acting as representatives of the community, asked the governor to enjoin the mayor from distributing titles to others, although at the same time they requested that their own holdings be given legal title. The mayor defended his actions by explaining that it was the only way to resolve the great confusion of claims and that he was not selling plots but only providing titles to existing holders. Some of the current holders, he asserted, had been harassed and intimidated by the complainants, whom the mayor accused of redistributing lands that had already been partitioned and titled. They had acted in concert with armed *comuneros* and had provoked "judicial disputes and disagreements" within the village. The governor sided with the mayor and accepted his explanation of his actions and his opposition to Bolaños.

Nevertheless, Bolaños and his followers continued to ask the national government to intervene. In 1904 they again petitioned for the orderly distribution of whatever communal lands might still remain unassigned. They requested that a surveyor be appointed to serve as *partidor y administrador* in order to resolve pending matters and represent "a [legally] abolished society in the process of being liquidated."[74] This time they accompanied their petition with a long account of the conflicts in Dolores and of the "thievery" of previous *partidores* who had distributed the lands in a most inequitable manner. They recalled the difficulties they had encountered over lands that bordered on neighboring *haciendas,* and they described how most of the eighty ladino tenants who had farmed community lands before 1881 had attempted to title the lands they rented. Bolaños claimed that he had respected Morán's partition as long as no disputes emerged. In response to this petition, the National Assembly asked the president to commission a new outside *partidor,* as Bolaños and his followers had requested.[75] The results of this decision remain a mystery, although any revision of extant arrangements was unlikely after decades of possession and occupation by *indígenas* and ladinos alike. Most of the complex changes of the previous twenty years were irreversible. A few years later the community of Dolores ceased to appear in Izalco's documentary record.

Although there are few sources that provide information on the links between Izalco and national factional leaders, the 1898 "revolt" reveals an important connection between the locally grounded context of Izalco's Indian politics and the development of national politics.[76] As the twentieth century began, most of Dolores's *comuneros* were able to retain access to and continue farming parcels that had previously belonged to their community. But the partition process itself, filtered through a community whose ethnic solidarity had become compromised by commercial, cross-ethnic, and political networks, also weakened the internal cohesion of the community. Despite the rhetorical flourishes by leaders who called for justice and fairness, all of the identifiable groups within Dolores seem to have behaved in a similar conflictive and competitive fashion, although all managed to obtain the support of a significant number of *comuneros.* In the end, privatization only served to reinforce the emerging differentiation within both ladino and Indian peasant groups, while allowing various factional leaders and their closest allies to benefit unequally from the distribution of land and the sale of lots.

In land-wealthy communities like Dolores, in which intense ethnic rivalries, expanding commercial agriculture, and important political alliances had already created a complex maze of interests and alliances, the privatization of land hastened the weakening of indigenous solidarity. Indigenous communal organization and identity suffered from Indians' becoming subordinate to emerging ladino commercial and landowning elites. But this did not always occur in a straightforward fashion. The partitioning process exacerbated existing resentments toward ladinos of all classes, although it also encouraged alliances between community factions and ladino entrepreneurs and political actors (including military officers).[77] The decades-old links of Izalco's Indian communities to larger commercial networks and political alliances had already set the stage for the conflicts that emerged during the privatization process. The personal and kinship ties necessary for any form of communal cohesion could not be easily maintained given the increasing number of community members, the fixed resource base, the external pressures, and the nature of political alliances forged during the 1880s and 1890s.

Although the privatization of community lands in Izalco created a landed peasantry, it also led to competitive and conflictive land distribution among community factions. At the same time, privatization reactivated and heightened conflicts with bordering *haciendas* and peasant communities while inviting the participation of ladino peasants and elites, who both arbitrated and took advantage of the complex maze of indigenous claims and counterclaims. The privatization of communal lands debilitated the Indian communities of Izalco. This eventually led to the disintegration of what was left of the community of Dolores during the early twentieth century. By 1932 there was nothing left of this once prosperous Indian community, which by then had become identified merely as a ladino barrio.[78]

While we should be careful not to generalize from the experience of Dolores, many other Indian communities in El Salvador did indeed experience similar internal crises when faced with the privatization of their corporate lands. Repeatedly, the commercial networks and political alliances that these communities maintained with regional and national society were crucial in determining how land was distributed and whether ethnic or corporate solidarity survived. The partition process fostered endemic conflict among *comuneros* and weakened their ability to compete (or negotiate) with ladinos for control over local resources and power. But conflicts over privatization also demonstrated that the internal solidarity of Izalco's Indian communities had already been weakened. This should force us to reconsider the idea that Indian peasant communities of the nineteenth century retained the politically autonomous character they had during the colonial period. By the late nineteenth century, decades of change had already tied these communities to larger political struggles and a new commercial economy that involved new markets and entrepreneurs. This laid the foundation for potential challenges to the stability of communities' internal hierarchies and ideologies.

After suffering through the conflictive process of privatization, the Indian peasants of Izalco could not always count on community solidarity in their efforts to organize in defense of their interests. For centuries the Indian community of Asunción had relied on its internal organization to ensure that the subsistence needs of its members were being met. But after privatization, the community—damaged by its own divisions and conflicts—would organize around a more abstract principle: a sense of identity based more on kinship and political ties than on land ownership. A reduced core of *indígenas* based in Asunción continued to identify themselves as members of an Indian community, even after the conflicts of the turn of the century and the dissolution of the communally controlled lands and resources that had formed the basis of Izalco communities for over two centuries. Until at least the 1920s, Asunción continued to elect an Indian *alcalde* (mayor) and *regidores* (council members) and identify itself as a *comunidad* (community).[79] Yet their position within the larger political economy of the region had changed drastically, and within their own municipality they were now merely a minority group.[80]

The weakening and near dissolution of communal ties also undermined the ability of Izalco's indigenous communities to act politically as strong autonomous allies of larger elite-led factions. The weakening of the community facilitated the privatization of political power, reducing community life to a distorted, ritualized, and defensive function that became, by the 1920s, one more node in an emerging national political system based on patron-client relations and the mobilization of votes but not militias. During the first decades of the twentieth century, community organization in Asunción provided a means of generating Indian electoral support for presidential candidates. But the possibility of autonomous military and political mobilization had been eliminated. It was not until 1931 and 1932, in a vastly changed context, that Izalco's indigenous leaders would again independently mobilize, this time in a failed alliance with communist leaders.

Víctor Hugo Acuña Ortega

The Formation of the Urban Middle Sectors in El Salvador, 1910–1944

In the history of Central America, the fall of the dictatorships in Guatemala and El Salvador in 1944 has been associated with the social and political emergence of the middle class. Similarly, the social and political conflicts of Costa Rica in the decade of the 1940s have been related to the actions of urban middle sectors, whose first organizational and political expression was to form the Center for the Study of the National Problems, one of the sources of the National Liberation Party of José Figueres Ferrer.[1]

Strangely, despite the existing consensus about this interpretation, few historical studies have analyzed the process by which these middle sectors emerged in the structure and social life of Central American countries in the decades before World War II. We still do not know when they formed, what kind of occupations they had, or how they related to the liberal governments of the early twentieth century, nor do we know what bonds they had with the working classes and their receptivity to socialist and revolutionary ideas. Although few historians have investigated the formation of the middle sectors in the subcontinent, the Central American case does not seem to be exceptional in Latin America.[2] There are, however, more sociological essays inspired by John J. Johnson's thesis on the role of the middle sectors in the region.[3]

For El Salvador we have Everett A. Wilson's study, which, based on Johnson's ideas, begins to examine the formation of the urban middle sectors during the 1920s; and we have Patricia Parkman's work, which evaluates Wilson's arguments and the role of the urban middle sectors in the fall of dictator General Maximiliano Martinez in 1944.[4] These studies are rare in their emphasis on the middle class. However, although they contribute important elements, they leave many aspects of the origin and composition of these social sectors in the dark, beyond their insistence on the urban character of the political movements they discuss.

This is the point of departure for this chapter about La Concordia Artisans Society (Sociedad de Artesanos del Salvador, hereinafter La Concordia)—a well-established artisan's organization that by its practices and speeches, and by its great public visibility, seems to have represented the interests of certain middle-sector groups and their clientelist relations with the state as well as with economic and political elites.[5] There were other associations of urban middle-sector groups in the capital—such as the public employees, the commercial employees and teachers, and societies of craftsmen—as well as in other cities like Santa Ana, San Miguel, and Santa Tecla.[6] In short, during the first three decades of the twentieth century, especially after World War I, El Salvador experienced the remarkable development of its worker and craftsmen societies—and there were far more than in other Central American countries. Around 1920 there were more than fifty *mutuales* (working class and artisan self-help societies) throughout the country. This extensive development affected workers as well as the proprietors of small workshops and factories in the main cities. During the early development of these associations, employers and wage earners participated together in the same groups. It was not until the 1920s that a process of ideological and social differentiation of the associations occurred, with some *mutuales* becoming unions that radicalized ideologically under the influence of anarchist and socialist ideas, whereas others reaffirmed their mutualist traditional direction as they confronted the new forms of working radicalism. All of these transformations constituted the context within which the Regional Federation of Workers of El Salvador (Federacíon Regional de Trabajadores Salvadoreños) expanded and radicalized when it came under the influence of the recently created Communist Party during the early 1930s.[7] At the same time, other groupings emphasized their character as middle-class organizations, loyal to the prevailing social and political order. This was the case with La Concordia.[8]

History of La Concordia

This association of craftsmen was founded in 1872 under the auspices of the government of Field Marshal Santiago González. All evidence points to its being the first long-established mutualist artisan grouping not just in El Salvador but in all of Central America. On January 22, 1860, 213 master craftsmen convened at the university in San Salvador, invited by the government of President General Geraldo Barrios; they founded the Society of Craftsmen of El Salvador and named its first board of directors. It is clear that the initiative for this association came from the government, and it appears that this short-lived grouping was La Concordia's predecessor.[9]

The organization's 1899 statutes explain some of its history: Article 2 states that the organization is dedicated to the "moral, intellectual, and material improvement of its members, especially of all workers, fomenting the education and improvement of their habits, exercising charity, and cultivating friendship." Article 3 states that the organization will have a savings bank, a library with a reading room, and a night school. Article 5 calls for the organization of industrial competitions. These are all familiar elements of a mutualist society composed of craftsmen, employers, and self-employed workers. It is significant that article 20 of the statutes calls for its president, vice president, and vocales to be artisan craftsmen. This disposition was removed from the statutes in 1918 perhaps because in the first decades of the twentieth century the organization welcomed members of the military, professionals, and educators.[10]

In 1874 La Concordia opened night and day schools for artisans.[11] However, the organization's status was rather precarious during its first years. In 1878 La Concordia's president summoned the general assembly in order to reorganize the society, and in 1886 its secretary, Francisco A. Funes, who would soon become an outstanding Salvadoran politician, asked for the government's support to print the organization's stationery on the government's printing press in an effort to formalize the organization definitively.[12] From its inception La Concordia had its own building. It was destroyed by an earthquake in 1873, and in 1883 the Salvadoran government financed the construction of new premises.[13] Successive earthquakes damaged this building, so the organization was constantly repairing and maintaining its facilities, which included a meeting room, a reading room, and a classroom for the night school. During the 1930s, managing the building became the organization's almost sole reason for being.

In February 1904 La Concordia decided to merge with other artisan societies of San Salvador—Excelsior and the Union of Workers—but revoked the decision in March of that year.[14] However, as a consequence of that insolvent merger the organization lost its building, resulting in a long legal battle with the Society of Craftsmen of El Salvador, the organization that emerged from the aborted fusion. La Concordia won the lawsuit in 1913.[15] These years were otherwise the greatest for La Concordia. In 1911, as a patriotic gesture, it lobbied the National Assembly to build a monument to ex-president Francisco Menéndez; although the funds were granted, the monument was never built. It also participated actively in the commemorations of the centenary of the first declaration of Central American independence.[16] In general, the group enjoyed the support of the governments of the Meléndez-Quiñónez dynasty (1913–1927). When La Concordia recovered its facilities in 1914 it opened a library and reactivated the night school. In 1915 and 1916 the organization sponsored industrial contests and exhibitions that brought great attention from the Salvadoran press.[17] In 1916 La Concordia paid for an advertisement in the *Blue Book,* a prestigious monograph highlighting El Salvador's accomplishments.[18] In those years La Concordia was considered the oldest and most respectable artisan organization of the country. Its dynamism in this period is attributable to a great extent to the leadership of Coronel Salvador Ciudad Real, first secretary and later president of its directive council.[19]

During the 1920s La Concordia experienced a period of change. From 1922 to 1927 its members participated little in the life of the organization, which kept a low profile on the national scene.[20] By 1927, with the presidency of reformist Pío Romero Bosque, the group began a new, more dynamic phase; for example, it organized the celebrations surrounding the Day of the Teacher, coordinated with the national celebration of ex-president Francisco Menéndez, on June 22.[21] However, it was during the 1930s and especially after the massacres of 1932 and the consolidation of the dictatorship of General Maximiliano Hernández Martínez that the organization lost all presence in national life—both the night school and the library were closed. Unlike the presidents preceding him, including the ephemeral Arturo Araujo (1931), Martínez never participated in any events connected to La Concordia. However, although the organization's board of directors did not meet during most of 1932 because of restrictions placed on political and most forms of social organizing, La Concordia's eventual decay cannot be attributed solely to the government's repression, because after that year the organization worked without major interference from the dictatorship. Its decline was due more to the dictator's indifference to the organization. As a result, it became a small group that administered to members within its locale, an impoverished sector of San Salvador where popular dances were held.[22] Currently, the locale is a social center for craftsmen and professionals, and the organization no longer has the public prestige it once had, though it preserves the pride of being a very old institution.

Social Composition

La Concordia's membership probably numbered around fifty, and no more than a hundred attended its general assemblies. Among its membership were military officers, teachers, and some professionals, but the largest groups were the shop-owning artisans and small-scale manufacturers; this seems quite evident, at least during the 1910s. For example, in the *Blue Book,* we found the following members listed:[23] Francisco Funes, lawyer, journalist, and politician, board secretary in 1886; Leopoldo Cuéllar González, proprietor of the Great Hairdressing Salon and Perfumerie El Comercio, *regidor* (alderman) of the municipality of San Salvador, and treasurer of the organization in 1916; Alberto Casati, proprietor of a silversmithing factory, francophile, treasurer of the organization from 1921 to 1923; Manuel Bertrand, proprietor of a *sastrería* (tailor shop), president of the organization from 1913 to 1914; and Joaquín Mancia Varela, proprietor of a *sastrería.*

Salvador Ciudad Real, a president of La Concordia in 1917, participated in the organization from 1910 to the 1920s. In 1927 he published the pamphlet *The Silk Industry* printed by the undersecretary's office of industry and commerce. The government distributed the pamphlet for free to encourage the promotion of silkworm cultivation in the hopes that El Salvador would become "the Belgium of Central America." Ciudad Real had a farm near San Salvador where he grew the plant and installed a processing facility in his house. He entered his products in contests organized by La Concordia in 1915 and 1916. The journalist Alejandro Bermúdez described Ciudad Real as a blacksmith, bookkeeper, clerk, agriculturist, and soldier, and he was considered to have stood out in all those capacities.[24] He became a general in the reserve during the government of President Romero Bosque, and during Martinez's dictatorship he held several political and military positions, among them the governorships of Sensuntepeque, Sonsonate, Cojutepeque, Ahuachapán, and San Vicente.[25] During the 1930s, Ciudad Real became distanced from the organization though he continued to belong. On August 29, 1932, he entered the Gerardo Barrios Cooperative Society, a group similar to La Concordia but over which the military had a greater influence.[26] Members of La Concordia also belonged to other organizations, such as the Athenum, thirty-three teacher's organizations, and other mutualist and cultural associations.[27]

Among La Concordia's membership were typesetters who were also fond of writing and literature. Juan Antonio Solórzano was a poet, a member of La Concordia, and a journalist for the newspaper *Diario del Salvador* when he died in 1921; both institutions organized solemn funerals for him. He was described as an "untiring worker of intelligence," who composed hymns for his own organizations as well as for several other working-class organizations of El Salvador.[28]

Adrián Meléndez Arevalo was an important member of the literati, a typesetter, and owner of the largest printing shop. He was closely allied to the governments of the Meléndez-Quiñónez era (1913–1927) and was mayor and municipal councilman of San Salvador; he was also a deputy in the Salvadoran National Assembly.[29] In the electoral campaign of 1918 Meléndez Arevalo published *El Aventino, Semanario Político, Órgano del Comité Central de Obreros Quiñonistas* (El

Aventino, political weekly magazine, organ of the central committee of quiñon-istas workers).[30] He also published several novels, was a sort of official spokesman for La Concordia, and wrote a history of the organization during the late 1920s.[31] In June 1939 La Concordia organized a tribute in honor of Meléndez Arevalo, and it was attended by delegates from different worker-artisan associations. The main speaker at this event affirmed that "Meléndez Arevalo is an example for the working-class movement because he is a person who by his own merits and love of the work has managed to distinguish himself."[32]

Although in 1919 a member of La Concordia's board of directors denounced the "frock coat proletariat" that lived off the national budget, by the end of the 1920s teachers had acquired influence within La Concordia. In 1928 the board of directors decided to "ask the National Assembly to decree the Day of the Teacher on June 22, the day in which the revolution of General Francisco Menéndez came to power."[33] The National Assembly created a committee to promote the Day of the Teacher, and the organization participated in the celebrations during 1929 and 1930.

In summary, La Concordia was dominated by the small-scale manufacturers, artisans and skilled workers, as well as professionals, military officers, teachers, and public employees. These were people who came from occupational groups which expanded greatly in El Salvador between the end of the nineteenth century and the first decades of the twentieth century, and that despite their hetero-geneity can be referred to as urban middle sectors.[34]

Social and Political Ideas

Liberalism was at the center of La Concordia's ideological world, as was frequently the case among Central America's working class and artisan circles. However, La Concordia's literature rarely contained any explicit discussion of ideology, in part because its statutes prohibited formal discussion of political and religious subjects. In 1882 the government invited two delegates to participate in the inauguration ceremonies for the first railroad in El Salvador (connecting the port of Acajutla with the city of Sonsonate). Paschal Monterrosa, one of the delegates, gave a speech in which he stated, "It has been some time since a great revolution has been at work in El Salvador, one of progress, with peace as its flag and work as its objective."[35]

In 1919, during the inauguration of the organization's new director, Adrián Meléndez Arevalo gave a speech in which he presented the key ideas of the organization—all derived from nineteenth-century liberalism: the moral and material improvement of the worker, by means of his own effort, improvement through education, and an evolutionary vision of society. This speech is the only text that clearly articulates the organization's ideological position, one in which communism is denounced from a Christian perspective, a surprising statement because the worker-artisan groups of this period were quite secular, and La Concordia was no exception: "Here is why, gentlemen, the members of the institution in whose name I speak, do not belong to the demolishing phalanx that, under the bloody fulgor of the red flag, preaches free love and the community of interests, this procedure is a brutal socialism that, by the same fact, does not rest, or rather, it is not a corollary of the doctrines that had their sanction twenty centuries ago in Monte Calvario."[36]

In 1919 the organization asked the government for protection for weavers and small shop owners who were being affected by a new textile factory. Later, the director of La Concordia created a permanent commission for the study of the promotion of small-scale industries.[37] These initiatives clearly demonstrate the organization's preoccupation with shop-owning craftsmen.

Before and after the 1932 massacres under Martínez, La Concordia showed its anti-Communist position firmly.[38] And some of its members participated in Martínez's repressive anti-Communist campaign. For example, professor Francisco R. Osegueda, president of the organization in 1928–1929, gave a radio speech in February 1932 on the peasantry and the "anti-social" doctrines of communism.[39] During the 1930s, as was the case during the previous decades, La Concordia was very deferential toward the government even as the dictatorship was indifferent to the group.

In sum, La Concordia shared the liberal ideals and enlightenment ideas of moral improvement of the worker by means of personal effort and education.[40] Radical social ideas were alien to those associated with the organization. This reflects the organization's middle-class character, as clearly enunciated by its members. For example, in a 1918 article published in *Diario del Salvador* Ciudad Real states that, "Like this, the Salvadoran craftsman (artisan) marches with firm step by the footpath that the civilization indicates, until arriving at the place he must occupy in the concert of modern society. With their savings banks, the day will arrive in which they will be self-sufficient and make the bourgeoisie respect them."[41] In this text Ciudad Real offers examples of the importance of social mobility and liberal notions of social progress. He also celebrates the manner in which "the craftsmen had managed to occupy honorary and important positions in public administration."

In a still more explicit acknowledgment of the importance of La Concordia to the middle-class consciousness, the organization's president, in a 1929 speech during the inauguration of its new director, Domingo Melara, states:

I feel intimately satisfied to belong to this grouping of the so-called middle-class. Middle-class, not because he is incapable of rising to the heights of thought and the excelsitudes of feeling; middle-class not because he is incapable of descending to the darkest of the miseries, in which those below teem and moan. . . . Middle class, I repeat, gentlemen, because in the fight for life it contributes its arms as well as its brain, because it resorts at the same time to the nerve and the spirit. And indeed because the need for survival has imposed on him the need to discipline all his faculties, it is the middle-class that is called to handle one day the destinies of the world. But for this it needs to organize itself on the bases of harmony and order.[42]

In October 1932, a few months after the *matanza* (the massacre that followed the 1932 revolt), La Concordia sent a memorandum to the other artisan societies of El Salvador explaining its disposition to collaborate with them and maintain warm relations. This was a typical attitude of the organization throughout its existence. In effect, it tried to maintain warm relations with other artisan and worker associations and supported some joint efforts. For example, it sent a representative to an important working-class congress held in Armenia in June 1918, during which most of the Salvadoran labor groups formed a confederacy. However, it never joined a larger alliance and always maintained its organizational independence.

La Concordia maintained a more permanent and daily connection with labor organizations by lending or renting its premises for their board meetings as well as for social events like dances and celebrations. It generally granted requests to use its premises, though in some instances denied them for ideological reasons. In March 1931 La Concordia's director approved a regulation stipulating that its premises would not be used for "communist propagandas, nor strikes, nor any other work that jeopardizes its social interests."[43]

Concordia, the Dominant Classes, and the State

In 1930, in the context of increasing social and political discord, La Concordia published a note explaining that it was not party to the militant organizing and agitation of the period. However, its statutory prohibition on political alliances did not exclude its forming alliances with the state, the political elite, and entrepreneurs. On the contrary, its members were eager for the respectability and social recognition these alliances would bring, while the dominant sectors were interested in gaining support and legitimacy for their policies. The relationship was paternalistic, with the middle sectors expressing deference to the elites and receiving respectability in exchange for subordination and submission.[44] Clientelism was an important component of Salvadoran politics during the administrations of Meléndez and Quiñónez, although there was a big difference in the way the elites related to urban groups as opposed to the rural sectors—the urban groups of artisans, workers, employees, and bureaucrats were simply closer and could have more direct contact with those who controlled political power though, of course, always in a subordinate position. The active participation of these groups in the electoral processes and in political life in general offered a democratic façade to these governments and it granted them a certain legitimacy.[45]

The presidents of the republic attended or sent delegates to the inauguration celebrations for the organization's new directors. In 1929 President Pío Romero Bosque christened a new wing of the organization's building.[46] Romero Bosque was an honorary president and member of the La Concordia, a resource the organization frequently relied on when interacting with governors, politicians, and industrialists. All the Salvadoran presidents, including Hernandez Martinez, were honorary members of the organization, and the organization's hall of honor contained a gallery with pictures of its most distinguished members. Governors supported the organization with subsidies and aid for its night school or for repairs of the facilities. And La Concordia knew how to be thankful. It participated visibly in public activities, such as the funeral of ex-president Carlos Meléndez, who had been a "member and firm protector."[47]

Although the organization's statutes prohibited it from political participation, individual members were not prevented from doing so. Thus, in the electoral campaign of 1918 the following members of La Concordia *participated* in the Central Committee of Quiñonista Workers: Manuel Bertrand, Emilio Sanchez, Liberato Galindo, Adrián Meléndez Arevalo, and Domingo Melara.[48] It is evident that urban middle sectors were well inserted into the networks of political clientelism of the Meléndez-Quiñónez era and were actors in the theatric rituals of democracy.

La Concordia maintained close relationships with some of the richest men in the country. This was the case with Miguel Dueñas—perhaps the country's wealthiest man—who gave many donations to the group, among them an urban plot on which to build offices and a school of arts. La Concordia honored Dueñas by giving him the title "protector of the Salvadoran working class."[49] Arturo Araujo and the tycoon David Bloom received similar titles. La Concordia, like many *mutuales* of the time, behaved deferentially toward the state and dominant sectors. Its uniqueness lay in its high level of respectability.

Rituals of La Concordia

La Concordia's membership showed a great predilection for rituals and ceremonies that served to express their social difference from other subaltern sectors of Salvadoran society and their deference to the dominant sectors. Their ceremonials elaborated the membership's social condition and served not the familiar function of solidarity, frequent among the working-class and artisan societies, but instead expressed the organization's exclusivity and respectability.[50] Its taste for ritual manifested at different levels. For example, the organization was preoccupied with its own symbols: a shield, standards, hymns, and marches that members composed for it. Rituals were used in the initiation acts for the board of directors that, in the years the organization was in its greatest splendor, were carried out according to a strict program, including a military band provided by the Salvadoran government, the presence of the president of the republic or some of its ministers, and the attendance of delegations from other groups. Rituals framed the relations of La Concordia with its benefactors from the dominant classes to whom they knew how to pay tribute with respect and good manners.

The organization's ritualism manifested in a certain legalism expressed in its preoccupation with its own statutes. The legal ritualism had, of course, a practical side but was also evidence of the organization's respectability. Its legalism included the scrutiny of its financial agents; sometimes procedures were not respected and some treasurers of the association were found to be embezzling.

The minutes of the board of directors and of the general assemblies reflect its formalism, which served as a mechanism for ensuring the organization's exclusivity; for example, the statutes established a procedure for accepting new members. In theory members joined only by invitation of two members and after a study of the applicant's qualifications. As the group declined, however, so did its ritualism.

Ceremonial and Civic Duties

The organization best expressed its taste for ritual in the organization of events and civic ceremonies. In this sense it acted as a producer of patriotic spectacles. It had a conscious will to invent traditions, to create or to promote events, and to sanctify heroes and founding fathers. According to article 42 of its statutes, "The only celebration that will be celebrated with the participation of all the partners is the national holiday in which the Mother country celebrates its independence. Its object is highly noble, because the Corporation will celebrate the idea that the artisan looks for the light and well-being, emancipating himself from ignorance." La Concordia played a key role in the Salvadoran national liturgy that the liberal state elaborated during the first decades of the twentieth century.[51] In 1882 it participated in the inauguration of the first section of the railroad in El Salvador, the celebrations in 1911 of the centenary of the first declaration of independence, the celebrations in 1912 of the adoption of the new Salvadoran flag, and the centenary of Independence in 1921. La Concordia also celebrated September 15, the day the new board of directors was elected, and October 12, the Day of the Race (Columbus Day).

The middle class expanded in Central America under the shadow of the growth of the state apparatus, the development of urban life, and the demand for services and functions by the agroexport economy. From the beginning these sectors were heterogenous and included the military and bureaucrats as well as artisans and small industrialists. La Concordia articulated the interests and ideas of a sector of the middle class, the industrial sector of the city of San Salvador. It seems to have had a central place in the relations between the state and the elites and the Salvadoran working class, mainly from 1910 to 1930. In its relationship to the state and the dominant sectors it maintained an air of respectful deference unlike similar organizations in the worker-artisan movement, and its position of preeminence was reflected in its treatment by the dominant sectors of El Salvador.

It valued respectability, social mobility, and patriotism. In this sense, it could not be more distant from the world view and radical ideology that was expanding among Salvadoran workers and peasants during the late 1920s, especially with the radicalization of the Regional Federation of Workers, controlled by the Communist Party.

Clearly, La Concordia was strongly oriented toward the middle class. Less clear is whether it had a democratic vocation. It is likely that its deference to elites and its need to distinguish itself from other organizations would limit its interest in democracy. As is well known, the political role of the middle sectors in Salvadoran history during the twentieth century has been heterogenous; these sectors have spawned as many reformists and revolutionaries as servants and defenders of the authoritarian state.

The middle sectors played a critical role in the fall of the Martinez dictatorship in 1944 and in other frustrated attempts at democratization. But the middle sectors did not systematically adopt the democratic ideal as their own, perhaps as a result of their traumatic experiences during 1932—many of them embraced anticommunism and supported authoritarian politics. These sectors preferred order over democratic political participation. The authoritarian inclination of some groups among the middle sectors was consolidated by their reliance on the military career as an important path of social mobility and the militarism acquired by the political regimes of El Salvador after the events of 1932. In contrast, in Costa Rica the middle sectors became the base of the democratic regime in a nearly unanimous way, mainly after the civil war of 1948 and after the defeat of the Communists, enhanced by the absence of the military institution and the possibility of social mobility through education, which the state promoted.

Erik Ching

Patronage and Politics under General Maximiliano Hernández Martínez, 1931–1939

The Local Roots of Military Authoritarianism in El Salvador

Despite, or perhaps because of, their profound impact on twentieth-century El Salvador, the military regimes of the 1930s to the 1970s remain profoundly enigmatic. Until recently, studying the military was politically hazardous and practically difficult. Archival documentation was off-limits to researchers until the late 1980s, and researchers and subjects alike were silenced by terror. This lack of information on the military has greatly hindered our ability to understand twentieth-century El Salvador, for the nearly five decades of military government (the longest period of uninterrupted military rule in modern Latin America) left an indelible imprint on both state and civil society.

Because the military regimes remain so understudied, we lack answers to some basic questions about their politics, such as how they governed, forestalled opposition, and generated support—in short, how the military stayed in power and what it did while it was there. The study presented in this chapter follows the lead of recent work on the military in El Salvador[1] but employs new archival evidence in the study of a specific period of military rule, the initial decade of the first regime of General Maximiliano Hernández Martínez (1931–1944).[2] The main sources for this study are records from El Salvador's Ministerio de Gobernación (Interior Ministry), particularly correspondence among offices at the local, regional, and national levels.

I argue that patronage was the defining characteristic of Martínez's political system. This system consisted of a nationwide network of patron-client relations that tied local, regional, and national actors together in a highly centralized, hierarchical pyramid. The existence of this system represented the continuation of a long process of political centralization and state formation dating to the nineteenth century. Martínez and his cohorts at the national level presumed to hold determinant power; however, they needed substantial local involvement. Without a solid foundation of local allies, the sustainability of military rule would have been seriously jeopardized.

Thus, while there is good reason to focus on the domineering, authoritarian, and centralized aspects of Martínez, we need to "decenter" his regime.[3] Decentering carries a two-fold methodological implication, one cultural, the other social.[4] The former calls for viewing politics and political identities as discursive constructs, the by-product of anonymous narrative, collective consciousness, or performative language. The latter calls for viewing national, centralized political systems from the perspective of subnational actors. In the absence of a cultural methodology, decentering defines politics as the arena in which actors pursue supposedly stable or fixed interests vis-à-vis rivals. For instance, *peasant* is assumed to be a coherent category of political interest, typically in conflict with landowning elites. While acknowledging the risks of "imposing oversimplified models on society," this study decenters the Martínez regime solely from the social angle.[5] In the case of El Salvador, a major actor at the subnational level was economic elites, particularly the famed coffee planters. But we must also recognize the agency of subalterns—peasants, workers, and smallholding farmers, both Indian and ladino. In their ongoing battles with local elites, they shaped the political system, even if they did not end military rule, democratize politics, or substantively alter their material existence.

Martínez Comes to Power

It is tempting to cast the Martínez regime in a light of invincibility on account of its longevity and brutality.[6] Indeed, Martínez's thirteen-year tenure was the longest in Salvadoran history, and his regime committed some draconian acts of terror. These issues should always remain at the forefront of any discussion about Martínez. Yet we must also go beyond them if we hope to learn more about the inevitable complexity of his regime. For instance, in its first few weeks in office, the regime was anything but stable; confronted by a host of destabilizing pressures, its survival was anything but guaranteed.

One of the foremost challenges before Martínez was the Great Depression and the accompanying collapse of coffee prices. With its export-driven economy, El Salvador felt the downturn in myriad ways: growers faced declining profits; laborers endured falling wages; and the government confronted a budget deficit as import duties, its main revenue source, dried up. Between 1930 and 1932, the value of both imports and exports in El Salvador declined by more than 50 percent.[7] This economic crisis had wide-ranging social and political implications, including the removal of President Arturo Araujo. Elected as a reformer in January 1931, Araujo responded to the crisis in a manner consistent with his political platform; he maintained the already limited social spending and cut back in other areas, most notably military pay. As salaries shrank or fell into arrears, the military grew restless. Finally, a group of midlevel officers launched a coup in December 1931 that ousted Araujo and brought Martínez to power. Martínez may have had the financial crisis to thank for his new position, but he now confronted the same financial quagmire as his predecessor.

Another problem before Martínez was a rapidly escalating social crisis in the west. Throughout the second half of 1931, peasants in the four western departments of El Salvador—Sonsonate, Santa Ana, Ahuachapán, and La Libertad—had been mobilizing against local authorities. In late January 1932, less than two months after Martínez came to office, they rose up in rebellion. Hundreds if not thousands of rebels attacked roughly a dozen municipalities and occupied six of them for as long as four days before military units arrived and squelched the uprising. The rebellion represented a major challenge to the Martínez regime and threw the nation into a state of emergency.[8]

In addition to these economic and social crises, Martínez faced a diplomatic challenge on account of the coup that brought him to power. Martínez denied involvement in the conspiracy, thereby justifying his claim to the presidency as Araujo's legal vice president. Historians still debate his participation in the coup, but many foreign governments at the time believed him complicit.[9] Most prominent among these was the United States, which invoked the 1923 Washington Treaty, of which both countries were signatories. The treaty mandated that no government in Central America would receive recognition if it came to power in a nondemocratic manner. The United States sent a special diplomat, Jefferson Caffrey, to El Salvador to negotiate Martínez's resignation, but Martínez rejected the demand. For the next three years the United States refused to recognize his regime; of course, in late December 1931 no one knew that the dispute between the two countries would drag on for so long. More immediately pressing for Martínez was the possible range of U.S. responses. It does not appear that either the U.S. State Department or Caffrey threatened Martínez with a more substantive action, but knowledge of past U.S. interventions in the region, including its lack of support for loans, was not lost on El Salvador's leaders.[10] Furthermore, in the midst of the diplomatic impasse, U.S. and Canadian warships arrived on El Salvador's coast in response to the 1932 uprising. Officers from these ships traveled to San Salvador to inform Martínez of their readiness to land troops to defend North American lives and investments. Martínez informed them that this was not necessary, and indeed the intervention did not occur. Nevertheless, the arrival of foreign warships was an inauspicious moment for Martínez.[11]

In addition to foreign pressures, Martínez faced domestic opposition. Araujo still had substantial support, both in and outside government, especially among working people who had embraced his reformist agenda. Other domestic opponents included people who were not Araujo adherents but who supported democratic reforms. Finally, there was the military, arguably Martínez's greatest threat. The military had a long history of overt involvement in politics, and military officers had been constant fixtures in government, particularly the presidency. This pattern began to change around the turn of the century. Whereas coups were the customary mode of power transfers, 1898 was the last time a sitting president was ousted in a coup prior to 1931. After the victor in the coup, General Regalado, completed his term in 1903, only one other military officer held the presidency prior to Martínez. Nevertheless, the military remained a potent force. Coup attempts and conspiracies were a constant feature of political life in El Salvador. Martínez had to be wary, for the coup of 1931 awakened the ambitions of many power-seeking officers.

Yet another problem for Martínez was his lack of nationwide political networks. The few political alliances he had established during his brief campaign for the presidency in 1930 had withered away. In fact, the small political party that had sponsored his candidacy, El Partido Nacional Republicano, withdrew its support when he joined the Araujo ticket as vice president, and as Araujo's vice president during 1931 he was not able to build a support network outside of the military.[12] Once he became president, Martínez received numerous offers of fidelity; however, his challenge was determining how many, if any, were genuine.

In short, Martínez's first weeks in office were marked by a multitude of perils. His government was isolated, indigent, and opposed on many fronts. He obviously overcame these challenges, given that he remained in office until 1944. The manner in which he survived these pressures says much about his overall governing strategy. The British chargé d'affaires described it in Bismarckian terms as balanced use of an "iron fist and a velvet glove," meaning that Martínez rewarded supporters and repressed adversaries.[13] This strategy was evident in Martínez's response to the fiscal crisis. He slashed social spending, suspended payment on a 1922 loan from a U.S. bank, and paid military salaries. This rewarded his most im-

portant ally, the military, and further estranged those already opposed to him, adherents of democracy and the U.S. government.

Martínez's response to the uprising of January 1932 provides another example
of his counterbalanced use of repression and reward. The regime's immediate response to the rebellion was merciless violence. Military units swept through the
insurgent zone and killed at least 10,000 people in less than three weeks. The
harsh response squelched the rebellion, returned local authorities to power, and
consolidated the regime's support base. Opponents of Martínez prior to the uprising were now likely to choose him over peasant rebels. Not least among
Martínez's new adherents was U.S. secretary of state Henry Stimson, who despite
his official opposition to the regime lauded Martínez in his personal diary as "the
man who . . . is the only pillar against the success of what seems to be a nasty
proletarian revolution . . . we are unable to recognize under the 1923 rule."[14]

Once the immediate threat had passed, Martínez reversed his repressive approach toward the countryside and adopted a reformist stance. Believing that the
key to avoiding future uprisings was to lessen abuses of the rural poor by local
elites, Martínez ordered that the most egregious abusers be sanctioned and that
local government officials defend workers' interests. Peasants, both Indian and
ladino (non-Indian), remained wisely skeptical of the regime's motives, but they
recognized its willingness to help and occasionally appealed to it for assistance.[15]

Martínez's response to other domestic opponents remained consistent with his
iron fist/velvet glove strategy. He dispensed with the leaders of the 1931 coup by
reassigning them to remote posts or sending them abroad. Prominent civilian
politicians were either offered high-ranking positions in government or repressed
by police surveillance or exile. Finally, in his response to the United States,
Martínez simply waited. The United States did not pursue a policy beyond non-
recognition, which allowed Martínez to outlast its resolve.[16] In summary, Martínez confronted a mélange of challenges during his initial months in office. He
overcame them with shrewd action and adroit politicking, the same traits that
went into the making of the political system that would sustain him for the next
thirteen years.

Politics and Elections Prior to Martínez

It is not known whether Martínez intended to remain in power for as long as
he did. He declared initially that he would remain in office only for the remainder of Araujo's four-year term (1931–1935) and then retire in accordance with the
constitutional mandate against presidential succession. But shortly thereafter,
Martínez claimed that he had the right to hold his own four-year term, declaring

his intent to run for the presidency in 1935. After an uncontested victory, he gained an additional four years in office (1935–1939). As this term wound down, Martínez and his supporters installed a new Constitution (1939) that allowed a president to succeed himself for one term. The Constitution also changed the term in office to six years and turned the selection of the president over to the National Assembly rather than to the popular vote. The National Assembly dutifully elected Martínez to a six-year term in 1939. Near the end of this term, Martínez was preparing to change the Constitution to allow him another six-year term, but mass protests drove him out of office in 1944.

Martínez's rise to power certainly signified an expanded role for the military in politics. Officers occupied many high-ranking posts once reserved for civilians, including the Ministry of War and departmental governorships. For instance, in 1930 only two of the fourteen governors were officers, but by 1934 twelve were.[17] Nevertheless, it would be inaccurate to describe the early Martínez government as a military regime per se. Most of the executive cabinet, the entire National Assembly, and all municipal offices remained in civilian hands.

Regardless of this significant civilian presence, the Martínez regime was fundamentally an antidemocratic dictatorship. The manner in which Martínez rejected democracy, however, was consistent with the patronage system of the previous decades of civilian rule; he retained some electoral procedures but without the substance of popular rule. Elections occurred regularly and often; people registered to vote and voted; and results were tallied and published. Politics under Martínez involved a vigorous electorate and electoral process. However, beneath the surface something else was at work. The functioning of this system is perhaps best understood in the context of a brief history of electoral procedures in the decades prior to 1931.

Until the procedure was changed in the 1950 Constitution, voting in El Salvador was conducted publicly and orally. This was perhaps the most salient feature of El Salvador's political system. Oral voting allowed a person's vote to be known and subject to influence or threat. Elections for both local and national offices were conducted in the municipalities under the watchful eye of incumbent municipal authorities. Before the election these officials supervised the selection of a *directorio,* a commission of four or more local citizens who would run the voting process. Once chosen, *directorio* members assembled inside the polling site, usually the *cabildo* (municipal hall), and had voters pass by and declare their vote.

Ostensibly democratic, these elections were heavily managed affairs. Local patronage leaders, often the same people conducting the election, utilized the machinery of patron-client networks to influence voters and control the outcome.[18] Patronage networks were the foundation of political power. Persons who aspired to hold office themselves, or influence those people in office, needed a body of dependable patronage allies at their command. These included their personal clients as well as other patrons who hoped to join forces and built a network large enough to contest for power on election day. The accumulation of patronage alliances and the nurturing of patron-client bonds were ongoing processes in which elections represented only a fleeting, albeit critical, moment of culmination.

Elections usually involved competitions between rival patronage networks over the machinery of voting. The faction that determined which voters passed before the *directorio* likely emerged victorious at day's end. Success in municipal elections enhanced the possibility of building alliances with patrons at the regional or national levels, for they were always in search of reliable locals who could secure votes in national elections. Thus, politics consisted of a mosaic of alliances spread across the nation. A local network might be autonomous, concerned only with local affairs, or it might be connected to larger networks. Votes constituted the most ubiquitous exchange in patronage alliances, but they were hardly the sole request. When politics and elections turned violent, which occurred often, patronage demands turned to the human and material resources needed to wage battle. In either case, political life revolved around the making, breaking, and maintaining of patronage alliances.

In a society like that of early twentieth-century El Salvador, with substantial inequalities in wealth and power, patron-client relations were commonly rooted in class relations. The archetypal patron was a landowner, and his clients were dependent laborers. Through coercion, cajoling, or some combination of the two, rich and powerful patrons ensured that clients did their bidding on election day. But this rigid portrayal of patrons as rich landowners and clients as poor workers needs to be tempered, for it was far from the universal condition. Salvadoran society was highly complex, and the patronage system mirrored that complexity. For instance, some patronage networks were built on religious, ethnic, or family foundations rather than simply on class.

The municipality of Nahuizalco in the early twentieth century offers a revealing example of this complexity. Located in Sonsonate Department in the foothills of the coffee-growing highlands, Nahuizalco was a predominantly Indian village, with about 90 percent of the population classified as Indian in 1930. Nahuizalco was also a sizable municipality with 15,000 inhabitants in 1930, 10 percent of the population of Sonsonate Department. Throughout the first half of the twentieth century, Nahuizalco's Indians controlled large portions of the region's agricultural lands, despite the existence of a small ladino elite with sizable properties. During the privatization of their communal properties in the 1880s and 1890s, Nahuizalco's Indians did not lose most of their lands to outside speculators or coffee barons. Rather, they gained title to their individual plots. This conversion to a smallholding peasantry did not eradicate the Indians' sense of community. Both before and after privatization, Indians participated actively in municipal politics. Their large numbers, material resources, and history of mobilization made them an important political force. Outside political and military leaders often sought them out as allies.[19]

Always a focal point for ethnic issues, Nahuizalco became a hotbed of ethnic politics in the late nineteenth century when the small, but increasingly powerful ladino population began vying with the Indians for control over municipal government. Over the next five decades, the village was divided into two camps, each roughly united. On account of their numerical disadvantage, ladinos had to resort to classic patronage-style tactics to achieve electoral success. They controlled the machinery of voting and ensured that only their supporters passed before the *directorio*. Indeed, they won a number of elections over the years. One might suspect that Indians would conduct their electoral affairs differently owing to their decided numerical advantage. But, in fact, the Indians ran elections in much the same manner as their ladino adversaries. They controlled the polls and allowed only known supporters to vote. All elections in Nahuizalco, regardless of whether Indians or ladinos were victorious, tended to be decided by unanimity. The only difference between Indian and ladino victories was the number of votes cast. During ladino victories, the number of voters seldom reached 20 percent of the number during Indian victories.

This case of Nahuizalco suggests that patronage was the de facto rule of politics across the country, and whoever participated in the system did so according to its norms. Thus, an entire group of so-called subalterns—that is, smallholding Indian peasants—could constitute a patronage network and thereby complicate any presumed images of patrons as rich landowners and clients as dependent laborers. Admittedly, Indian society exhibited its own hierarchies. It would be erroneous to assume Indian politics as necessarily egalitarian. But Indian society was not marked by vast disparities in wealth. Instead, Indian authority rested at least partly on religious, gender, family, and generational lines rather than simply on accumulated land and wealth. It is likely that these same issues were important for ladino society as well. Clearly, ethnicity was a key variable for both sides of Nahuizalco's political divide.

If Nahuizalco exemplifies the complex makeup of local patronage networks, it also symbolizes the patronage foundation of the political system in El Salvador in general in the late nineteenth and early twentieth centuries. In one municipality after another, across the entire nation, patronage networks battled one another for control over municipal government and the opportunity to build alliances with regional and national patrons. The system tied together people in disparate geographical locales. But until the 1920s, decentralization was its defining characteristic. No single network at the national level was able to consolidate authority and institutionalize patronage by welding the local and regional networks into a single, national whole. But slowly, steadily, if unevenly, the system did centralize. The culmination came in the 1920s under the Meléndez-Quiñónez family. For thirteen years between 1913 and 1927, three members of this family controlled the presidency and centralized patronage. They were able to do so largely because of steady economic growth and an accompanying increase in state power. Political advancement now meant rising within the ranks of the solitary network rather than trying to overthrow it from without. We should be cautious not to overstate the power of the Meléndez-Quiñónez family. They enjoyed an unprecedented degree of authority, but El Salvador was still a poor country with a rudimentary infrastructure, and large areas of the country remained remote from national politics.

Over the next four years (1927–1931), President Pío Romero Bosque subjected the patronage system to a relentless attack. He and a coterie of loyal bureaucrats promoted democratic reforms in a vigorous campaign directed from their offices in the National Palace in downtown San Salvador. Their goal was nothing less than changing elections from objects of patronage to expressions of popular will. Despite the enormity of this task, they made impressive strides. The highlight was the presidential election of January 1931 when the reformist candidate, Arturo Araujo was elected in what appears to have been a democratic process.[20] Notwithstanding Romero's success, his reform program failed to eradicate the old patronage system. After the 1931 coup, patronage networks reemerged as the dominant medium of politics. Interestingly, Martínez initially stated that he would continue Romero's incipient democratic reforms. And the municipal elections of January 1932 were quite competitive in many places; the Communist Party even ran a candidate for mayor in San Salvador.[21] But this election proved to be the exception. With each passing month, Martínez's opposition to democracy became more apparent. He pushed aside the Romero reforms and installed a new, or better said, an old, system that bound together the local, regional, and national levels.

Pro-Patria and the Return of Patronage

The political system that Martínez eventually put into place greatly resembled that of the Meléndez-Quiñónez years (1913–1927). A strong central authority presided over a pyramid of patronage networks, linking local and national levels together in mutually dependent relationships. Martínez received votes for himself or his supporters in the National Assembly, and the networks ensured that opposition movements would have little opportunity to emerge. In return for their loyalty, local patronage leaders were free to go about their affairs. In the event that a problem arose, such as the emergence of a challenger, the national government would likely support local patronage leaders. For those locals wanting to climb the political ladder, loyal service translated into advancement.

We do not know if Martínez came into office with the intent of making patronage the basis of his political system. The tensions of his first months in office meant that he focused initially on little more than political survival. Controlling elections in all of the nation's 257 municipalities was an impossible task. It appears that for the first two municipal elections, in December 1931 (postponed to January 1932) and December 1932, Martínez left the municipalities to their own devices, doing little more than issuing an order stating that the government would not tolerate violence and disorder.[22] As long as visible opposition movements did not emerge, Martínez appears to have been content to let the elections run their course. This meant that patronage returned in force. Needless to say, popular opposition was unlikely in the wake of the government's repressive response to the uprising in January 1932.

Martínez was less lax about elections for the forty-two deputies in the National Assembly. A loyal Assembly was crucial to presenting a united front before foreign diplomatic pressures. But lacking established lines of electoral control in the municipalities, the regime could not count on the results of widespread voting. Thus, for the first two Assembly elections, in January 1932 and January 1933, the government made up candidate lists and allowed hardly anyone to vote. For instance, in the capital city of San Salvador, which had roughly 20,000 eligible voters, only 379 votes were cast during the three days of voting in the 1932 election.[23] Comments from the U.S. chargé d'affaires reflect the extent of control: "The official returns indicated that the entire membership of Congress will be composed of deputies backed by and favorable to the Martínez regime and there will apparently not be any opposition group in the new Assembly."[24] *Diario Patria,* a newspaper, commented that the 1932 election represented "the adoption by the new government of the old procedures which discredited the exercise of suffrage among us."[25]

These first two deputy elections demonstrate the ability of the Martínez regime to control the results of a specific contest. But the formal patronage system and its intimate integration of local and national politics was still under the surface. The impetus to change this was the presidential election of 1935. Martínez announced his candidacy in June 1933, and shortly thereafter he oversaw the establishment of a new official political party, the Partido Nacional Pro-Patria (National Party of the Fatherland). Pro-Patria's immediate objective was to mobilize support for the presidential campaign, but by any other definition it was the framework of a patronage system. No alternative parties were allowed to exist, and all political offices, whether elected or appointed, local or national, would be filled through its channels.

Pro-Patria's inaugural *consejo supremo* (supreme council) gathered in San Salvador in July 1933 to devise a recruitment strategy. The plan that emerged from this meeting called for Pro-Patria *delegaciones* (chapters) to be established in every neighborhood. The first chapters were to be established in the fourteen departmental capitals. Their members would travel to outlying municipalities to organize local chapters, whose members, in turn, would go to the *cantones* (neighborhoods) and do the same. Each chapter could have an unlimited number of rank-and-file members, but an organizational committee of only a select few would lead it. In the municipal chapters this committee was called the *directiva* (executive committee) and consisted of up to twenty-four members; in the neighborhoods it was called a *sub-comité del barrio* (neighborhood subcommittee) and would have no more than fifteen members.[26]

Given its design, this organizational strategy had exponential growth potential. Thousands of chapters with hundreds of thousands of members could be created in a very short time. Indeed, comprehensive data from Sonsonate Department, and partial data from the remaining thirteen departments, reveals that the strategy produced impressive results. In Sonsonate, nine of the department's sixteen municipalities had Pro-Patria chapters by October 1933, and by June of the following year all sixteen did. Of those sixteen, seven had complete neighborhood chapters, and more than likely so did the other nine, but we lack membership lists to say for certain. By October 1934, Pro-Patria had 10,000 card-carrying members in Sonsonate Department, with an additional 6,500 waiting for cards to become members. Two months later the total number of members had risen to 20,000. This figure is all the more impressive in light of the fact that only men could join Pro-Patria and Sonsonate's adult male population was roughly 30,000.[27] This level of membership does not necessarily reflect genuine support for Martínez, but it does demonstrate Pro-Patria's organizational capacity. An indication of the degree to which these activities in 1933 and 1934 laid a foundation for Pro-Patria's dominance in later years comes from a study conducted by the government in 1940. The object of the study was to survey all the "societies, organizations, and clubs in the nation." Its results showed that, "in almost all the populations, there does not exist any society except for the sub-committee of the Partido Pro-Patria."[28]

The administrative ranks of Pro-Patria were synonymous with government bureaucracy. Martínez, his cabinet members, and other high-ranking officials made up Pro-Patria's supreme council. Governors and commandants, the two ranking officials in the departments, presided over Pro-Patria's executive committees in the departmental capitals. And in the municipalities, the *mayors,* councilmen, and local commandants were in charge of Pro-Patria's chapters. This combined military and civilian presence in Pro-Patria reflects the diverse makeup of Martínez's regime. It also reveals a link between political structures and state security. Civilian officials and their military counterparts worked alongside one another and were incorporated into a vast intelligence network. One of the party's mandates stated that its leaders were expected to "submit lists of labor union supporters and communists so that they can be watched and prevented from posing as *Martinistas.*"[29]

Just as Pro-Patria was synonymous with government, it also reproduced the country's social and economic hierarchies. Local economic elites held the positions of authority, and workers and peasants made up the rank and file. The municipality of Nahuizalco in Sonsonate Department, once again, provides a revealing case study. As of July 1934, Nahuizalco's Pro-Patria apparatus consisted of roughly 3,000 rank-and-file members presided over by its executive council of twenty-nine members and seventeen neighborhood sub-committees with a total of 283 members. The executive council was composed entirely of ladinos, most of whom were prosperous landowners. Their names—Brito, Magaña, Mejía, and Olivares, among others—dominate lists of the village's *finqueros* (coffee planters), cattle ranchers, and generally "well-to-do" citizens. By contrast, not a single one of the 283 names on the neighborhood subcommittees appears on these lists of prominent commercial farmers. Moreover, the subcommittee lists are dominated by recognizably Indian surnames, such as Lile, Galicia, Tépaz, Cúmet, Zetino, Crúz, Shúl, and Campos. If we include other surnames common to Nahuizalco's Indian families, such as Pérez, Cortés, and Hernández, we can safely conclude that Indians accounted for at least 70 percent of Nahuizalco's subcommittee members.[30]

Sonsonate City, the departmental capital, provides a similar example. The executive committee consisted of thirty-five of the city's most prominent citizens. As might be expected for a departmental capital, some of these individuals were of national stature. Héctor Herrera, for instance, served as Martínez's national auditor in 1932 and also owned four haciendas around Sonsonate City. Lisandro Larín had been the governor of Sonsonate Department once and the *alcalde* of Sonsonate City twice. By contrast, laborers dominate the list of rank-and-file members. Only the first four pages of the alphabetized list have survived, but they are sufficiently revealing. Of the 119 names on those four pages, 82 are listed as *jornaleros* (day laborers), and only 2 of the remaining 37 names are listed as *agricultores* (commercial farmers). The remaining 35 members are artisans.[31]

This evidence from Nahuizalco and Sonsonate illustrates the extent to which Pro-Patria bound together broad swathes of society and integrated local, regional, and national politics into a unified whole. As this evidence suggests (discussed in greater detail later), everyone in the system was bound by a series of mutual obligations and reciprocal relationships. Everyone had a role to fulfill, and all expected that in return for doing so the system would respond to their needs. These expectations varied with the interests of the solicitors, but they typically revolved around requests for government aid in local politics, promotion within the ranks of Pro-Patria, or simply to be left alone. Obviously, elites had bargaining power in this system, not only to reproduce or extend their social and economic standing, but also because the Martínez regime defined them as the driving force behind the nation's economic development.

But the Martínez regime did not side with elites to the exclusion of workers and peasants. In fact, as briefly mentioned earlier, the regime instituted a populist reform program in the wake of the 1932 rebellion that had as its goal the incorporation of popular needs into the regime's development program. This program defined peasants and workers as organic, albeit unequal, partners with landed elites and the military in the national body. The military believed that peasants and workers provided labor, elites offered knowledge and skills, and the military represented honor and order; all three were necessary for the nation to progress. Based on this corporatist, pseudofascist formulation, the military sought to defend workers and peasants against the most egregious abuses by local elites. It also pursued an array of modest but highly publicized measures designed to lessen the material burdens on the working masses.

Skeptical readers might dismiss the military's reforms as empty posturing by a regime dedicated to elite-led development.[32] But while the program was not designed to radically restructure the distribution of wealth or power, dismissing it out of hand would be a mistake. As limited as it might have been, the reform program created a space within which workers and peasants, Indian and ladino alike, found room to maneuver. Furthermore, worker and peasant agency was at least partly responsible for the creation of this space. The most overt expression of this agency was the 1932 uprising. Less dramatic, although more numerous, examples were the repeated requests and demands directed at the regime. Thus, between 1932 and 1934 an important series of convergences occurred. At precisely the same moment that it was constructing the edifice of Pro-Patria and institutionalizing patronage as the mode of political interaction, the Martínez regime was also incorporating broad sectors of society into its ranks and instituting a populist reform program designed to lessen the burdens on working people. It is not clear to what extent the channels of Pro-Patria served as a vehicle for popular demands; this remains a topic for future inquiry. But it is clear that popular agency was a foundational component of the Martínez period.

A look at municipal elections starting in 1933 reveals how patronage fueled politics. The edifice of Pro-Patria was sufficiently in place by the end of 1933 to allow the party to control the elections that December. Roughly six weeks prior to the election Martínez sent a circular to his governors informing them that Pro-Patria's supreme council would have final say over all municipal candidates but that governors were to use their contacts in the municipalities to assemble lists of acceptable candidates. Acceptable was defined as, "persons that most meet the needs of the nation, the department, and the Partido Nacional."[33] This selection process was a key moment in the construction of patronage. Governors, appointed by and already dependent on Martínez, accumulated loyalty from their contacts in the municipalities. These contacts in turn gathered favors from the candidates. Everyone in the system owed something to someone.

This process of dispensing patronage, as well as the risks that came with it, is revealed by the case of Guillermo Barrientos, member of a prominent landowning family in the region of San Julián in Sonsonate Department. Barrientos was chosen by the governor to select candidates for three municipalities: San Julián, Cuisnahuat, and Ishuatán. Barrientos dutifully followed his mandate by assembling his lists and forwarding them to the governor's assistant. However, in the process he angered some candidate hopefuls. This was one of the risks of dispensing and accumulating patronage—namely, alienating those excluded. Barrientos described the situation in a note to the governor's assistant: "There is no lack of persons in these places, motivated by one reason or another . . . who want to undermine our sincere efforts and change these names." Since it was in Barrientos's interest to ensure the success of his selections, he lobbied on their behalf: "These persons are the best we could hope to find for being in agreement with the aspirations of the National Party; for this reason I encourage you to have a prompt interview with the Governor, putting before him this list of names."[34]

Another example of the contested nature of candidate selection comes from a series of letters from Gabino Mata Jr., a wealthy cattle rancher and coffee grower in the region of Nahuizalco and Juayúa, to the governor of Sonsonate Department in November 1937. Mata objected to the governor's choice of candidates for the forthcoming election and was hoping to change his mind. Mata first suggested an alternative for *alcalde* in Nahuizalco and then turned to the department's three seats in the National Assembly. One candidate, Ricardo Vilanova, particularly irked Mata, and he encouraged the governor to choose Alfredo Salaverría of Juayúa instead. The governor followed Mata's advice on Nahuizalco, but we do not know if he did so regarding Vilanova. Regardless, Mata's correspondence illustrates the personal and local dynamics that went into candidate selection and the competing interests that high-ranking party officials had to balance when compiling their lists.[35]

The criteria governors used to select local agents remain speculative. Presumably they chose a friend, confidant, established political ally, or someone who came highly recommended. Their written correspondence frequently refers to decisions made in personal conversation, suggesting familiarity with the involved parties.[36] If a governor did not have a particular individual in mind, he turned to the formal channels of the local Pro-Patria chapters, which then submitted lists of candidates in official *actas* (records of proceedings). Once the upper echelon of Pro-Patria had received and approved the lists of candidates, it returned them to the municipalities with instructions to follow through on election day. A typical example was sent from the governor of Ahuachapán to the municipal officials in Ahuachapán City: "You are informed that the superior authorities have approved definitively the following personnel for that Municipality. . . . It is recommended that this list not be altered."[37] A similarly explicit example is contained in a coded telegram that one governor sent to the municipalities in his department on the eve of the 1937 municipal election: "Avoid all possible disorders in the next elections. Do not allow mixed *directorios* or contrary elements to form."[38] In short, municipal officials were instructed to make sure the election occurred as planned.

The final stage in the electoral process was voting day, when the candidates brought the clients out to the polls. Pro-Patria kept extensive records of local elections, especially after 1935, consisting mostly of telegrams, letters, and memos sent back and forth on election day. These records offer a day-to-day, and in some cases an hour-to-hour look at voting as local officials informed their superiors. The records are revealing in their monotony, for it was rare that voting was anything other than unanimous. A prototype of these reports is the telegram arriving from Guazapa in San Salvador Department on the conclusion of voting for the municipal election of December 1937: "Voting has been closed with seven hundred twenty (720) votes in favor of Alcalde Joaquín Mayorga Melara. . . . The most complete order reigned."[39] Often the reports would not bother to mention the candidates' names given the absence of competition.

In addition to being foregone and unanimous, elections also resulted in limited turnover in office. The same people, or, rather, the same political networks, tended to monopolize office once they gained Pro-Patria's approval. A comparison of lists of municipal office holders in three departments (Sonsonate,

Ahuachapán, and San Miguel) for three consecutive election years—1937, 1939, and 1941 (elections were held every two years after 1935)—reveals the extent of continuity in office holding. In thirty-seven of the forty-eight municipalities in these three departments, the same person held the position of *alcalde* for at least two of the three elections. When the other municipal offices, régidor and síndico (alderman and trustee), are included, the level of continuity is even more apparent. In all but one of the remaining eleven municipalities the same person held these offices in at least two of the three elections. This evidence is even more revealing when we take into account two unofficial rules of municipal politics: (1) Members of opposition networks did not serve on municipal councils together; and (2) individuals rarely changed patronage allegiances. So when the same names appear from one list to the next, almost certainly the same political network is monopolizing office.

It is no great surprise that Pro-Patria relied on the same coterie of local political players. Martínez got what he wanted, and so did locals. The system was designed to be mutually rewarding for those who had the privilege of participating in it. But what about those who were excluded? As I described earlier, the process of selecting patronage allies could be a zero-sum game; choosing one person or faction meant snubbing another. The dilemma of any centralized political system is to find the balance between limited largesse and the expectations of the upwardly mobile. How did those who were overlooked respond?

Electoral Irregularities

Notwithstanding the utter predictability of most elections, sometimes opposition factions in the municipalities did emerge and refuse to accept their outsider status. In these instances, opposition leaders relied on any one of the old tricks, such as controlling the selection of the *directorio* (electoral council), or seizing control of the polling place on election day. One example comes from the village of Santiago de María in Usulután Department in 1936. According to reports from the official candidates, "just after we had formed the *directorio,* at the last minute . . . a nucleus of men in favor of Pablo Mejía as *alcalde* came forward to advance his candidacy." Both sides immediately sought the governor's support, and over the next few days a flurry of telegrams were exchanged. Despite a voluminous correspondence, it is not clear what actually transpired. It appears that Mejía or his supporters tried to gain control of the polling place shortly after the formation of the *directorio.* In making his case to the governor, Mejía adopted a legalist standpoint and claimed that the original *directorio* was illegitimate due to a technicality. The official candidates employed a more foolproof method by accusing

Mejía of inciting violence: "The various members of the band supporting Pablo Mejía," they wrote, "continue to agitate the people by carrying weapons in the park with malicious intentions." The paper trail for the case ends here, without revealing the governor's specific response. But final election results show that Mejía failed and the official candidates won.[40]

The national government's aversion to disorder tended to result in quick responses to electoral irregularities, as a case from Aguilares in San Salvador Department illustrates. On the morning of the election of 1937, a faction emerged opposing the official candidates. The incumbent mayor immediately sent a telegram to the governor requesting assistance: "I ask that you give orders to the National Guard regarding the designated candidates. Adversaries preparing to assault the village. . . . Urgently request your position." The message was forwarded to both the Ministers of Government and War, who sent explicit orders to the nearest National Guard post less than an hour later: "Maintain order." The National Guard arrived in the village, but for reasons that are still unclear, they were unable to "reestablish order" in time to avoid a postponement of the election. Regardless, this case reveals the rapidity with which military force was used to defend political order. It took only a few hours for news from Aguilares to result in soldiers arriving in the village with orders from the highest levels of government.[41]

Repression was not the government's sole response to upstart candidacies. In line with Martínez's velvet glove approach, the government occasionally accepted opposition movements, seemingly recognizing that they grew out of genuine frustration on the part of ignored factions. In short, a little disorder was sometimes necessary to attract the government's attention. An example of this comes from the village of Nueva Concepción in Chalatenango Department. On the morning of the election of 1937, the official candidates informed the governor that an opposition movement had appeared and was trying to "upset the public order and openly oppose higher orders by dissolving the official candidacies." Instead of sending in troops and defending the status quo, the governor ordered that the candidates be changed and the upstarts be allowed to win the election.[42] We do not know if this indeed transpired. But we do know that it was not uncommon for the government to change candidates at the last minute. For instance, in 1937, there were thirty-seven other municipalities, along with Nueva Concepción, in which at least one of the candidates was changed in the week before or after the election. Nueva Concepción was the only one, however, in which the change can be directly linked to an active opposition movement.[43]

"Disorders" like these in Santiago de María, Aguilares, and Nueva Concepción merit close examination, for they expose the cracks in Martínez's political system and highlight its complexities. But how frequent were they? Unfortunately, the government did not compile lists of these incidents, or at least such lists have not survived in the historical record, so only a schematic picture is possible. If we look at only 1937, a year especially rich in electoral documentation, only 14 of the nation's 257 municipalities witnessed an opposition movement that employed physical mobilization rather than simply the standard verbal and written lobbying. None of these movements appear to have been particularly violent, and only two of them, including Aguilares, caused an election to be postponed.

Disturbances appear to have been inspired primarily by local variables rather than opposition to Martínez or patronage in general. Outsiders simply wanted a turn in the system. And despite its aversion to disorder, the Martínez regime granted them some freedom of movement, however limited, as long as they confined themselves to local issues. This was an astute strategy on the part of the regime because the regime sought not only efficiency from its municipal allies but also effectiveness. In other words, changes in local conditions might necessitate changes in personnel. This was another of the challenges before the regime's bureaucrats, balancing the needs of the system with those at the local level.

This evidence invites a brief digression on the evolution of local politics leading up to the 1930s. Every municipality likely had multiple political factions wanting to control local government and enjoy the accompanying rewards, however provincial they might be. In years past it was not uncommon for election day to turn violent as rival factions scrambled for control over the electoral machinery. During the Meléndez-Quiñónez era, violent clashes between patronage gangs were a regular feature of elections. Under Martínez, electoral violence was less likely. The state had the power to sanction locals who engaged in destabilizing activity. Instead of fighting it out, patronage bosses had to lobby it out by cultivating relations with higher officials. The infrequency of violent disorders under Martínez testifies to Pro-Patria's ability to create an atmosphere in which working outside the system was perceived as counterproductive.

The Presidential Election of 1935

The presidential election of January 1935 provides an example of the patronage system operating at maximum efficiency. When Martínez announced in mid-1933 that he would run for the presidency in 1935, he made no public mention of competition. But whoever might have thought that opposition would be allowed quickly learned the contrary. Any person with national-level political standing was either brought into the government, placed under surveillance, arrested, or exiled. Martínez was the only candidate, but his election was not to be a rote exercise in protocol. Rather, it was to be a mass demonstration of his capacity to carry out his functions as the supreme patronage boss. The more voters that came out to the polls, the more power his regime could claim.

The primary mechanism for getting out the vote was, of course, the patronage networks. It was the duty of local political bosses to mobilize their retainers on election day. Pro-Patria also realized that a little largesse to encourage voting never hurts, so Pro-Patria chapters devised strategies to encourage voting. The Sonsonate City chapter offered food and a movie: "This chapter has decided on the eve of the election to entertain the public with a movie in the early evening and then invite everyone to a designated place at 3:00 in the morning for coffee, tamales, and bread, so that they will be gathered together and organized to go to the polls when they open." The national government offered its own version of beneficence—electricity and water flowed without the customary rationing.[44]

In the days leading up to the voting, the standard mass of correspondence was exchanged between local and national offices relating to the composition of *directorios* and the candidates for the National Assembly. One governor's orders read: "Serve instructions to the *alcaldes* to ensure that no variations are reported in the election of the *directorios* from those names which have been sent to them by the Supreme Council of Pro-Patria."[45] One *alcalde* acknowledged the receipt of the names for the deputy candidates: "I understand which candidates should be elected as deputies."[46]

When election day finally arrived, voting occurred as planned. According to the government's reports, 329,555 votes were cast, every one of them in favor of Martínez. This represented 77 percent of all registered voters, which in a nation of 1.5 million people testifies to Pro-Patria's success in mobilizing the electorate. This was also a 20 percent increase over the turnout in the 1931 election. Throughout the three days of voting, municipal leaders submitted daily, and sometimes twice or thrice daily, reports on the voting. The report from the commandant of Cabañas Department is typical: "Throughout Cabañas Department, elections for supreme authorities are being conducted in the greatest of order. Voting is unanimous in favor of the noble cause postulated by General Maximiliano H. Martínez. . . . People are providing a civic and patriotic demonstration. We expect complete success."[47] A report from Juayúa reads: "The number of votes recorded to date is 1,214, being the number recorded today 394. All voting is being gathered with total spontaneity in complete calm."[48] The British Minister effectively described the results: "The election itself, on the 13th to the 15th of January, was the usual farce. There was no other candidate, but the people were nevertheless urged to record their votes. . . . The elections for the National Assembly took place, all the candidates elected . . . being Martínez men. There is no opposition."[49]

Martínez's complement to this highly structured political system was militarism and a vast security apparatus. As previously mentioned, civilian officials were expected to perform security functions by reporting on potential radicals. However, the bulwark of security operations and intelligence gathering was carried out by formal military personnel—roughly three thousand soldiers, five hundred National Guardsmen, and five hundred municipal police. Martínez also created a special intelligence unit whose agents were at the disposal of governors and commandants. A vast network of civilian informants and collaborators known as *orejas* (ears) supplemented the security forces. Some *orejas* were formally employed, such as the schoolteacher in Sonsonate Department who submitted regular written reports to his superiors.[50] The more typical *oreja* was an otherwise normal civilian willing to pass on information to security agents out of a sense of duty or in exchange for a favor or a few pesos.

By 1935 intelligence gathering was a prominent feature of Martínez's regime. Virtually every identifiable organization or social group in the nation was under surveillance. University students and intellectuals received special attention because, as one intelligence report put it, they possessed "socialist tendencies." The government had an on-going *lista negra* (blacklist) of people considered undesirable. Between 1934 and 1939 Martínez faced five military conspiracies; three were discovered while still in the planning stages, and the other two were squelched immediately after they attempted to seize power.[51]

Martínez in the Context of Twentieth-Century El Salvador

Martínez's rise to power may at first appear to be a classic example of a "regime change," a sharp and lasting break with past political structures.[52] After all, Martínez turned a civilian democracy into a military dictatorship. But when looked at more closely, the profundity of this transition might not be so readily apparent. Certainly, Pío Romero's democratic reforms were profound, but lingering beneath the surface of the Romero era were some old patterns that would come back to life after 1931. Perhaps Romero said it best from exile in 1934: "I established an innovation, whether the people will allow a return to the old methods remains to be seen."[53] Indeed, Martínez returned to the old methods of patronage. He and his associates sat atop a pyramid of patronage and through their political machine, Pro-Patria, presided over a vast network of patron-client relations that integrated the local, regional, and national levels. While Martínez and the upper tiers of Pro-Patria had a monopoly on violence and presumed to hold final say over all things political, they relied on constant negotiation with locals, both elites and workers. The evidence presented here suggests that historians should "decenter" the regime, as, say, Jeffrey Rubin has done for Mexico. Admittedly, Rubin's definition of *decentering* involves a cultural framework that is not explicitly employed here. But it also signifies the need to consider the formative role of regional and local actors in a centralized, even authoritarian, national political system: "National politics [should] be understood as something partial and complex that coexists with, but is different from, regional and local politics, and that is only one among several locations and kinds of politics."[54]

This study of patronage during the Martínez era poses some questions about El Salvador in the second half of the twentieth century. For example, to what extent did the Martínez regime serve as a blueprint for the regimes after 1944? If patronage was the foundation of Martínez's system, to what extent did it survive? Is there a relationship between patronage survivals and the descent into civil war in 1979? Answering these questions is beyond the scope of this chapter, but posing them is worthwhile. Comparative studies illustrate the durability of patronage-based political systems even when a military regime initiates an explicit antipatronage campaign. For instance, Frances Hagopien shows that the military regimes in Brazil between 1964 and 1983 carried out an aggressive and highly visible antipatronage program.[55] Despite their efforts, though, the program failed.[56] Hagopien's findings suggest that future studies on El Salvador would benefit by asking if patronage was ever challenged in El Salvador as it was in Brazil. If so, how successful was the campaign? If not, how could patronage have diminished? A good starting point for approaching these issues is the recent work of Philip Williams and Knut Walter. In their overview of the military regimes, they argue that each administration had its distinct characteristics, but each also exhibited a high degree of continuity with its predecessors. Admittedly, Williams and Walter focused on the national level and were not looking for patronage per se. But in their well-researched overview, they failed to find sharp or lasting breaks that might signify political renovation.[57]

Kati Griffith and Leslie Gates

Colonels and Industrial Workers in El Salvador, 1944–1972

Seeking Societal Support through Gendered Labor Reforms

How do military regimes seek support or legitimacy from society? What strategies, besides violent repression, do military leaders use to remain in power? In other words, how do military leaders try to achieve hegemony? El Salvador's long period of military rule (1931–1979) gives researchers ample opportunity to investigate the mechanisms whereby military regimes try to gain societal support. Erik Ching's chapter shows that General Martínez's regime sought support through locally based patron-client relationships. Some analysts of El Salvador's subsequent military regimes find that these regimes pursued a political alliance with urban industrial workers in order to gain support.[1] Nevertheless, the alliance between the state and urban industrial workers during the 1950s and 1960s remains overgeneralized in the literature. Even those who specify Salvadoran governmental policy during this period as "repression with reforms" do not fully elaborate the mechanisms whereby military leaders formed an alliance with urban industrial workers.[2] Moreover, research on these later military regimes has not explored the role that gendered labor reforms played in solidifying the alliance. As a result of this oversight, researchers may have underestimated the reformist tendency of Salvadoran military regimes from 1944 to 1972. Drawing on newspaper accounts and government publications, we show that adopting labor legislation designed to protect women workers was an element of a broader government strategy to ally with urban industrial workers.

Examining how military regimes seek societal support is important because each strategy to secure regime legitimacy may have different social implications. For example, gendered labor legislation can have important social implications for industrial women workers. Research on other countries suggests that labor laws giving women special protections tend to make employers less willing to hire them and that special legal protections for women workers can depress women's participation in the industrial labor force.[3] Therefore, by illuminating the gendered nature of the reforms pursued by the Salvadoran military regimes, we hope to contribute to future research on the potential relationship between labor reforms and women's industrial labor force participation in El Salvador.

Building an Alliance with Urban Industrial Workers, 1944–1972

After 1944, Salvadoran military leaders made a commitment to industrialization.[4] This brought with it, however, the danger that urban workers would unionize, mobilize, and destabilize the country politically. As table 1 indicates, the percentage of El Salvador's gross national product (GNP) contributed by industry increased from 9.5 percent in 1942 to 19.2 percent in 1971. Tax exemptions for industry (1950–1956) and an import substitution industrialization policy during the 1960s (which promoted domestic production of industrial products previously imported) stimulated industrialization.[5] The Central American Common Market, in place from 1961 to 1969, spurred El Salvador's industrial growth. Industrialization attracted migrants to the cities and converted urban poor into workers. The percentage of workers in the industrial sector increased from 11.4 percent in 1951 to 20.9 percent in 1971 (see table 1). The participation of urban workers in the general strike that helped bring down the Martinez regime in 1944 inflamed the military's fear of the burgeoning ranks of urban workers. Furthermore, between April 1944 and December 1947 there were at least ninety-three labor conflicts.[6] Urban workers organized themselves into various types of organizations, including unions.[7] By 1956 there were 14,088 union members in El Salvador affiliated with fifty-one unions; although in 1956 only 27 percent of these were industrial workers, by 1971 industrial workers represented 45 percent of unionized workers.

Mexico's success in quelling urban worker militancy inspired El Salvador's military leaders during this period of industrialization. Mexico's president in the late 1930s, Lazaro Cardenas, successfully transformed militant oil and railroad workers into an important base of political support. Cardenas did this by granting these union leaders privileged access to government decision making through the ruling political party, the Institutional Revolutionary Party (Partido Revolucionario Institucional, PRI), and by responding to demands by rank-and-file

Table 1. Indicators of Industrialization, Union Growth, and Industrial Union Growth

Year	Industrial sector, percentage of GDP	Industrial sector, percentage of total workforce	Number of unionized workers (total)[a]	Number of unions (total)	Industrial sector, percentage of unionized workers
1942	9.50	—	—	—	—
1945	10.60	—	—	—	—
1951	14.07	11.42	13,521	40	—
1956	16.37	—	14,088	51	27
1961	16.76	12.84	21,566	72	32
1966	18.80	—	24,126	78	51
1971	19.20	20.93	47,000	124	45

Sources: Column 1: 1942, 1945, Henry Wallich and John Adler, Proyecciones Económicas de las Finanzas Publicas: Un estudio experimental en El Salvador (Mexico City: Fondo de Cultura Económica, 1949); 1951–1971, "Indicadores Económicos y Sociales"; 1964 and 1973, Consejo Nacional de Planificación y Coordinación Económica. Column 2: Eduardo Colindres, Fundamentos economicos de la burguesia salvadorena (San Salvador: Universidad Centroamericana Editores, 1978), 124–25, chart 17. Column 3: 1951–1956, Memorias; 1961–1971, Estadísticas del Trabajo. Column 4: 1951–1956, Memorias, Ministry of Labor; 1960–1971, Estadísticas del Trabajo, Ministry of Labor. Column 5: Estadísticas del Trabajo.

a. 1951–1956 data represent totals as of 1 September; 1961–1971 data represent totals as of 31 June.

workers for social reforms. Like Mexico's semiauthoritarian leaders, El Salvador's military leaders attempted to convert this potential menace into a base of social support. Instead of relying solely on violent repression, they pursued an alliance with urban industrial workers. Military leaders allowed certain unions to organize and to publicly advocate for social reforms in exchange for assurances that union leaders and workers affiliated with their unions would remain loyal to the regime.

Like leaders in Mexico, El Salvador's military leaders marginalized Communist and radical labor leaders but granted privileged decision-making access to a select group of moderate union leaders. Moderate union leaders were able to advocate for labor reforms from this vantage point. For example, on February 11, 1947, the executive branch of the Salvadoran government appointed two moderate labor representatives to the six-member commission charged with drafting a labor code.[8] The commission's proposals became the basis for groundbreaking labor legislation contained in the 1950 Constitution.[9] The constituent assembly charged with writing the Constitution summoned the Salvadoran Committee for Union Reorganization (Comité de Reorganización Sindical Salvadoreño, CROS) and selected labor organizations to participate in the debates regarding labor legislation.[10] CROS included key industrial workers, such as railroad workers, bread makers, cobblers, and tailors.[11] Labor representatives were in the assembly "day and night" and "many of them spoke up and intervened in discussions" and "demonstrated large popular support."[12] Throughout the 1950s, military leaders invited moderate sectors of labor to send representatives to the National Assembly to discuss decisions regarding labor law.[13]

Salvadoran military leaders further imitated Mexico's model by institutionalizing labor's participation in decision making through political parties. In Mexico the state gave the Mexican Confederation of Workers privileged access to decision making in the PRI. Similarly, the Salvadoran Revolutionary Party of Democratic Unification (Partido Revolucionario de Unificacíon Democrática, PRUD) (1948–1960) and its successor, the National Conciliation Party (Partido de Conciliacíon Nacional, PCN) included certain labor unions within its decision-making structure, albeit in a subordinate role.[14] As López Vallecillos states, Colonel Osorio (1950–1956) aimed to "affiliate the labor movement with party politics."[15] PRUD officials did this by rewarding moderate labor leaders with PRUD-affiliated government posts.[16] They also initiated a union central to be incorporated into the government decision-making apparatus in 1958: the General Confederation of Unions (Confederacíon General de Sindicatos, CGS).[17] Like PRUD, PCN granted labor leaders access to decision making and positioned itself as a party that could reconcile economic class divisions: a party in which "capitalists and workers . . . could all find a home."[18] The first PCN president, Colonel Julio Rivera (1962–1967), even dressed in "workman's clothes" on ceremonial days to appeal to urban industrial workers.[19] PCN leaders developed a close relationship with the CGS during the volatile years after the fall of President Colonel José María Lemus in 1960.[20] The PCN subsequently included CGS as labor's representative in state decision-making bodies.[21] For example, the PCN appointed a key CGS leader to be the under-secretary of the Ministry of Labor. Many CGS union leaders also held seats as PCN delegates in the National Assembly.[22]

Between 1944 and 1972 El Salvador's military leaders introduced social reforms designed to secure legitimacy from urban workers and their families. In the early 1960s President Colonel Rivera expressed a sentiment shared by other military leaders during the 1950s and 1960s: "If we do not make the reforms, the Communists will make them for us."[23] PRUD officials instituted price controls on basic goods, and increased state subsidies for education, housing, healthcare, and sanitation projects. In addition PRUD officials gave benefits to urban workers in the formal sector by mandating a minimum wage, a bonus system, paid vacation and leaves, a social security system, a forty-four hour work-week, industrial training programs, and disability payment for accidents on the job.[24] PCN presidents, including Colonel Rivera and his successor Colonel Fidel Sánchez Hernández (1967–1972), reduced rents and increased the urban minimum wage. These social reforms benefited urban workers, helping the government gain societal support from this important group. Thus, Salvadoran military leaders sought societal support by building a limited alliance with urban industrial workers. The cornerstone of this strategy was giving privileges to moderate unions, including limited access to decision making within political parties and the government. As a result, labor leaders were able to exert some influence within these military regimes. One of the issues that labor leaders pursued was protective legislation for women workers.

Labor's Demands

In the late 1940s industrial workers wanted not only social reforms but also governmental intervention in the workplace to protect workers from employer abuses. Industrial workers expressed their desire for intervention in more than half of the conflicts that occurred between April 1944 and February 1945. They particularly wanted help ensuring that women workers had special protections. To do this, however, workers first had to convince El Salvador's military leaders to establish a Department of Labor and to develop labor laws.[25] Organized industrial workers felt that a Department of Labor would give them more state protection in the workplace as well as increased influence over state policy.[26] Thus, the demand that women be given special protections was part of a broader political strategy to increase government intervention in the workplace.

Organized industrial workers demanded special protections for women from dangerous and arduous work. In its 1944 manifesto the National Union of Workers (Unión Nacional de Trabajadores, UNT) declared that it would fight for "the prohibition of women's involvement in dangerous work and night shifts."[27] The Fraternal Union of Workers (Unión Fraternal de Trabajadores, UFT) stated in its manifesto, "the U.F.T. will fight so that the woman neither works in dangerous factories nor in heavy lifting work and in principal that she takes care of herself during pregnancy."[28] In 1946 Salvadoran labor leader J. J. Valencia told government officials, "another major concern [of ours] is . . . to remove them [women] from public spaces and to rebuild the home in order to build families with good values."[29] In March 1950 the Society of Salvadoran Workers was commemorated for its "pro woman-worker campaigns," calling for special considerations for women workers.[30] In 1951 labor leader Carlos Salinas argued that the first phase of labor protections for workers should focus on the "weakest part: the woman worker . . . whose body suffers more as a consequence of long, tiring work."[31] Julio Cesar Tejado, a labor delegate at the 1954 Ministry of Labor Conference, asked for "immediate legislation" regarding women and minors and asked for protections against women's work in construction, and work involving cement.[32] Labor delegate Jorge Alberto López said that the state should not "permit women and minors to work in night-time restaurants and billiard halls where alcoholic beverages are served." He argued that "women and minors who work in environments of vice sacrifice themselves and warp their personalities; in contrast, if they work in a healthy environment, they are more likely to acquire good habits and customs."[33]

In the 1950s labor leaders demanded a reduced workweek for women workers. During the debates regarding the 1950 Constitution, a labor representative, Rafael Gamero, proposed a woman's maximum workweek be thirty-nine hours, compared to a man's maximum workweek of forty-four hours.[34] At the 1954 Ministry of Labor Conference labor delegate López stated that "because of her social role and her condition, it is humane and practical to reduce women's maximum daily shift to seven hours and to prohibit women from working overtime for any reason." He justified his request saying, "reducing the women's shift, because of her sex, will ensure that she doesn't wear herself out physically and that a strong, capable, and responsible future generation of workers will be possible."[35]

Once the government legalized special protections, organized industrial workers pressured state leaders to enforce these special protections and conduct special studies on appropriate working conditions for women and minors. At the 1954 Ministry of Labor Conference labor leaders pressured Ministry of Labor officials to increase government enforcement of regulations regarding women and minors' work. Labor delegate López stated that the ministry should be doing more inspections in environments where women and minors work.[36] He solicited the ministry to budget for studies regarding women and minors. Labor delegate Tejado argued for increased enforcement of the law prohibiting women and minors from working in unhealthy and unsafe environments.

Labor leaders also promoted sex-segregated industrial training programs. One of labor's demands at the 1954 Ministry of Labor Conference was to establish training centers. In 1958 various unions in San Salvador petitioned the Ministry of Labor to create a separate Center of Home Economics for Women.[37] After 1963 labor representatives in the National Department of Apprenticeship were in a position to pressure the Ministry of Labor for more sex-segregated industrial training. They approved and supervised training programs and played a role in hiring apprentices.[38]

Labor's Demands or Female Worker's Demands?

Even though female industrial workers comprised close to a quarter of the industrial labor force, they were underrepresented in unions and nearly excluded from organized labor's leadership. We cannot assume, therefore, that labor leaders expressed the interests of women workers. As table 2 shows from 1951 to 1953 women made up only 12 percent of the unionized workforce.[39] Men historically dominated Salvadoran labor leadership.[40] Labor leaders and representatives continued to be almost exclusively male in the 1940s and 1950s. Between May 1944 and May 1946, thirteen unions listed their executive committees in the newspaper; eleven of them were exclusively male, and the remaining two each had only one female member.[41] Of the 180 labor representatives listed in the newspaper during this period, 175 were male. Moreover, throughout the 1940s to the 1960s, male union leaders represented labor in most of the important labor assemblies.[42] For example, all of the delegates representing all "existing labor societies" at the meeting held to coordinate efforts in the key months after the fall of Martínez in 1944 were men.[43] Male union leaders also exclusively represented labor's interests to the government. Thus, labor representatives in the three labor delegations to the government in the 1940s, the Labor Law Defense Committee, the 1953 union delegation to the National Assembly, the 1954 Ministry of Labor Congress, and the 1964 Minimum Wage Commission were all male.[44]

Rather than relying on the organized labor movement to represent them, organized women workers represented themselves to government officials when they had a grievance. For example, in 1946 an all-female labor delegation visited the president to request help to resolve a labor dispute.[45] The strategy of a leading women's organization in the 1950s, Fraternidad de Mujeres Salvadoreñas (Fraternity of Salvadoran Women), further emphasizes women's minimal participation in union leadership. These women leaders advocated for increased participation of women workers in union leadership.[46] Their concern reflected the historical tendency of women to participate in unions as wives and supporters.[47] A union newspaper reporting on the 1918 Workers' Congress, for instance, announced that "the woman, who is in the working man's home, the great bearer of our equilibrium . . . receives the affection of our white flag."[48] Moreover, at the regional general assemblies in the 1920s, it was reported that "every member brought his wife, kids, and neighbors" to the meetings.[49]

Although sources on female industrial workers are sparse, evidence suggests that in the mid-1940s organized female workers did not appear to share male workers' concerns for special protections.[50] Women prioritized increased industrial wages and called for increased safety protections for *all* workers. Nine of fourteen newspaper articles reporting female workers' concerns (between June 1944 and July 1946) highlighted salary as their major concern.[51] Six of the fourteen articles highlighted female workers' demands for labor rights for all workers.[52] None of the articles mentioned the need for protective legislation for women or sex-segregated training programs. Labor leaders Angélica Trigueros

Table 2. Women's Participation in the
Industrial Labor Force and Unions

Year	Female industrial workers, percentage of total[a]	Female unionized workers, percentage of total
1951	20.5	12.7
1952	—	12.8
1953	—	12.5
1956	17.1	—
1961	21.7	—
1971	25.5	—

Sources: Column 1: 1951, 1956, 1961, 1971, *Censos Económicos,* Ministry of Economy; column 2: *Memorias,* Ministry of Labor.
   a. Includes only industrial workplaces with five or more workers.

and María Luisa Bonilla did not promote protective legislation for women during their speeches at the 1946 Labor Day celebration.[53] Instead, they called for improvements in the working conditions for both men and women. In 1956 female industrial workers even *opposed* a proposal to prohibit women from working the night shift.[54] Some female workers preferred to work night shifts so they could take care of their children during the day.

Moreover, major women's rights organizations at the time did not make special protections for female workers a priority.[55] A leading women's group, Liga Femenina Salvadoreña, founded in 1947, did not appeal to state leaders for special protections for women.[56] After significant discussion of the issue at the 1951 National Women's Seminar, women made no demands in favor of special protective legislation for women in the workforce. Instead, women sought improved educational and training opportunities and full political participation.[57] The scant participation of women in union leadership and the tendency for female workers and reformers to avoid calling for special protections for women suggests that they may not have supported organized labor's gendered demands.

In the 1944–1956 period industrial workers led by a predominantly male leadership sought protection for workers through greater state intervention in the workplace, particularly through gendered labor reforms. Industrial workers wanted the government to legalize and enforce special protections for women workers and to provide sex-segregated industrial training programs. As part of the military's effort to build an alliance with moderate urban unions, the government promoted gendered labor reforms that mirrored labor's specific demands during this period.

The State's Gendered Labor Reforms

El Salvador's military leaders during this period were not the first to advocate for gendered labor reforms. They echoed sentiments first expressed by two democratic reformers from the late 1920s and early 1930s. President Pío Romero Bosque (1927–1931) prepared labor laws that included protections for women and minors.[58] Presidential candidate Araujo's "Plan de Trabajo" expressed the government's commitment to "persistently protect" Salvadoran female workers. Furthermore, Araujo (March–December 1931), like many labor leaders of the time, highlighted a woman's primary role as mother. According to Araujo, the woman is, perhaps, "the principal spring" of the next generation of male workers.[59] Pío Romero Bosque and Araujo employed gender in their political discourse with workers, although they stopped short of implementing any labor laws.

Military leaders after 1944 again recognized that responding to labor's gendered demands might help them gain societal support. In the mid-1940s General Castañeda Castro's government (1945–1948) stated that the National Department of Labor would give special attention to "women and children's work."[60] The Labor Code Drafting Committee's 1947 statement affirmed that "one of its [Ministry of Labor's] principal goals is to protect the life and physical, mental, and moral development of minors and women, as they, because of their special conditions, are at greater risk than adult men. . . . For their own good, they will be prohibited from working in certain jobs, and they will be put in situations that guarantee their safety."[61] President Colonel Lemus (1956–1960) often mentioned the primary role women play as mothers. In 1958 Lemus provided state-funded bonuses for selected female workers and wives of male workers who had recently given birth. As Lemus stated, "it was an act of justice, for the noble function of motherhood."[62] In the 1960s, the Christian Democrat Party (Partido Demócrata Cristiano, PDC) candidate and then mayor of San Salvador, José Napoleón Duarte, called for legislation "to protect" the economic rights of wives and mothers. According to the PDC, only with economic protections could a Salvadoran woman be free "to accomplish her grand mission as queen of the home and educator of her children."[63] Salvadoran military regimes during the 1950–1972 period took these promises seriously and legalized special protections for female workers through the Constitution, labor laws, and labor codes.[64]

Legalizing Special Protections for Women

El Salvador's 1950 Constitution diverged from earlier ones by gendering labor legislation.[65] It gendered the definition of worker by mandating that "the state will employ all of the resources in its reach to provide employment for the worker . . . and to make sure that he and his family have the economic conditions for a dignified existence." It identified the family as the "fundamental base of society" that should be "specially protected by the state."[66] It assumed that women's primary social roles were as workers' wives and mothers. The new labor legislation protected pregnant women from losing their jobs and gave them the right to paid leave before and after pregnancy.

When the Constitution considered women as workers, it posited that they merited "special legislation" beyond protections for pregnant workers. Article 183 was the first to restrict women from working in "unhealthy and dangerous labors." At the 1954 Ministry of Labor Conference, labor, state, and business representatives further fleshed out what special legislation for women would mean in El Salvador. The conference included gendered labor reforms among its six agenda items.[67] The final recommendations at the conference included reforms prompting government officials to state that the law about "women and minors" was one of the "most important and delicate" laws the state promoted.[68]

The labor sections of the 1962 Constitution, the 1963 Labor Code, and its subsequent revisions in 1972 all further amplified the "protective" legislation. Chapter V of the 1963 Labor Code, dedicated to "the work of women and minors," established that jobs "should be especially appropriate to a worker's sex, age, physical state, and development." It specified that "oiling, cleaning, inspecting, or repairing machines or mechanisms in motion" or jobs in which workers handle toxic substances, including gas, vapors, or dusts, which could potentially poison them, were too dangerous for women workers. Women were also prohibited from working underground or underwater, in industries such as mining, or in work involving the "fabrication of explosives." The revised 1972 Labor Code further specified that women should not work in jobs involving "construction of any type" and work related to "demolition," "repair," and "conservation." Chapter V of the 1972 Labor Code states that "minors under eighteen and women of any age are prohibited from working in unsafe or unhealthy workplaces. . . . Dangerous work includes the oiling, cleaning, revision, or repair of machines or mechanisms in motion and any job that uses automatic or circular saws, knives, cutters, drop hammers, and all other mechanical apparatus that require precautions or special knowledge, except kitchen or butcher utensils, or other related tasks."

Enforcing Special Protections

Salvador's military leaders demonstrated their commitment to special protections for women by enforcing the new legislation. In the 1950s and 1960s state officials restructured the Ministry of Labor and enhanced personnel capacity in order to improve enforcement of special protections for women workers. In 1951 the National Department of Social Services, a section of the Ministry of Labor, was reorganized into three divisions. One of these, the Division for Women and Minors, was dedicated solely to enforcing laws related to women and minors through factory inspections and special studies. In April 1951 Ministry of Labor representatives officially expressed their willingness to increase inspections and conduct more special studies to develop and enforce "effective mechanisms of protection" for women workers.[69]

After the 1954 Ministry of Labor Conference, an expert committee was formed to further develop criteria for identifying unhealthy and unsafe work environments.[70] The division conducted eight studies in 1956 focusing on women's limitations, conditions, and opportunities in the labor force.[71] Ministry of Labor inspectors identified and fined factories with unhealthy and unsafe working conditions for women as well as those out of compliance with maternity regulations. The number of inspections conducted each year increased throughout the 1960s (105 inspections were conducted in 1954, 190 in 1956, 287 in 1957, 333 in 1963, 655 in 1964, 1,975 in 1965, and 5,238 in 1967).[72] The Ministry of Labor also trained and expanded its personnel and progressively extended the work of the Women and Minors' Division in 1952 and again in 1955.[73]

Segregating Industrial Training Programs

Reports from as early as 1949 indicate that El Salvador's military governments promoted sex-segregated training programs. For example, in 1949 and 1950 state leaders founded home economics training schools for young women in San Salvador.[74] In December 1950 government leaders reported that the *Casa del Niño,* a vocational school for children, offered shoemaking, mechanics, and carpentry workshops for boys and cleaning, ironing, sewing, cooking, and bread-making workshops for girls.[75] The rising interest by the Ministry of Labor in defining what constituted sex-appropriate industrial training after the 1954 conference suggests, however, an increased commitment to training programs as a means of segregating the industrial workforce by sex. After the conference, the officials from the Women and Minors' Division visited twenty-two training programs between September 1954 and September 1955, including the School of Domestic Economics and the Female Vocational School of France to determine criteria for sex- and age-appropriate industrial training.[76]

The Women and Minors' Division subsequently administered sex-appropriate training programs in the late 1950s.[77] Male industrial workers received training in higher paying occupations considered too dangerous for women, such as electronics, mechanics, shoemaking, and shoe repair.[78] Male minors received government grants for vocational training in mechanics, electricity, and construction.[79] When women received training, it tended to be in lower paid industries involving cooking, cleaning, and sewing. In 1956 Ministry of Labor officials reported that young women attended state-funded cooking and sewing courses.[80] From 1957 to 1958 state-funded programs trained about 150 women in "domestic" industries such as sewing, culinary arts, food management, and typing. In Morazán and other regions state leaders established similar industrial training schools exclusively for women in the late 1950s.[81]

The 1963 Apprenticeship Law strengthened the military's commitment to sex-appropriate industrial training. It mandated that the state establish a National Department of Apprenticeship, under the auspices of the Ministry of Labor, and include representatives from the Women and Minors' Division.[82] The law charged a seven-member National Council with designing a new law and dictating general norms that would regulate industrial apprenticeships. The department supervised public and private training programs and implemented the National Council's recommendations to develop state-funded sex-segregated training programs and on-the-job apprenticeships.[83]

In the early 1960s the state began monitoring whether "trainings are appropriate to a workers' sex, age, physical state, and development."[84] Industrial job announcements listed in several Salvadoran dailies during the 1960s suggest that employers almost exclusively recruited men for state-sponsored on-the-job industrial apprenticeships.[85] A photo series in the publication *Industry,* of the Association of Salvadoran Industrialists (February 1963–March 1966), also suggested that men were most likely to benefit from these on-the-job apprenticeships. As a Ministry of Labor official active in the 1960s expressed, "These programs were for men, they were designed to train men in more skilled positions, and women never participated, only when there were trainings on sewing."[86]

What is particularly noteworthy here is not that the military regimes between 1944 and 1972 legalized special protections for women workers but that they took such an active role in enforcing these regulations and in redirecting women out of higher paying industrial jobs and industries. The latter indicates that the Ministry of Labor committed considerable resources to this endeavor.

With the exception of a few recent studies, scholars traditionally portray El Salvador's military leaders as monolithically repressive and commonly refer to the military as a repressive political instrument of the economic elite.[87] Nevertheless, the evidence presented here suggests that Salvadoran military leaders from 1944 to 1972 did try to persuade society to support their regime and that one of the ways they did so was by introducing special protections for female workers.[88] Because gendered labor reforms may not challenge the profit margins of industrialists as much as significant increases in minimum wage, we might expect the military to be more open about negotiating with labor leaders for these type of demands.

Intervening in the workplace to protect women and minors constituted a way for military leaders to demonstrate a political commitment to urban labor leaders that did not tax the relationship between military leaders and industrialists too severely. Therefore, a focus on gendered labor reforms gives us an opportunity to document the extent of the state-labor alliance during this period. By enforcing special protections for women workers and by promoting sex-segregated industrial training programs, the government demonstrated that it was willing to respond to the labor leadership of urban workers. Because gendered labor reforms constituted such an important aspect of the state-labor alliance, gender-neutral analyses of the state-labor relationship during this period risk underestimating the reformist nature of these military regimes.

A gendered reading of the state-labor alliance may help us understand why many industrial workers joined the ranks of the leftist anti-government movement in the mid-1970s. The fact that the military repeatedly responded to labor's gendered demands between 1944 and 1972 helps to explain why, by the early 1970s, many industrial workers and their moderate labor leaders expected to be included in the government's decision-making process. Government leaders also responded to some of labor's nongendered demands for labor reforms favorable to urban workers. Many industrial workers may have joined antigovernment forces of the left when they realized that military leaders had retracted from the alliance in the mid-1970s. Explanations of El Salvador's civil war have often noted the incomplete nature of the government's reforms during the 1944–1972 period. The explanations highlight that the state-labor alliance was confined to urban workers and that rural labor relations remained unchanged throughout this period. Although the failures of the military to redistribute in the rural sector are an important explanatory factor, future research on the causes of El Salvador's civil war should more fully consider the legacy of the development and decline of the state-labor alliance in El Salvador.

Our analysis raises several questions: What were the social implications of the military's strategy to build an alliance with moderate unions during the 1950s and 1960s? How did special protections affect women workers? Research on other countries suggests that the gendered nature of labor regulations can affect women's participation in the labor force as well as the wages they receive. For example, in Mexico the participation of women in the industrial labor force sharply declined after Mexico put similar labor regulations in place in the 1940s.[89]

The history of gendered labor reforms in El Salvador may help us understand the dramatic changes in the composition of El Salvador's industrial work force. Although the special protections for women remained legal until 1994, they decreased in the late 1970s. Moreover, the state's commitment to enforce these regulations waned in the 1970s and during the decade of war in the 1980s.[90] In 1994 the government repealed the protections altogether.[91] The proportion of women workers in industrial jobs in El Salvador has increased from roughly a quarter of all industrial workers in 1950–1970 to roughly half in the late

1990s.[92] In the export-processing industrial sector, the *maquiladoras,* women made up over 80 percent of the workforce in 1998.[93]

El Salvador exemplifies a trend toward increased women's participation in industrial work throughout Latin America. Prominent analysts link this change to the preference of *maquiladoras* to hire women.[94] Yet analysts disagree about why foreign companies might prefer to do so. Some argue that foreign employers believe women are more docile than male workers, and others argue that women are less expensive; hiring women allows the industry to devalue its wage levels.[95]

Yet the research has not considered how employer hiring preferences may interact with domestic legacies of state-labor relations such as gendered labor reforms. Could it be that the aggressive role of El Salvador's political leaders in segregating industrial work in the 1950s and 1960s contributed to the notion that women as workers were less valuable than men, or that, unlike men, they did not need to be paid enough to support a family? Did foreign companies establish *maquiladoras* in the early 1990s simply to take advantage of the artificially depressed wage expectations of women workers and thereby create lower wage expectations for both women and men working in the *maquiladora* industry? By tracing the origins of gendered labor reforms we have provided the groundwork for understanding the role that the state-labor alliance may have played in paving the way for the recent upsurge in women's industrial employment in El Salvador.

Carlos Benjamín Lara Martínez

The Formation of a Rural Community

Joya de Cerén, 1954–1995

The study of historical processes is essential for understanding contemporary sociocultural dynamics in a community. This kind of research provides a diachronic understanding of the principal sociocultural systems that condition the way a community functions in the present. This is particularly true for rural communities that have emerged in the second half of the twentieth century, that have constructed their social and symbolic systems from the historical conditions that gave rise to them.

During El Salvador's recent history many rural communities (*cantones,* or villages, and *caseríos,* or small hamlets)[1] have been disarticulated and reorganized, a process stemming most often from agrarian reforms that have sought to reduce social conflict. Joya de Cerén, the community examined in this chapter, is no exception. Joya de Cerén was established through a 1954 agrarian reform by President Lieutenant Colonel Oscar Osorio and administered by the Institute for Rural Colonization (Instituto de Colonización Rural, ICR). That Joya de Cerén was formed by an agrarian reform conditions the kinds of social actors who participated in constructing its social and symbolic systems. Groups and institutions at the local level that shaped the community include agriculturalists who benefited from the land reform and small-scale producers previously established in the area. At the level of national institutions, administrative and technical personnel from the ICR had important roles, and international actors, including delegations from the American Friends Service Committee and the Mennonite Church, also influenced the community's formation. I argue that the social and symbolic systems of the community resulted from a coalescing of forces among social actors at these three levels who at times worked together and at others found themselves in conflict.

Since the birth of the village of Joya de Cerén dates to 1954, I concentrate here on the second half of the twentieth century. I drew on four types of primary data: (1) official documents from state institutions like the Rural Colonization Institute, the Salvadoran Institute for Agrarian Transformation (Instituto Salvadoreño de Transformación Agraria, ISTA), and the General Statistics Directorate (Dirección General de Estadística); (2) documents from independent (nongovernmental) institutions that were involved in the founding of Joya de Cerén, including the American Friends Service Committee; (3) contemporary newspaper accounts of President Oscar Osorio's agrarian project; and (4) oral accounts I collected from project beneficiaries and local landholders.

Oral histories let us see the story from the perspective of those who were at the center of the founding of Joya de Cerén as an agrarian reform community: the recipients of land in 1954 and the small-scale landowners who were already settled in the area. I drew on twenty oral accounts of the history of the community as it was narrated by founders of Colonia Joya de Cerén and their children. In addition, I maintained a constant dialogue with current residents of the region, state officials who participated in the Joya de Cerén project, and people who worked with American Friends Service Committee during the community's founding. This approach allows us to contrast the oral accounts of current members of the community as well as state and NGO figures with the documentary record. This approach will enable us to construct a complete portrait of this period in the history of Joya de Cerén.

While socioeconomic analysis is clearly important to understanding a community founded through land reform, this research also seeks to understand the role played by social and religious factors in the community's founding. Locating the particular or individual forces that shaped the community within the context of the larger society may reveal the local social dynamics in their full complexity. In the final part of this chapter I describe the current sociocultural dynamics of the community, with the goal of showing the interplay between historical continuity and rupture in shaping the community's contemporary configuration.

General Characteristics of Joya de Cerén

The village of Joya de Cerén belongs to the municipality of San Juan Opico, located in the northern part of the Department of La Libertad, in the county's central region. San Juan Opico is composed of a municipal or county seat *(cabacera municipal)* and twenty-seven villages. The village of Joya de Cerén sits in the southern part of the municipality, forming part of the Valle de Zapotitán. These are the flattest and most fertile lands in the area, and while hillsides and ravines cut across some of the village, the central hamlet—Colonia Joya de Cerén, the focus of the 1954 land reform—sits on the best farmland in the area.

Joya de Cerén officially includes five small hamlets. As noted, Colonia Joya de Cerén lies in the village's center, ringed by four other hamlets: Plan del Hoyo and La Ranchería, which existed before the 1954 agrarian reform, Agua Zarca, and part of Estacón Bandera. There are also three recently formed hamlets that are effectively part of the village, although they do not appear on official maps or other documents: El IRA, Santa Bárbara, and Colonia El Progreso. In 1996 roughly 5,834 people lived in the village, representing 11.28 percent of the municipality's total population. The population is distributed within the village as follows: Colonia Joya de Cerén, 304 homes; IRA, 80 homes; Plan del Hoya, La Ranchería, and Agua Zarca, 296 homes.

An average of 8.57 people live in each household in the village. Based on the number of households in each hamlet, the estimated population of the hamlet of Colonia Joya de Cerén is 2,605 inhabitants, representing 44.65 percent of the total population of the village. In the central hamlet the distribution of housing is relatively concentrated owing to the planning and designs of the ICR technicians. The more recently founded of the outlying hamlets also show concentrated settlement patterns, whereas the older peripheral hamlets are more sparsely settled.

The Founding and Organization of the Village of Joya de Cerén

On October 28, 1932, the government of El Salvador created the National Social Defense Board, which became Social Improvement on December 22, 1942. These were the predecessors to the Rural Colonization Institute (Instituto de Colonizacíon Rural, ICR), founded on December 29, 1950, and the Institute for Agrarian Transformation (Instituto de Transformacíon Agraria, ISTA), created on June 26, 1975. In the words of ISTA officials, these institutions were dedicated to contributing to the economic improvement of the people, offering houses and lots in urban centers or parcels in rural areas, to rationalize agricultural production and improve rural housing.[2]

This social policy had direct repercussions in the municipality of Opico: on August 12, 1942, seventy-four-year-old Dr. Francisco Dueñas sold two important lots of his plantation, the *hacienda* San Andrés, to the National Social Defense

Board. The plantation contained 5,509 hectares, of which Dr. Dueñas sold 3,309 hectares. These two properties would become the village of Joya de Cerén and the community of Sitio del Niño. During the twelve years between the government's purchase of this land and the ICR's organization of Joya de Cerén, Social Improvement simply rented the resulting parcels at low cost without planning a community. This policy attracted a peasant population, who settled on the banks of the Río Sucio. A local resident whose parents had moved to the area from Nejapa seeking to improve their lives recalls this period. In Nejapa his parents had worked on a large plantation called El Angel. On this plantation workers were expected to dedicate every day to working for the landowner, leaving no time for *milpa,* the traditional agriculture of Mesoamerica in which corn, squash, and beans are grown together. *Milpa* agriculture is the basis of subsistence production throughout the region. "When we came to Joya, these lands were part of the *hacienda* San Andrés. The land was worked for *censo,* which means they paid in crops or grain. Later, an institution called Social Improvement showed up and they started to make things better for us poor people. Things got better because they gave us more land to work and made sure [the parcels] were sold at a very low cost."

On September 4, 1954, the ICR delivered materials for the first eighty homes, thus beginning the organization of the Colonia Joya de Cerén. The hamlet of La Ranchería already existed, as did Plan del Hoyo, but the lands that were used for the settlement of Joya de Cerén were uninhabited cane fields. The ICR was in charge of building the first eighty houses. Most of the lots were a thousand square meters, and the houses were eight by ten meters. The houses had two bedrooms, a living room, dining room, kitchen, and storeroom, as well as a patio or garden area large enough to allow the cultivation of fruit trees. The settlement also included a communal building, the *casa comunal,* for holding community meetings and other community-oriented events. A health center was built, and roughly 3.5 hectares were left open as green spaces. The government charged only 3,000 *colones* (about US$1,200) per house and lot, with a twenty-year payment plan, so the new home-owners paid about 150 *colones* (US$60) annually. Those who received larger properties paid more; some of the new owners paid annual rates of 230 *colones* (US$92). After several years, a second phase of forty houses was completed. These new houses were built through a partnership in which the ICR provided materials and the beneficiaries provided the labor. When the forty houses were finished, they were distributed by lottery among the workers. The third and final phase was overseen by ISTA. The houses built in this phase were sold at the same prices as the initial eighty homes.

In 1954 the ICR registered the families that were to live in the new settlement.

Most of the recipient families were from the municipality of Opico, where they had lived on agricultural properties, which they sold to friends or relatives when they left for their new homes. ICR workers found it difficult to convince the intended beneficiaries to accept the project: local peasants feared participating with what they suspected was a communist endeavor. According to one informant, "The people here didn't want to accept the houses, because they said this was communism and they would be consigned to slavery." The anticommunist repression and campaign of the Martínez military government (1931–1944) and subsequent administrations had clearly affected the peasant sector to the extent that many people equated land distribution with communist ideology. Other locals expressed different objections, as in the case of a man who did not want to accept a home because he feared being indebted.

In spite of these obstacles, on September 4, 1954, ICR authorities officially inaugurated Joya de Cerén. In a solemn celebration, the eighty keys were handed over to the new homeowners. The directors of the ICR declared that these kinds of communities "would, in time, be able to solve the agrarian problem in our country, primarily in the areas of education for rural people, creating the human resources able to serve effectively in the great transformations that are currently taking place in all the countries of the world."[3] We now know that the ICR projects did not solve El Salvador's agrarian problem—not because they were poorly designed, but because there were too few of them. The projects took an integrated approach to community development, addressing the social, cultural, and economic aspects of the community. The far-reaching achievements of the reform policies are reflected in the low level of social conflict in the community over time. Such long-term stability is notable in rural El Salvador, particularly during the 1980s, when there was considerable conflict in the country as a whole.

Families, rather than individuals or single-parent households, were the envisioned beneficiaries of the project. The residential plots and agrarian properties were distributed in accordance with an understanding that "family well-being" was central to the community. According to ICR documents, "families are considered to be members of groups made up of a father, mother, and children, legitimate or illegitimate; or groups formed by kin related by third-degree consanguinal ties, legitimate or not, or second-degree affinal relations, when the qualifications of the first definition are not met."[4] This requirement may have been crucial to the community's social stability.

As part of the project, the ICR created an agricultural cooperative in the community, Finca de Beneficio Propocional (Proportional Benefits Farm). Its objective was to improve the material conditions of peasant farmers through community organization. Land the ICR owned was given over to the creation of the producer's cooperative. The majority of the workers from the new community of Joya de Cerén belonged to the cooperative, whose principal crop was sugarcane, with some land dedicated to the subsistence crops of corn, beans, and squash. The farmers were paid roughly two *colones* (US$.80) a day. In the Joya de Cerén cooperative workers' yearly incomes ranged from 123 *colones* (US$49.20) to 248 *colones* (US$99.20). Members of the cooperative also received dividends on completing the *zafra,* the intense period of sugarcane harvesting and processing that ran from late December into March each year. Part of these dividends went toward payments on the ICR housing.

Corn was also distributed among members of the cooperative. One informant recalls that in this period (1954–1960) it was distributed according to the time spent laboring: those who worked longer received more corn. The corn was distributed in *quintales* (one hundred pounds); as the informant put it, "it was all brought together and then given out according to how much one had worked."[5] The ICR supplied land, which was rented at 30 *colones* per *manzana,* machinery, which was also rented, and various other materials. It also provided technical support, which the cooperative paid for, and it charged interest at 3 percent over the investment. Production costs and profits for sugarcane in the 1958–1959 season are shown in the table; the profits were shared among the sixty-nine members of the cooperative in that year.

The cooperative's administrator played an important role in the community. The ICR named the administrator in an effort to guarantee the cooperative's economic success. The ICR also sent technical experts to advise farmers about types of seeds, fertilizers, and other aspects of farming. The prevailing assumption was that the *campesino* needed technical assistance in order to advance the nascent enterprise of the cooperative. The cooperative's farmers also received advice on production, marketing, and financial management. Nevertheless, and in spite of the presence of an administrator and technical advisors from ICR, the cooperative was not sustainable for long.

After a few years, around 1961, the members requested that the cooperative be dissolved and the land be distributed among community members. The ICR subsequently subdivided the communal land and gave each head of household 2–3 *manzanas* (1–2 hectares), depending on the quality of the land. Farmers paid about 3,000 *colones* (US$1,200) for each parcel. The payment plan was the same as for the houses, with residents paying 150 *colones* (US$60) annually. Initially, beneficiaries were prohibited from reselling their parcels, but this condition was later removed, and Joya de Cerén became a community of small property owners.

These smallholders continued producing sugarcane, but over time the cultivation of subsistence crops increased. "In those days," said one informant, "almost

Sugarcane Production Costs and Profits, 1958–1959 Season

Sugarcane produced	4,143 tons, 8 *quintals*, 7 pounds[a]
Area cultivated	75 *manzanas*[b]
Median production	55.24 tons per *manzana*
Direct production costs	
Materials	5,035.78 *colones*
Labor	24,875.66 *colones*
Administration	2,789.04 *colones*
Total	32,700.48 (US$13,080.19)
Indirect production costs	
Interest (at 3%)	981.01 *colones*
Agricultural machinery rental (2.5% above nominal value)	244.73 *colones*
Tractor (2 mos. labor)	2,250.00 *colones*
Rental of 75 *manzanas*	3,455.74 *colones* (US$1,382.29)
Total cost of production	36,156.22 *colones* (US$14,462.48)
Cost per ton	8.2885 *colones*
Income from sale of sugarcane produced	52,672.92 *colones*
Net income	16,516.70 *colones* (US$6,606.68)

Note: Profits were shared among the co-op's sixty-nine members that year.
    a. One *quintal* equals 100 pounds.
    b. One *manzana* equals 0.7 hectares.

everyone worked in cane fields because only a few grew corn and beans. Today there's more *milpa* than cane, and others have sold out." When I asked why the cooperative had dissolved, all the old members and their children insisted that the farmers only saw a small part of the profits from the cooperative and that the better part of the income simply disappeared. Some blamed the ICR authorities for this, and others pointed to the cooperative's directors, who were also members of the community.

But there was another factor motivating the dissolution of the cooperative: the lack of value assigned to collective property. Most small farmers preferred having their own plots, and in the peasant economy farming was a family enterprise. As one informant put it, "I preferred having my own [land], because you can make your own decisions." In other words, the peasants valued most their ability to control the process of production, and at the time only private property guaranteed small farmers the ability to make those decisions. According to these peasants, in a cooperative with collective land there was always someone above the actual producer deciding what would be produced: the ICR technicians or the cooperative's directors. These people did not always act in the best interest of the small-scale farmers. When small-scale farmers could decide, they tended to favor subsistence crops against the advice of the ICR advisors, who favored the commercial crops, in this case sugarcane.

Some of the community leaders—specifically, the directors of the Joya de Cerén Community Development Association and the current growers' cooperative—felt that the ICR representatives played an important part in the emergence of this preference for private property by convincing peasants to request the subdivision of the land. Yet as far as I could ascertain, the bulk of the members preferred the subdivision of the land even when that meant they would have only 1.4–2.1 hectares, and it seems unlikely that they were manipulated by outside agents.

But this was not the only cooperative created at Joya de Cerén in the 1950s. A consumer cooperative was formed, working out of a store that sold basic necessities such as soap and household articles. There were conflicts in this cooperative as well and accusations of corruption. Some people pointed to ICR directors, particularly the accountant, and others leveled their charges at the cooperative's directors. Resolving these sorts of conflicts was of great importance for the future of the cooperative movement in El Salvador. Many cooperatives are still threatened by problems of corruption.[6] In the case of Joya de Cerén most informants assert that corruption and abuse of power by authorities were the chief causes of the breakup of the first two of the community's cooperatives. But it should be noted that the ICR's mandate was not simply to create cooperatives. It also sought to create and support forms of social organization that would guarantee community development and the practices it fostered contributed to improving the quality of life of the residents of the village. The cooperative was administered by the *central directorate,* or central committee. "The [central committee] was in charge of community improvement programs," recalls one informant. "Family assistance, if someone was ill, if someone needed financial or psychological help, or advice and the like—[the members of the central committee] were all with the community." The central committee was also in charge of coordinating all social-improvement efforts. Committee members were elected for two-year terms in a general assembly in which the majority of the community participated. "The members of the [central committee] were named by a unanimous decision, through a hand count, so many for, so many against."[7]

The community held general assemblies each week. In these assemblies people discussed the problems facing the collective. Decisions were taken by vote, establishing a system of majority rule. "Generally, it was well known that each week, on Tuesday or Friday, there were meetings of the whole community. All the men and the majority of the women came. They were meetings, like assemblies, that were held in the communal house."[8]

The ICR also built a health center in order to meet the community's health needs permanently. A doctor came every day from San Salvador, and the ICR hired a full-time nurse. "I came here when I was twenty-three," said Doña Celina. "I came as an assistant nurse, to work in the health center, which at that time was part of the ICR. I'm from Santa Ana. I went to San Salvador to take a nursing course, and from there I went to a training course in rural [health] in Quetzalte-peque. It was in 1954 that I came here to the community to be the nurse." The ICR also hired a social worker with the goal of introducing new patterns of behavior and inculcating a community spirit among the settlers. The social worker took on a range of projects, such as housekeeping, appropriate trash disposal, and rational water use.

In 1956 a group of North Americans and Europeans came to support Joya de Cerén and El Sitio del Niño. They were international volunteers with the Latin American Program of the American Friends Service Committee, headquartered in Pennsylvania. "This group was called 'Los Amigos,'" noted one informant, who added that "they were pacifists—not from the Peace Corps, but pacifists." The group maintained a presence in the community until about 1968 or 1970. During this period foreign volunteers came for stays of one to two years to participate in social and economic programs. They supported the health center with volunteer nurses and doctors. They also helped out with agricultural projects, the school, and with diverse groups like the 4-C Club, which worked on reforestation projects, and the Cooking Club, which taught women how to cook. "The Americans and the social worker gave classes on cleaning, the right way to use the house and its latrine, the right ways to use water. . . . One lived here in the community, [and] we became used to this pattern, of having these people here. In the afternoons they played indoor [soccer], and all the little kids and old men would sit around and watch, the youngsters playing soccer, because the ICR gave them all the things they needed for sports."

These volunteers organized diverse groups and activities that created a sense of community, such as a carpentry shop, a sewing group, and a painting group, although the last of these was short-lived. They and the social worker were supported in these activities by the central committee. "In those days it was really nice, because people collaborated, and if someone said, We're going to have such-and-such an activity, and we need you all to help out, you'd say, Okay, I don't have to donate anything but my time [*mi persona*], I'll help out with whatever you need, and someone else might say, I can give you this, or I can give you that; if it was a matter of going to a fair [to benefit the project] . . . some gave corn, others rice. . . . That's the way things were here, all of it."[9]

The ICR also built a school that, after three years, taught five grades, helping greatly to improve educational achievement in the community. The community received further assistance during the 1970s when a group of Mennonites came to teach bread-baking. "Lots of women took the classes, but of all of them only one still makes bread to sell, two or three times a week. Besides her, the rest of us just make bread for our own homes, we just bake a little," said one informant.

Religion was important to the community's residents. As it happened, the ICR never considered it necessary to build a church in the community. Nevertheless, the community, supported by the parish of Opico, petitioned the ICR for a property for the Joya de Cerén church. The ICR gave them a plot of 2,247.3 square meters for 10 *colones* (US$4.00). "When the community was first begun, religious services were performed in the community hall, where we also held dances, social events for the youth and for the friends of the land. The priest from Opico, who at that time was Monseñor López, organized religious activities. He came every Sunday at five in the afternoon to celebrate mass, and when we asked him, he'd come at other times to celebrate mass for weddings, funerals, and so on. Then Monseñor López said we had to make a church, and one day after mass he called on the whole community. A group of men had already asked for the land. Monseñor [López] took everyone to the river to gather up stones to lay the first stone, and from then on the church was here, and the first board of directors of the church was founded."[10]

The church was completed in 1972, seventeen years after the project was initiated. Its construction was a testament to the importance of religious activities for the people of Joya de Cerén, who, in spite of their low incomes, financed the construction of the church themselves. Community members came up with various strategies for raising money for the church. "One man farmed a piece of land and gave the earnings from this plot to the church, but he got tired of bearing the burden by himself," according to one informant.

In general the residents of Joya de Cerén regarded this as a positive time in which a strong sense of community was established and maintained. When I asked if mutual assistance was a regular feature of community life, all my informants pointed to this period (1954–1970) as a time of solidarity and collaboration among residents. One informant suggested that if there is a sense of belonging in Joya de Cerén today it is precisely because in this earlier period they were taught to live in community: "We became used to this pattern in the community."

We must acknowledge that the cooperative project in Joya de Cerén failed primarily because of poor financial management, particularly of profits, and because the majority of members preferred to own their own property. Private ownership was more desirable, principally because in this arrangement the individual farmer could decide what would be grown, whereas under the cooperative arrangement the technical staff of the ICR or the cooperative's directors made this decision. The subdivision of land made Joya de Cerén a community of smallholders. As a cooperative the agricultural economy was based in sugarcane, but after the cooperative was dissolved, farmers assigned greater priority to subsistence agriculture. However, residents of Joya de Cerén were not able to satisfy their basic needs through agriculture alone, and they had to seek other sources of income to complement their farm earnings.

The project made a lasting contribution to residents' lives; in particular, it fostered high levels of cooperation and solidarity among residents, and, at least until 1994, a socially stable community, free of internal social conflicts. In addition, Joya de Cerén served as a refuge for its inhabitants during the conflicts elsewhere in the nation during the 1980s. While some residents supported the growing revolutionary movement, the community as a whole stayed on the margins of it.

The agrarian reform of the early 1980s did not affect Joya de Cerén because its land had already been divided into small plots. Nevertheless, the remainder of the *hacienda* San Andrés did fall within the purview of the land reform, which created the San Andrés cooperative association. The reforms did affect the hamlet of Plan de Hoyo, which had not been part of the 1954 project. Although many of the local farmers joined the San Andrés cooperative at the time, today only eleven heads of household are still members; most farmers are independent producers.

Joya de Cerén in 1995

By 1995 Joya de Cerén was a community of private, smallholding farmers: 84 percent of household heads reported agriculture as their primary economic activity; 64.2 percent are landowners and only 29.9 percent work on rented land. Most of the plots in the community (32.6 percent) are 1.4 hectares in area, 26.08 percent are 0.7 hectare, 19.56 percent range from 0.2 hectare to 0.6 hectare, and 13.04 percent are 1.75–4.2 hectares. Although there may be properties larger than those identified here (one informant referred to a property of 21 hectares) most of the landholdings in Joya de Cerén do not exceed 1.4 hectares. According to the criteria established by the Economic Commission for Latin America and the Food and Agriculture Organization of the United Nations, these properties are all categorized officially as *microfincas* and *subfamiliares* (microfarms and subfamily)—that is, farms that do not satisfy all household needs.[11] Nevertheless, agriculture continues to be the principal source of income for this population. Most of these smallholders (72.65 percent) produce corn and beans. Sugarcane growers represent 11.36 percent of the group; while 5.6 percent grow vegetables. Of the remaining households, 3.45 percent grow sorghum, 2.3 percent fruit, and 2.3 percent rice. These data confirm the aforementioned tendency of small farmers to convert their production to subsistence crops once they have private properties.

The production of corn and beans in Joya de Cerén is first and foremost about satisfying basic household needs and is not a commercial endeavor. Subsistence agriculture is typically highly effective, and growing beans, corn, and certain vegetables guarantees small producers daily subsistence in spite of the national and international economic fluctuations. For this reason, subsistence agriculture has come to form the basis of Joya de Cerén's economic system. It has been combined with other economic activities, such as small-scale cattle-ranching (usually four to six head of cattle, though some ranches have fifteen to eighteen head), small stores, and raising domestic animals like pigs and fowl. Around sixty-five households (11.36 percent) combine subsistence agriculture with sugarcane production. Growing sugarcane is an entirely commercial endeavor, so it provides some liquidity to farmers. In thirty-seven years the cane growers of Joya de Cerén have significantly increased their production, from 55.24 tons per *manzana* in 1958–1959 to 100 tons per *manzana* in 1995–1996, suggesting that those growing it have a more business-oriented approach than other farmers.

Salaried labor is another important complement to income-earning strategies. Wage labor is performed by two kinds of social actors: farmers themselves, who are contracted at certain times of year, when they do not have work in their own field, such as during the sugarcane and coffee harvests, and young men, who are incorporated as full-time labor in the service and industrial sectors. Work in the industrial sector, which currently represents 11.88 percent of the economically active population of Joya de Cerén, is spread across diverse domestic groups in Joya de Cerén.

Some households receive income from families in the United States (10.59 percent of households). They typically receive US$100–200 a month, an important resource for these families. Nevertheless, we must not forget that the majority of Salvadorans in the United States do not have permanent labor contracts but are instead underemployed, making their contribution an unstable source of income for their relatives in El Salvador.

Families depend on all these sources of income to function. Consequently, Joya de Cerén is currently a "semipeasant" community where subsistence agriculture remains the basic form of economic activity; note, however, that this is not a transitory, short-term state but an established system. Its significance in the village is clearly revealed when we move the analysis beyond the level of the individual to that of domestic unit or household. The household constitutes the unit of consumption and, in the case of subsistence agriculture, of production as well. The combination of different income strategies is only understandable from the perspective of the division of labor inside these domestic groups.

This semipeasant character produces polyvalent social subjects that move in distinct social spaces simultaneously in order to guarantee their survival.[12] As Lourdes Arizpe shows, the combination of different income sources within a household permits small-scale farmers to continue to pursue subsistence agriculture under adverse conditions.[13] Thus, the persistence of subsistence farming is not simply the result of the incapacity of industrial and service sectors to absorb this labor force as has long been insisted in Latin American sociology. In the case of Joya de Cerén, we can also see a kind of resistance by the residents to being completely incorporated into the commercial economy. The combination of diverse income sources allows residents to continue their subsistence farming practices, which give them a certain degree of autonomy without isolating them completely from the dominant capitalist economy.

Ethnographic research with the residents of Joya de Cerén has made clear that the community's subsistence economy should not be understood as merely an economic choice. It is a cultural option that privileges social life over purely economic interests. Rather than simply investing in the constant improvement of material conditions, the residents of Joya de Cerén invest in social capital, in the capital of their social relations, an option created by their collective work over the years. In this context, the system of domestic groups in the village is of fundamental importance.

Domestic groups form the basis of the social fabric in the hamlets that make up the village. They are residential entities that constitute the units of consumption in the community. Inside these groups are a range of family formations. In Joya de Cerén we have seen the following kinds of family: nuclear family, 68.52 percent; incomplete nuclear family, 9.26 percent; one nuclear family and one incomplete nuclear family, 12.26 percent; and fragmented nuclear family, 9.26 percent. The last two categories represent extended families, including relatives beyond the nuclear family. Notably, in Joya de Cerén an extended family never included two complete nuclear families. Instead, extended family households typically consisted of a nuclear family with an incomplete nuclear family or members of a fragmented nuclear family. This indicates that the extended family, when it forms part of a single domestic household, is a type of association brought together to provide economic and social protection for incomplete nuclear families, whether they are new couples beginning married life, single-mother families, or families headed by a widow or widower. It is important to emphasize that extended family households tend to change frequently. A typical household may move from being an extended family to a nuclear family to yet another formation over the course of time.

In 45.5 percent of the households studied, when family members married (or formed life partnerships) they went to live with parents, most to the household of the man's family, although some went to the homes of the woman's parents. This creates a household with a nuclear family hosting an incomplete nuclear family. Some new couples stay in this situation even after the birth of their first child, although most move away and build their own households at this time. Typically, couples live in the house of one spouse's parents for one or two years while they gather sufficient resources to be able to move out. At this point the new couple constitutes a nuclear family, a unit that will be maintained until the children grow and begin to marry. This is one of the reasons that 68.52 percent of family groups are nuclear families, the type of family structure that endures most of the time. Once the first child is married, the extended family is again established. If for some reason a daughter's marriage fails, or if she simply has children outside of a stable relationship, she and her children are reintegrated into the paternal household. Finally, if one of the parents is widowed, or is of advanced age, one child with his or her family takes care of the parent. This is an ideal reconstruction of the functioning in Joya de Cerén of the life cycle of a domestic unit, and it corresponds to the pattern seen throughout Mesoamerica.

In Joya de Cerén, 51.5 percent of adults declared that when they married or made life partnerships they left their parents' home to form a new home of their own. This tendency toward neolocality breaks with the traditional cycles as described above. Neolocality represents the influence of contemporary capitalism on Joya de Cerén, whereas patrilocality (maternal or paternal) represents the influence of traditional peasant society. Thus, the semipeasant character of the village is seen in the composition of its household groups, which are shaped by both traditional, patrilocal dynamics and capitalist, neolocal dynamics, within a shared system.

The overarching importance of domestic groups in the community can be seen in the way the community constructs its system of solidarity and mutual aid. This system begins with the actual household unit, of course, the primary entity through which solidarity relationships are developed. Beginning with this primary group, the system establishes the association of households headed by brothers and sisters. Second-tier relationships are established through households headed by cousins (the extended family). The solidarity of household units and extended families is maintained through vertical relationships, which may be through parents and children or grandparents and grandchildren. When this vertical relationship disappears, the group tends to disappear, although some households connected by sibling relationships may maintain systems of mutual aid and solidarity.

There are other associations that generate solidarity relationships in the village, and religious associations are the most effective of these. Nevertheless, at the center of these are the domestic units and extended families that constitute the basis of social solidarity. The same could be said of the political organizations, like the Community Development Associations (Asociación de Desarollo Comunal), whose support base is grounded in the system of domestic groups. But the domestic groups of Joya de Cerén do not merely constitute the solidarity universe of the village. They are the center of the community's biological reproduction. It is through them that property is transmitted from generation to generation, and they are the conduit for passing on cultural norms and values that guide the social life of the community's members. This multifunctionality points to these domestic units as structural elements in the community and in the totality of social interactions and processes.

Lessons from Joya de Cerén

An outstanding feature of the agrarian project of 1954 is its emphasis on a holistic, integrated vision of community development. The project was not limited to the community's economic development; it was also concerned with social and cultural development, particularly the development of community solidarity and a system of mutual support among residents. Such an integrated vision has proven essential for successful rural development efforts. Based in community cooperatives, the economic development of Joya de Cerén encountered numerous obstacles. Yet the larger communal project made significant achievements, notably in the construction of a community that, at least since the early 1990s, has been socially stable and functional. This demonstrates that development projects that incorporate diverse aspects of a community, both economic and social, bear more fruit than those focusing solely on the economic component.

The economic difficulties of the project can be attributed to two factors: poor management of the association's utilities and the preference of the small farmers for private property and the concomitant ability to make their own land-management decisions. Farmers' decisions differed from those recommended by the ICR technicians in that farmers opted for a subsistence-based economy over one geared to commercial markets. The subsistence-based strategy, combined with other economic activities, allowed for a certain fluidity in working within the national economic system. In this sense, farmers' favoring subsistence-based agriculture should not be interpreted as an isolationist tendency but instead as an interest in conserving a measure of socioeconomic autonomy without being kept wholly on the margins of the world and national economies.

This experience provides a lesson that promoters of rural development should keep in mind: development projects need to take into account not only the technical aspects of production and the commercialization of products (such as the quality of the ground, types of seed, mechanization of the agricultural work, networks of commercialization) but also the expectations and inclinations of the benefactors. Because macroeconomic conceptions do not focus on specific local culture, the expectations of the benefactors often do not coincide completely with the plans of the project's promoters. Projects to improve the living conditions of small farmers that do not conflict with cultural norms should be developed through dialogue between promoters and benefactors. In the case of Joya de Cerén, such a dialogue could have taken place among the small farmers, the technicians of the ICR, and the international volunteers. Unfortunately, the agrarian reforms the Salvadoran government initiated during the 1980s (and later) did not take the comprehensive approach established in the ICR projects of the 1950s. This failure constitutes a serious limitation in the effort to create better living conditions for small farmers.

Finally, although the local level has its own dynamic, and the characteristics and influence of local phenomena are revealed only when they are observed from the local point of view, local history cannot be fully understood exclusive of the context of the larger society. As we have seen, even minute local phenomena are closely tied to larger processes. This dialectical relationship (between the macro and the micro) is particularly important to understanding the dynamics that brought about the 1954 agrarian reform, including that in Joya de Cerén. Three social forces participated in the project: the local population (the benefactors), the national government, and the international community. These three social groups were organized around two overarching concerns: the interests of the local community and the desire of the national state to organize successful examples of reformist development policy as sources of political support. The international community developed the project based on these two sets of concerns, to a certain degree identifying the local interests but also supporting the national development program, which was based on sugar production.

Section Two

Civil War and Its Aftermath
Local Politics and Community

El Salvador's revolutionary civil war of 1980–1992 was by far one of Latin
America's most dramatic experiences in recent times. A persistent guerilla army
successfully confronted a military force micromanaged and funded by the United
States in a terrain so small that most experts would not have conceived of the
possibility of a long, drawn-out conflict. Parallel to the war, El Salvador experienced at least a partial transition to a "tutelary" electoral system, while the
United States negotiated its attempt to manage and finance the imposition of
"reforms" whose goal was to "modernize" El Salvador's oligarchic state and social
institutions (banking, export, land, labor, rural development, police) in an attempt to remove the social bases of support for the insurgency. This period is
perhaps the best-known part of the country's history. But the ending of the war
in 1992 and the complex social and political transitions that have followed
should not cause us to desist in questioning the origins and process of the revolution, as well as other slighted themes not so closely tied to the political
chronology of the 1970s and 1980s.

The chronology and major turning points of the revolutionary civil war are
relatively well understood, although a more careful and comprehensive study of
both the political and military aspects of the conflict would be welcome. How-

ever, the myriad local experiences of Salvadorans during this period are much more obscure and worthy of further attention. The war had a tremendous and extremely differentiated impact on local communities, and the many dilemmas that have emerged in its aftermath require the kind of careful local studies provided by the chapters that form this section of the book.

Despite the significant attention given to the revolutionary process of the 1970s and 1980s, few studies have focused on its principal protagonists.[1] The chapters by Leigh Binford, Elisabeth Wood, Vince McElhinny, Lisa Kowalchuk, and Irina Carlota Silber provide important insight into the transformation of rural El Salvador during the 1980s and early 1990s. Binford's chapter helps dismiss arguments that El Salvador did not experience a genuine social-revolutionary movement during the 1980s. By examining the history of catechist organizing in Morazán, Binford reveals an important and little-known aspect of the revolutionary movement. His work helps us understand the ability of the People's Revolutionary Army (Ejercito Revolucionario Popular, ERP), one of the guerilla armies of the Farabundo Martí National Liberation Front (FMLN), to recruit peasants in this region as well as the local grievances that fueled support for the insurgency (particularly state repression). He argues that peasant catechists were "organic intellectuals" in the Gramscian sense and that they served as the "transmission belts" that conveyed, interpreted, and adapted urban-based revolutionary ideologies to relatively remote rural areas. Furthermore, Binford adds complexity to the history of the Salvadoran Catholic church during the late 1970s and early 1980s by arguing that the church was not only divided by its grassroots practices and its hierarchy but also by its reformist and conservative tendencies. Binford's investigations into the importance of local intellectual activists provide a sound basis for further research in other regions.

Wood examines the experience of a repopulated community in Tenancingo, Cuscatlán. After intense local conflicts and a major military engagement in 1983, most of Tenancingo's population fled into Honduras. Repopulation in Tenancingo by its former residents started while the war was still raging, in 1986, as an unarmed zone in which neither guerillas nor army would carry out military activities. Seen as a limited victory for political negotiation in the midst of civil war, the Tenancingo experience also revealed the need for local peasant and other movements to gain autonomy from both the state and rebel organizations, in an effort to construct a reformed community to some extent inspired by the larger goals of the revolutionary movement. The challenges of local community organizing, the formation of cooperatives, and other efforts led by local people or assisted by the few outside institutions that provided support made of Tenancingo an early laboratory for the challenges of reconstruction.

McElhinny's chapter links the revolutionary war period with the postwar dilemmas of reconstruction and democratization. By examining a locality that firmly connects peasants with the revolutionary actors of the 1980s, McElhinny's work provides a window into the challenges posed by the need for postwar integration and development and the ambiguity of postwar resolutions. The chapter highlights the construction of communitarian values and development programs within Ciudad Segundo Montes, one of El Salvador's most successful communities of civil war ex-combatants. McElhinny uses survey evidence to compare Ciudad Segundo Montes with other rural communities. He shows that the attitudes and behaviors found within the community demonstrate high levels of participation, tolerance, and political efficacy, yet they also exhibit a conflictive and distrusting orientation toward the state. Conflictive orientations do not necessarily disqualify Ciudad Segundo Montes for lacking a vibrant "civic culture" but rather ask us to reconsider the cultural and institutional requisites that are most congruent with a stable democracy. Finally, by comparing groups within Ciudad Segundo Montes, McElhinny finds that the formation of a collective identity is a necessary local component of postconflict transitions to democracy, and the breakdown in this crucial attribute helps explain the limitations that Ciudad Segundo Montes has faced as a development model.

Kowalchuk also considers some of the difficult dilemmas of postwar society for rural workers and peasants. By focusing on postwar contestation over land in the confusing context of sometimes corrupt and self-serving peasant leaders, Kowalchuk revisits the theme suggested in the chapters by Lauria-Santiago and Lara Martínez: the problems stemming from internal organization within peasant movements and communities. Kowalchuk finds that the institutional, ideological, and political ambiguity of the postwar period has left the door open to many problems with the way peasant demands are filtered through a relatively dispersed, disorganized, and corrupt leadership. Given continuing demands for land reform and development investment in the Salvadoran countryside, the difficulties Kowalchuk identifies in this chapter will continue to be part of Salvadoran reality for some time. Silber's chapter examines the lives of repatriated people in Chalatenango who live in organized repopulated communities and have been involved in postwar reconstruction. Her study details what happens to revolutionary peoples and places after a negotiated peace by investigating the competing local ideologies and practices that comprise and at times compromise everyday rebuilding processes. Silber focuses on the problematic relationship between rural folk, particularly women, and several historically allied nongovernmental organizations in the region. She examines the contradictions within the discourse of *asistencialismo* (assistentialism, or self-help organizations) that suggest that those in whose name the war was fought are, on the one hand, blamed for "loosing" their revolutionary identities and traditional war-time organizing and, on the other, accused of having received years of handouts as refugees and thus unwilling to incorporate themselves into the national productive economy. By carefully listening to these conflicted discourses as used by local people, Silber moves us beyond the limited explanations described here. Instead, she suggests that what is taking place is a search for alternative survival strategies. These efforts address a shifting reality that many local residents describe as one of broken promises and bankrupt dreams left in the wake of the war. As war-time social relations, strategies, and activism are held up as the ideal for community life, Silber suggests that patterns in postwar Chalatenango demonstrate a remarginalizing and reexcluding of people who for some period had new identities—a tragic wasted opportunity in El Salvador's transition from war to peace.

Leigh Binford

Peasants, Catechists, Revolutionaries

Organic Intellectuals in the Salvadoran Revolution, 1980–1992

Social scientists writing on the Salvadoran revolution (1980–1992) generally agree that the popular wing of the Catholic Church played a crucial role in consciousness raising and organizational development among urban and, especially, rural populations. However, discussion of that role tends to focus on the martyred Archbishop Oscar Arnulfo Romero, or on priests such as Rutilio Grande, José Incencio Alas, and Octavio Ortiz, who worked in and around the capital and were threatened, tortured, or killed by Salvadoran military and security forces or deaths squads linked to them.[1] The army of lay peasant and worker catechists, that is, the "noncommissioned officers" of liberation theology trained by these priests, tend to be discussed in generalities, when they are discussed at all. In fact, the paucity of specific information about liberation theology in the countryside led Yvon Grenier to conclude that that church's role in raising consciousness in rural areas has been overestimated; he argues that the Catholic Church contributed to the development of the resistance mainly through its support for the Christian Democratic Party and the politicization of middle-class students and intellectuals who worked in or attended Jesuit schools, such as the Central American University or the Externado San José, based in the capital.[2]

It is true that the archbishopric was the only Salvadoran diocese, among five nationally, in which progressive Catholicism received official support. The bishops who controlled the other four dioceses (centered in the departments of Santa Ana, Usulután, San Miguel, and La Unión) were conservative supporters of the religious status quo and discouraged pastoral agents—many of whom grew up in impoverished rural areas and until 1972 trained in the Jesuit-run San José de la Montaña seminary—from implementing programs that challenged elite ideologies.[3] Nonetheless, progressive Catholicism did take root in many rural areas when there occurred fortuitous meetings of progressive clergy and catechists trained at one of seven *centros de formación campesina* (peasant training centers, also known as *universidades campesinas,* or peasant universities) scattered around the nation. Indeed, in her *Martyrdom and the Politics of Religion* Ana Peterson argues that "although CEBs [Comunidades Eclesiales de Base, Christian Base Communities] have received more scholarly attention," the peasant training centers were "probably the most important element of the popular church in El Salvador."[4] Montgomery claimed that about 15,000 (mostly peasant) leaders received training in the centers between 1970 and 1976.[5] Despite these assessments, neither the centers nor those who trained in them have been studied, partly a result of the capital-centric bias that has historically plagued social science writing on El Salvador, and that is in the initial stages of being redressed.[6]

The study presented in this chapter represents a first effort to examine progressive Catholicism from a regional perspective, focusing on the training centers and those who trained in them. I argue that peasant training centers were instrumental to the development of a group of progressive, peasant intellectuals who, in concert with local clergy, introduced into rural communities a more integral religious vision that took account of people's material and spiritual needs as well as promoted historical and sociological analysis of the human condition. Violent repression by state agents probably led most Farabundo Martí National Liberation Front (FMLN) recruits into guerrilla ranks; however, catechists and members of Christian Base Communities in northern Morazán, the focus of this chapter, formed a significant percentage of the people who joined the People's Revolutionary Army (ERP) out of political conviction during its early, clandestine phase (1975–1980). Because of a lack of written material about the centers, this study is based primarily on interviews and discussions with catechists and former catechists who lived and worked in northern Morazán before, during, and after the civil war.

Catholicism in Northern Morazán

Northern Morazán is a roughly defined 200-square-mile area situated north of the Torola River in Morazán Department. In 1970 this mountainous, volcanic upland, marked by altitudes ranging from 600 to 5,000 feet (south to north), contained over 35,000 inhabitants, many among the poorest in the nation. Peasants

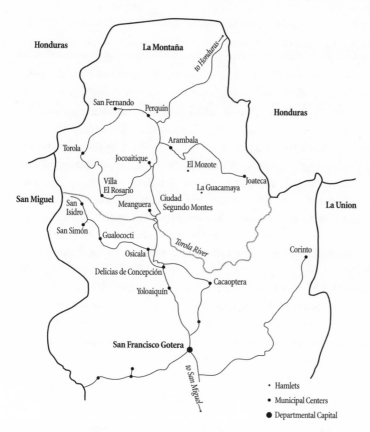

Northern Morazán

planted thin soils and steep, eroded hillsides in corn, beans, sorghum, and henequen, depending on local rainfall and altitude. A few of the higher and better watered areas sustained small coffee plantations, the basis of the region's only agricultural enterprises that merit qualification as capitalist. Elsewhere in northern Morazán merchant capital reigned supreme over a dispersed peasantry and landless rural proletariat. Low soil fertility and small land holdings compelled many northern Morazanians, especially those from drier, more heavily populated areas around Meanguera, Torola, and Villa El Rosario (see map) to seek seasonal work harvesting cotton, sugarcane, and coffee in El Salvador's agro-export zones.

Until 1973 the region contained only one Catholic parish, centered in the important regional market town of Jocoaitique. From this home base—the only community with regular Sunday services—Padre Andrés Argueta traveled by jeep to the area's other seven municipal centers and a few of the dozens of rural *caseríos* (dispersed communities) distributed over the rugged countryside. Argueta represented a traditionalist current of Catholicism that emphasized spirituality and subordination before the will of God. His liturgies focused on the self-sacrifices of the saints. He interpreted poverty, disease, and infant death as trials mandated by God for which those who bore them with dignity would be rewarded in the hereafter. Argueta's own material well-being was secured, however, by the payments he received for presiding over baptisms, christenings, weddings, and funerals, as well as special masses celebrating the patron saints. Religious practice in northern Morazán was little different from that described for the Aguilares region by Carlos Rafael Cabarrús in his seminal *Génesis de una revolución:* "an important cult of the saints; an abundant conformity with the present while awaiting a future life, and a definite consecration of the established order. Only a miracle by the saint permitted the peasant to alter his position. Only a miracle could convert him into a rich person, given the belief that the quantity of goods are limited."[7] According to Fabio Argueta, a catechist from Meanguera, "Many people only gave their love and affection to saint's images. By loving only the image, they had ceased loving and serving one another. The people had become so pious that they displayed no spirit of service toward those who were most in need."[8]

These beliefs established Catholicism as an important underpinning of the regional hegemonic order, defining *hegemony* here as a system of beliefs and practices that favor dominant groups and that serve as frames that shape people's lived experience, even their experience of struggle against oppression.[9] Like many priests, Argueta benefited materially from a rural class system that kept most people subordinate to a few rural merchant and agrarian capitalist families. In Jocoaitique he ate without cost at the homes of the local economic elite, who increased their cultural capital by associating with him. And when he visited poor, outlying areas, he was often met at the entrance of the community by officials and welcomed with fireworks and music from a local band. For most people a visit from the region's only priest was a rare and important occasion. After mass Argueta ate alone in a local home or the church sacristy, for no one would dare to break bread with a literate man of God—nor did the priest ever invite them to do so. The community served him its richest fare: chicken, eggs, cream, and milk that most peasants rarely consumed. People who required the priest's council, or wished to request a favor, usually sought out the assistance of an intermediary, whether a judge, church official, the mayor, or another person of status. The priest's relationships with his "flock" were marked by the paternalism exercised by large rural landowners and merchants toward peasants and rural workers. Surely Argueta was aware of the relationship between his practice and the dominant order, for on the occasion of elections he sometimes used the pulpit to urge people to vote for the National Conciliation Party (PCN), formed by the military government in 1961.

The conservative role of the church in northern Morazán began to change in 1968, when Bishop Graciano of San Miguel, Argueta's immediate superior, ordered priests in his diocese to seek lay candidates for catechist training in Centro Reino de la Paz, recently opened in El Castaño, San Miguel. Obligingly, Argueta began to identify and invite *mayordomos,* sacristans, and other pious churchgoing males from around northern Morazán to attend a month-long catechism course. Over the following three or four years thirty to forty northern Morazanian peasants and, in a few cases, rural workers attended courses in El Castaño or San Lucas (city of San Miguel) and Los Naranjos (Jiquilisco, Usulután), other training centers in eastern El Salvador that opened shortly after El Castaño.[10] Among the various goals of the centers was the training of lay catechists who could help administer the faith to a rural population that outnumbered parish priests 30,000 to 1 nationally.

Unbeknownst to Argueta, however, the centers informed their theory and practice according to the dictates and recommendations of Vatican II (1962–1965) and especially the 1968 Episcopal Conference at Medellín, Colombia, where Vatican II was adapted to Latin America's distinct reality. Most of Argueta's charges returned from the intense, month-long course eager to make real the "preferential option for the poor" around which much of the didactic material revolved. Not surprisingly, many soon entered into conflict with Argueta, whose theory and practice of Christianity contrasted with a new and potent teaching that urged people to take responsibility for their development and that of their fellow human beings. I will discuss these conflicts later, but first it is necessary to outline the experiences in the training centers that contributed to the catechists' transformation.

The Training Centers

Abraham Argueta (no relation to Padre Andrés Argueta) was working as a tailor in Joateca when he was asked in 1969 by the priest if he would like to attend El Castaño. In 1995 he explained his initial reaction to the school in the following terms: "[There] I suffered a sort of mental transformation because before [going to the center] I didn't relate much to people. I kept apart, they said that I focused on my own affairs and didn't get involved in other things. When I went [to El Castaño] I suffered a kind of . . . I don't know what. . . . I awoke but didn't

Descriptive Information on Catechists from Northern Morazán and Adjacent Regions

Name	Municipality	Born	Sent by	Catechism center	Year sent	Age	Land	Occupation	Activity during civil war
Cristobal	Joateca	1930	Argueta	El Castaño	1969	39	no	Carpenter	Displaced, San Martín (near San Salvador)
Felipe	Joateca	1927	Argueta	El Castaño	1969	42	yes	Mailman/peasant	Displaced, San Miguel
Abraham Argueta	Joateca	1936	Argueta	El Castaño	1969	33	no	Tailor	Refugee, Nicaragua
Miguel Angel Benítez	Cacahuatique	1950	Irish	El Castaño	1976	26	no	Peasant	FMLN combatant/catechist
Samuel Vidal Guzmán	San Fernando	1950	Argueta	El Castaño and San Lucas	1971	21	yes	Peasant	FMLN health sector/catechist
Fabio Argueta	Meanguera	1943	Argueta	El Castaño	1970	27	10 mz.[a]	Peasant/merchant	FMLN political organizer
Maximino Pérez	Cacaopera	1929	Argueta	El Castaño	N.A.	early 40s	N.A.	Peasant	FMLN combatant/catechist
Román Díaz	Delicias	1925	Irish	El Castaño	1969	44	yes	Peasant/day worker	Social Base/refugee, Honduras 1983
Secundino Chicas	Meanguera	1930	Argueta	El Castaño	1969	39	2 mz.	Peasant/artisan	Refugee Honduras/health worker
Anastacio Portillo	Osicala	1932	Ventura	Los Naranjos	1976	44	yes	Carpenter/peasant	FMLN political activist/refugee, Honduras
José Clemente Luna	Cacaopera	1945	Irish	El Castaño	1975	30	1 mz.	Tailor/bricklayer	Social Base, tailor/refugee, Honduras
Pedro Rodríguez	Tarola	1950	Argueta	El Castaño and San Lucas	1972	22	10 mz.	Peasant	FMLN health sector/refugee, Honduras

Name	Municipality	Born	Sent by	Catechism center	Year sent	Age	Land	Occupation	Activity during civil war
Anastacio Caballero	Jocoaitique	1930	Argueta	San Lucas	1978	48	4 mz.	Tailor/peasant	Refugee Honduras/pastoral worker
Natividad Pérez	Cacaopera	1940	Irish	El Castaño and San Lucas	1976	36	6 mz.	Peasant/day worker	FMLN kitchen/social base/political activist
Rodolfo Vasquéz	San Fernando	N.A.	Argueta	El Castaño	1969	N.A.	yes	Peasant	Assassinated in La Unión, 1979
Cristobal Chicas	Joateca	1958	Argueta	El Castaño and San Lucas	1975	17	yes	Peasant	FMLN musician, Radio Venceremos
Sebastian Chicas	Joateca	1955	Argueta	El Castaño and San Lucas	1975	14	yes	Peasant	FMLN musician, Radio Venceremos
Aparicio Orellana	Guatijiagua	1953	Irish	El Castaño and Los Naranjos	1973	20	yes	Peasant	FMLN combatant/catechist
Andrés Barrera	Meanguera	1939	Ventura	El Castaño and Los Naranjos	1973	34	yes	Peasant	FMLN musician, Radio Venceremos/refugee, Honduras
"Mauricio" (pseudonym)	Cacaopera	1940	Irish	El Castaño	1971	31	yes	Peasant	FMLN logistics and supply
"Pancho" (pseudonym)	Cacaopera	1950	Irish	El Castaño	1976	26	yes	Peasant	FMLN
"Tito" (pseudonym)	Cacaopera	1946	Irish	El Castaño	1972	26	yes	Peasant	FMLN political organizer

Source: Direct investigation.
a. Manzana.

even know where I was. . . . A strange thing happened to me, I was seeing everything in a different way. Everything felt to me as if I was someone else and in some other place. It was like a psychological metamorphosis. I felt an awakening to a different world and it caused me to take in everything that was there."[11]

Abraham Argueta offered unusually dramatic testimony of personal transformation as a result of attending El Castaño, but the general terms in which he expressed his experiences were echoed by many other catechists. They spoke of "being transformed," "awakening as if from a long sleep," "feeling like a new man," or "having a veil removed from the eyes."[12] These feeling were responses to the messages imparted by the priest-teachers, but they were shaped by the particular form and structure of the educational experience. The El Castaño training program was driven by liberation theology, which emphasized the development of the whole or integral person as a spiritual and material unity through collective struggle. The religious units of the course focused less on miraculous saints than on the historical Jesus, whose spirit, the students learned, resides in every human being, regardless of wealth or social status. Whereas the poor are dignified (and deserving), liberation theology teaches that God promises no special honor or celestial reward for accepting such misery, for poverty is not a transcendental condition mandated by the deity but a historical and social product that Christians have the responsibility to remedy. Accordingly, to units on theology the El Castaño curriculum appended others dealing with agriculture, community organization, and cooperative development designed to supply workers and peasants with the knowledge necessary to develop their communities socially and economically.

Of course this was all new to the students, many of whom arrived thinking that they were going to learn more about the Bible and prayer. Both the secular and religious features of the curriculum generated confusion and consternation. Of every class of forty or so, a small number dropped out, resistant to the new teachings, unable to adapt to the strict discipline that characterized life in El Castaño, and chastened by the sight of casually dressed priests playing soccer with the students. Miguel Angel Benítez, a small-scale agriculturalist from the Cacahuatique area who became an outstanding catechist until his premature death from cancer in 1996, expressed his initial reactions as follows: "When I arrived at the center [El Castaño], I was a bit concerned and I asked myself, 'What are we going to do here?' At that time the schedule for each day had been written up and I was looking at it. Well, at such an hour [one class] and at such an hour another class. They had themes on community development, health, education, agriculture, and free themes. I asked myself, 'To combine these things as a Christian, how's it going to happen?' I had thought that they were going to teach us things about the

Bible and to pray. . . . The other thing that bothered me a bit was that I was accustomed to seeing the priests dressed in pants and cassocks. But as I watched them wearing tee-shirts and playing soccer with the masses . . . well, when one has a preconception, all that is a bit strange."[13]

Besides their preconceptions, the would-be catechists possessed generally poor reading skills, a dependent relationship to authority, and a reticence about expressing themselves in public, particularly when it came to sharing personal beliefs and life history experiences. For instance, most recruits had completed two or three years of schooling, often the maximum available in rural areas away from municipal centers. Apart from the limited availability, academic competence had little value among a population dedicated to agriculture and small-scale stock raising, where the skills necessary for making a living were learned through observation and performance. Aphorisms expressed the objective *necessities* that everyone *knew* to be true: *Las letras no se come* (You can't eat the alphabet), intoned by parents to keep children home from school once they had learned enough reading and writing *para defenderse* (in order to defend themselves). Such attitudes reflected socioeconomic realities, but they also contributed to perpetuating them.[14]

Still, most people sent to the centers had at least a minimum level of reading proficiency, which would improve with practice and through special classes there. Fewer recruits were experienced speaking in public before large groups. A number of informants mentioned their initial bashfulness and timidity. Ramón Díaz said that each person "felt fear the first time he was called upon to speak in the midst of a group," although he noted how, "in the end, one gains the force to stand up in front of a group of people head-to-head." And Miguel Angel Benítez stated that on arriving at El Castaño, "one feels timid, that one can't break through these barriers that keep him from deepening his understanding of the church." We might consider these attitudes the corporal embodiment—the "body *hexis*" in Pierre Bourdieu's terms—of a long history of abuse at the hands of priests, government officials, doctors, soldiers, and the local merchant elite.[15] Northern Morazán's poor had learned that because of the vast inequalities in access to power, direct confrontations with authority invariably ended in disaster.

In El Castaño priest-teachers employed a variety of studied methods to break down peasant and worker reserve. For instance, they ordered students to deliver extemporaneous speeches while facing a wall, after which other members of the group debated the positive and negative points of their style and discourse. In a more intricate version of the same technique, students formed two concentric circles around the speaker, with the first circle assigned the task of critiquing the speech and the second observing and critiquing the commentaries of those in the first circle. The instructor then had students change positions so that eventually each would experience speaking, observing the speaker, and observing the observers.[16] Over time most students overcame their shyness; they returned to northern Morazán with the personal confidence and many of the technical skills to become protagonists of change at the local level. Abraham Argueta, who testified earlier to an abrupt transformation, described his return home as follows: "I passed that first level and arrived home full of enthusiasm. Other friends had attended [El Castaño] but they had not called together the community to speak about development. But I arrived and began to make house visits and had a meeting in my home. I motivated the people so much that we were offered a house so that we could meet every Wednesday. Soon I proposed the cooperative, invited the other comrades [*compañeros*—he refers to catechists here] and told them, 'Let's speak to the people about cooperatives.'"[17]

Most aspiring catechists were in their late twenties and thirties (average age was thirty-one at the time of first attendance) and already had formed independent households when they began their studies (see table). The majority cultivated a few *manzanas* of land; others worked as artisans (bricklayers, carpenters, tailors) or combined artisan work and agriculture. The centers paid students' transportation costs and gave them food and housing while in attendance, but they did not provide monetary subsidies to maintain family members who remained behind in northern Morazán. Although courses were often scheduled during the slack agricultural season, the lack of family financial assistance resulted in an overrepresentation of the middle economic strata in El Castaño. Landless and land-poor peasants and workers spent the November–April dry season earning cash income by weaving rope, bridles, hammocks, and other products from locally grown henequen fiber or left Morazán in order to harvest cotton, sugarcane, and coffee on the plantations of the rich. The catechists' solid social and economic status—pious adults who had proven that they could meet their families' basic needs—probably lent their voices considerable weight when they introduced novel ideas and forms of organization. Perhaps younger people would have adjusted better to the centers' conditions and curriculum, but age and dependent economic status probably would have reduced their effectiveness as community organizers.

Another feature of the centers that bears mentioning (and merits detailed historical study) is the role that time discipline played in forming new subjectivities. While the evidence is thin at this point, the disciplinary regime made enough of a mark on several catechists that they commented on it twenty to twenty-five years later. U.S.-born Jesuit Dionisio Santamaría, formerly the parish priest in Chirilagua, San Miguel, and his El Castaño team removed recruits from their flexible daily routines at home and imposed a tight programming of wake-up, prayer services, classes, recreation, and meals not far removed from their own seminary training. Although attendance at the centers was voluntary, and students could leave anytime they wanted, the priests' high social status and moral authority bound most attendees to what was practically a "total institution." The structured social routines provided a conducive environment for the propagation of the new ideas the priests sought to communicate. The El Castaño regime involved a training of body as well as mind through the calculated employment of many of the disciplinary apparatuses discussed at length by Michel Foucault in his analysis of the modern microphysics of power/knowledge.[18] To varying degrees the students were subject to surveillance, normalization procedures, and even examination. But instead of generating Foucault's "docile subjects" adapted to preexisting social conditions, the priests aimed at producing change agents. The dynamic practices they employed can certainly be interpreted as means to this end.

On many occasions priests used their status and authority—cultural capital, in Bourdieu's terms—to subvert ingrained conceptions of low self-worth.[19] Maximino Pérez, at sixty-six years one of the oldest catechists I interviewed, recalled that once Padre Dionisio Santamaría placed Maximino (under five feet tall) and another short student at his sides and asked the class to state which among the three was the largest (*más grande*). The class selected Santamaría because he was "very large" (*grandote*) and a priest. But Santamaría said that they were wrong because "all people were equal, whether large, short, dark-complexioned, lame, or blind." All people, he stated, had the same capacity.[20]

In the abstract all students might have had the same capacity, but the priests did evaluate them, even if informally, and in the words of Abraham Argueta, "if one had advanced sufficiently, they invited him to the second level," and if not, "they left him to work in the community."[21] The first-level introductory course ("initiation") was followed by advanced levels ("deepening" and "advancement"), usually taken at six-month intervals for those who were invited back. In addition, the San Lucas center (located in San Miguel) offered a special month-long health course, and the Guadelupe center trained female catechists.

On one occasion some forty of the best students nationwide, Abraham Argueta among them, were invited to compete for the opportunity to become trainers in the centers. In 1972 the ten who excelled took a course in intergroup interaction in Centro de la Providencia in Santa Ana, run by Padre Walter Guerra; after practicing in Salvadoran centers for a time, they were sent to Guatemala to the Jesuit-run Rafael Landívar University for advanced training in group dynamics (*dinámica del grupo*) and existential laboratory (*laboratorio vivencial*). On their return they worked in teams of three or four at peasant training centers throughout El Salvador, teaching the critical first unit used to "loosen up" new arrivals. Space limits prevent a detailed discussion of the very sophisticated techniques that the rural trainers put into practice. Briefly, they attempted to provoke the students to openly display their emotions and, as these reached their maximum flowering, devised situations in which they would come together as a group and reject the authority of (and thus their dependence on) the teacher. In a marathon session on the final day, following a week of programmed provocations, the groups attained a degree of internal cohesion that allowed them to confront the teacher and share personal histories and inner thoughts with one another. It is difficult to overstate the brilliance of this strategy. Who could be more familiar with the beliefs, attitudes, dispositions, and subtle aspects of body language of the recruits to the centers than trainers who shared their rural social roots and were fluent in the relevant cultural codes? Once "opened up" by the shock therapy of that first, intense, week-long course, the students would be more receptive to the religious alternative—and the practical implications that followed from it—offered by the priests in the units that followed. Interestingly, Argueta stated that apart from the regular service they provided the centers, the teams were also invited to impart courses in group dynamics to urban intellectuals, priests, lawyers, and professors working in nongovernmental organizations.[22]

It would be a mistake, however, to characterize the centers as sites designed to breed resistance and rebellion. As originally conceived, the programs were of the self-help variety, oriented toward the development of local organization and the acquisition of technical skills that poor people could put to work in order to resolve pressing material necessities. Hence El Castaño and other centers included courses on modern agricultural techniques, cooperative formation, and planning, along with theology and religion. To impart courses outside their areas of expertise, priest-administrators recruited intellectuals, technicians, and even people from the Ministry of Agriculture, a practice that would hardly have been the case had they been out to overthrow the state—as they were later accused of attempting to do.

The Catechists in Northern Morazán

In northern Morazán the ability of newly trained catechists to put the lessons to use depended to a considerable degree on the level of support that they received from the local priest. True to his past Padre Argueta did everything possible to dampen the impact of the new teachings and return "wandering" catechists to his fold. Once Fabio Argueta (no relation to the priest) asked him, "Look Padre, when you read the Bible and open [it to] the gospel of the rich, I see that you prefer to take up a theme related to the Virgin and don't want to talk about the wealthy. What's going on?" Padre Argueta replied, "If I begin to talk about the rich, then don Pablo Ventura [a wealthy Jocoaitique merchant] won't continue to feed me."[23] (Argueta had a standing invitation to eat for free in Ventura's home.) Pedro Rodríguez recalled that at monthly meetings, Argueta warned the catechists not to take up the theme of the rich and the poor.[24] He tried to orient the work toward the "missionary" type, that is, to have the catechists urge couples to marry in the church and prepare their children for communion.[25] Argueta told catechists who resisted his mandates that they were doing subversive work, that *he* was the religious authority in the region, and that they had to follow his orders.[26] Many catechists did submit to his demands, but others sought ways to concretize the lessons of the centers without instigating a confrontation. For instance, Abraham Argueta and five other Joateca catechists threw themselves into setting up a savings-and-loan cooperative through which local people could obtain low interest loans to buy chemical fertilizers, which were just becoming available in northern Morazán. Building on several years of success, the co-op took out a bank loan in the mid-1970s, which it used to purchase forty hybrid steers, a feed lot, and a mill for machinery for processing grain, corn husks, syrup (produced locally from sugarcane), and other raw materials into cattle feed. In 1980 following the assassination of one of its founders, Cooperative San Antonio collapsed. Prior to this it had grown to 113 members.[27] The six Joateca catechists who spearheaded the co-op's formation, legal recognition, and development drew heavily on the lessons of El Castaño (and in the case of Abraham Argueta, his experience as a teacher of group dynamics and existential laboratory), but Padre Argueta never supported the project.

In 1973 bishop Eduardo Álvarez, who took over the San Miguel diocese from bishop Graciano, reassigned northern Morazán's easternmost three municipalities (Villa El Rosario, Torola, and San Fernando) to a new parish centered in Torola township and headed by Padre Miguel Ventura, who had studied at San José de la Montaña seminary in San Salvador. In an earlier clash between the radical young priest and the conservative middle-aged bishop, Álvarez, a member of Opus Dei and chaplin to San Miguel's Third Army Brigade throughout the civil war, had held up Ventura's ordination for several months.[28] Placing Ventura in the northern Morazanian "backwater" may have been Álvarez's way of punishing him, although according to Ventura it was common practice for newly ordained priests to be "sent to areas where there was little communication."[29] It is also possible that Bishop Álvarez wanted to keep an eye on Ventura by locating him close by Andrés Argueta, who just happened to be the younger priest's uncle (his mother's brother). Although Ventura's father had died shortly before his ordination and he had requested to be posted closer to the family home in Yayantique (La Unión),

Torola was far from the earthly purgatory that Álvarez might have imagined. Ventura had traveled to northern Morazán in the mid-1960s and once even organized a retreat there for San José de la Montaña seminarians, hosted by a retired schoolteacher who spent thirty years in service to area youth.[30] Also, he had already met many of the region's progressive catechists, recruited by Argueta, through a relationship with El Castaño that began in 1970. During the two years following Ventura's appointment Padre Argueta struggled to maintain control of rebellious catechists in Jocoaitique and elsewhere in his parish, while Padre Ventura embarked on a campaign to practice the preferential option for the poor by developing Christian Base Communities in the Torola/Villa El Rosario/San Fernando region.

By 1975 Padre Ventura's parish contained many Christian Base Communities whose members attended services, assisted the very poor, and in some instances even organized collective work parties that divided the income from the fields, unusual in a region with a strong private-property ethic and no history of land reform. According to Ventura, Torola area peasants were even beginning to discuss creating a peasant organization with "new characteristics" *(nuevas características)* when the political situation deteriorated.[31] These successes owed a great deal to Ventura's display of fairness, compassion, and humility, as well as the dignity he acknowledged in others. He visited remote communities on a regular basis; insisted that people address him with the familiar *vos* rather than the formal *usted;* ate rice, beans, and tortillas with the peasants; and refused payment for performing masses, baptisms, funerals, or rendering other services. All these behaviors, which to some degree characterized progressive priests elsewhere in El Salvador, set Ventura apart from Argueta in the opinions of many northern Morazanian peasants residents. In fact Ventura's reputation spread beyond the frontiers of his parish, and he was invited to conduct services in outlying areas of Jocoaitique and Meanguera municipalities that technically were under his uncle's authority.[32]

However, Ventura's personal qualities and admirable comportment were as effective as they were only because he had the active support of an energetic team of more than a dozen progressive catechists with intimate knowledge of the communities in which they worked. Information on five of these catechists (Samuel Vidal Guzmán, Fabio Argueta, Secundino Chicas, Anastacio Caballero, and the deceased Rodolfo Vasquéz), originally recruited by Padre Andrés Argueta, is included in the table. The table also lists another substantial group of catechists from Cacaopera municipality, of which three villages (Agua Blanca, Junquillo, and Guachipilín) lie north of the Torola River and thus form part of northern Morazán. Cacaopera was under the authority of progressive Irish Franciscans based in San Francisco Gotera, and they sent many people to take courses at the centers.

The generalized poverty in northern Morazán also affected Ventura's plans. The region was marked by land fragmentation, a high percentage of rural wage laborers, straw houses that often lacked walls, and an effective absence of services (health, electricity, potable water) everywhere but in the municipal centers, where the regional elite resided. Referring to Torola, Fabio Argueta noted, "The people ... were really poor, and it was difficult for them to leave off working and to go to El Castaño or some other place. Every fifteen days, every month, they had meetings that lasted two or three days. ... Thus the people thought that it wasn't necessary to go to El Castaño, that [they could be trained] in the same place at lower cost, less expense."[33] Padre Ventura gained a few additional recruits, such as Andrés Barrera, to El Castaño, but preferred to train new catechists locally, banking on the "multiplier effect" of those who trained earlier in the centers.[34] Ventura met with the catechists every few weeks for training classes, to draw up pastoral plans, and to critically assess ongoing work. The priest had a great deal to do with the overall shape of the parish plan, but he granted catechists considerable freedom of action in their local practices.

A first step involved establishing "catechism centers" in each community in which the progressive church had a presence. Catechists working in these centers brought residents together and presided over a celebration of the Word, after which they discussed a "problematic" (social problem), followed by a catechism lesson. When Ventura made his monthly visit to the centers, he sought to avoid taking the central role, because "the priest is a motivator [animador], not a centralizer." Then community leaders from the rural areas attended courses in Torola and became "multipliers," that is, locally trained catechists. According to Ventura, he was drawing on his experiences as a seminarian, which included courses with people like Rutilio Grande, extensive work in rural areas during weekends and vacations, and teaching classes in El Castaño.[35]

Fabio Argueta, who lived near the town center of Meanguera, discussed Catholicism in northern Morazán in the course of more than a dozen interviews with me between 1993 and 1995. He noted that the catechists sought to move Catholics away from the cult of the saints toward a greater recognition of Christ as well as to encourage them to seek Christ in others. Basing their approach on Biblical texts in which Christ spoke of the love of one's fellow human beings as a prerequisite for loving God, the catechists struggled to promote "a spirit of brotherhood, of companionship, fraternity, of mutual aid."[36] Ventura said that they aimed for a reencounter, at both individual and community levels, of the poor person as a human being: "Through the Bible [the poor would] discover themselves as human beings with the capacity to transform their own history, not [to have to live] as slaves or as persons condemned to die young or to be illiterate."[37]

To concretize the lessons, the catechists formed Christian Base Communities. The first stage involved promotion of a sense of community, for which reading the Bible and discussing it in the context of liberation theology played an important role. As group unity increased, members decided to carry out collective projects. Putting to work the lessons they had learned in El Castaño about community organization, the catechists helped select local councils *(directivas),* which assessed needs and developed plans to address them. With the catechists at the forefront, taking up pick-axe and shovel, communities constructed roads and schools, or they assisted the poor or infirm: "For example, if a house of some poor person was falling down, we went to the community, met, planned, and built the house. If someone was sick and had no medicine with which to cure the illness, they were taken to a doctor and attended to. There were people who had nothing. They had no time to weed the corn field because they were working for their employer. Together we tried to resolve the most urgent problems of the community."[38] Some of these projects, particularly those related to road construction, received assistance from the Catholic charity Caritas, which supplied participants with food baskets to partly compensate for the time taken away from productive activities.

However, the inhabitants' poverty and their lack of access to resources limited the scope of self-help projects. For instance, peasants were unable to obtain bank loans unless they supplied a deed or registered title to property (land, house, animals) as collateral. As became clear during the Land Transfer Program following the 1992 Peace Accords, very few prewar land transactions met legal requirements. In El Castaño catechists learned that by forming cooperatives they could obtain production loans from state institutions at below-market interest rates and get better prices for products, thus reducing their dependence on local moneylenders and merchant monopolists. Because most earlier cooperative experiments in northern Morazán had failed or benefited economically better-off groups, strong prejudices existed among the poor against collective organization. These would take time and much work to overcome. Catechists like Fabio Argueta were attempting to move the population in the direction of cooperative organization when government repression halted the Christian Base Communities and related experiments and forced catechists into exile or underground.

By 1975 Padre Andrés Argueta had lost considerable ground. Even before he was banished from Meanguera by local authorities—after a conflict over his removal of a valuable gold chalice from the Santa Catarina church there—he had ceded practical control over much of that municipality. Two months after returning from El Castaño in 1970, Fabio Argueta organized three "catechism centers" *(centros de catequesis)* in Meanguera; Andrés Barrera, another El Castaño-trained catechist, established centers in the village of La Guacamaya, also in Meanguera, as did other catechists elsewhere. But as long as Padre Argueta controlled the parish, the Christian Base Communities remained without coordination. Ventura acted as a catalyst, supporting the catechists' efforts, organizing work in local areas into an overall parish plan, and training new catechists. He also incorporated some catechists from Perquín, Jocoaitique, and Meanguera when they approached him because they were not being attended by Padre Argueta, who customarily limited his visits to rural areas to the personally profitable patron saints' celebrations. Ventura's "incursions," albeit in response to requests from the Christian Base Communities, provoked hostile reactions from the older priest, who railed against his interloper nephew in his Sunday liturgies in Jocoaitique. In 1975, two years after Ventura took up his post in Torola, Bishop Eduardo Álvarez transferred him to Osicala, a few miles south of the Torola River. Over the next few years catechists in northern Morazán became targets of state repression, and many of them joined the ERP, which entered the region for the first time in 1974, or its mass organization, the February 28 Popular Leagues (LP-28), formed in 1978.

Priests, Catechists, and the People's Revolutionary Army

The popular church in northern Morazán enjoyed a brief political opening in the late 1960s and early 1970s, but the liberationist message and the collective projects to which catechists dedicated themselves eventually captured the attention of the authorities, who placed the Christian Base Communities and priests who supported them under close surveillance. The municipal seats (cabeceras), as bases for the repressive security forces (National Guard, Treasury Police) and home to merchants and landowners linked to them, remained pretty much off limits for liberation theology practitioners. But even in its rural strongholds, the new teachings often provoked confusion and resistance among those people who held strongly to a belief in destiny and the power of the saints and the superiority of the priest or were susceptible to elite claims that collectivist solutions to material problems were incontrovertible evidence of Communist influence. By 1974 the situation in northern Morazán had become tense. National Guard personnel staked out meetings in Torola and elsewhere, and a widely circulated leaflet portrayed a catechist with a Bible in one hand and a gun in the other.[39] Through church-sponsored news media and especially contacts in El Castaño, northern Morazanian catechists learned that elsewhere in El Salvador repression of the popular movement and the Catholic church was intensifying. The army, security forces, and death squads fired on organized students and workers and threatened priests and catechists, at times kidnapping and torturing them. Some were convinced that it was only a matter of time before physical repression arrived to northern Morazán. As the harassment intensified regionally, and the political situation deteriorated in other parts of the country, catechists working with Padre Ventura sensed that they needed to link up with a broader organization that might provide them protection. A detailed version of this history has yet to be constructed, but it appears that in response to the catechists' entreaties, Ventura arranged for Rafael Arce Zablah, one of the founders of ERP, to meet with a small group of catechists and others in order to share that organization's analysis of the national political situation and proposals for addressing it.[40] The first encounter took place in San Salvador and was followed by at least two more meetings in northern Morazán before Arce died in combat during ERP's first armed takeover of a town in El Carmen, La Unión, in 1975.

Arce proposed the creation of clandestine military committees that would prepare for the civil war he believed to be inevitable. Some catechists agreed and began to collaborate with him. Three early foci of ERP organization were Santa Ana (Jocoaitique), code-named "El Centro," La Guacamaya (Meanguera), known as "El Escondido," and Progreso (Torola), called "El Tancho." All were important sites of Christian Base Community influence. During the period between 1975, when Ventura was transferred to Osicala, a few kilometers south of the Torola River, and November 1977, some catechists continued their work with the church even as others became increasingly involved in clandestine political and military activities. With Arce's death, ERP operatives Santo Lino Ramírez and Juan Ramón Medrano, who traveled to and around the region disguised as cattle merchants, linked the urban-based ERP leadership with rural, northern Morazán.

Progressive religious organizing practically ceased following the death of Juan Ramón Sánchez. A catechist trained in El Castaño, Sánchez had dropped his catechism practice to become an important early organizer of ERP military committees. In November 1977 army commandos from the San Francisco Gotera barracks conducted a surprise search of a bus in which Sánchez was traveling; knowing that his forty-five pistol would be discovered, he engaged them in a shoot-out that left himself and three soldiers dead. Within a few days the National Guard picked up Padre Ventura and the catechist Fabio Argueta; each was tortured extensively—Argueta for about two weeks—before public pressure forced their release.[41] With these events government military and security forces began an all-out pursuit of catechists regardless of their political sympathies. When the intended victims proved elusive, the authorities sometimes took vengeance on their families, threatening or even murdering elderly people, women, and children.[42] Many catechists and members of Christian Base Communities who were not displaced within El Salvador or forced into exile in Honduras, Nicaragua, or elsewhere joined ERP or served the revolutionary struggle in a support capacity.

During wartime the catechists put the skills they developed in the training centers at the service of the revolution. Samuel Vidal Guzmán and Secundino Chicas, who attended Centro San Lucas, joined FMLN health brigades. Fabio Argueta and Anastacio Portillo worked as political organizers. Andrés Barrera ("Felipón") formed an FMLN musical group, Los Torogoces, which counted two of the Chicas brothers, both of whom attended El Castaño, among its members. And "Tito" (wartime pseudonym) served as a supply officer *(logístico)* charged with obtaining food, batteries, clothing, and medicines for the guerrilla army. Finally, Abraham Argueta, who took refuge in Nicaragua, formed a clothing cooperative in the northern city of Estelí that provided a valuable service to the Sandinista Revolution there. Each of these prewar catechists, and many others besides, utilized the analytical, oratorical, and organizational skills developed in the centers and sharpened through practice in their communities in the service of a revolutionary project consistent with the preferential option for the poor. Finally, in 1982 ERP command released a dozen former catechists from combat and subsidiary duties to meet the spiritual needs of the guerrilla army and its civilian support base.[43] These catechists, and others who returned from the Colomoncagua refugee camp between November 1989 and March 1990 (see Vincent J. McElhinny's chapter), became the core of the postwar popular church in northern Morazán. By 1994 their voices were among a small number that continued to project a message of hope and struggle in a depressing, postwar economic and political climate.[44]

Catechists as Organic Intellectuals in the Salvadoran Revolution

Grenier argues that there is little evidence that the Catholic church played an important role in the development of a mass insurgency: "By and large, virtually none of the most commonly quoted books on the Salvadoran internal war have strayed away from the relatively meager information found in *Génesis de una revolución,* a few publications on the development of unions proposed by Salvadoran social scientists and/or militants, and the few first-hand testimonies on the pilot project of Aguilares."[45] But all the projects mentioned by Grenier originated in the "center," that is, San Salvador parish, where Archbishop Chávez y González provided official support and encouragement to progressive Catholicism. In my discussion of the popular church in northern Morazán I have tried to evidence the limitations of a centrist vision. Centers like El Castaño and Los Naranjos trained thousands of progressive catechists who returned to their rural communities to challenge the dominant culture both through word and deed; through

them religious ideas and practices formulated by urban intellectuals—albeit rein-
terpreted on the basis of the rural experiences of numerous priests—penetrated
deeply into the Salvadoran countryside. By virtue of their initiative and leadership, catechists fulfilled the role of "grassroots" or organic intellectuals. They
worked with ideas served up in the centers but adapted them to differentiated, local social fields of power, as the example of the San Antonio cooperative formed
by Abraham Argueta and other catechists in Joateca demonstrates. They continued to farm or provide valuable services in order to sustain their households, and
they used most of their remaining time organizing Christian Base Communities
and collective projects through which they interpreted and disseminated a vision
of the future society. In the process they helped generate the very sense of community among sectors of the northern Morazán population that Kincaid viewed
as a necessary condition for the development of organized resistance in El Salvador.[46]

It is true that the catechists' roles as change agents depended a great deal on
the level of priestly support: high in the case for those who worked with Miguel
Ventura between 1973 and 1977, low or nonexistent for those who remained sub-
ordinated, whether by choice or necessity, to Andrés Argueta. The more important point, however, is that progressive catechists promoted the interests of the
poor (which tended to be their own) within the church. That they had few disagreements with Ventura can partly be explained by the priest's modest roots as
the son of a small, rural storeowner and farmer in La Unión as well as his determination from his first years of seminary to represent the poor in his evangelical
practice.[47]

The northern Morazán case also shows how progressive religious ideologies
and practices could develop in parishes within dioceses staffed by conservative
bishops. According to Miguel Ventura, by the time Eduardo Álvarez took charge
of the diocese of San Miguel, El Castaño had already attained a certain level of
autonomy. Álvarez held up Ventura's ordination and transferred him to the "safer"
Osicala parish south of the Torola River once he proved a thorn in Argueta's
side, but he could not force him to change his ideas or alter his religious practice.
From Osicala Ventura expanded his work into southern areas of Cacaopera and
Delicias de Concepción, even as he continued to meet with catechists from northern Morazán. Perhaps Morazán's relative physical isolation from the seat of
diocesan power in San Miguel proved useful, as did a certain convergence of
Ventura's beliefs with those of Archbishop Chavez y González. However, I have
emphasized that as energetic and intelligent as he was (and is), Ventura would not
have accomplished nearly as much without the willing help of several dozen
peasant and worker catechists, intellectuals (of the organic variety) in their own

right. Against Grenier, I believe that examination of other areas of El Salvador where the insurgency developed a significant rural presence will also reveal historical traces left by the training centers and the organic intellectuals—rising from the peasantry and the rural work force—who attended them. One such area deserving careful study is the department of San Vicente, an early and important site for the development of the Popular Forces of Liberation, and which contained the parish home of Padre David Rodríguez, a radical priest and teacher at Los Naranjos who became known as the Ché of Central America.[48] Others include the San Francisco Gotera parish staffed by Irish Franciscans and eastern Chalatenango, organized by Mexican nuns.[49] The historical ethnography of these areas, which is just beginning, would make further important contributions to our understanding of differentiated, regional developments in a nation that has, for far too long, been subject to overgeneralized and uniform interpretation.

Elisabeth J. Wood

Civil War and Reconstruction

The Repopulation of Tenancingo

Beginning in the mid-1970s, widespread political mobilization in the Salvadoran countryside was met with brutal repression by military and paramilitary forces. As mobilization and repression deepened to civil war, both sides of the conflict relied on local peasant participation. The resulting political polarization of the countryside reinforced bitter divisions among the rural population as peasants chose, were chosen by, or were reputed to have chosen sides in the emerging war. As the violence continued in the early 1980s, up to a quarter of the rural population—peasants and landlords alike—fled their homes for the relative safety of urban areas, or, in some cases, refugee camps or exile.

Beginning in 1985, many poor rural residents returned to the countryside, a trend made possible by evolving military and political strategies of both parties to the civil war. The earliest repopulation effort was that of Tenancingo, a municipality in the department of Cuscatlán. Nearly a decade of social conflict in Tenancingo between peasant organizations, landlords, military and paramilitary forces, and guerilla groups culminated in the September 24, 1983, attack by members of the Farabundo Martí National Liberation Front (FMLN) on the command post of the military forces in the municipal seat. In an action that Americas Watch described as the civil war's single most devastating attack (to that date), government aircraft bombed the town for several hours. Approximately one hundred civilians died, including thirty-five who were killed as the Green Cross attempted to evacuate the group along the main road.[1] The town and much of the surrounding area were deserted as the remaining families of Tenancingo joined the hundreds of thousands of other rural families displaced from their homes by the civil war.

Beginning in 1986, many families returned to Tenancingo under the terms of an unprecedented set of agreements negotiated by the archdiocese of San Salvador in which the FMLN and the Salvadoran military agreed that the area could be repopulated as an unarmed zone *(zona inerme)*. Hundreds of residents returned to Tenancingo and began to rebuild under the direction of a private Salvadoran development agency, the Salvadoran Foundation for Development and Housing (Fundación Salvadoreña de Desarrollo y Vivienda Minima, FUNDASAL). This audacious effort in the midst of ongoing civil war took many observers of Salvadoran politics by surprise, given the extreme political polarization of nearly all aspects of life in El Salvador. As a result of the support of several European governments, which gave the project a high profile internationally as well as domestically, both sides sought to shape and control the subsequent evolution of the Tenancingo project to their political advantage. And both the military and FMLN-allied political organizations subsequently launched their own tightly controlled repopulation initiatives, some in the same region. These competing visions of repopulation and rural reconstruction, and of the reconstitution of agrarian social relations, formed the political context of the project's subsequent evolution.

The story of Tenancingo—the emergence of mobilization, the deepening violence and repression, and its reconstruction—illustrates not only the course of civil war at the local level but also the constraints that history poses for local reconciliation and rural reconstruction, particularly when they are attempted while a war is still unresolved.

This chapter draws on research conducted in Tenancingo on various occasions from 1987 to 1991 as well as on unpublished documents. The primary sources are interviews conducted with thirty-two residents and ex-residents of Tenancingo and with representatives of various governmental and nongovernmental organizations, including the archdiocese of San Salvador, the Salvadoran military, opposition leaders, the U.S. Agency for International Development, and FUNDASAL. Observation of many community meetings in Tenancingo itself also inform the analysis. Given the political context of the Salvadoran civil war, those interviewed are not identified by name, except for high-level officials.

The Displaced Population, Counterinsurgency, and Repopulation

As described by Binford and McElhinney in their chapters, rising mobilization in both rural and urban El Salvador was met with deepening repression by both public and private forces in the late 1970s. The brutality and arbitrariness of the repression led many activists to join the hitherto small guerrilla groups or to leave their homes. Other families fled insurgent threats and executions. Approximately 50 percent of the displaced population left their homes between 1979 and 1982, a period that includes the agrarian reform of 1980, the accompanying militarization of the countryside by the army and National Guard, the "final offensive" of the FMLN, and the subsequent brutal repression of a broad spectrum of peasant organizations by state security forces.[2]

The number of displaced families continued to increase after 1983 as a result of the government's new counterinsurgency strategy, the "National Plan," which combined a campaign to separate civilians from the guerrillas by indiscriminately bombing certain contested areas with the stabilization of government control through the building of rural political loyalty in others. The plan in part reflected the growing acceptance within the Salvadoran military of an analysis of revolutionary movements that emphasized undercutting the roots of insurgency by constructing democratic regimes and counterrevolutionary institutions.[3] The 1986 counterinsurgency campaign "United to Reconstruct" (*unidos para reconstruir,* UPR) continued to emphasize the building of civilian loyalties as well as the bombing of conflicted areas. According to campaign documents, the civil conflict was a result of El Salvador's structural crisis and rigid social stratification; therefore, satisfaction of basic needs had to be combined with the political and ideological control of the population.[4] The FMLN responded to the new strategy by dispersing throughout the country in small units. Together, these strategies resulted in further displacing rural families.

By 1987, there were approximately 500,000 displaced persons in El Salvador—10 percent of the population. Immersed into the cash economy at a time of national economic crisis, displaced families suffered dire poverty as well as the loss of family members and a way of life. Most of the displaced (94 percent) lived dispersed throughout the marginal zones of departmental capitals and San Salvador, with little access to water, health care, or regular employment.[5] In response to the flood of displaced people into the urban areas, the government set up the National Commission for Aid to the Displaced of El Salvador (Comisión Nacional de Asistencia a los Desplazados de El Salvador, CONADES) in 1981 to minister to the displaced population with food distribution, health, and job programs. The remaining 6 percent of the displaced population (estimated to number between 80,000 and 125,000 people) lived in restricted sites under the protection of some institution, such as the Catholic and Lutheran refugee camps.

These relief programs were set up under the assumption that the displacement of such a large fraction of the nation's population would be temporary. However, after the failure of the 1984 negotiations, the war looked like a stalemate with no end in sight. Given the likelihood of a protracted civil war, various agencies—increasingly concerned about the growing dependency of the population on the programs and the possible irreversibility of war-driven rural to urban migration—began to reevaluate their aid strategies. At the same time, organized displaced persons began to assess alternatives to the ongoing misery of life as displaced peasants.[6] On July 25, 1985, the archdiocese of San Salvador announced its intention to rebuild the town of Tenancingo and thereby inaugurated a period in which repopulation became a volatile political issue. Beginning in 1986, a significant portion of the displaced population began to return to the countryside: some through projects initiated by organized groups of displaced people with support from development agencies, others through projects controlled by government and military agencies. Still others returned to the countryside by themselves, preferring the difficulties and uncertainties of the "journey home" to urban misery.[7]

The repopulation of Tenancingo—the first organized repopulation project—changed the terms of the debate on the future of the displaced: it signaled the support of the Catholic Church for the *right* of the civilian population to return to their places of origin. To some extent, the position of the church made the return home imaginable and feasible. By focusing national and international attention on repopulation, the Tenancingo project helped to open a limited political space for subsequent repopulation initiatives launched by the National Coordinator of Repopulation (Coordinadora Nacional de Repoblacíon, CNR), a committee of communities of displaced persons with close ties to the Christian Committee for the Displaced (Comite Cristiano Pro Desplazados de El Salvador, CRIPDES), an opposition organization founded in 1984 to represent the interests of displaced persons. Beginning in June 1986, CNR led a series of *unauthorized* repopulations of displaced families to highly conflicted areas in the northern third of the country, several within fifteen miles of Tenancingo. The CNR also played a supporting role in the repatriation of refugees from Honduras to conflicted areas of the country on various occasions from 1987 to the end of the war.[8]

In contrast to the Tenancingo case, many of the refugees returning from exile in camps in Honduras and other Central American countries brought with them a high level of social organization, political homogeneity, and political sophistication. For example, those who founded Ciudad Segundo Montes had participated for a decade in a complex system of governance in exile that mixed widespread participation in the self-management of the camps with overall political and military control by one of the five FMLN factions (see McElhinney's chapter in this section). The political and organizational cohesion of many repatriations enabled the communities to initiate and promote development projects and to rapidly build community resources, including strong local organizations and regional, national, and international political alliances.

In 1986, after the Tenancingo repopulation and shortly after the first CNR repopulation initiative, the military began its own repopulation projects as part of the UPR counterinsurgency campaign, an attempt to coordinate—under military control—the delivery of services by governmental and nongovernmental agencies to fourteen areas.[9] The campaign's showcase projects were located in the southeastern and eastern foothills of the Guazapa volcano, approximately fifteen miles north and west of Tenancingo. Few families returned to the UPR sites, owing in part to the prevailing political tensions and their inadequate resources.[10] By 1990, these communities no longer received attention from the Armed Forces except for occasional incursions during military campaigns against guerrilla units in the Guazapa area.

After the 1989 election of Alfredo Cristiani of the ARENA party (Alianza Republicana Nacionalista, Nationalist Republican Alliance) as president, the emphasis in governmental agrarian policy shifted from repopulating under military control to supporting individual private property, markets, and an open economy. The government began to restructure the agrarian reform through policies that strongly encouraged the breaking up of agrarian reform cooperatives into small holdings organized as service cooperatives. This titling of individual parcels to cooperative members was clearly intended to reinforce ARENA's rural base among conservative peasants.

Thus, by 1990 the northern repopulated and repatriated communities and the Salvadoran government offered competing visions of repopulation, rural development, and rural social relations. The communities advocated a collectivist vision, the government a neoliberal and individualist model. This ongoing competition for rural political loyalties formed the political and military context for the evolution of the Tenancingo repopulation project. While the Tenancingo project was the first formal repopulation initiative, the uniqueness and importance of the Tenancingo case rests on its independence from both sides (government and FMLN) and its commitment to repopulation as an effort in local reconciliation.

Tenancingo (1975–1983):
A Microcosm of the Salvadoran Civil War

The history of the civil conflict in the municipality of Tenancingo, 1975–1983, is one of profound divisions: divisions within *cantones* (villages, the administrative subdivisions of Salvadoran municipalities), between villages and the municipal capital, within the capital itself, and between the northern and southern villages.[11] The rising tide of violence that swept through the area beginning in the mid-1970s culminated in the 1983 bombing of the municipal capital, called the Villa by residents. This history of diverging allegiances, of the bitterness with which former neighbors viewed each other across these divisions, and the trauma that the years of violence left in their wake were among the most difficult legacies the people of Tenancingo faced in their efforts to rebuild their lives.

Tenancingo, a municipality in the department of Cuscatlán lies in steep hills to the southeast of the Guazapa volcano in north-central El Salvador. Most of the soil is fairly poor; better soils occur in the area surrounding the Villa and along the dirt road that runs from the Pan American highway to Suchitoto, the next town to Tenancingo's north. Before the war, these more fertile and accessible areas were controlled in relatively large holdings by a few families in the Villa; in the villages, peasants worked the fields as smallholders and under a variety of tenancy arrangements. According to a household survey of residents in 1975, 43.4 percent farmed land they owned, 34.5 percent were tenants, 13.2 percent farmed land lent to them by relatives, 5.0 percent were *colonos* (resident workers) and 3.9 percent were wholly landless.[12] The average holding of those who owned land in the village was 1.6 hectares, of the tenants only half that. Of those families farming 1.5 hectares or less, 97 percent claimed to use all their harvest for food for the family.

Since colonial times, the local economy was also based on the production of hats made from braided palm leaves. Peasant women and children braided palm leaves into long braids of palm fiber; workers in the hat factories of the Villa sewed them together, pressed them into the shape of hats, and bleached them in ovens. Tenancingo hats were marketed nationally and internationally. The stratification between the Villa and the village deepened in the twentieth century due to the increasing commercialization of exchange as families in the Villa developed and controlled markets, means of transport, and services. By 1975, only the three villages along the main road were accessible by vehicle; none had electricity or running water; several had elementary schools. Males, including male children, worked the fields, and women managed the household, including preparing food, carrying water, caring for children, and braiding palm leaves for cash.

Thus, by the mid-1970s social relations in the Villa were a complex mixture of capitalist and noncapitalist relations: some large landowners were still traditional *hacendados* who divided their land among land-poor peasants for rent or share-cropping; others hired wage labor to produce tobacco (not of export quality), oranges, and eggs for sale in Cojutepeque and San Salvador; others combined features of both noncapitalist and capitalist agriculture.

Although elite families controlled far less wealth than Salvadoran oligarchs, they dominated the municipality's political and social structures. Relations between the elite families and the poor families followed the classic patron-client pattern, mediated by god-parenting *(compadrazgo)*, marriage, and patron-saint practices. As population increased through the twentieth century, land became increasingly scarce despite the nonagricultural employment in the Villa and substantial out-migration. The decline in access to land between generations (from an average of 1.43 hectares for the previous generation to 1.10 for that of 1975) meant a substantial deterioration of the ability of peasant families to obtain even a minimal subsistence.[13] Based on his 1975 survey of 254 peasant households, William Durham demonstrated the critical importance of access to land (whether owned or rented) for family well-being: family income depended closely— indeed, nearly exponentially—on access to land.[14]

In this context of increasing scarcity, in the mid-1970s some peasants— among them smallholders, tenants, and landless laborers—mobilized to challenge local social and economic structures. According to former residents of the northern villages, political organization began with the formation of Bible study groups in 1975 or 1976. Initially, participation in the study groups seems to have been fairly widespread in those villages. The catechists, not all of whom were local, met at least occasionally with the Alas brothers, active priests of the nearby Suchitoto parish.

The authorities responded immediately to the growth of the Bible-study groups. The Democratic Nationalist Organization (Organización Democrática Nacionalista, ORDEN), an auxiliary group to the National Guard and later notorious for its death-squad activities, was active in each village at least as early as 1975, with some thirty members scattered throughout the municipality.[15] The first displacement of peasant families occurred in 1976 in the northern village of Rosario Périco when state security forces shot some participants in the study groups and threatened others. One interviewee believes that the repression against Périco and the neighboring village of El Pepeto was particularly brutal because those villages had voted for the Christian Democratic Party candidate in the 1977 election.

In response to the initial repressive measures, some participants joined more radical organizations. The Popular Revolutionary Block (Bloque Popular Revolucionario, BPR), a national alliance of trade union, student, and peasant groups, began to recruit peasants from the villages in 1978. The BPR also organized in the Villa, particularly among teenagers; in 1979 and 1980 the BPR led a series of unarmed marches and rallies in the Villa. By 1979, the Popular Forces of Liberation (Fuerzas Populares de la Liberación, FPL), one of the five guerrilla organizations that would soon comprise the FMLN, had established a presence in the area.

In their response to the emergence of these organizations, the security forces made no distinction between peasants who participated in political groups and FPL guerrillas. On March 22, 1980, the National Guard attacked the village of Rosario Périco, leaving nine dead. The remaining population fled, some to refugee camps, others to join the guerrillas, others to the Villa. According to one of the most knowledgeable sources interviewed, it was in the aftermath of the assassinations that some residents took up arms. In 1981 the National Guard began making more frequent forays into the villages, particularly El Pepeto, where they attacked families whose younger members had left to join the guerrillas. By 1981, the villages of Rosario Périco, La Cruz, and Copalchán had been abandoned, and El Pepeto nearly so. After the National Guard killed three teenagers in the Villa, others left to join the guerrillas. This trajectory of mobilization, repression, insurgency, and further repression culminated in 1983. The FMLN attacked the Villa's military post on July 3, 1983. Most Villa residents left for Santa Cruz Michapa (the nearest town) and Cojutepeque. The local army commander insisted that the families return to the Villa. A few months later, the FMLN again attacked military forces in the Villa. In response the Air Force bombed the town.

After the battle, most of the poor families initially fled to Santa Cruz Michapa, San Martín, and Cojutepeque. The five southern villages were never completely abandoned, although some families left the area. In contrast to the northern villages, residents of three southern ones (Santa Anita, Hacienda Nueva, and Ajuluco) joined civil-defense patrols. Residents attempted to disband the patrols after a 1985 attack by the FMLN, but the military refused to allow them to do so.

By 1983, nearly all of the elite families had left for Cojutepeque and San Salvador. Some continued to supervise their enterprises in the southern villages during relatively quiet periods. Life in exile for these families was difficult, but for most it was possible to start over. One hat-factory owner established new factories in San Salvador, another began again with just a few sewing machines, and a third specialized in marketing rather than production.

This turbulent history left a complex social and political legacy among the former residents of Tenancingo, a legacy that shaped the evolution of its repopulation. The presence within the same small town of families who supported the guerrillas and others who supported the government proved a source of ongoing social and political tension. Nonetheless, from the beginning of the project there existed a near consensus against the presence of a military post in the Villa because such a post could provoke another FMLN attack, military retaliation, and the displacement of the population from the Villa once again.

The Tenancingo Accord

The repopulation of Tenancingo as an unarmed zone in the midst of a full-blown civil war was a remarkable and unlikely event. The project was an initiative in local conflict resolution—with national implications—at three levels. First, the Tenancingo project was based on a unique set of agreements the archdiocese of San Salvador negotiated separately with the FMLN and the Armed Forces, in which both entities agreed to limit their presence in the area. By negotiating a limited local agenda, sponsors sought to build bridges between the armies at a time when there was little hope for dialogue. Second, in affirming the status of the displaced population as civilians with the right to return to traditional liveli-hoods and the right not to choose sides the project attempted a limited human-ization of the conflict. Moreover, the project asserted the principle of respect for the human rights of civilians even in civil war. Finally, the project sought to ad-dress the roots of the conflict through a limited redefinition of social and eco-nomic relations in the municipality as a model of rural reconstruction.

One key factor in negotiating the accord was Tenancingo's geographical loca-tion in a highly conflictive and strategic frontier between areas generally held by the FMLN and the Armed Forces. This battlefront position made necessary the acquiescence of both sides to the project and hence its independence. A further essential factor for the project's success was its timing: the initiative was launched at a time when a balance of political tensions created a brittle national political space that could be exploited by sufficiently astute proponents of an independent project. In 1984 José Napoleón Duarte had been elected president on a platform of negotiating an end to the civil conflict. Both sides sought to blame the other when these negotiations broke down. In this context both were reluctant to alien-ate the only institution trusted by both sides to mediate, the archdiocese of San Salvador. The political and military stalemate also increased the importance of other third parties and international actors to both sides. The international politi-cal attention focused on El Salvador, the debate over the degree of democratiza-tion signified by the elections, continuing international concern over violations of human rights, and a public commitment by some sectors of the military to the need for limited structural change were also conditions that could contribute to an agreement.

When Auxiliary Bishop Rosa Chávez announced the initiative on July 25, 1985, during a pilgrimage to the deserted town, the archdiocese had obtained ini-tial agreement to the project by both the Armed Forces and the FMLN. Indicating that the particulars of the accord had not yet been reached, Rosa Chávez offered a challenge to both sides: "Today all will be witnesses as to which party (government or guerrilla) is more firm in fulfilling its commitments. Tenancingo will be a privileged testimony of the seriousness of the committed parties in the process of dialogue."[16]

As part of the church's commitment to reconciliation, the archdiocese stressed that the project was open to *all* former residents of Tenancingo, regardless of their previous political involvement. Fearing a repetition of the traumatic history of Tenancingo, even many local elites supported the proposed conditions for the return.

The involvement of the archdiocese in the Tenancingo initiative thus went well beyond the church's traditional humanitarian role and ministry to the displaced. The archdiocese saw in Tenancingo both the opportunity to further the process of dialogue between the armed parties of the conflict and the "opportunity to create an alternative that might be a model of what we can do to construct peace with nonviolent methods."[17] This high rhetoric on the part of the church raised the political profile of the project from that of the physical reconstruction of a provincial town to one of national political dialogue with international consequences.

The archdiocese invited FUNDASAL to serve as its "right arm" in the project, and FUNDASAL staff members carried out much of the detailed negotiating and planning.[18] Financial and diplomatic support from the European Economic Community, the governments of Sweden, England, France, and Australia as well as from international development agencies (including, importantly, one U.S. agency) was secured by November 1985.

The content of the draft accord evolved during the subsequent process of negotiations. The Salvadoran military and U.S. embassy officials objected to the project on three grounds: the lack of trustworthiness of the FMLN, the unconstitutionality of a direct agreement between the FMLN and the Armed Forces, and the unconstitutionality of any commitment that would violate the military's responsibility to maintain the territorial integrity of the nation by the creation of "neutral" territory. Nonetheless, both the military and the U.S. embassy repeatedly offered financial support, which FUNDASAL declined.

These three objections were met by modifications in the character of the proposed accord as project sponsors sought common ground between the parties that could be sustained. Archbishop Rivera y Damas was to serve as the witness and guarantor of the accord. To elide the constitutional objection, each entity would enter into separate agreements with the archdiocese. In answer to the neutrality objection, negotiators devised a new formulation: members of either military force could pass through Tenancingo but neither was to have a *permanent presence* there.

In essence these issues involved the fundamental issue of *sovereignty*—hence the military's reluctance to enter into an accord directly or on equal terms with the FMLN. Thus the final form of the accord, separate and parallel accords with the archbishop, was for the military an unwelcome one. Furthermore, various aspects of the project—the welcome extended to all former residents, the creation of a special zone limiting the use of arms, the insistence on the integrity of the population as civilian—contradicted the military's emphasis on the building of civilian loyalties as the means to the military defeat of the guerrillas.

Given the political advantage to the FMLN of entering into the accord on formally symmetric terms with the military, why did the Armed Forces agree to the project? The Armed Forces could not afford to oppose it because international criticism of its policy of bombing of conflictive areas had put the government on the defensive. In addition the Salvadoran government and military had publicly embraced counterinsurgency policies that emphasized economic development. They could not easily publicly oppose such a concrete project lest the military aspects of those policies be confirmed as primary, as critics claimed. Finally, that the proposed initiative was to take place in Tenancingo, the only town the military admitted to having bombed, made it still more difficult for the military to oppose its reconstruction.

The FMLN representatives also objected in the negotiations to certain aspects of the project's philosophy, particularly what they viewed as its pacifism and autonomy from existing political organizations. But the FMLN could not afford to oppose a project that promised to address the structural injustices it was struggling to change. And maintaining its ongoing public readiness to enter into dialogue with the government would have been difficult if its representatives blackballed a concrete initiative by the archdiocese.

Moreover, it would be difficult to overestimate the political importance to the FMLN of the public recognition of dual structures of power in El Salvador implied by its entering an accord (even if technically an accord with the church) on the same terms as the Armed Forces. That is, the Tenancingo accord "recognizes that the guerrillas continue to be a force to be reckoned with in the country: that they hold territory, have a defined political and administrative structure, and can enter into and be held accountable for specific agreements."[19]

Thus in the eyes of the guerrillas, the accord affirmed the government's inability to control territory. Though he made no reference to the Tenancingo project, Joaquín Villalobos, one of the commanders of the FMLN, stressed the importance of such duality of power in a 1986 article: "In a country as small as El Salvador and with its population density, each square kilometer where the Armed Forces cannot sustain its military power in a stable manner, where they cannot maintain the juridical-political power of the government, and where, in an embryonic or partial manner, another power begins to develop, ends up reflecting an evident duality of political-military power between the FMLN and the army, which constitutes a grave strategic weakening of the North American counterinsurgency project."[20]

Yet the mere absence of the Armed Forces and government does not necessarily entail a duality of *political* power. In a press release, the FMLN stated its commitment to respect the reconstruction of streets and to collaborate in bringing in electricity and maintaining health services, recreation, and education.[21] The FMLN issued its own regulations for Tenancingo, another way in which it insisted that it was a political structure capable of delivering services and enforcing proclamations. According to one source, the FMLN's acquiescence to the project was conditioned on there being no funds from the U.S. Agency for International Development. Independently of the FMLN's objection, FUNDASAL opposed U.S. government involvement on the grounds that it would undermine the project's independence.

That the archdiocese and FUNDASAL succeeded in launching the Tenancingo project also depended on the ambiguities in the accord's terms, which proscribed the maintenance by either side of a "permanent presence" in Tenancingo. Would this proscribe an ongoing presence in the town by one group if they did not construct a permanent infrastructure? Did "Tenancingo" refer to the Villa, the municipality, or something in between?

According to one source familiar with the details of the negotiations, both parties agreed to the project because each believed it could shape the ambiguous terms of the agreement to its political advantage. As the project continued, de facto definitions of these terms were worked out "on the ground" in the political struggles over the project.

A Question of Sovereignty:
Dual Structures of Power in Rural El Salvador

On January 28, 1986, fifty-six families returned to Tenancingo in a caravan of Red Cross vehicles. The same morning, Colonel Amaya Pérez, the commander of the army's departmental detachment, convened a meeting of former Tenancingo residents in Santa Cruz Michapa, offered the displaced families new shoes and circus tickets if they refused to return to Tenancingo, and threatened to maintain strict control over the flow of food to the area.[22] In statements to the press, he claimed that Tenancingo was the first of the government's UPR repopulations.[23] Soon after Monseñor Rivera y Damas celebrated a mass of thanksgiving in Tenancingo on January 31, after which the FMLN held a press conference in the Villa, which reportedly enraged the Armed Forces.[24]

Clearly the Tenancingo repopulation project was not going to go forward unchallenged in the fragile political space defined by the accord. The project's sponsors had to defend, reassert, and redefine its independence. On various occasions the military attempted to claim the project as its own and to found competing government projects in the area. And to the FMLN, Tenancingo was a tempting public platform to demonstrate its claim that it constituted a rival structure of political and military power.

The ability of the archdiocese and FUNDASAL to oppose threats to the project was constrained by two conditions. First, the project's high public profile, while essential to its initiation and the defense of its independence, ensured that, indeed, such a defense would be necessary. The project's independence and survival depended on the support of the archdiocese and its international backers, yet the available political and institutional resources of the archdiocese were quite limited and had to be stretched to cover the whole range of issues and problems it sought to address nationally.

Second, the accord was negotiated with the leadership of the Armed Forces and the FDR-FMLN (Frente Democrático Revolucionario), yet the project depended on the understanding and respect of the accord by the members of both sides present in the area. That is, the security of the returning families depended not on the abstract agreement itself but on the day-to-day local respect for its spirit and letter. Any lack of communication between the leadership and the local actors of either side (whether intentional or not) had potentially serious implications for the project.

The Armed Forces frequently put military objectives before compliance with the accord, a pattern established within three weeks of the project's initiation. On February 16, 1986, approximately three hundred troops attacked ten guerrillas on the main streets of the Villa after having received an order from the Armed Forces high command that countermanded the local officer's understanding of the accord.[25] The troops shot indiscriminately as they entered, conducted a search of all the houses, killed one unarmed resident, reportedly raped a woman, and captured two guerrillas.[26] In response, FUNDASAL asked its European diplomatic contacts to send messages to the government and Armed Forces expressing concern about the incident.

In the early days of the project, the Armed Forces were quite responsive to such lobbying. In a meeting two days later, the head of the high command, General Blandón, reassured project sponsors of his support for the project and agreed to carry out several concrete actions in response to the incident.[27] In the following months—until November 1986—military troops occasionally entered the Villa while passing through the area, with only minor incidents. The ability of the archdiocese and FUNDASAL to occasion respect by the Armed Forces for the civil population in a highly conflicted area during this period was one of the most important initial successes of the repopulation project.

During the first months of the project, the guerrillas visited the Villa frequently. For example, in the first two weeks after the return to Tenancingo, guerrillas visited the Villa almost daily, leaving their weapons at the edge of town—clearly interpreting the unarmed zone literally. After the February 16 attack, the guerrillas continued to visit but carried their weapons. Throughout the first months of the project, the guerrillas avoided contact with military troops within the Villa, frequently leaving town as soldiers entered, with no exchange of shots. However, in instances of purported collaboration by residents with the military, military considerations overruled respect for the accord; suspected collaborators were usually kidnapped for a few days and released with warnings to leave town.[28] However, the FMLN refused to allow the expansion of the project into the northern villages until 1991 and continued to attack the civil-defense patrols in the southern villages, killing three people between March and mid-June 1986. Because of the ambiguity of "Tenancingo," the attacks were not denounced as violations of the accord even though they violated its spirit.

Although day-to-day relations between the guerrillas and residents during the first year of the project were generally cordial, the presence of the guerrillas was a source of increasing concern to residents. The guerrillas regularly attended the Saturday night dances held by the community and occasionally bought small amounts of food in the stores on their way through the area. After an incident in which a group of guerrillas retreated before a large group of soldiers, the village's community council asked the FMLN to reduce its presence.[29]

As guerrilla visits to the Villa increased, the Armed Forces upgraded the roadblock in Santa Cruz Michapa, two kilometers north of the intersection of the Tenancingo road and the Pan American highway. The roadblock was a source of intimidation and inconvenience to the residents as they found it increasingly difficult to bring in food and clothing. In spite of the violence and difficulties, including those of the roadblock, families continued to arrive in Tenancingo.

Explicit conflict over the independence of the Tenancingo repopulation project began in May 1986, when the military attempted to claim the Tenancingo project as its own, during what Americas Watch referred to as an "intense propaganda war."[30] The "war" began with the visit of General Blandón to Tenancingo on May 6, accompanied by eight to ten colonels and a hundred troops.[31] On May 7 a national newspaper carried the story of Blandón's visit under the headline

"Tenancingo is protected by the Armed Forces." The story stated that the officials had assured the population that "Tenancingo will no longer be the 'town without law' as it had been called because of the lack of authority in the region," a clear rejection of dual sovereignty. The troops left on May 8, after the arrival of national and international press. Colonel Carranza, the new head of the departmental detachment, asked the Estado Mayor (high command) for permission to carry out civic-military actions in Tenancingo. After project supporters lobbied against the proposal, the request was denied. Shortly after the regional inauguration of the military's "United to Reconstruct" campaign, Colonel Carranza visited the Villa with the mayor on June 11 and declared the Armed Forces' support for the project.[32] He stated, "more than ninety families have returned . . . and are working in different productive activities, *due to the help of the Armed Forces. . . .* In the coming days other working groups will be created to develop productive projects *in cooperation with all agencies of the government* [emphasis added]."[33] Subsequent press reports asserted that "many persons asked the Departmental Commander to establish a military base to improve their security."[34] A September article reported that Blandón had said that the "army will reestablish a military presence in the town whenever it is deemed necessary."[35]

In response to the attempts by the military to claim the project, FUNDASAL sought to clarify the origins and philosophy of the project in its own press release in which it explicitly denied that the project was part of the UPR campaign.[36] It also stated that the project counted on the support of the government and Armed Forces to understand and respect the accord, "which in part consists of an agreement not to establish a permanent military base in the Villa."[37] Because the Armed Forces generally distinguished a military post from a permanent presence (and thus, by not establishing a post, they were respecting the accord), this public characterization of the accord by its sponsors as prohibiting a *base* rather than a permanent military presence was a victory for the Armed Forces. Nonetheless, civic military actions were not carried out until 1987, nor did the military ever establish a base there.

Twice in early 1987 the FMLN carried out well-publicized actions in Tenancingo that attempted to demonstrate equivalence between the FMLN and the government in terms of military control of territory and social service delivery. The first anniversary of the repopulation provided the first opportunity. The vehicles of visitors—including the papal nuncio, as well as ambassadors and representatives from France, West Germany, Spain, England, Italy, Mexico, and Peru—were stopped at a national police roadblock four kilometers from the Villa, an FMLN roadblock two kilometers from the Villa, and an army roadblock a kilometer later.

The second public assertion by the FMLN that it represented a structure of power equivalent to the government's took place on January 31, 1987. As part of a vaccination campaign sponsored by UNICEF, government nurses visited Tenancingo, where they were joined by guerrilla nurses in the central park in what seemed a graphic demonstration of the FMLN's ability to deliver services equivalent to that of the government. *Diario Latino* published two photographs of this joint delivery of services under the headline "Guerrilleras and government nurses vaccinate [residents] together." In the foreground of one of the photos, two women guerrillas are vaccinating a small child, with machine guns at their sides. A government nurse is a few yards away attending to someone else. According to the captions, "In Tenancingo the first real dialogue has occurred. The children do more than the politicians. In these unusual photographs, taken the day before yesterday in the town of Tenancingo, *guerrilleras* of the FMLN and nurses of the Ministry of Public Health vaccinated children who passed to one or the other alternately."

The response of the Armed Forces to the vaccination photographs was immediate and severe. According to one source close to the project, the head of military intelligence argued that such events tended to demonstrate the existence of another army, which was unconstitutional, and to challenge the sole responsibility of the Armed Forces to extend security throughout the country. Within days of the vaccination incident, the departmental commander once again formally requested that a military base be established in Tenancingo.[38] Although his application for a base was denied, Air Force troops were stationed in the area of the Villa beginning shortly after February 15 and occupied the Villa nearly continuously until September 1987. The troops threatened residents, killing one and detaining several, among them a Tenancingo resident who worked with FUNDASAL as an organizer.[39] That local troops insisted on viewing FUNDASAL staff as guerrillas indicates the difficulty in conveying the project's independence at the local level.

In response FUNDASAL publicly threatened to withdraw from the accord, and a series of high-level diplomatic efforts by the archdiocese and FUNDASAL were carried out in defense of the project.[40] As a result, the troops subsequently withdrew from the Villa proper but occupied the area immediately surrounding it for some weeks. From November 1987 until the end of the war, military troops and guerrillas both occasionally visited Tenancingo but rarely remained in the immediate area. Tenancingo was relatively peaceful, although troubling but usually isolated incidents continued.

Although the diplomatic campaign did not result in the complete withdrawal of the troops, the project's supporters were able to successfully defend the bottom-line of the accord despite the contested sovereignty surrounding the project.

They did so in the context of the civil war at a time when the issue of repopulation had become highly politicized. Both sides were held accountable to agreements that constrained their ability to act against the civilian population. Although the Tenancingo project did not prevent violations of human rights, it raised their political cost and brought about an unprecedented—if still far from perfect—respect for the rights of civilians in the midst of the war.

Rural Reconstruction in Tenancingo

For the archdiocese and FUNDASAL, reconstruction did not mean a return to preconflict social relations. In their vision of reconstruction, the project sponsors emphasized the need for the social and economic transformation of the inequitable structures at the root of the civil conflict.[41] Within the political space of the project, they attempted to redistribute wealth and power in the municipality under a set of political, military, social, and economic constraints, including the ongoing military conflict in the municipality and region.

The attempted transformation of social relations could not rely on a direct redistribution of existing assets, which was considered impossible if the government were to agree on the project. Rather, FUNDASAL hoped to achieve a redefinition of social relations by extending credit and technical assistance to build up the productive and organizational capacity of peasant smallholders, creating alternative sources of employment in the Villa, enlisting the participation of the poor in organizations to define and protect their common interests, and consolidating those organizations into a set of alternative democratic institutions through which the poor could confront the eventual return of the preconflict elite.[42] This experiment in local democracy in the midst of a civil war proceeded despite the ongoing conflicts over the project: fields were planted, crops were harvested, and transport of inputs and products was usually possible. Moreover, the absence of the Villa elite gave the project several "years of grace."

FUNDASAL made most major decisions throughout the first three years of the project, occasionally consulting with the archdiocese. FUNDASAL founded and subsequently tutored various community organizations, including farmer organizations and the *consejo comunal* (community council) of the Villa. The transformation of the displaced person into an active participant in the resolution of the conflict was an important theme in early FUNDASAL literature describing the project, but FUNDASAL's highly directive role threatened to undermine that objective.[43] Sponsors were aware to some extent of this tension. As the project developed, the fledgling organizations were gradually to assume the responsibilities that FUNDASAL bore initially. The extent to which the organizations assumed and redefined project leadership would be one measure of the project's success.

An essential part of FUNDASAL's vision of reconstruction was thus the empowering of the municipality's poor families. Yet many families were no longer self-sufficient and relied on donated food and make-work programs. To diminish this dependency on assistance, FUNDASAL's programs offered subsidized credit, limited the donation of materials to emergency programs to rebuild a minimal physical infrastructure, and provided *initial* food, shelter, and employment. FUNDASAL envisioned that after a few years of increasing participation and responsibility by the local committees, it would be able to turn the credit program over to the groups as a rotating fund of working capital under local control.

The farmer committees were the most successful aspect of the reconstruction efforts. Default rates were low and a marketable surplus was produced. Levels of participation were quite high during the first three years of the project, a significant accomplishment given that few participants had ever received credit before. The committees gradually assumed responsibilities for the credit program from FUNDASAL. For example, in the second year of the project, the farmer organizations negotiated rents with the landowners, arranged contracts for agricultural inputs jointly with FUNDASAL, rented a tractor for the spring plowing, and participated in the review of credit applications. However, in subsequent years, the number of participants declined as the farmer organizations denied credit to those who failed to pay off previous loans (with some allowance made for extenuating circumstances).

The Tenancingo project failed to create significant nonagricultural employment in the Villa. Considerable resources went toward founding a cooperative to produce palm hats, an endeavor that collapsed within a few years of FUNDASAL's withdrawal of its sponsorship. While some households produced palm hats and other unsophisticated handicrafts for sale in national markets (some thanks to initial loans from FUNDASAL), the resulting income was insufficient to support families. Moreover, repayment rates for housing and other nonagricultural loans were extremely low. Tensions over repayment of these loans increasingly threatened to undermine the community council.

In the view of project sponsors, the essential role of the council was to peacefully resolve local conflicts. Its democratic structure was deemed essential to that goal. The council would ensure that the diversity of political loyalties among residents would be represented, it would function as a forum for discussion and clarification of common interests, and it would represent the residents of the repopulation before the Tenancingo elite, as well as national and international organizations. That is, the council was conceived as a countervailing structure of power to the traditional economic and social forces of the municipality.

Yet, if the community council were to evolve into a viable and autonomous organization, it would have to meet two different challenges: escaping the protective wing of FUNDASAL paternalism and defining its own goals and structure independently of FUNDASAL and its vision. And it would have to define the extent of its local authority and defend its legitimacy against increasing pressure by the mayor's office.

The council's most immediate responsibility was to convene and lead the general assembly, the monthly community meeting of all residents in which issues were raised and discussed. In the first year of the project, council members were elected as representatives of four local teams (*equipos locales,* a rough equivalent of ward meetings). FUNDASAL promoters worked very closely with the council. Meetings were frequently held with FUNDASAL staff present, and often in the FUNDASAL office. FUNDASAL trained new members in skills such as agenda planning and public speaking, oriented the council to the objectives and programs of the project, and advised the council on thorny issues that came up. The FUNDASAL staff occasionally withheld its opinion and supported the independent decision of the council; in other cases FUNDASAL played a more active advisory role.

To some extent, the council did take on the role of representing the project to political authorities. In their relations with the archdiocese, council members grew increasingly self-confident and articulate in expressing the community's concern and opposition to the military presence. In the second and third years of the project, the council negotiated with government ministries for the restoration of services, particularly the naming of teachers to the local schools. The council's spontaneous assumption of authority in August 1987 when confronted with the theft of community trees by outsiders was an example of its development. After failing to convince the thieves that its authority was final within the community, the council traveled to the regional office of the Ministry of Natural Resources to denounce the theft, and its authority was supported. The council also negotiated with local representatives of the FMLN. It occasionally requested the FMLN to reduce its presence in the Villa. In 1987 the council successfully negotiated the reopening of the village of Jiñuco, but the FMLN refused for several years to allow further expansion of the project to the north. Despite some objection, the council did not make a systematic effort to end the FMLN's expulsion of purported military collaborators.

However, with a few exceptions in the early days of the project, council members did not participate in meetings of project sponsors with the Armed Forces either on a regional or national level. For example, throughout 1987 the council's actions against the increasing militarization of the area were limited to lobbying the archdiocese and publishing in national newspapers denunciations of the military's ongoing presence in the Villa. Military elites ignored the council and communicated directly with the archdiocese or FUNDASAL.

While the absence of the prewar elites created an opportunity to develop alternative social structures, social tensions between families originally from the Villa and those from the villages as well as political tensions among groups with different political loyalties contributed to a high rate of turnover in council membership. In the program's first year the council served as a forum in which such tensions could be defused to some extent through discussion and the reaffirmation of the community's support for the terms of the accord. The military's occupation of the Villa during 1987 increased the tension and anxiety in the council; internal relations within FUNDASAL became more hierarchical as well.[44]

Tensions between FUNDASAL and the council deepened when the agency insisted that the council collect utility payments. Residents resented the council's hesitant efforts to do so, arguing that the council should insist that international donors pay utility bills. Decreasing community participation (the number of council members declined from thirteen in 1989 to three in 1991) and the high turnover rate of the council membership reflected this tension as the council was increasingly perceived by some residents as lacking any autonomy from the development agency.

The Legacy of Tenancingo

The repopulation of Tenancingo was a unique experiment in conflict resolution and rural reconstruction in the midst of civil war. The evolution of the Tenancingo repopulation project illustrates both the possibility of limited, local conflict resolution in the midst of civil war and its limitations. The unlikely but successful negotiation of the Tenancingo accord by an independent third party demonstrates the possibility of intermediate political negotiation under certain conditions. Crucial among those conditions was their timing: the negotiations occurred at a moment when neither side could afford to oppose them, in the aftermath of explicit public recognition of the structural roots of the war by the military, and in a context of increasing national and international emphasis on the need to respect human rights and to democratize the state. The project also illustrates the crucial role of international actors: such actors supported the archdiocese (both politically and financially), protected the project's independence, and, most importantly, raised the costs for its abrogation by either side. Although the military, and to a lesser extent, the FMLN, maintained substantial pressure on the residents of Tenancingo, nonetheless the project achieved a limited humanization of the conflict within the political space defined by the accord.

However, the very success of the Tenancingo project made its replication ex-

tremely unlikely as the successful defense of the project's independence reinforced the military's hostility to any future initiative. Moreover, the internal evolution of the project illustrates the difficulties that the legacy of political mobilization and polarization poses for reconstituting a divided community destroyed
by civil war. In addition, the intended reforms and innovations were constrained
by the absence of negotiation and reform nationally. Key institutional reforms
were fraught with problems—many arising from the contradiction between the
project's local attempts at reform and the national absence of reform. Simply put,
the project could not supersede the fact of the war.

More fundamentally perhaps, the attempt to create a local democratic institution was isolated from national social forces. Aside from the archdiocese, FUN-
DASAL, and some international agencies, there was little interest in the effort.
While the project demonstrated that given a significant commitment of international funding and political resources as well as the services of an experienced
development agency, communities could be rebuilt such that former residents returned irrespective of political allegiances and despite a history of high levels of
political violence, other project ambitions of fundamental social change were not
realized. The project's neutrality meant that aspirations for participation and redistribution that in El Salvador were identified with the insurgency were not
tapped as they were in other repopulation projects such as that of Ciudad Segundo Montes (see McElhinney's chapter).

Nonetheless, the returned families participated in organizations with unprecedented democratic assumptions and intentions. Perhaps this legacy of participation, even if in organizations founded "from above" by a development agency,
contributed to the postwar political evolution of Tenancingo. Despite the absence
of vigorous opposition organizations during the reconstruction project, FMLN
candidates won municipal elections in Tenancingo in 1997, 2000, and 2003.

Vincent J. McElhinny

Between Clientelism and Radical Democracy

The Case of Ciudad Segundo Montes

Control of large parts of the Salvadoran countryside by the Farabundo Martí National Liberation Front (FMLN) during the civil war created unprecedented political space for experiments in participatory rural development. How much did these experiences alter the political culture and institutions of postwar El Salvador? The FMLN projected an image of a transformed insurgent culture as the basis for a collective, egalitarian, and participatory political-economic alternative to traditional rural power relations marked by clientelism, coercively sanctioned exclusion, and individualist peasant survival strategies. The counterinsurgent policy of the Salvadoran government and its U.S. sponsors portrayed the revolutionary movement as social deviants, whose socio-psychological rehabilitation was essential to restoring political stability.

This chapter critiques both the insurgent and counterinsurgent arguments for failing to help us understand the structural-institutional circumstances under which the very real democratic aspirations of an ex-combatant political experience might provide the basis for a stable democratic transition. I focus on the case of Ciudad Segundo Montes, a community that gained international recognition in the early 1990s as a model for alternative economic development and participatory self-governance. Ten years after repatriation to northern Morazán, this community remains enmeshed in a complex and unfinished struggle to define and assimilate revolutionary expectations of equality, economic security, and political opportunity.

Interviews conducted during six visits to Ciudad Segundo Montes between 1990 and 1999 as well as a representative community survey of 155 residents carried out in 1995 reveal a community that confounds both the pessimism of neoliberals and the optimism of the project's radical democratic European and U.S. supporters. The residents of Ciudad Segundo Montes are at once highly participatory and self-confident yet alienated and remarkably conflictive in their orientation toward political change. These contradictory attitudes and behaviors become more understandable only when the community's experience of collective self-defense, participatory decision-making, a certain leveling of privilege, and unity against a common enemy are considered within a changing political and economic opportunity structure. In this chapter I highlight the historical construction of communitarian values within Ciudad Segundo Montes and the challenges its development model has faced in the changed opportunity structure of the postwar period.

The Formation of Ciudad Segundo Montes

Ciudad Segundo Montes originated in Colomoncagua, a small Honduran border town, in 1980—the destination of some 8,400 refugees fleeing parts of Morazán, San Miguel, and La Union in the wake of the massive campaigns by the Salvadoran Armed Forces to annihilate the FMLN. The repatriation of these refugees to El Salvador in 1989–1990 represented an awakening of a peasant population to its own capacity for self-governance. At the same time, the political experience bore the imprint of a participatory experience severely deformed by the civil war.

Conjecture about how much of a break the Ciudad Segundo Montes experience made with prewar vertical and exclusionary political culture must begin with what we know about life in northern Morazán prior to the civil war. Prewar life in northern Morazán has been most vividly reconstructed by Leigh Binford.[1] Morazán was and is El Salvador's poorest department, recognized for having what the United Nations Development Program (UNDP) refers to as "African levels of poverty"; it ranks last in human development among fourteen Salvadoran departments, as well as below Cameroon, the Gabon, and Ivory Coast, according to the UNDP.[2] The terrain of northern Morazán is mountainous, and the soil is thin and rocky, unsuitable for most types of crop production for which the country is known.[3] Residents were mostly smallholding, independent farmers who cultivated some mix of corn, beans, sorghum, fruit, or henequen during the rainy season (April to October), or harvested lumber in the higher regions. Agricultural activities were complemented by production of *jarcia,* or artisanal goods (hammocks, rope, and harvesting sacks) produced from henequen plant fiber.

The 1961 Agrarian Census reports that Morazán had one of the highest percentages of smallholding farmers (57 percent of all farms cultivated by their respective owners were less than or equal to 3 hectares) in El Salvador. The cultivation of coffee within Morazán (on 2,977 farms, or 20 percent of the total) and sugarcane (on 1,647 farms, or 11 percent) was limited to small-scale production.[4] Many more farmers cultivated henequen (4,849 farms), although farm size was equally small. Inequality in land tenure was considerably lower in Morazán than in other parts of El Salvador.[5] The largest farm in northern Morazán was 550 *manzanas* (385 hectares), small by comparison to holdings in the central coast and western coffee highlands of El Salvador. Farming income was usually insufficient to provide for the family year round, forcing migration to the haciendas in the southern and western areas of El Salvador, even as far as the banana plantations in northern Honduras, and the sugarcane, coffee, and cotton harvests in Guatemala and Nicaragua.

An important advantage afforded by life on the economic margin in Morazán was autonomy. Robert Williams describes Morazán as a zone of "peasant refuge," populated by peasants displaced by the previous expansion of export agriculture in the more fertile zones.[6] It represented a territorial borderland, containing *bolsones,* or pockets of land whose ownership was contested by both Honduran and Salvadoran governments but attended by neither. Prior to the war, except for a single road opened in 1960 that scarcely penetrated into the northern part of Morazán, hamlets above the Torola River were quite isolated, with social interaction beyond one's closest neighbors limited to the nearby weekly markets in Jocoatique or Osicala. The weakness of the state's administrative capacity is reflected in the relatively low population of the departmental capital, San Francisco de Gotera (pop. 7,500), compared to other Morazanian municipalities before the war. There were twenty-two local government employees and no more than ten justices of the peace, indicating that the smallest of Morazán's twenty-six municipalities had no salaried officials.

Rural life in northern Morazán prior to the war relied on highly individualistic, subsistence agriculture, with little interdependence among neighboring households except through kinship and patronage networks. The Salvadoran peasant was characterized by deeply rooted feelings of fatalism, distrust, and low self-esteem.[7] One's own poverty and the assignation of wealth to a few, were considered God's will, which mitigated class indignation. Conflict typically pitted families against each other, often involving violent disputes over land, debts, or commercial exchanges. Individualist survival strategies prevailed, although such strategies were complemented by clientelistic alliances, including *compadrazgo* (ritual co-parenthood) as a means for securing some minimal socioeconomic insurance.[8] Patrons were usually the local merchant who extended credit or a nearby landowner who contracted seasonal labor. By the same token, many local merchants were also appointed as mayors by the then dominant National Conciliation Party, thereby closing ever more tightly the patronage network through which they could assure the quiescent provision of labor by the surplus poor of the region.

There was little evidence of communal solidarity, beyond an unspoken understanding of the common destiny of all *campesinos* to endure the exploitation of an unfair system dominated by large landowners and enforced by the National Guard. The practices of the Catholic Church were deeply implicated in the preservation of this local power structure. Fabio Argueta, a former catechist and later political organizer for the People's Revolutionary Army (ERP) during the war, recalls that "for many people, love and kindness were only shown to the image [of the Virgin Mary, or the local patron saint]. By worshiping only the image of God, they had stopped loving and serving one another. People had become so overly pious that the principal of loving one another no longer translated into the spirit of service toward the most needy. Everyone would attend the mass, but no one would lend a hand to others in tasks with which they needed help."[9] Convinced that the "lot of the poor" could not be changed, consolation was found in preparing for individual salvation. The role of the prewar church, Ignacio Martín-Baró argues, was to make social docility a religious virtue.[10]

Peasant values may also have been rooted in the risk aversion attributed to smallholder farming, the incidence of which was higher in Morazán than other departments, and the isolation from urban influences. This confluence of factors may have contributed to a somewhat different process of political formation than that which occurred in Chalatenango, Cuscatlán, or San Vicente in the 1970s. Jenny Pearce claims that these factors explain why no "independent peasant movement" emerged in Morazán, like the Christian Federation of Salvadoran Peasants (Federacion Cristiana de Campesinos Salvadoreños, FECCAS) or the Union of Farm Workers (Union de Trabajadores del Campo, UTC) in other regions of El Salvador.[11]

If an independent peasant movement did not emerge on its own in the 1970s, two outside forces converged to create one—the progressive wing of the Catholic Church and revolutionary organizers from the capital. Despite tremendous disincentives, political organizing in northern Morazán began in the early 1970s through Bible study groups and producer cooperatives.[12] Although most people had little experience participating in discussions of local problems or cooperative solutions, the "discovery" of these unlikely peasant capacities and the abatement of suspicion of collective projects began to take hold in northern Morazán. The work was catalyzed by a cadre of politically trained catechists and an activist priest, Miguel Ventura.

State repression followed closely on the heels of local organizing, with individual assassinations of political activists by the National Guard, the police, and death squads beginning in 1976. With the escalation of the civil war in all of El Salvador, the Salvadoran Armed Forces undertook several massive "search and destroy" campaigns in northern Morazán. A "scorched earth" strategy began in 1980, punctuated by over twenty civilian massacres and steady aerial bombardment, decimated much of the population, their homes, and their means of livelihood. The war forced many to seek refuge in the departmental capitals and neighboring countries.[13] Of the prewar population of 55,000 living above the Torola River, only 10,000–15,000 remained in this highly conflictive zone during the war.[14]

Displacement and exile closed a first chapter of prewar organizing, resistance, and repression for some. For many others, however, it marked the beginning of a collective experience of forced exile and collaboration with the ERP over the next ten years. People from all parts of northern Morazán fled to Colomoncagua, Honduras, a border town strategically designated by the ERP as a refuge for displaced but sympathetic peasants. Assistance arrived in the form of food, clothing, medicines, and materials for marginal shelters, formally administered by the United Nations High Commissioner for Refugees (UNHCR), though in a tense coordination with ERP-designated representatives of the refugee community and several other international nongovernmental organizations (NGOs). Aware of their collaboration with the ERP, the Honduran army viewed the refugees with hostility and regularly terrorized camp residents. During nine years in exile in Colomoncagua, Honduran soldiers killed forty-six refugees, caused thirty-four to disappear, deported eleven, and raped at least three women.[15] The logistical, relief, and security demands of exile forced the refugees to organize distribution and self-defense committees. Widespread and decentralized participation in the management of the refugee camp represented a dramatic departure from the individualistic, passive, and hierarchical way of life before the war, especially for women, who assumed many decision-making roles. The refugees eventually negotiated with international NGOs for a literacy program, training as health promoters, and the initiation of small workshops that would provide needed household items in the camps as well as the means for a future livelihood.

During a decade in exile (1980–1989), the refugees developed a complex system of governance based on participatory decision making and egalitarian resource distribution that served as the political model of *auto-gestión* (self-management), which would shape the expectations of life after the war. The governance structure in Colomoncagua, which peasants adapted on their return to El Salvador, placed the ultimate decision-making power in a general assembly of over two hundred delegates—representing all geographical (five sub-camp neighborhoods) and social (health, nutrition, education, sanitation, water, children, women, elders) constituencies within the community. The relatively closed nature of life in the refuge permitted broad-based discussion of how to distribute resources and work responsibilities, inculcating a capacity for resolving conflicts by open, nonviolent means. Acquiring new vocational and management skills elicited a sense of political efficacy that encouraged the refugees to hold the UNHCR more accountable, as well as developing, albeit fragile, internal accountability mechanisms for elected camp leaders.

These achievements were made under conditions that could hardly be considered ideal for democratic experimentation. As part of the government's strategy for defeating the FMLN, northern Morazán and the refugee camps in neighboring Honduras were virtually cut off from the rest of the country. Almost all other basic social services were nonexistent. While demanding recognition from the international community as civilian victims of the ongoing conflict, which they undoubtedly were, the refugees in Honduras consistently channeled donated materials across the border to ERP combatants. Also, Colomoncagua served as a convenient source of recruitment and a recovery station for wounded or pregnant ERP combatants. This strategy of *doble cara* (showing one civilian face to the Salvadoran Armed Forces and another to the FMLN) was practiced within the refuge by the mid-1980s in order to leverage the political discourse of human rights emanating from the Christian Democrat government (1982–1988) and its U.S. benefactors. One estimate of the level of clandestine patrimony from the camps suggests that as much as 30 percent of the assistance received was sent directly to the ERP.[16]

This symbiotic relationship between the refugees of Colomoncagua and the ERP represents one of the early fault lines in the model of governance designed in the camps. Clearly the residents of Colomoncagua demonstrated a striking capacity for *auto-gestión*, including the ability to bargain forcefully and effectively with international NGOs over the conditions of assistance. There were frequent conflicts between the UNHCR and camp leaders, with one outside observer noting that "UNHCR officials were uncomfortable with the responsibility for these people, who were politically embarrassing, unwilling to play the role of docile and grateful recipients of aid, and insistent on developing their own path for their future."[17]

At the same time, ERP commanders exercised primary authority over most major decisions within the camp; for example, ERP leaders appointed the camp leadership. Still, there was considerable accountability to the broader community within the camp as well, as in instances of collective decisions to remove negligent or less competent leaders for problems related to unequal distribution of resources. Nonetheless the lines of autonomy between civilian and combatant and between refuge governance and ERP authority were fundamentally blurred. An atmosphere of insecurity and dependence tended to censor complaints about perceived corruption and opportunism. The experience of FMLN internal and external military sanction/punishment of war crimes, including executions, reinforced a verticalist discipline and fear that weakened the capacity of the Colomoncagua residents to develop a stronger experience of participatory democratic self-governance.

If we may speak of a value change from the prevailing individualist habits in prewar Morazán to the orientations that characterized the collective identity in Colomoncagua, its origins are rooted in this combined experience of collaborating with the ERP in resistance to the Salvadoran state and acquiring economic and political skills within the refugee camp. The radical effects of this political socialization are illustrated in the following observation by a youth coordinator at the height of optimism about the future at the time of repatriation: "We learned so much. . . . Most of us were very little when we went into the refuge, and we hadn't yet accepted the values of capitalism, individualism, and selfishness; they hadn't yet entered our consciousness. . . . We consider that a very favorable condition of our development. If we'd lived longer in El Salvador, it would have been more difficult to become organized, to think about serving the community. . . . We've come back into a capitalist system, the same one our parents lived in, but we've had the experience of being in an autonomous community, or deciding for ourselves what our values are."[18]

In late 1989 at the height of the FMLN offensive, and continuing into 1990, the refugees returned to northern Morazán to occupy a strategic position along the single road that traversed the zone of conflict.[19] In a short time the entire camp infrastructure was transported and reassembled at a site just north of the Torola River, unfolding on either side of the *calle negra* (asphalt artery road). The new settlement was named in honor of Father Segundo Montes, the martyred Jesuit sociologist-priest who had studied and been so inspired by the achievements of the refugees (he was murdered by the military in 1989). From 1989 until the signing of the Peace Accords in 1992 the ERP, in collaboration with organized communities like Ciudad Segundo Montes, consolidated its effective authority in Morazán north of the Torola River.

The refugees who populated Ciudad Segundo Montes brought with them an ambitious vision for the economic and political development of the entire region, based on the participatory egalitarian model that had been developing throughout the war, not only in Colomoncagua but also among other regional peasant organizations aligned with the ERP as well.[20] With the financial backing of international NGOs, Ciudad Segundo Montes was intended as part of a larger integrated rural development scheme that would replicate the educational, health, and occupational training experiences of Colomoncagua in other parts of northern Morazán.[21] The optimistic economic expectations shared by many returning refugees were linked to the hope that Ciudad Segundo Montes would serve as the industrial engine that would reactivate the economy of northern Morazán, an ideal combination of factory and farm inspired and financed by European NGOs.[22]

One of the most successful aspects of this model has been education. While in exile, camp residents had achieved a literacy rate of approximately 85 percent, which is extraordinary compared with the 40 percent average for rural El Salvador at the time. The establishment of Ciudad Segundo Montes raised the number of qualified teachers in northern Morazán from less than twenty to several hundred. Some eighty-seven students obtained the equivalent of a high school diploma in May 1995, and post–high school education was established within Ciudad Segundo Montes in collaboration with the Spanish University of Salamanca. Prior to 1960, only a handful of students had gone beyond the secondary education level in all of northern Morazán.

Ciudad Segundo Montes has faced its most complex obstacle in the reconciliation of internal and external challenges to the democratic and economic goals of the project. The high-water mark of political participation in the community may have occurred in 1991, when over 250 elected delegates of the community's general assembly facilitated substantive discussions of key community issues in all neighborhoods . The delegates elected an executive twelve-person board of directors—a significant step toward greater autonomy from the command structure of the ERP. In addition to political organization, approximately 1,700 residents were formally employed, if only symbolically compensated, in community projects (which included carpentry, metalworking, clothing, and shoe factories, a bakery, and animal feed, auto-mechanic, and construction projects) or services (education, health care, and production administration, child care, a dental clinic, cultural center, radio station, and the communal bank). These projects experimented in giving workers voice in workplace decisions, anticipating the eventual transformation of each enterprise into individual cooperatives organically linked through stock ownership or voting rights to the entire community. Each workshop elected a representative to the general assembly, as did most social constituencies. A local radio station and community musical group disseminated relevant information and endowed various issues of local interest with a public forum.

A 1989 community newsletter that echoed these collective values declared, "the necessity of repatriation as a community [comes] not only from the concrete advantages that this model for life offers people for resolving their problems, but also because in the current circumstances of the country, there is no space to resolve problems from an individual perspective."[23] The apparent leveling of hierarchical social relations, and the experimentation with collective, participatory, and contentious modes of political and economic behavior, challenge the characterizations of prewar peasants as passive and resigned to a predetermined fate, as well as the extremist and pathological motivations attributed to peasant communities that rebel. However, adapting these strengths to the postwar transition has also revealed that the expectations of a radical departure from the previous peasant economy built from a social scaffolding of deep, collective commitments were also wide of the mark.

The Postwar Political Opportunity Structure

In the postwar period Ciudad Segundo Montes has had to adjust to a dramatically different environment. The concept of political opportunity structure is useful for evaluating how changes in its political and economic institutional structure, the availability of elite alliances, and the state's propensity toward repression all intervene in the relationship between political behavior and aggrieved local groups.[24] Whether political and economic institutions are open or closed reflects the pluralism and porosity of the formal legal-institutional structure and is indicated by both access and influence, since access without influence leads to co-optation. The likelihood of alliances between local and international elites, including foreign NGOs and multilateral agencies, which played roles in the postwar reconstruction process, is also part of the opportunity structure created in this sort of context. The political behavior of aggrieved local groups reflects both the correlation of forces between challenging and defending groups and the cultural component of past practices.

International allies have proven to be increasingly relevant supporters of local solidarity, providers of resources, and transmitters of ideas and values in their roles as transnational advocacy networks and counterinsurgent patrons of besieged states. Development donors and their respective intermediary NGOs have staked out localities in their competition with or support of the state. Shifts in the composition of these international allies have set important limits to the political-economic model of Ciudad Segundo Montes. The leverage provided by international elite allies has depended on the composition of local elites, namely the FMLN, which has transformed into an opposition party. In Ciudad Segundo Montes, the political opportunity structure has improved because of its more open institutional structure and the near elimination of state repression but it has

also deteriorated as a result of the diminished availability and stability of elite allies. I briefly address each of these conditions in turn. Reforms embodied in the
1992 Peace Accords opened some political space by legalizing the FMLN as a political party, eliminating most elements of the state security apparatus, and mandating regular elections for local and national offices. The 1994 "elections of the
century" delivered very modest gains to the FMLN in its debut as a legal political
institution. It polled strongly in San Salvador but poorly in the countryside, especially in areas where its support during the war should have translated into votes.
Murray estimates that as many as 225,000 eligible voters (17 percent of votes
cast) were passively or actively denied their right to vote through incompetence
or fraud by the elections board.[25] Many of these disenfranchised voters lived in
municipalities supportive of the FMLN. In all, the FMLN coalition won only 15
of the country's 262 municipalities in 1994. Support for FMLN mayors and
councils has grown since 1994.

In northern Morazán the electoral pattern has been somewhat different. In
1994 five FMLN mayors were elected in northern Morazán. This strong showing
in an ERP zone presents a somewhat unexpected response to the ERP's strategy
of rejecting municipal government during the war. In Ciudad Segundo Montes,
winning local office was initially viewed as a means to gaining access to government-funded reconstruction projects that were refused to unrecognized local and
national NGOs. Despite government recognition, the municipal government has
mainly played a symbolic role in conferring legal authority to the communal organizations and local NGOs, such as the Segundo Montes Foundation, and their
network of international sponsors, who had exercised the dominant influence on
the early development decisions. One representative of the 1994 Meanguera
town council confessed frustration in conducting the business of an underfunded
local government that residents viewed as simply a predatory tax collector.

A poorly defined parallel authority structure emerged between municipal government and traditional communal groups. A process of decentralization has
heightened expectations that effective local governance might go beyond the
provision of services to play an active role in economic development.[26] Yet where
a productive division of administrative authority was possible, duplication and
competition have occurred. Communal organizations might have delegated broad
representational authority to the municipal government and taken on the role of
a social movement. Yet the *junta directiva* of Ciudad Segundo Montes has fought
to preserve overall governance authority in the community, not only duplicating
the work of the municipal council but also regulating social-movement activity
within the community. The underspecified roles for the mayor and council and
the lack of coordination among local actors have contributed to the loss of faith

in the municipal government institution, resulting in the decay of early FMLN political strength at the local level in Morazán. In northern Morazán, only two FMLN mayors were elected in 1997, one in Meanguera.

Despite greater institutionalized political access, an unfavorable realignment of Ciudad Segundo Montes's political allies has neutralized many of the benefits of gaining a political foothold in local and national office and aggravated local divisions. A political crisis within the FMLN was touched off by a poorer-than-expected showing in the 1994 presidential elections and latent political strategies that have always divided the five-member organization. Demands by the Popular Liberation Front (FPL) for greater unification motivated the exit of the ERP and elements of the National Resistance Party (Resistencia Nacional) from the FMLN in December 1994 to form a separate Social Democratic Party (Partido Democratico, PD).

As the FMLN was splitting, the Nationalist Republican Alliance (ARENA) had solidified its political control, having profited from five years of aid and remittance-subsidized economic growth during the Cristiani administration (1989–1994). Yet ARENA was also suffering internal divisions between the landed, hardcore right-wing elements of the party and the ascendant self-described modernizing elements whose interests were more diversified in finance and commerce. The leadership of PD rejected the FMLN's broadly socialist goals, instead favoring strategic alliances with the modernizing element within the ruling ARENA party. The remaining three leftist parties consolidated the FMLN into a single party but have continued to fragment into "democratic-revisionist," "orthodox-socialist," and "institutional" tendencies. In an unprecedented move, three PD deputies reversed a prior opposition vote and joined ARENA on May 31, 1995, in passing a 3 percent increase in the highly regressive value-added tax. The tax had an almost immediate impact on the poor by increasing prices for basic consumption. The decision so alienated many of the ERP/PD's northern Morazanian supporters that the party has become politically ineffective in the region.

The divisions between Ciudad Segundo Montes and ERP/PD leaders can be traced back even further. As preparations for repatriation and negotiation of the war were being planned in 1989, questions of distribution and ownership of communal assets in ERP zones of control were debated but never resolved. Ciudad Segundo Montes was perceived as the "favored child" of the donor community, having received substantially more support than surrounding municipalities. There is little doubt that Ciudad Segundo Montes has struggled to incorporate over 1,000 demobilized combatants and provide for over 600 *lisiados,* or war disabled, in addition to the already highly vulnerable local population.[27] The ERP leadership extracted loans from Ciudad Segundo Montes' coffers, secured employment for selected combatants, and attempted to appoint community leaders much as they did in Colomocagua. The political autonomy accumulated by Ciudad Segundo Montes' leaders enabled them to resist certain ERP demands. Yet disagreements over postwar resource allocation deepened tensions between the ERP and Ciudad Segundo Montes, ultimately influencing the decision by the community's leaders to abandon the PD in 1995 and affiliate with the now FPL-dominated FMLN—a less influential set of allies.

Perquin's loss of the municipal government to an ARENA-led coalition in the 1997 municipal elections signaled a low point in the Left's political organizing in northern Morazán. The crisis caused by the PD's defection from the FMLN stripped a formidable political vehicle of the former ERP base of its ideological engine. Many of the former ERP base—humbled by being abandoned by PD representatives and disillusioned by the ineffective accompaniment of PD NGOs—are now following the decision of Ciudad Segundo Montes to reintegrate into the FMLN. However, fights within the FMLN between the *ortodoxos* and *renovadoras* wings have continued to exacerbate local power struggles. The Ciudad Segundo Montes *junta directiva* initially affiliated with the *renovadora* wing of the party but has since shifted to the *ortodoxo* wing for reasons that will become clear later. The reorganization of the FMLN in the zone since 1995 has helped it recover lost ground—six municipalities returned to the FMLN fold in the 2000 elections, polling its highest absolute percentage of votes yet in Morazán.

Electoral gains in the region have been possible due to greater institutionalized controls on state repression in the postwar period. Nevertheless, Ciudad Segundo Montes has had to defend itself using unconventional means. Beginning in Colomoncagua and during the population's return to northern Morazán in the midst of the war, repeated instances of successful, sometimes confrontational negotiation with local military authorities legitimated strategies of collective political action as essential civic behavior. During the war, the community frequently used mass mobilizations to free members of the community captured by the Armed Forces, persuaded guards to allow the transfer of supplies through military checkpoints, stopped military interventions in the community, and held the government accountable for fulfilling its promises to protect human rights. Extra-institutional mobilization tactics have complemented traditional advocacy efforts in the postwar period as well. Residents of Ciudad Segundo Montes have regularly participated in mobilizations to pressure the government to fulfill the various economic conditions of the Peace Accords, including resolving the complicated problems associated with land transfer, forgiving agrarian debt, and indemnifying war-wounded and families of war victims, as well as correcting voter registration anomalies in FMLN zones and prosecuting human rights cases identified by the Truth Commission.

The space and effort necessary for participatory democracy has also been curtailed by the closure of economic opportunity in northern Morazán. The FMLN's formal surrender of arms in 1992 was followed by a steep decline in external aid to the community, beginning in 1991 and accelerating in 1993. The collapse of the Soviet Union struck a dual blow to the Salvadoran revolutionary movement of which Ciudad Segundo Montes was a part. Not only did ideological support for alternative development models evaporate, but also European and U.S. allies turned their attention and aid to rebuilding Eastern Europe and the former Soviet states, quickly consigning Central America to a lesser policy arena. Food aid ended in 1991, one year after the community returned to northern Morazán, and faced with the constraints set by external donors, its general assembly voted in favor of introducing wages for work in community workshops.

Economically, the structure of opportunity has not improved, and many interviewed feel that conditions have worsened, especially for those dependent on the rural economy. Expectations of a regional recovery have proven to be far too optimistic. Morazán remains predominantly rural (73 percent) and agricultural (69 percent of the economically active population); over two-thirds of residents do not earn enough to purchase the minimal goods considered sufficient for meeting basic needs.[28] With no regional economy in which to integrate, permanent employment in Ciudad Segundo Montes workshops has collapsed. Estimates of formal employment fell from 600 in 1995 to 150 in 1998.[29] Wages in the clothing factory dropped from a peak of 1,500 *colones* per month in 1993 (US$172, more than twice the national minimum wage) to an average of 650 *colones* per month in 1995, with periodic layoffs due to lack of work. Other factories sit idle, donated equipment has been sold, and people have returned to prewar survival strategies in subsistence agriculture or employment in the informal sector, which includes small restaurants, stores, and other micro-enterprises, or they work as domestic servants outside the community. People have also left the community to seek employment in cities and the United States. The actual population of Ciudad Segundo Montes declined dramatically from about 11,000 in 1994 to about 5,000 by the late 1990s, although the entire department of Morazán has experienced the country's highest rate of emigration during the postwar period.[30] This downward economic trajectory was brought into even sharper relief by a 1997 census conducted by Fundación Segundo Montes, which found that over 50 percent of the community's residents live in extreme poverty.[31]

In evaluating this downturn, critics of Ciudad Segundo Montes both within and outside the community have attributed local problems to the leadership's mismanagement of local resources, lack of transparency, and inflexible decision making. The Ciudad Segundo Montes *junta directiva* and their supporters counter that the shortage of credit (related to problems legalizing the community's land

and assets within the criteria set out in the Peace Accords) and a state policy that has abandoned the rural economy are to blame. Both groups recognize the decisive impact of the decline in external aid: an end to the policy of work as an entitlement and the beginning a difficult transition toward a market-based economy.

Between 1995 and 1998, the local governance structure of Ciudad Segundo Montes has evolved—although some might say unraveled—in response to these structural changes, toward a more decentralized and delegative model where each organization (production, education, health, communal association, women, bank, radio, Fundación Segundo Montes) has its own assembly and elects two delegates to a central coordinating council with ultimate decision-making power in the community. This model was intended to give the council, the mayor, and NGOs working in the community specialized roles and prevent any one institution from monopolizing decision-making authority. While this is a unique arrangement for rural communities, in practice it has not been the panacea many community residents expected it to be.

In February 1995, during this difficult transition, "Juan José Rodríguez" (Hugo Meléndez), president of the community board of directors for five years, died of a brain hemorrhage. Rodríguez, brother of ERP zone commander Jorge Meléndez ("Jonás"), served mostly as a technician in northern Morazán before being sent to Colomoncagua after an injury suffered in a munitions accident. He was appointed camp leader by the ERP in 1986 but became a widely respected and visionary leader as well as an important political broker between opposing political factions and international agencies. Rodríguez's vision may also have unified the different social and political currents within Ciudad Segundo Montes toward the larger goal of community development. The loss of Rodríguez contributed to the unintended increase in authoritarian treatment of dissent within Ciudad Segundo Montes and a hardening of political positions.

A combination of factors—poor resource management, a stagnating rural economy, the state's passive asphyxiation of FMLN zones, and the political crises within the FMLN—spawned heated debate in Ciudad Segundo Montes over proposed market-oriented reforms and outright opposition to elected leaders. Consistent with its defensive, almost siege-like posture during the war, the Ciudad Segundo Montes leadership has tended to emphasize the limitations imposed by a hostile external political environment and the complexities of decentralization under conditions of *assistencialismo*—a term invented by donor agencies that attributes beneficiary apathy to dependence on donations.

An opposition movement, the Workers Association of Morazán (Asociación de Trabajadores de Morazán, ATM), formed within Ciudad Segundo Montes as a result of bitter divisions with elected leaders over questions of communal property ownership and the rights of workers and citizens. ATM organized several public demonstrations, with estimates of participants ranging from several hundred to 1,500. On December 8, 1993, opponents of the Ciudad Segundo Montes board of directors and mayor accompanied workers who seized the electrical-generating plant to protest the board's refusal to turn the plant and other workshops over to the workers as independent cooperatives. On a visit to the community in January 1994, just after the takeover, I encountered the community in crisis. The gravity of the situation was palpable as I approached the locked and guarded community power station, damaged from sabotage during the occupation. A painted graffiti message on the building housing the generator accused community leaders of authoritarian rule. As an outsider to the community, I was greeted by the man guarding the small power plant by his demanding, "which side are you on?" He explained to me that force had been necessary to "liberate" the plant. The damage to the generator and the costs of lost production in the local factories when power was cut were substantial for the poor community. However, the social scars left by the first open contest for power between community members had cut much deeper. It was instantly clear that whatever cooperative solidarity that bound Ciudad Segundo Montes' residents as a community was under severe strain. The structural forces that held it together during the war had been loosened. This instance of civil disobedience motivated by internally rooted grievances marked a turning point in the community's development, shattering the image of political consensus that structural forces had held fast during the war. Ironically, the effectiveness of employing a public discourse of human rights as part of an insurgent strategy left the Ciudad Segundo Montes leadership politically vulnerable to the same tactic from an internal opposition.

Local political competition brought with it a growing bitterness within the community over unanswered questions of property ownership, indemnification for losses during the conflict, and a diminishing capacity to meet the needs of all its residents. The blueprint for decentralizing control over community assets is vaguely outlined in the document *Target 2000: The Strategy of Comunidad Segundo Montes—In Search of Utopia North of the Torola River*. The document reflects the culmination of a consultation process begun in July 1992 over how to decentralize governance of Ciudad Segundo Montes' social and production activities and assets in autonomous, self-sufficient enterprises.[32] The proposal of self-sufficiency as the central assumption of the decentralization plan was made by community leaders who saw on the horizon a dramatic decline of external assistance and attended to the advice of European donors that the workshops must adjust to market competition.

Although the plan was initially presented as consensualized, *how* decentralizing would be accomplished soon became the source of division within the *junta directiva*. The question tapped deep fears in a community that was moving away from communitarian principles. The dispute ultimately resulted in the disintegration of the *junta directiva* and the decision to expel twenty-one foreign technicians (of twenty-three then present) from the community in June 1993, two of whom were later involved in the December electrical plant occupation. One U.S. volunteer who participated in the takeover argues from the point of view of the ATM that the pressure to spend aid money and a power hungry (Ciudad Segundo Montes) leadership were forcing the community to abandon a relatively democratic parliamentary system and resort to an autocratic leadership, monopolized by the *junta directiva*. In the new *Asamblea Amplia*, "composed of work-site representation rather than geographic representation," the participants were carefully selected by the *junta directiva*, and opposition voices were excluded.[33]

The legacy of the clothing workshop best captures the complex political and economic difficulties faced by the Ciudad Segundo Montes development model.[34] Thirty to forty people were employed producing clothing for the community in Colomoncagua, but the clothes did not sell in northern Morazán. An investor attempted to convert the workshop to *maquila* production, paying workers to sew "Made in the USA" labels to sweatshop apparel assembled in San Salvador. However, the venture quickly failed for a variety of reasons. Negotiated agreements embedded in the Peace Accords stipulated the delivery of a contract to make uniforms for the newly formed National Civilian Police (Policia Nacional Civil, PNC). This contract alone produced a small economic boom in the community beginning in late 1992. Piecework salaries jumped to as high as 1,500 *colones* per month (US$172, or $0.85 per hour), and jobs were added as the workshop was capitalized with eleven new $1,000 sewing machines. Workers were grouped in teams, sewing pants or shirts, and produced over eighty uniforms a day. When construction of a new building to house clothing production was delayed, workers volunteered their labor to finish the building on their own. Representation at the workplace was through a grievance committee of four elected workers, who could bring complaints to the supervising staff and participate as delegates in the Ciudad Segundo Montes general assembly.

By 1994, the bloom was off the rose. As the financier and manager of a highly centralized production system in Ciudad Segundo Montes, CODEMO was uncertain of its role under a more decentralized system. Self-interest perhaps explains why members of the *junta directiva* who were also employed at CODEMO switched to opposing the decentralization plan when its implications became clearer. In 1994 workers were divided about the emerging questions of equity, offering complex critiques of themselves as "privileged" community members yet suggesting that opportunism motivated the leaders of the ATM including any concern for the community's elderly or infirm. Both workers and supervisors expressed a principled sympathy for the ATM and its primary egalitarian demand that some economic opportunity be shared with all members of the community. And not everyone supported the takeover as an act of protest, because the two-week outage reduced income just before Christmas and threatened the loss of the production contract. By mid-1995, a greater number of interviewed workers at the clothing factory, perhaps the most lucrative employment in Ciudad Segundo Montes, described the work less as a transformative, collective project than in terms of traditional clientelist relations.[35] In response to discontent over periodic layoffs, declining wages, and the fallout over the treatment of the ATM, CODEMO tightened its control over workshop production. The clothing work-shop's grievance committee was recomposed to include only trusted friends of the plant supervisor, certain workers were not invited to participate in community assemblies, and others were fired for public disagreements with CODEMO. Sev-eral informants, speaking anonymously, confirmed that many workers felt intimi-dated by the plant supervisors and CODEMO. However, open criticism of the lack of workplace democracy was muted by fear of losing one's job at a time when fewer and fewer people were working.

At the end of the uniform contract with the PNC the clothing workshop never recovered its initial production levels. High transportation costs and low technical capacity made it virtually impossible to compete with a brutally efficient *maquila* sector in San Salvador. Similar fates have befallen a bakery and the poultry farm.

For over a decade, the unifying project of survival against an oppressive state had channeled these grievances outward or at least kept them bottled up. Greater personal liberty in the postwar period produced what many ex-combatants have described as a process of postwar decompression, refocusing the optic of persist-ing grievances inward in the search for local causes and solutions. Criticism of the increasing incapacity of the Ciudad Segundo Montes project to provide uni-versal opportunity shifted from the complete abandonment of the rural economy and foot-dragging on fulfillment of the Peace Accords by the ARENA govern-ment and many of the donor countries to the personal defects, administrative mistakes, and opportunism of local leaders, neighbors, and family members. This shift parallels a structural transformation of the political project of the FMLN and its external allies from a broader goal of social transformation to a moderate one of incremental, "acceptable" improvements

By the late 1990s, FMLN and Ciudad Segundo Montes leaders concluded that the New Popular Economy proposal for a network of decentralized light indus-try and nontraditional agricultural cooperatives as the stimulus for reviving the economy of northern Morazán was a bust. The plan vastly underestimated the state's commitment and financial investment required to achieve self-sufficiency or any of the other goals in *Target 2000*. Morazán held the dubious claim of having received a full o percent of nationally budgeted public investment in 1998. Despite a slew of multimillion dollar targeted rural development programs operating since 1992 in Morazán, an Inter-American Development Bank (IDB) loan officer who is familiar with the region remarked that he, "wasn't sure whether the IDB or any other institution should be investing in programs that encourage people to stay in Morazán."[36]

Looking back, we may now fully appreciate the complexity of and ambition inherent in the model of local governance and shared economic goals of Ciudad Segundo Montes, as well its collision course with donor expectations of market competition and self-sufficiency. The unfulfilled expectations of a better life, one of the key promises to combatants and their families during the war, is now a constant threat to the single most important resource on which the success of Ciudad Segundo Montes depends—a collective commitment to creating an alternative community, both economically and politically. Dissent has succeeded in inspiring a transition, if unintended, toward political pluralism at the local level and a reexamination of these expectations and the means to achieve them. Beginning with the influence of an activist church in the early 1970s and the adaptation to exile, Ciudad Segundo Montes peasants have forged a radical new political culture based on experiences of collective self-defense, participatory decision-making, a certain leveling of privilege, and unity against a common enemy. Postwar events suggest that this alternative path is not without its pitfalls.

The Road Ahead

In preparations for the mayoral and deputy elections held in March of 2000, the residents of Ciudad Segundo Montes were deeply divided over the next mayoral candidate. The *junta directiva* is now under the banner of the *ortodoxo-socialista* wing of the FMLN, which supported Mercedes Ventura, the head of the local school system. An opposition coalition, aligned with the *renovadora* wing of the FMLN and centered around the Segundo Montes Foundation, backed the reelection of the current mayor, Francisco Pereira. Ventura, the *junta* candidate, narrowly won the FMLN convention nomination, after a first vote was annulled due to irregularities. However, she lost the general election by ninety-five votes to a centrist candidate from the United Democratic Convergence Party (Convergencia Democratica Unida)—of which the PD is a coalition partner—after Pereira, the Segundo Montes Foundation (Fundación Segundo Montes, FSM), and the *reno-*

vadoras threw their support behind him. For the first time, the *junta* faction has lost control of the municipal office of Meanguera and must share power with an opposition force. Both parties have now set their sights on winning the upcoming vote for FSM officers, lobbying strenuously within the community for support. Despite the bitter in-fighting that has strained the democratic process in Ciudad Segundo Montes, the intensity of local political competition represents an expression not only of the divisions that could pull the community apart but also a commitment to hard-won political right of participation that could form the basis for a new postwar social contract.

The emergence of inequality and privilege, the promotion of private versus collective economic initiatives, and the less polarized relationship with the Salvadoran state have forced Ciudad Segundo Montes to adapt the formative experiences and expectations of its collective identity to a new set of parameters. Disputed shifts in decision-making power within the community have tracked similar contests within the constellation of political allies that represent the political left in El Salvador, forcing many to rethink their revolutionary ideals as related to political equality. Idle productive workshop infrastructures now sit as icons to poor development planning and the truncated neoliberal aid commitments to reconstruction that focused on the minutia of small enterprise self-sufficiency while ignoring the deeper structural failure of the larger rural economy.

I have argued that the Ciudad Segundo Montes collective identity is frayed, indicated by widespread discontent about participation in decision making, divergence over problem-solving strategies, and greater tolerance for economic inequality among the more privileged. These results call into question Ciudad Segundo Montes's one true advantage and the foundation of its political culture—a collective identity of resistance to an exclusionary, authoritarian, and repressive political-economic system. Recent events hint that this internal solidarity may be breaking down, or simply adapting to an unfinished democratic project. Whether Ciudad Segundo Montes, one of the most highly organized and successful opposition communities in El Salvador, can adapt to and surmount these challenges has particularly salient implications for the democratic transition underway in the country as a whole.

Irina Carlota Silber

Not Revolutionary Enough?

Community Rebuilding in Postwar Chalatenango

> *Civil wars are, at best, about opening up political space for the development of alternatives to capitalist social relations; they do not resolve the contradictions that gave rise to them, even though the disruption of capitalist markets, flight of landlords, and elimination of most signs of the state apparatus may provide a fertile field for social experimentation.*
>
> —Leigh Binford, "Hegemony in the Interior of the
> Salvadoran Revolution: The ERP in Northern Morazán"

Wartime survivors, their remembrances, their present practices, and future trajectories have become increasingly the focus of El Salvador's postwar reconstruction and development. This is the case for rural residents in the northeastern department of Chalatenango, a former conflict zone and site of a wartime repatriation movement. This chapter concentrates on Chalatenango's postwar reconstruction, focusing on the explosion of grassroots and nongovernmental organization (NGO)–led development efforts that characterize the department's transition from war to peace and nation rebuilding. While successful postconflict rebuilding cannot be solely the responsibility of NGOs, or popular organizing for that matter—for this erases the nation-state's responsibility completely—NGOs have come to be seen as part of local people's tools for negotiating an unjust system. In order to shed light on this matrix of reconstruction, I describe and analyze local processes in three primary sites: the repopulated community *(repoblación)* of El Rancho,[1] the grassroots organization Coordinator of Communities in Development of Chalatenango (Coordinadora de Comunidades en Desarrollo Chalatenango, CCR), and the NGO Foundation for Cooperation and Community Development of El Salvador (Fundación para la Cooperación y el Desarrollo Comunal de El Salvador, CORDES). This is a focus from "below" that hones in on the increasing differentiation and growing unevenness between and among overlapping groups, NGOs, grassroots organizations, and women and men in communities who for a long while shared a life of struggle and survival. Specifically, I argue that in postwar times, historically oppositional practices and discourses have lost their meaning for many residents struggling under close to a decade of neoliberal, privatizing, and structural adjustment policies. In doing so, I expose some assumptions about grassroots mobilizing that romanticize and essentialize rural people's suffering, their struggles, and their daily lives.

This chapter forms part of my larger project that documents the rise of a palpable disillusionment in Chalatenango. My discussion of the effects of postwar demoralization takes up a *reconstruction paradox:* In a formerly revolutionary population characterized by high organizational capacity, residing in an area targeted by various reconstruction projects that emphasize participation as necessary for sustainable development, there is a *decline* in participation—particularly by women—and a stagnation of development work. This analysis builds on Elisabeth Wood's argument that El Salvador's transition from war to peace to democracy was "forged from below via a revolutionary social movement."[2] Scholars suggest that the pursuit of peace was characterized by a series of "bargains" between the FMLN (Farabundo Martí National Liberation Front) and the Salvadoran government. A central bargain was this: elites conceded political democracy and the FMLN conceded a liberalized market economy. However, in their practices and discourses, many women and men in *repoblaciones* challenge the national and local bargain of political participation that denies them economic empowerment as they continue to live in poverty. Residents reject the terms of this bargain, as women in particular cease participation in reconstruction projects. In doing so, they engage in a politics of memory that contests local NGOs and grassroots groups' narratives about the war that privilege political inclusion for the FMLN, which has occurred, over economic restructuring, which has not. In response, NGOs rationalize their development struggles by blaming residents for reconstruction failures.[3] Ultimately, as residents reclaim spaces of violence, they are accused of being either "too revolutionary" or "not revolutionary enough." Meaning that they are simultaneously chastised for ceasing to participate in traditional wartime community organizing and for the failure of micro-enterprise development projects.

James Ferguson's analysis of the development industry provides a theoretical framework for examining this paradox.[4] However, rather than exploring the effects of hegemonic development models, I suggest that the processes occurring in postwar Chalatenango indicate the importance of problematizing NGO-led development, in particular the logic, impact, and ramifications of a politicized "counterhegemonic" project. This is important because one of the legacies of the war is the transformation of a revolutionary social project into alternative models of development that both resist and accommodate neoliberal development. NGO-led and grassroots-complicit development efforts and interventions produce unintended consequences, or "side-effects." While hegemonic development depoliticizes, it is critical to focus on the development industry that emerges from polarized conflict and is ultimately driven by politics. In this context, development "problems" are constructed at the grassroots level, and they are politicized through claims to a uniform past. These "problems" deligitimize and depoliticize residents from *repoblaciones,* the intended development "beneficiaries" and targets of empowerment strategies. Thus, contradictory side effects of alternative development projects arise: rural residents, their abilities and deficiencies, are mapped out in a combination of opposing faults or characteristics. They are critiqued simultaneously for (1) "losing" their revolutionary identity and "forgetting" the past, the war, and their struggle; and contradictorily (2) for failing in recent microenterprise development models because they do not have entrepreneurial capabilities or a "culture of credit."[5] The unintended consequences of NGO and grassroots-complicit efforts generate processes and structures that gender both community reconstruction and its critiques. They place blame on women, who are held responsible for alternative models of development.

Today, Chalatenango's history of a strong social movement informs regional reconstruction expectations, assumptions, critiques, and efforts. These emphasize community organization as a key component of projects aiming to achieve sustainable local development and national reconciliation after a protracted civil war. While it is critical to explore this legacy of "organization" and by extension the place of "community" as residents negotiate between performing collective, regional, oppositional identities and surviving in a rural economy where it is increasingly difficult to make a living, what follows is a quieter story about what happens in the interstitial moments of daily life marked by decreasing collective action. What happens when we take this less exotic path as our point of entry for a region and people carrying the weight of a history of revolutionary consciousness? How can we talk about the shift from insurgents to citizens who move in and out of individual and collective work, keeping in mind that "it may be precisely after the revolution that the long struggle for democratization and economic justice will be waged."[6] Vincent J. McElhinny's analysis (in this volume) of postwar processes in neighboring Morazán, also a former conflict zone, cogently describes the contradictions of rebuilding in terms of a "postwar decompression." Critically, he too points to the ways in which wartime expectations of societal transformation have been replaced by more moderate goals. These unfulfilled promises have created a situation in which local inhabitants place blame on local or national actors rather than on more elusive global forces. The struggle is one between empowerment and alienation that may undermine the very hope for building a future collective identity.

The sections that follow detail ethnographically what happens to "revolutionary" peoples and places after a revolutionary struggle. The chapter begins by briefly describing the history of present practices, discourses, and assumptions. This is followed by a brief discussion of the ethnographic context. The chapter concentrates on several ethnographic moments. The first is an analysis of an evaluation session led by a director of CORDES. The encounter exemplifies "bottom-up," "community-led" events intended to identify the problems and solutions to the present "woman problem" in *repoblaciones*. This NGO-driven moment is then juxtaposed with the alternative imaginings of three women in the community of El Rancho. Through these ethnographic examples I problematize the discourse and practices of "organization" and "community" and the manner in which they are gendered. I aim to demonstrate how a historically politicizing project is transformed into an alternative development model that creates unintended consequences. In this case the model constructs Chalatecos as "not revolutionary enough." For many in leadership positions on the Left, this ascription threatens democratic rebuilding, because it erases the power of the wartime experiences and knowledge of "participatory outsiders" or "recently retired revolutionaries."[7] However, others implicitly critique Chalatecos as ex-combatants or formerly displaced peoples with many challenges to confront or with little to offer.[8] The chapter concludes by situating this case study within recent discussions on NGOs and theories of civil society and exploring the power of "community." In short, this work offers an entryway into the local logic of a palpable disillusionment, one of broken promises and bankrupt dreams.

Chalatenango: From *Tierra Olvidada* to Conflict Zone

[Chalatenango] with its thin soils, de-forested, misused, exhausted, and eroded, its primitive agriculture unassisted by capital investment or modern supervision, and its social cohesion weakened by economic decline, dispersal of settlement, and migration, gradually became the country's poor, backward, and neglected tierra olvidada *[forgotten land] of the present century.*

—La Prensa Grafica, November 23, 1965

Chalatenango is of no value to the nation.

—*Director, Programa de Desarrollo Humano*
Sostenible Chalatenango, December 1997

The department of Chalatenango, located in northeast El Salvador, is a rural, mountainous region, historically a frontier land and one of the nation's most marginalized departments. By the late 1970s, the new teachings of liberation theology were spreading throughout the region. This consciousness-raising project contributed to a radicalized peasantry and the "reawakening" of popular movements organized around land rights, increasing wages, and access to education and health care. These movements were met with increasingly violent repression, and in the early 1980s, the military and paramilitary instigated a regime of terror. The department became a key conflict zone and a strong site of oppositional mobilizing. As a result of the twelve-year civil war (1980–1992), which claimed the lives of 80,000 people, left 8,000 "disappeared," and displaced one million of El Salvador's five million people,[9] most community residents in Chalatenango were forced to flee their homes. Many joined guerrilla forces and formed a militant revolutionary movement; others became internally displaced. But most civilians crossed the border into Honduras and lived in refugee camps for varying amounts of time. Scholars, development practitioners, and activists have documented this phase of the war and tracked the historic repatriation that began in 1987, as refugees mobilized to return to their place of origin while the war was still ongoing (see Elisabeth J. Wood's chapter).

With the signing of the United Nations–brokered Peace Accords on January 16, 1992, between the Salvadoran government and the Farabundo Martí National Liberation Front (FMLN), the war officially ended. El Salvador's internationally recognized "negotiated revolution" marked a historic transition to peace that focused on opening up the political system, creating a representative democracy, reducing the armed forces, strengthening the judicial system, and reforming the electoral process.[10] For war-torn areas such as Chalatenango, the government's five year (1992–1997) national reconstruction plan to oversee the challenges of massive rebuilding and a land-transfer program (Programa de Transferencia de Tierras, PTT) for ex-combatants and their supporters have been important though contested initiatives.[11] Additionally, in Chalatenango, internationally sponsored relief and emergency assistance shifted to the rebuilding of communities, in some cases attempting to incorporate women's needs. Yet, according to a high-level overseer of Salvadoran reconstruction efforts from the U.S. Agency for International Development (USAID), neither the state nor international donors offered a well-thought-out postwar development plan[12] nor was there a cogent gender perspective.[13] Today, these *repoblaciones* have been resettled for more than a decade, and residents have shifted from wartime organizing to peaceful rebuilding within a complicated postwar context where the root causes of the war—political and economic power inequalities—have not been resolved. Most Salvadorans still lack access to resources, political participation, and social services; many of them problematize the meaning of peace and the quality of democracy.[14]

Building Peace: Grassroots Chalatenango

For many Chalatecos and people working in Chalatenango, "history" is the recent past; it begins with the civil war and is called on to inform present-day reconstruction efforts. Rene Morales, director of Chalatenango's UN funded Sustainable Human Development Program (Programa de Desarrollo Humano Sostenible, PDHS), frames current development efforts in the history of war. He explains, "One has to begin with a society in crisis and in various levels of crisis."[15] For Morales, the key postwar challenge is to unite what he terms the "two maps of Chalatenango": a southern Chalatenango emerging from a *low-intensity* war that was characterized by continuous government and institutional presence with a northern Chalatenango, site of a *high-intensity war* with ten municipalities abandoned, entire communities destroyed, and the birth of alternative popular organizing structures. The challenge is to address the *doble institucionalidad* (double institutionality) to coordinate the legacy of these alternative community structures with the post-1994 election return of municipal government bodies. My study focuses on residents of northern Chalatenango who negotiate this *doble institucionalidad* in their everyday lives: one *repoblación,* a grassroots group, and an NGO.

El Rancho

In El Rancho, a large village in the municipality of Las Vueltas, the legacies of the war are layered.[16] Early postwar reconstruction addressed infrastructure needs: repairing destroyed homes through projects that brought in new cement-block houses, reestablishing and expanding schools, rebuilding churches, and paving roads. Early national and international funding was invested in urbanizing the municipal core of Las Vueltas. The *alcaldía* (city hall—with its now twice-elected FMLN mayor) was rebuilt, a telephone station erected to facilitate communication, a Ministry of Health clinic staffed, a rehabilitation center instituted, and electricity installed, starting from Las Vueltas and trickling to the surrounding villages.

Along with a slowly moving land-transfer program, a local development plan emphasized gendering reconstruction by implementing women's projects such as chicken and pig farming, cattle raising, arts and crafts, sewing workshops, and day-care centers that would enable women to work. These efforts were intended to incorporate former combatants, injured war veterans, and women (many of whom lost their male kin during the war through death, separation, or abandonment) into the productive economy and the development process. As the transition from war to peace continued, early optimism gave way to the daily challenges and struggles of rebuilding.

In El Rancho, development "failures" have cast the *repoblación* as a "special" community *(una comunidad especial)*, meaning a difficult community to work with, as a representative of Plan Internacional explained.[17] This assessment of El Rancho is not unique, for El Rancho is a community mapped out and critiqued by many actors, from community residents themselves to grassroots groups, political NGOs, and other development institutions working in the region. During the course of my fieldwork in El Rancho (1993–1997), the physical improvements were striking, yet the community experienced some trying times. Various actors told me that the popular organizing that characterized the war was in "crisis." Community structures like the community council *(directiva)* were unraveling, coveted "sister city" status was never achieved,[18] and the women's projects placed in Chalatenango as vehicles for development had in almost all cases collapsed. Even the women's center—intended to serve and unite the region's women through regular meetings aimed at discussing women's issues and continuing with a long-term consciousness-raising project—was unused, closed, and covered with bat feces. Only the arts and crafts workshop still operated, providing erratic employment for six marginalized women, as orders for Salvadoran arts and crafts in the international solidarity market were decreasing during my fieldwork in 1996. A grassroots needs-assessment conducted in 1996 listed a series of necessities for the region. Lack of organization *(falta de organización)* ranked as a top problem.[19]

The CCR

The CCR was established in 1988 and grew out of a national repatriation movement organized by the Christian Committee for the Displaced (CRIPDES). With the transition to peace, CCR—initially named Coordinator of Repopulated Communities (Coordinadora de Comunidades de Repoblaciones)—refocused and renamed itself Coordinator of Communities in Development of Chalatenango (Coordinadora de Comunidades en Desarrollo Chalatenango). It continues to be composed solely of residents from *repoblaciones.* In 1997 the organization reported serving 30,000 people in thirteen municipalities and claimed fifty-two community councils. CCR concentrates on promoting community organization in order to contribute to economic, political, and social development. It does so by establishing community councils, democratically elected community governing bodies.[20] Importantly, these councils charter communities, allowing them to propose community-based development projects and garner funds. The sections that follow build from ethnographic research on one branch of CCR, the Secretaría de la Mujer (Women's Secretariat), and its attempts to address community issues from a woman-centered perspective that privileges a transformative gender mission through organizational work, trainings, and projects. Throughout, CCR is theorized as a grassroots group that operates under certain constraints, frameworks, ideologies, and histories. The ethnographic section documents a grassroots meeting attended by women who were recruited from CCR's constituency.

CORDES

While CCR operates on exceedingly scarce resources, its focus on social and political organization is structurally complemented by its well-funded sister institution CORDES, which focuses on economic development issues.[21] CORDES presents itself as very much a grassroots, politically engaged NGO (associated with the Popular Forces of Liberation, Fuerzas Populares de la Liberación, FPL).[22] CCR is hierarchically related to it in everyday practices. CORDES's pursuit of "participatory development and community self-sufficiency" follows from the foundation's general objective to "promote communities' self-sufficient agricultural development in order to contribute to the construction of an alternative socioeconomic project for the nation."[23]

CORDES has successfully made the transition from wartime oppositional organizing to well-funded international reconstruction and development. Regionally, it attempts to create programs and practices that build from a history of opposition and are palatable to funders. As one of its directors explains, CORDES's role is to translate a community's needs into a language that funding agencies want to hear. Although most of CORDES staff in Chalatenango are not originally from *repoblaciones* nor do they live there presently, most are Salvadoran FPL members (as are most residents of the region they serve), and they have a long history with the popular movement and with wartime survivors now living in the area. Like CCR staff, they share with community residents a history of violence, loss, struggle, survival, and witness. For example, one of CORDES's directors, Daysi, is a vital presence who powerfully exemplifies how some of the problematic practices of NGOs are often overcome by history. Organizations like

CORDES have meaning beyond the development work they do. Narratives depicting Daysi's wartime capture, torture, and survival circulate throughout the region and validate CORDES's efforts. As a result, CORDES, one of the first NGOs in Chalatenango, remains one of its most progressive, politically committed organizations and wields considerable social capital in the region.

La Problematica de la Mujer

In November 1997, fifty women "community leaders and representatives" (organized under CCR) participated in a two-day CORDES needs-assessment workshop designed to identify, evaluate, and address local development, most specifically to repair the crises in women's lives—*la problematica de la mujer.* At this meeting, the women, ranging in age from twenty to fifty-five, were called on to represent women from their respective communities and their "problems." Daysi, CORDES's regional executive director, led the workshop.[24] The three women from the "gender and training team" assisted, as did Carlos, the director of CORDES's credit program, run entirely by men.

This event would be an inclusive, integrated, bottom-up analysis, reaching from the home, community, municipality, and department, and covering the economic, political, and social realities of women's lives, a rather large task for a two-day meeting that ultimately served to plan CCR and CORDES' gender strategy for the following fiscal year. Throughout the event, Daysi negotiated a difficult position of authority easily and well. She spoke from a position of common history, invoking the language of "us" *(nosotras)* and the informal you *(vos),* a marker of intimacy, equality, and solidarity, that women rarely use at present.

The meeting began by all being asked to write down on index cards as many "women's problems" as they could think of. Daysi then read each card aloud, taping some on the wall, discarding others, redirecting some, and debating the meanings of many. After a few hours, with index cards covering an entire wall, women's multiple realities had been constructed in terms of "problems" that could be intervened in either through technology or ideology. These problems included illiteracy, domestic violence, crime within communities, and lack of employment opportunities, women's projects, and credit for women. Not surprisingly, poverty came up again and again in the index cards. But this problem was translated in a particular way that elided women's economic disempowerment through a discourse on the lack of "communal values" and "organization" that structured the remainder of the workshop. A deficit model, rather than one emphasizing assets, guided the session.

Importantly, Daysi qualified the role of NGOs for the participants as providing a way to negotiate present-day injustices. While NGOs are spaces validated by international donors, she eloquently voiced NGO's limitations, saying that, indeed, they should not have to exist. "We exist because the state marginalizes. We exist to support the people. We are not going to solve the problem of potable water, of orphaned children. That is a lie. NGOs cannot resolve the economic problems of all women in communities." With this statement, Daisy both validated and refuted growing complaints from residents that situated blame in local terms and on local institutions, organizations, and actors. However, her statement was followed by the familiar slippage into organizing rhetoric: "until one day when we get power, and then we will see what we can do in the face of this terrible globalization."

As the workshop continued, "the problem" was translated into a language of crisis and blame was placed on "women," "community," "values," "organization," and the combination of these. Indeed, Daysi, too, places blame locally. For example, Daysi, supported by her staff, shifted the discussion to analyzing why already existing CORDES women's projects do not work. She suggested that the (donated) projects are not appropriated by women. Carlos added that it was a problem of organization. Rosario from the gender and training team opined that it was in fact also a problem of dependence on external assistance, *asistencialismo*, where women (and men) only like to receive aide.

Isabel, an elderly resident of one of the repopulated communities, challenged this perspective. She offered that the projects do not work because they create difference, they cannot empower all women, and this breeds envy and individualism rather than community. But Isabel's perspective was silenced as Daysi launched into a discourse on "history." She began, "Now remember. We are going to review a little bit of history [*Recuerden Uds. Vamos hacer un poquito de historia*]. When this war started, right, remember, remember how we survived? What did we do back then? We were united. We had those Sundays, those Farabundista days. Together we would all work the *milpas* and the *frijolares*. The war united us. And the formula was: All owners, all responsible [*dueños todos responsables todos*]. That's how it was."

Her call for women to remember their lived history, rooting it in a shared moment, continued as she walked the women through the second phase of the war, where she collapsed life in refugee camps with repatriation to devastated communities. She focused on one element of these varied experiences, the strength of the "communal spirit." Interestingly, she located the crisis in community organizing in the peace process, in the third phase, the cease-fire. She stated, "In this phase came land transference. But we are still struggling over which piece of land belongs to whom. So this brought on a crisis in communal projects. Who are the owners? Everybody *compañeras,* we are all the owners [*todos compañeras, todos somos dueños*]."

She ended her story in the present, by critiquing women en masse for losing this spirit. The fifty women representatives came to stand for all women, decontextualized, nameless, unspecified. Daysi provided an example of how in one community no one helped two old women working in a communal store—a CORDES project. She asked, "So, when have you"—and here she used the formal "you," *usted,* shifting away from intimacy—"gone to help those poor old women carry their heavy loads? Never!" She explained that the ideology has become "What can I take, not what can I give?" Yet in her narrative she did not address the way in which the war destroyed families and erased the household social and economic unit, nor how this created present-day socialization challenges for a generation of wartime survivors negotiating their own and their children's transition. Daysi concluded by articulating for the women the key problems: loss of community practices and ideology. She linked this to how "the community needs to rethink itself, to see what it should do, should be. How it will organize." This was an attempt to harness old strategies, successful strategies from a very different context, for use in a new terrain where the Left has no cogent answer.

By the end of the day, the "women's problem" had been defined as "we, as a community, are not clear about our future," with the root cause being "poor community organizing." Through various twists and turns, women agreed with the analysis that the current crisis in community, in women, stems from the loss of values learned during the war. This was evidenced through one of the key terms to emerge from the workshop—*organization*. One of the term's many meanings is well-run development projects, where *development* is defined as the repayment of small-scale loans; but *organization* also invokes revolutionary ideals, a cause, a common history of struggle. It is a claim of identity rooted in everyday practices. However, in the postwar context the call to organize rings hollow at a time when socioeconomic differences are increasing. As scholarship across Latin America suggests, "democracies may be in the process of political consolidation, but they also show signs of their inability to meet basic social demands such as civil and economic rights." Chalateco citizens are stuck between lowered expectations for the state and higher expectations for rights.[25]

In a recent study, Leigh Binford shows how a fundamental FMLN model centered on participative democracy and self-management, how involvement and participation reflected an "acceptance of more responsibility for one's situation and an active effort to confront and resolve difficulties rather than lament them."[26] Daysi's workshop, which focused on community organization and participation and how they have become "lost" (evidenced by the failures of women's projects), was grounded in this expectation of "involvement." But calling for "organization" is a contradictory endeavor. It asks generations of marginalized women and men to reeducate themselves to become successful small-scale entrepreneurs and repay their loans, yet it critiques community members for losing their "revolutionary" ideology and practices, as evidenced by their lack of mobilization. The solution to economic injustice falls on the backs of the very poor, on women, who become the embodiment of what is lacking. Economic restructuring or empowerment, key to the struggle, is elided, erased as a proscriptive to the lives of community members. Instead, the extreme poverty, sacrifice, and unity of the wartime period is held up as the model replacing a struggle against economic marginalization. Thus, NGO assertions idealize and homogenize a revolutionary past, mask difference, and mystify the challenges of reconstruction.

Addressing the Postwar Call to Remember

In Chalatenango, I spent considerable time participating in the ebb and flow of women's activism, tagging along and listening to women's stories about the past, the present, and their occasional hopes and frequent worries for the future. Indeed, Chalateco survivors negotiate the contradictions of peace building by actively turning to their memories of the recent past, to their lived history of mobilizing, sacrifice, and loss. They seek to remember the past as a time of heroic participation, a triumphant though suffered-through period in which Chalatecos were oppositional *luchadores,* armed and political fighters creating community. The recent past is called on selectively and politically to build a community and a postwar citizenry that still struggles. However, this meta-narrative is often contested in a variety of community spaces as many residents place the survival of their household economy over community politics. In the following two sections, stories from three women who are positioned differently in El Rancho illustrate the ways in which a politics of memory confront NGO and grassroots politics of development that gender community problems.

In El Rancho, a short-lived women's group was initiated outside of both CCR and CORDES; it named itself "Grupo de Animación" (animation group).[27] Thirty-year-old Chayo, one of the eight participants, explained that the group's objective was to "animate [*ánimar*] all the women who are depressed in order for them to defend themselves and meet their basic needs." For this group, *ánimo* was synonymous with "development," and indeed Chayo explained that the motivation for forming the group derived from the many failed development projects in El Rancho. She also complicated the discussion of development by referring to it as both a communal social project and an inherently personal one. During an interview conducted in October 1997 she discussed development issues: "To me, the meaning of development involves personal development, to have the time to devote oneself to both the family and the community." She emphasized the importance of incorporating women in community life: "I wish that all women were active in some kind of work so that they might feel alive and not feel isolated and alone, full of shyness. I want them to have personal development and participate in the different community activities. That is what I desire."

Although Chayo made the connection between development and community organizing, her analysis of the past provides an alternative reading to Daysi's uniform rendering of "community organization." For Chayo, the past holds both the glories of unity and the legacy of its deceit. Her depiction of the early organizing of the struggle is one of broken promises and bankrupt dreams. Her story is one of deception, lies, and loss, as she explained, "When we first started organizing, they used to tell us, 'In twenty-four hours the country is going to be liberated,' . . . but you can see that war is quite painful and it's not an overnight matter. Many people have to struggle and die. . . . So that was a big lie, what they said about the country's liberation in twenty-four hours. And you can see it, the costs are too high to liberate a country. Right?"

From these founding "lies" at the root of organizing efforts, Chayo sees the seeds of present-day community disorganization, lack of mobilizing, and community-wide lack of faith in present-day efforts. She continued, "So I thought it was a deceit . . . and that is why since that time we have this great demoralization happening. Because you could say it's been a lie since then. So now you can tell people the nicest hopeful things to lift their spirits, but no one believes it at all."

Chayo is not alone in this perspective. Forty-nine-year-old Kasandra, an early and long-time participant in the movement, voiced the contradictions of the struggle by arguing that area residents were unable to take a neutral position during the war. She went further than Chayo and consciously and cautiously debunked a romantic vision of the Left. She did not deny the positive changes in postwar times but did not want to homogenize the past: "There have been a lot of things that have ruined us more. . . . There were hard times during the war, because not everything is pretty. The guerrillas were also quite cruel. It's the truth. If you didn't like me, or if you rubbed me the wrong way, I could say 'I don't like her because of this,' for whatever reason. I would go and tell a leader 'she is an enemy, a spy.' Entire battalions died, not just a group. . . . It was hard because the government's army was as cruel as the guerrilla forces."

As Philippe Bourgois poignantly shows, "the revolutionary movement in El Salvador was traumatized and distorted by the very violence it was organizing against. Through an almost mimetic process, the government's brutality was transposed into the guerillas' organizational structures and internal relations, as violence became a banal instrument of necessity."[28] Interestingly, Kasandra's critiques of the war took her to an analysis of community and its sense of unity. For her, unity as the basis for community was indeed rather characteristic of prewar social organization, kin relations, and everyday practices rather than a result or legacy of wartime organizing. This earlier sense of community characterized by strong kin ties is then broken by the war and its aftermath—the displacement of extended family, loss of kin, destruction of landscape, and an increasing socioeconomic differentiation within communities that leave many questioning their years of sacrifice. In the past, she says, "in the small communities we all lived as best we could. But we had more unity because back then when something happened to you, everybody came to help. Not now. People can see you dying and nobody does anything to help. . . . People were really united . . . before the war. If somebody was sick, everybody took turns and went to help."

Kasandra critiques wartime expectations of *unidad,* which she understands as equality. This is linked to her analysis of the distribution of postwar development at the local level and continued economic injustices. She compares her present concerns to the hopes she had when she joined the struggle: "I was so sincerely happy when they said that upon taking power we would achieve unity. What one person had, all would have. For example, if somebody ate *frijoles,* everybody would eat *frijoles.* If somebody ate meat, everybody would eat at least a little bit of the same. There was going to be unity. This is what the struggle was for, the search for unity."

Like Chayo, Kasandra engages in a discourse of deceit and is angered by lies and disillusioned by the aftermath of organizing for social justice. Kasandra and Chayo were not alone in remarking on present-day community differences. For many, this community difference could not be reconciled with a history of loss and sacrifice. And so Chayo continued, outraged by the "success" of some who did not "really" participate in the struggle: "What I don't like in these communities is that there is always this kind of preference, I'm going to call it that. So the people who have more possibilities are those who did not necessarily work hard during the armed struggle or in community organizing, those people have benefited most."

For Chayo, the unity characteristic of community organizing is different from both Daysi's and Kasandra's. Like Daysi, Chayo employs a discourse of community crisis located in the very emergence of postwar national reconciliation, but she focuses on the entrance of official, municipal government institutions—on the *doble institucionalidad* mentioned earlier. With the establishment of municipal government (although FMLN), community political structures are repositioned. This creates a new set of tensions as community councils struggle for autonomy and legitimacy within their communities and with official institutions. Chayo's visions of organization, community, and unity are mapped to wartime, they have a spatial component, and thus recent cartographic changes are seen as critical: "The community of El Rancho was united with the community of Las Vueltas. When we arrived they formed one single community. Then, after that Las Vueltas formed a sister-city project [with a foreign country], and that relationship continues to fund projects in Las Vueltas. And now El Rancho remains alone, becoming independent from Las Vueltas."

This landscape is marked by growing differences between municipal capitals and smaller, more rural villages. Unequal distribution of postwar benefits and resources aimed at rebuilding destroyed communities contributes to tense community-based politics: "And to top this, all the projects failed. Then El Rancho was left with nothing. All these things discouraged the women and men, seeing that, be it one thing or another, everything fails."

Ultimately, residents cannot forget, although Chayo hopes for new strategies and avenues to heal so that they lose the "culture" of war *(que se le vaya perdiendo el sistema de guerra)*. She reflects that, like so many of her neighbors, she will never forget such things as "how they killed our sons, that cannot be erased. What we have suffered in our own flesh. To walk and fall through those mountains. When you had to flee, pushed on by the bullets. These things one cannot erase. Some have even become wounded war veterans. This and other things makes one remember a lot. We cannot lose these traditions."

Fuí, Soy y Seguiré Siendo Revolucionaria

A final ethnographic example provides insight into the importance of context in understanding the logic of NGO-led development and responses to it, and complicates easy moral generalizations that label women as not revolutionary enough. For this I turn to Elsy, one of El Rancho's "women's leaders." In later postwar times, Elsy has shifted from survival to being able to engage in conspicuous forms of consumption for the first time in a long while. And so she buys rayon in Chalatenango to make pantsuits and purchases shoes with high heels and a purse to match, wearing flip-flops inside her home. She is no longer CCR's regional women's representative, nor does she hold community women's meeting or attend community council meetings. She "escapes" to San Salvador most weekends to be with her partner, who works in the new civilian police force and is now taking a college course. Also, Elsy is moody—*lunática,* her mother calls it.

Erratic, unpredictable behavior, unfocused anger, periods of depression, incessant complaining about all things—body pain, bad tortillas, and token social services. But this state of mind alternates with extreme highs and energized periods in which, for example, she tells stories that invoke her past participation in organizing for social justice.

Depending on context, Elsy constructs, frames, or positions herself differently, sometimes privileging her identity based on her history of strong grassroots activism, her face of *la mujer organizada* (organized woman). Over the course of five days, on three different occasions, Elsy narrated increasingly detailed versions of her "midwife *(partera)* story." Her first account was primarily factual. Elsy had participated in a ten-day midwife-training course offered by the Ministry of Health. The idea behind this workshop was to train women with past medical experience (that is, women with wartime experiences as nurses) to become local midwives. The course received no follow-up, and in many cases practicing midwives in rural communities were not invited to participate. But the project did affect Elsy in many ways. For weeks afterwards, she bought natural medicine pamphlets and began taking better care of her ill mother. Also, the workshop took over her imagination, as she repeatedly reflected on its contradictions, an example of the frustrated paths of her everyday life.

The second time Elsy talked about the workshop, she was attending to her youngest daughter's minor scrape. As asked, I passed her the first-aid kit distributed at the end of the sessions, and Elsy complained that the kit did not have the essentials, not even gloves. She explained that 31,000 *colones* (roughly US$3,560) had been budgeted for the training but that clearly not all of this money was spent on the workshop. Her analysis: "They ate the money [*se lo comieron*]." In this telling of the story she located the blame locally; it is not the sponsoring Ministry of Health she took issue with but the nurse Paty who led the sessions. Paty, who was not a participant in the revolutionary struggle, had denounced Elsy as a revolutionary because she contested the poor distribution and quality of supplies.

In her third recounting, Elsy embedded the midwife story within a series of other tales, the climax of a larger conversational exchange. Elsy had just participated in a heated community general assembly, called not by the community council but by CCR as an emergency intervention into community problems. Here, a CCR coordinator, Mardo, announced that the council had been defunct for over six months, and that a new one had to be elected. Residents were told that without a council they were going to suffer because, according to the CCR coordinator, "if you don't organize you will be a regular community, without projects." If they did not agree to hold elections and fill the vacant posts, they would be unable to propose and garner development projects. Thus, without a community council, they would be a dead community *(una comunidad muerta).* And because meaning has shifted spatially, the political landscape moving away from wartime zones of control that united communities, the CCR coordinator explained how the issue of organization and the election was a problem that El Rancho had to resolve on its own because other communities would not be affected in the least, and, indeed, El Rancho would be further marginalized. This was very much a chastising session, ending only by a sudden thunderstorm.

Perhaps it was the rain and the power outage, or perhaps the dark just lets people talk—whatever the explanation, Elsy launched into a series of stories. With an increasingly agitated yet forceful voice, she moved from critiquing how she had received nothing from the Peace Accords—no land, no credit, simply because of bureaucratic errors—to explaining why she had ceased participating in community decision making. She was outraged by accusations from neighbors that those on community councils, those who worked to represent the community, actually pocketed a substantial amount of incoming aid, they were, it was said, "eating the money" *(comiendo el pisto).* Elsy contested these claims saying that only once had she received a personal gift from a delegation. Interestingly, she was defending herself from the same accusation she had leveled at Paty, the midwife trainer.

In her narratives, Elsy engaged in a common postwar discourse of deceit, an analysis of corruption that local people make, theories for understanding their frustrated dreams (see Lisa Kowalchuk's chapter). The term *engaño* (deceit), as illustrated in the preceding section, is frequently used to explain a range of betrayals and injustices. How else were people to make sense of the growing stratification within and between communities, among people whom local history constructs as arriving from refugee camps equal (meaning, *equally poor*), *todos pelados* (all naked). Elsy's stories, like Chayo's and Kasandra's, suggest that decreasing participation, withdrawal from positions of power (like the community council), and challenges to authority may be indicative of people's emerging resistance efforts, claims of solidarity, and the collective over the individual at odds with postwar differentiation that NGOs are often forced into.

After asserting her own incorruptibility, Elsy said that those who were truly corrupt were the NGOs working in Chalatenango. In making this assertion, she lumped together organizations with a generally recognized track record of commitment to supporting popular organizing and local development efforts with more recent arrivals. Elsy claimed that the problem stemmed from international donors' actually believing that Salvadoran organizations serve people like herself. Moreover, she questioned the fairness of equating NGOs' extension of credit with development—that is, NGOs who receive money as donations turning around and charging folks like herself, a practice that from her perspective was an example of NGOs skimming from projects (other examples were NGOs' new cars, new offices, and new staff). Then she made a powerful connection, linking present development, with its contradictions, to the past, to the international solidarity movement active during the war. She explained how it was the same when internationalists arrived and sought out the most malnourished, orphaned, and injured children, took their pictures, and with these raised money in their home countries for the struggle. And those poor children received not a cent for the photographs and did not benefit from the resulting donations. Indeed, in El Rancho such a "poster-child" lives up the hill from Elsy. The "Save the Children" print, yellowing and torn around the edges, still hangs from the façade of the girl's house.

Our conversation ended as Elsy returned to the issue of the workshop, her voice becoming more agitated, louder, stronger, her speech faster. In this version, she presented herself as a leader, combating Paty the trainer, whom Elsy described as the only one who benefited from this kind of exercise, building her career by climbing upon the backs of women like herself, "like a ladder to success [*como una escalera para hartarse*]." This time, Elsy moved from criticizing the useless first-aid kits to talking about the cloth women received to make uniforms for themselves. All of this was a pittance compared with the 31,000 *colones* budgeted. Elsy began by saying how they had all seen the three rolls of cloth in Paty's truck, but how Paty had only brought in one roll to distribute. The trainer announced that the "fat women" *(las gordas)* would receive four yards of cloth and the "thin women" *(las pechitas)* would receive three yards.

In her story, Elsy said she turned to the women and asked if they would support her in contesting this injustice. Again invoking the 31,000 *colones,* the poor supplies, the lack of remuneration, unlike the previous year's participants, Elsy challenged Paty as she argued for at least equal amounts of cloth, regardless of size, saying, "*todas gastamos y perdimos el mismo tiempo* [we all spent and wasted the same amount of time]." Elsy laughed when telling me about Paty's fury, her exclaiming, "But you are revolutionary; you have to conform [*Pero usted es revolucionaria, se tiene que poner conforme*]." At which point Elsy reclaimed her revolutionary identity by saying, "I was, am, and will continue to be a revolutionary [*Fui, soy y seguiré siendo revolucionaria*]," and added that in fact people should not conform but rather *know* their rights. Elsy ended by saying that all the participants received four yards of cloth.

This moment of "victory" for Elsy captures the many contradictions and irritations of postwar processes where former revolutionaries redefine and reclaim their past, the weight of their history with consumption practices. Did she wear a cloak of revolution to legitimize individual consumption? Do sites and practices of consumption, as some argue, create new ways of thinking and produce a sense of belonging that grounds cultural citizenship?[29] Interestingly, Elsy invokes the history of revolutionary organizing in very much the same way Daysi does. She explained how she had mobilized the other participants by saying, "We who have organized to struggle against injustices, let's now organize for this, which is not even shit."

Organizing *La Gente* (the People) versus *La Comunidad* (the Community)

This chapter has detailed some of the contradictions of grassroots participation. CORDES's evaluation session, Chayo and Kasandra's theories of reconstruction, and Elsy's narratives of development injustices exemplify how survivors of El Salvador's protracted civil war have struggled against a series of postwar development processes. These processes converge on rural people's consciousness, on their "dependency" on external assistance, on their problematic organizational abilities as residents are told that they must reorganize, reanimate, and remember the past. Today, wartime social relations, activism, and survival are held up as the model and voiced as the ideal for community life. But an important question remains: How much community participation can be asked of people who experienced the wartime sacrifice of home, family, community, and lives?

In Chalatenango, the search for alternative models of development to combat neoliberal government policies is grounded in the revolutionary social movement of the recent past, a history of self-government and oppositional organization for survival and social change. Early studies of grassroots efforts document the foundation of present-day discourse and practice. Scholars discuss the repatriation movement by emphasizing that the most important economic gain was a shift from dependency to autonomy.[30] In postwar practices this expectation has not been met, and moving beyond a subsistence economy remains a driving force for communities. In order to meet this goal, "organization" remains a key focus in everyday life across social fields. Indeed, concern for organization, unity, and survival are seen as characteristic of *repoblaciones,* a marker of identity and the basis of success.[31] Recent work continues to depict *repoblaciones* in terms of the power of community organization, linking this material, moral, and spiritual discourse to survival. Some scholars focus on *sobrevivencia,* on survival and surviving, emphasizing people's alternative models in pursuit of social justice. In these accounts Chalatecos view organization as crucial to wartime survival, "Our organization was nothing more than obedience to the organized people. If it hadn't been like that, we would all have died."[32] They link survival with organization (as discipline). Hope for the future is rooted in wartime agency.[33] How else to overcome Chalatenango's many physical, geographic, and economic obstacles?

Indeed, renowned Salvadoran novelist, poet, and essayist Manlio Argueta introduces a recent text on two *repoblaciones* in Chalatenango. He writes, "Their life, on the other hand, continues like it always has, though perhaps now with more clarity about their rights and hopes. 'Something will change someday,' they say. They have become enriched with the experiences and values of the spirit of survival, which has its antecedents in the past century and is part of the motivation of those that were never defeated, . . . and they continue being the foundation of national identity."[34]

In this passage he collapses Chalateco history into a mythic, continuous past of marginalization, poverty, survival, and consciousness raising that ultimately romanticizes *campesinos*. The research presented here complicates these more hopeful accounts of people's past struggles and cautions against overly celebrating the power of community and women's resilience in the face of adversity. As Bourgois poignantly remarks, "People do not simply 'survive' violence as if it somehow remained outside of them, and they are rarely if ever ennobled by it. Those who confront violence with resistance—whether it be cultural or political—do not escape unscathed from the terror and oppression they rose up against. The challenge of ethnography, then, is to check the impulse to sanitize and instead to clarify the chains of causality that link structural, political, and symbolic violence in the production of an everyday violence that buttresses unequal power relations and distorts efforts at resistance."[35]

This chapter heeds this call through its study of community and organization. Whether invoking the war (Daysi) or prewar social organization (Kasandra), community organizing continues to be locally valued. Community status, along with women's status, is linked to the "success" of active organizing. More recent NGOs (many nonpolitical) and other government-funded development foundations have appropriated this discourse of organizing in the name of local development. Thus, they too help contribute to create Chalatecos as not revolutionary enough despite their history of revolutionary organizing. In a variety of contexts these organizations employ a discourse similar to that of CCR and CORDES, one that chastises the resident beneficiaries of their development efforts. For example, the director of the foundation Prochalate grants Chalatecos a degree of agency while also pointing to what he sees as a characteristic flaw—their sense of indemnification born from suffering: "Only the Chalatecos will resolve their problems. We can only present our suggestions, and the people will have to accept them in the best way. . . . The residents expect a prize for having survived the civil war."[36]

A representative of another organization, Plan Internacional, follows with a similar critique, invoking a language of "relief mentality" and revolutionary ideology: "Bringing infrastructure projects to these communities is very difficult because they want everything paid for." And he laments that, "You can't get rid of these ideological positions. They are already in the game."[37] A representative of another internationally funded group working in Las Vueltas describes the NGO's position of accompaniment by analyzing the challenges to his work in the present: "They [the people] are tired, . . . and they've started to fall asleep. It has happened in all places. The grassroots has lost respect for their leaders."[38]

Interestingly, these positions are similar to that espoused by one of the national women's directors of CRIPDES; she has a long history of revolutionary mobilizing and works closely with CCR's Women's Secretariat. Irma explains that "the long process of the organizational struggle has fallen, . . . and values have been lost."[39] While she understands the decreasing activism of postwar times, she places her hopes in the fact that the communities remain united, as they are composed entirely of FMLN supporters.

In Chalatenango, NGO-led development has marked postwar reconstruction. It has been attractive to institutions like the World Bank and USAID and to critics of hegemonic development practices. As in many parts of the world NGOs negotiate neoliberal desires on the one hand, and oppositional struggles that seek to politicize what development depoliticizes on the other. Scholarship in El Salvador indeed posits that sustainable development initiated by NGOs can challenge globalization.[40] In general, analyses of NGOs typically are concerned with the relationship between them and civil society, social movements, democratization, and alternative discourses and models of development; key terms include participation, empowerment, local, and community.[41] With their focus on long-term political effects rather than economic material benefits, NGOs are touted for strengthening, fostering, and promoting civil society. But as the romance with NGO-led development diminishes, they are critiqued for undermining social movements and masking the power relationships between donors and recipients.[42] This chapter has explored these relationships ethnographically through the lens of NGOs' intended beneficiaries: civil society. This is critical because in postwar times civil society groups—including women's groups, environmental groups, and community groups—have come to be seen as key building blocks for national reconciliation and for El Salvador's successful transition to democracy.

Lisa Kowalchuk

The Salvadoran Land Struggle in the 1990s

Cohesion, Commitment, and Corruption

If Salvadorans needed reminding that neither the 1980 Agrarian Reform nor the 1992 Peace Accords had resolved the problem of land hunger, they received it in the latter half of 1995 when events forced this problem to the surface of public consciousness. On October 23, 1995, over 1,100 landless and land-poor peasants—armed with cooking utensils, a few days' supply of corn and beans, plastic sheeting for temporary *champas* (huts), and copies of the Constitution— walked onto sixty-four agricultural properties, including seventeen coffee estates, in the western and central regions of the country. The peasants told private security guards and police that their actions were legitimated by Article 105 of the Constitution, which established an upper limit of 245 hectares on private agricultural land holdings. Since the Salvadoran government had failed to enforce this limit, the peasants claimed that their property "interventions" were a way of helping the government to fulfill its obligations.

In this chapter I analyze the local-level commitment to, and participation in, this renewed struggle for land reform in El Salvador in order to illuminate the effects of several structural, historical, and ideological factors on grassroots participation in the struggle. Three important factors in this regard are preexisting social networks, access to key resources, and ideological commitment to social movement struggle. Political ideology, in turn, has its roots in the peasants' civil war linkages with two influential agents for social change: the progressive Catholic Church and the Farabundo Martí National Liberation Front (FMLN).

I analyze the impact of these factors by examining four groups of movement participants that vary in members' commitment to the movement organizations, their participation in movement activities and in other civic and political affairs, and their longevity. They also differed in their vulnerability to destructive forces that preyed on rural poverty and illiteracy. One such destructive force that emerged around the land struggle was rural con men who used the peasant associations' ongoing efforts to organize new members for their own material gain. These petty criminals tended to target groups deficient in internal networks, resources, or ideological commitment to popular struggle. This kind of corruption ultimately destroyed two of the groups analyzed here.

The research for this study took place from September 1995 to August 1997. I conducted seventy-one semi-structured interviews with grassroots members of the base groups and observed social interactions in the communities where members of two groups resided. In a third group, I observed life in a protest encampment. In addition, I observed several dozen national, regional, and local meetings of the peasant organizations, and analyzed documents, news articles, and movement-generated materials of various sorts. I also interviewed a number of peasant leaders at the national level.

Historical Background

The 1990s land struggle was rooted in the 1980 Agrarian Reform. Under the first phase of the reform, the governing civilian-military junta expropriated agricultural properties larger than 500 hectares and transferred the land to the full-time employees on the estates. The state organized these beneficiaries into cooperatives, creating approximately 320 cooperatives comprising 38,000 individual members. In the third phase of the reform renters of small plots averaging 2 hectares each became individual owners. This group comprised 47,000 peasants, known as *finateros* in reference to the state agency that administered this component of the Agrarian Reform, the National Financial Institute for Agricultural Lands (Financiera de Tierras Agricolas, FINATA).

The second phase of the Reform, which would have expropriated and transferred holdings between 100 and 500 hectares, was blocked by the coffee oligarchy. Instead, the Constitution was amended in 1983 to establish a limit of 245 hectares (about 605 acres) on agricultural properties that could be owned by any individual. The amendment gave landowners three years to sell or otherwise transfer acreage in excess of the new, higher ceiling to small farmers. After this period of grace, the government was to expropriate surplus lands, or *excedentes* as they came to be called, and transfer them to landless and land-poor peasants.

Throughout the duration of the civil war, however, landowners either ignored the 245 hectare limit or found licit and illicit ways to circumvent it, the latter including transferring *excedentes* in name only. Successive governments under the Christian Democratic Party and later the National Republican Alliance (ARENA) made no move to enforce the Constitutional limit.

In 1994, the Democratic Peasant Alliance (Alianza Democrática Campesina, ADC), a coalition of over twenty peasant organizations, alleged that more than 300 properties exceeded 245 hectares. At the same time, land hunger remained a persistent dilemma for the majority of the farming population. At the end of the civil war, 52 percent of the population employed in agriculture was landless, a drop of only 8 percent relative to the pre-1980 agrarian structure.[1] The landless and land poor together made up 83 percent of the farming population.[2] Furthermore, this small improvement in landlessness had been offset by a troubling increase in the proportion of tenant farmers, from 27 percent of the rural population in 1971 to 38 percent two decades later.[3] The situation of farmers who rent land is precarious because they have access to less land on average than nontenants, and they are less likely to invest in productive improvements.[4]

The 1992 Peace Accords generated another major land reform in El Salvador, known as the Land Transfer Program (Programa de Transferencia de Tierras, PTT). The PTT provided land to demobilized government soldiers and members of the FMLN, as well as a smaller category of noncombatant supporters of the insurgents who had resided in conflict zones during the civil war—40,000 families in all. But the capacity of this program to reduce rural poverty is hampered by the beneficiaries' inadequate access to credit and minimal knowledge of farming techniques as well as the high prices for and marginal quality of the land transferred through the program. Given these problems, Salvadoran economist Pedro Juan Hernández referred to the PTT in 1995 as a program of "reinsertion into poverty."[5] Writing at the time the PTT was nearly complete, Paige observed that "Agrarian tensions in El Salvador have not diminished at all, despite declining birthrates, rural migration to cities, and land reform."[6] Indeed, recent research reveals a trend toward a reconcentration of land ownership in the 1990s.[7]

The persistence of rural poverty and inequality, and the fact that the government's obligations concerning the 245 hectare limit were reiterated in the Peace Accords, prompted a reactivation of the demand for land reform. In 1994 the ADC called on the government to create a joint commission to further investigate and expropriate properties with *excedentes*. The government finally consented, but the investigative commission, which began work in January 1995, collapsed in May when the Salvadoran Institute for Agrarian Transformation (ISTA) unilaterally dismissed findings that revealed surplus acreage on twenty-seven properties.

By mid-October, ADC leaders felt they had exhausted the *vía de negociación* (negotiation path) in their efforts to persuade ISTA to reconsider these properties. The land invasions began on October 23. Dialogue between ISTA and the ADC quickly resumed thanks largely to mediation by the FMLN and the UN observer mission, whose role was to oversee and ensure the implementation of the Peace Accords. Most peasants willingly left the properties as a show of faith in the renewed talks, with few incidents of repression. The peasants then set up encampments in nearby public thoroughfares and remained there until the property investigation resumed in late December of 1995.

The peasants who carried out the land invasions were members of six organizations of landless and land-poor peasants that belonged to the ADC. The oldest and largest of these was the National Association of Agricultural Workers (Asociación Nacional de Trabajadores del Campo, ANTA). Created in 1986, ANTA claimed 11,000 members in 1997. Like the other organizations involved in the land struggle, ANTA owed its formation to the logistical and financial support of the FMLN during the civil war. An additional organization pursuing the *excedentes,* with a membership of 6,000, was the Association of Agricultural Workers of El Salvador (Asociación de Trabajadores Agropecuarios de El Salvador, ATAES). ATAES helped to create the ADC in 1989 but left the coalition in 1995, when its secretary general, Guillermo Sánchez, was expelled for misusing donated funds while heading the ADC's sustainability committee. From that point, ATAES became an open enemy of the ADC. Although ATAES took part in a series of land invasions coordinated by the ADC in 1991, Sánchez claimed he was now opposed to this tactic on the grounds that it would "destabilize the peace process."[8] Sánchez did, however, participate in the land investigation commission.

Protest, lobbying, and media campaign work around the *excedentes* declined sharply with the reactivation of the property investigation in 1996. ADC leaders' efforts to pressure the government were directed primarily through UN Offices for Verification, which relayed information on progress in the Peace Accords to higher UN officials. Nonetheless, the ADC organizations continued to prepare their members to receive land; for example, ANTA provided information to local membership groups on how to attain legal status as agricultural cooperatives, and provided educational workshops on cooperative management and other economic, social, and political topics. It even organized and affiliated new landless and land-poor peasants for the *excedentes* struggle. ATAES also recruited new members during this period.

Four Grassroots Groups

Within the peasant associations involved in the land struggle, the grassroots participants were organized in *grupos de base* (base groups).[9] The majority of the members of most base groups lived within two to three miles of one another. Those who lived further away were typically relatives or close friends of members in the residential core of the group. In most of the organizations, the base groups were in the process of seeking official registration as agricultural cooperatives or had already achieved this status. The peasant associations adopted the cooperative as a membership structure to facilitate the transfer of land on a collective basis.

La Victoria

One of the most cohesive and participatory base groups in the land struggle was the ANTA cooperative La Victoria. This cooperative had forty registered members and approximately fifty *aspirantes*—people who were waiting to be added to the official membership list. A core group of about twenty members and their families resided in the same *caserío* (hamlet) near Lake Coatepeque, in the village of Santo Tomás. I interviewed seventeen of these members and spent about a month in the hamlet. Most of the other members lived in the cantón. Many La Victoria members had lived in this cantón for generations. Some could name ancestors who had been cheated out of their modest land holdings by the forebears of El Salvador's wealthiest families, who were said to have owned most of the land in the Department of Santa Ana before the Agrarian Reform. Their knowledge of the area helped them to identify a nearby coffee estate that exceeded 245 hectares, which they targeted during the land invasions.

The twenty residentially concentrated members of La Victoria constituted the core of the cooperative in another sense: they held the leadership positions and took on the day-to-day tasks that came with being involved in the land struggle. These included legalizing the cooperative, visiting ISTA to inquire about the status of the property that the cooperative was demanding, and investigating alternative properties.

This core group of activists in the La Victoria cooperative stood out from most other ANTA base groups in its level of participation in ANTA activities. For example, ANTA held biweekly departmental meetings for its base groups to update the affiliates on the land investigation process, to inform the members on a range of other ANTA activities, and to provide a forum for different base groups to communicate with one another. Whereas other base groups often failed to send anyone to these meetings, La Victoria representatives always attended. They also took part in ADC protest marches to demand the cancellation of land and bank debts that beneficiaries of previous land reforms owed to the state. Though many La Victoria members had benefited from the third phase of the Agrarian Reform, few had outstanding debts. Their participation in these marches was an act of solidarity with the broader peasant movement. Several members of La Victoria even helped other residents of the village to organize a base group and affiliate with ANTA. They attended this new group's early meetings to bolster the efforts of the ANTA promoter, and between meetings they talked to the members about their own experience with organized struggle.

La Joya del Lago

A second grassroots group in the land struggle, also an ANTA cooperative, was La Joya del Lago. Most of its thirty-one members lived in a relatively new *colonia* (neighborhood) in Valle Verde, a village adjacent to Santo Tomás. I interviewed twenty-four members and spent sixteen days in this neighborhood. In its layout and proximity to farmland, this neighborhood was more suburban than rural, unlike La Victoria, which was surrounded by fields of coffee and subsistence crops. The majority of La Joya del Lago members were related by blood or marriage to a large family that had founded the cooperative. This family had always resided in the Lake Coatepeque area, though before the agrarian reform they had lived and farmed on an island in the middle of the lake. As island terrain and land on the edge of the lake became colonized by lavish vacation estates, subsistence farmers and fishers were pushed further inland. La Joya del Lago members occupied a coffee estate in northwest Santa Ana during the 1995 land invasions.

La Joya del Lago's participation in ANTA activities was minimal after the land invasions. For example, they never sent representatives to biweekly departmental meetings, relying instead on their ANTA promoter to bring information about the land investigation to their cooperative meetings and grew resentful when her attendance became spotty. Because they did not obtain information on their own, La Joya del Lago members were reluctant to hold cooperative-level meetings in the absence of the ANTA promoter, whose many responsibilities made it hard for her to get to Valle Verde on a regular basis. In this sense they differed from La Victoria members, who held meetings even when their promoter could not attend.

In the fall of 1996, La Joya del Lago leaders began to demand direct material assistance from ANTA. According to their ANTA promoter, they threatened to turn to another source of support. In early 1997, the promoter made the journey to Valle Verde only to find that the president of the cooperative and several other members refused to meet with her. This precipitated an informal rift in the cooperative's relationship with ANTA. In the meantime, the cooperative developed a relationship with a corrupt peasant organizer named Alberto Sol, who claimed to have special access to French Embassy funds for demobilized FMLN guerrillas. In order to benefit from the French Embassy project, Sol said, they needed to present proof that they were ex-guerrillas. More than half the cooperative members paid Sol 200 colons (about US$30) each for phony documents attesting to their status as former combatants. Sol also claimed he needed to take over the presidency of the cooperative and would need its official membership list in order to proceed. When it finally dawned on the members that they had been swindled, the cooperative restored its relationship with ANTA and rejoined the land struggle.

La Filadelfia

This base group began forming five years prior to the 1995 land invasions. It was organized by a leader of one of the smaller ADC associations, but began to affiliate with ANTA in early 1996. During the land invasions, about a hundred members of the group entered a large coffee estate in the municipality of Jayaque, located in the Department of La Libertad. Afterwards they established an encampment across the road from this property in a rural subdivision that belonged to the estate's owner. Their encampment lasted longer than that of any other base group involved in the land struggle. While the others returned home at Christmas 1995, La Filadelfia members remained encamped until the following May. By January, however, the encampment had dwindled from about one hundred families to thirty adults and a few children and remained at this level until it was dismantled. A few members dropped by the encampment on weekends to give monetary contributions and to find out what was going on with the land investigation. I spent about ten days in the encampment, and interviewed twenty-eight members.

The uniqueness of La Filadelfia's situation, both in terms of the duration of their encampment and the sudden drop in membership, owed to the influence of a corrupt, alcoholic organizer named Antonio Rivera. He used the group, and the peasant organizations' style of recruiting members to the land struggle, as a racket. During the five years he had been holding meetings and bringing in new members with the promise of imminent land transfers, he had collected tens of thousands of colons in membership dues and other supposed expenses. Some members of the encampment estimated that the figure could easily be as high as eighty thousand colons (US$10,000).[10] In December, several group members questioned Rivera about his use of collective funds and other suspicious practices. He reacted angrily but then deserted the encampment, telling the others to leave as well. Those who stayed after December did so because they feared that Rivera would return with replacement members in their absence, which would have undermined their eligibility for the property.

With ANTA's assistance, the remaining leaders and two new ones reorganized the group's finances and membership list after Rivera's departure. They also started the process of obtaining cooperative status. There was a new sense of hope in the encampment. The results of the land investigation, however, deflated this optimism and eventually contributed to the group's dissolution. In March, ISTA ruled that the coffee estate they were awaiting did not exceed 245 hectares. Although this contradicted widespread local knowledge of the property, ANTA claimed that it could do nothing to change the verdict. At this point La Filadelfia leaders became deeply suspicious of ANTA. Several were convinced that the organization had sold them out to the government. Having previously confronted Rivera regarding his corrupt practices, they were undoubtedly conditioned to distrust movement organizers who could not deliver immediate results. At this time, peasants in the encampment were also being pressured by authorities to leave. Although ANTA was in the midst of finding the group an alternative property, the group did not reassemble after dismantling the encampment in May.

La Santaneca

Another base group whose members were victimized by petty corruption was the ATAES cooperative, La Santaneca, created in 1994. Because of ATAES leaders' disavowal of land invasions and its split from the ADC, this base group did not take part in the ADC's October 1995 mobilization. Due to new efforts of ATAES organizers in Santa Ana, La Santaneca's membership dramatically increased in size in 1997, ballooning from about fifteen members to over one hundred. Because the members resided in diverse municipalities, an urban locale— the headquarters of the FMLN in Santa Ana city—was used for the group's meetings. The only base group activity was the biweekly meeting where the organizer, Antonio Cartagena, collected money from dozens of people and promised that they were very close to obtaining land. My research on this base group consisted of observing one of these biweekly meetings, interviews with two members, and informal conversations with several other members.

Like Rivera in La Filadelfia, Cartagena made himself president of the group, which had attained its cooperative status earlier. Given that he was an engineer by occupation, this not only went against the norms of the peasant organizations but also violated Department of Agricultural Association regulations, according to which cooperative leaders must be employed in agriculture. Cartagena also had a drinking problem and had begun to show up drunk at meetings. Furthermore, he announced that the secretary of the cooperative had disappeared with most of the money. Though he claimed to be pursuing legal action against her, he continued to request the biweekly contributions from the peasants.

Several disturbing features stood out in the Santaneca meeting I observed. Although it was well attended, the meeting was extremely chaotic compared to most meetings of ANTA's base groups. Many people spoke at once, drowning the person who had the floor. Cartagena, however, was bright and articulate. He assured those in attendance that the government was about to start transferring properties to ATAES peasants. He also announced that ATAES needed 150 colons from the group every two weeks to cover the travel and living expenses of technical personnel who were working hard to investigate the property registers. This was in addition to the one hundred colons that each member had to pay into their *capital social* (individual membership fund). Astoundingly, no one questioned this justification or inquired about the use that the technical staff had made of earlier contributions. In light of these anomalies, the cooperative appeared destined to disintegrate.

Networks and "Movement Centers"

One of the factors that distinguishes La Filadelfia and La Santaneca from the groups that remained intact was the extent of preexisting social ties among the members. A broad consensus exists among scholars of social movements that people who are more socially integrated have a greater propensity to participate in movements. Considerable empirical research on social movements in the developed world as well as peasant movements in primarily rural societies supports this view.[11] Dense network ties draw people into movements by providing, for example, channels of communication to interpret grievances. As well, involvement in formal organizations cultivates knowledge and skills that are relevant to movement participation and leadership.[12] Since everyone is usually socially integrated in some way, the role of this variable obviously depends on the types of networks to which one belongs. In agrarian societies, for example, ties of dependency on landowning elites prevent peasants from taking part in revolutionary movements.[13]

More has been written about the role of social networks in leading people to join social movements than in sustaining their participation. But Staggenborg found that the cohesion of a local women's movement was maintained between peak periods of collective action through the existence of "movement centers." These are physical gathering places that allow participants to coordinate tactics and that "create solidarity and visibility" for the movement. Examples of such centers in the women's movement include cultural events and enterprises in urban settings, such as women's art galleries and bookstores.[14] The movement centers that Morris describes in numerous local manifestations of the civil rights movement emerged around the urban black churches.[15] Given deficiencies in transportation and technologies of communication in rural, less developed societies, more geographically localized spaces are required to sustain participation over several months or even years. In this respect, organizations whose members regularly interact within local communities would seem to have the best prospects for staying together during lulls in protest activity.

In El Salvador the presence of residentially based networks distinguished the two base groups that stayed together from the two that collapsed. In contrast to La Victoria and La Joya del Lago, La Filadelfia and La Santaneca members came not just from different villages but from different municipalities. In fact, those from La Filadelfia had originally come from several different departments. Although the majority of members in this group had been living in the Department of La Libertad when they joined, some came from Chalatenango, Cabañas, San Salvador, or La Paz. A few had recently moved to the central or western regions of the country from areas more directly affected by the armed conflict. People were mobilized to join these two base groups through small primary networks of immediate family and friends. But there were no movement centers in either base group to link these small networks together. The regular meetings that were held to motivate continued monetary contributions and, in the case of La Filadelfia, the land invasion and subsequent protest encampment, served as movement centers. But because they were temporary, these settings were inadequate for ensuring the continued existence of the group. When most La Filadelfia members left the encampment at the end of December 1995, their residential dispersion impeded them from learning about new interpretations of events. The members who remained placed their hope in the new base group leadership, and in ANTA, with which they had frequent contact.

The situation of La Victoria, La Joya del Lago, and other ANTA base groups suggests that it is particularly important for the activists and leaders of the group to be residentially concentrated. The leaders' information about the land investigation acquired during the department meetings or through contact with ANTA leaders and cadre provided a centralized means of keeping abreast of changing conditions. With most of the other base group members living close to the leaders in both La Victoria and La Joya del Lago, a critical mass of participants could be mobilized in response to new information. This was seen during the October land invasions. Upon withdrawing from the properties they had occupied, most of the peasants initially went home. The existence of movement centers in most of the base groups in the land struggle enabled national leaders to mobilize a wave of protest encampments a few days later. In La Santaneca, leadership was centralized in the corrupt organizers. In La Filadelfia, the men who resumed the leadership when Rivera left were from different municipalities. This would make it very difficult to coordinate activities when everyone finally left the protest encampment.

It was not only their residential dispersion that hurt La Filadelfia and La Santaneca. The fact is that these base groups were not organized with the intention of ensuring their cohesion but as a source of cash for the corrupt organizers. Without the demoralizing experience of being defrauded, other residentially dispersed base groups in ANTA divided and lost members, but core groups of committed members remained organized. The influence of corruption along with the lack of a movement center contributed to the demise of La Filadelfia and La Santaneca. But to some extent attitudes and behaviors in the larger networks with which the base groups were linked provided fraudulent leaders with opportunities they might not have encountered elsewhere.

Unethical practices at the highest level of ATAES suggest a tolerance for this kind of behavior, which undoubtedly influenced the way its base groups were organized. For example, more than a year after Sánchez was expelled from the ADC, a group of twelve peasants presented a notarized grievance against him and two other ATAES leaders to the FMLN's Secretariat of Agrarian Affairs. According to the peasants, Sánchez and a technical employee of the organization were pressuring them to sell the land they had received under the Peace Accords, even though the boundaries of each beneficiary's holdings had not yet been determined.[16] They complained of two additional anomalies. An ATAES engineer and several other professionally employed individuals were registered as beneficiaries of the property. As well, although he was not a recipient of land in this property, Sánchez was cultivating cash crops on it.

Social networks help to explain the different aftermath of corruption in La Joya del Lago. Unlike La Santaneca, this cooperative had ties with a peasant association that emphasized ethical and effective orientation of grassroots members and that instructed and monitored its promoters accordingly. Although for a time La Filadelfia's contact with ANTA helped sustain cohesion among those who remained in the encampment, this relationship was established only after the damage wrought by Rivera. La Joya del Lago's longer experience with ANTA provided it with a clear basis of comparison with the disappointing alternative they had explored. On mending their relationship with ANTA, La Joya del Lago brought in new members and made plans to take possession of a 130 hectare property that became available through ANTA's efforts.

Resources

A range of material and nonmaterial resources—such as money, leadership skills, technical expertise, and links with influential actors—are required for movements to emerge and develop.[17] Resources influence the capacity of movement organizations to engage in lobbying, protesting, and other means of expressing their demands. But at the individual level, they also affect whether people are able to participate in movement activities and the extent of their contributions. A type of resource that distinguishes the base groups in this study is the members' access to land and other sources of income. It is no coincidence that the most active and cohesive base group, La Victoria, was in the best resource position, and that of the three groups for which data on resources was systematically collected, La Filadelfia was the poorest.

Scholars of peasant revolt have debated how access to land affects participation in revolutionary movements.[18] Wolf argues that the "middle peasant"— whose income from land is sufficient to sustain a family without its members seeking wage work elsewhere—constitutes the class basis of many rural uprisings.[19] Cabarrús, on the other hand, identifies the semiproletariat as the numerically most important component of the radical peasant associations that emerged in El Salvador in the 1970s.[20] Despite differences in the specific class fractions they identify, Wolf and Cabarrús concur that the strongest participants in peasant organizations are those with a resource base to cushion them from the costs of the struggle. They both argue, moreover, that this is not found in the fraction of the peasantry whose income depends entirely on temporary wage work, but among those who have access to land.

Though Wolf and Cabarrús are concerned with rural revolt, their analysis may also be relevant to commitment and participation in noninsurgent peasant movements. Land ownership constituted a critical distinction between La Joya del Lago and La Victoria, reflecting the different impact of the 1980 Agrarian Reform on the two cooperatives. About twenty La Victoria members—almost all of the households with core members and a few others—had benefited from the third phase of the Agrarian Reform. Most of the reform beneficiaries owned only 1 or 2 *manzanas* (excluding the president, Don Alejandro, who had eight). But these *finateros* were unusual in that they had profitably transformed their small parcels, which had been severely eroded and steeply inclined to begin with, through agro-ecological cultivation methods. Soon they were able to grow jocote, an egg-sized fruit with a high retail price on the local market. Many were using jocote revenues to gradually substitute coffee in areas previously dedicated to corn and beans and had been harvesting and selling coffee for several years. Because of jocote and coffee, several of the *finateros* no longer worked for wages, although their sons and daughters still did.

In contrast, none of the members of La Joya del Lago had benefited from the Agrarian Reform, and only two of its members owned any land at all. Most of the male heads of household in the cooperative made their living through a combination of temporary wage work on local farms and in nonagricultural occupations, particularly construction. In this respect, the proliferation of private vacation homes and exclusive tourist resorts around Lake Coatepeque provided employment to men in the area. While many of the younger men in La Victoria supplemented their families' earnings this way, for the men in La Joya del Lago it was a more important (although unsteady) source of income. As well, a few of the men and women in La Joya del Lago worked as caretakers in lakeside vacation homes.

The more acute shortage of land among La Joya del Lago members helps to explain the lack of caution in their response to the mythical French Embassy project. Furthermore, the members of this cooperative had made several unsuccessful and enormously costly attempts to obtain land prior to 1995. Xiomara, the sister of the cooperative president, recalled that by 1995 they were already exhausted by their participation in the peasant movement. Don Alejandro, the president of La Victoria, persuaded them to "make one more attempt" by joining the *excedentes* struggle. Given their morale and their expectations at that point, it is not surprising that they became frustrated with the outcomes of the struggle by late 1996. For the members, paying in order to qualify for an internationally supported project must have appeared easier and surer than waiting for ANTA to legalize their access to the *excedentes*.

The more secure material position of La Victoria members—especially the core leaders and activists—relative to La Joya del Lago, afforded them more autonomy and discretionary time for peasant movement activities. The leaders often spent entire days away from their crops to take part in errands on behalf of the cooperative and ANTA activities, invariably paying for their own transportation. Moreover, La Victoria's core members were also community activists. They had taken the main initiative to obtain all the vital services and infrastructure the community now had: a surfaced road, electricity, running water, a primary school, and the only telephone line in the hamlet (installed at a small grocery store owned by a nonmember). They continued to be active in the upkeep of these utilities, which demanded considerable perseverance given the unresponsiveness of state agencies. The most onerous responsibility involved maintaining the recently installed potable water system, which frequently broke down despite a steady climb in the rate charged per household. An additional difficulty for La Victoria members was resistance to their involvement from non-leftists in the community who, by their accounts, banded together to vote them out of the various committees and yet often proved incompetent or apathetic in the roles they took over. Hence, even when they were no longer part of the community water committee, Don Alejandro and other La Victoria members continued to carry out much of the legwork involved in pressuring the state water company for repairs.

On average, the La Filadelfia members who stayed in their encampment after 1995 were poorer than La Victoria or La Joya del Lago members. None had access to land. A few of the men had rented land previously but in recent years had found rental prices too steep. A great many of the interviewees did not have homes of their own and had been living *de posada* (as guests), usually with parents or siblings. One forty-five-year-old member, Tomás, together with his twenty-seven-year-old wife and their five children, had literally nowhere else to live other than the encampment. One of their children, a three-month-old baby, had been born there. Many in the encampment were not working in agriculture at the time of the land invasions. Several of the women had quit jobs as domestic servants—one of the least remunerative forms of employment in El Salvador—to take part in the land struggle. Two men were former members of Agrarian Reform cooperatives, one of which had been subdivided into individual parcels.

Ideology

Not all social networks are conducive to oppositional collective action. Rather, attempts to change social and political conditions arise within networks that become ideologically "alienated" from those conditions.[21] This is another factor that distinguishes the behavior and fate of the base groups in this study. The groups varied in their prior exposure to agents of attitudinal transformation. The ideological influence of external agents can be crucial for social movement participation among people who have experienced decades of impoverishment, exploitation, and authoritarianism.[22] Peasants and other subordinate groups devise myriad private ways of resisting oppressive elites. But, as Tarrow observes, such mentalities of resistance among the poor are "largely passive interpretations of the status quo detached from agency—and are often part of the deadening culture of poverty."[23] In other words, counterhegemonic values, beliefs, and practices do not necessarily become articulated as explicit demands to alter the socioeconomic and political status quo, nor lead to active confrontation of authority. And if "cognitive liberation" is necessary for oppressed people to join social movements, it must also play a role in their ongoing commitment to the movement struggle.[24]

In El Salvador, FMLN insurgents influenced the beliefs and values of Salvadoran peasants, whose support they solicited during the civil war. This occurred even in the western region of the country where there was little combat but where the guerrillas needed to ensure the movement of arms. They also attacked economic targets in the western region, such as the properties of the oligarchy. FMLN influence sets La Victoria and La Joya del Lago apart from the other two base groups. In La Joya del Lago, contact with the insurgents in the 1980s decisively changed political beliefs and values. The head of the core family in this cooperative, Don Lorenzo, became persuaded through conversations with guerrilla leaders that they were fighting for a just cause. He recalled that they made him more aware of rural injustice—miserable pay for farm laborers, repression in the workplace, and the increasing mechanization of farm operations. "I realized that what they were saying was right, that I had spent my sweat just for the rich," he said. "I realized these guys were good people."

La Victoria and La Joya del Lago members provided clandestine support to the guerrillas during the civil war. They provided patrol services for the FMLN operations, guarded arms caches, channeled funds to the guerrillas, and transported food, medicine, and other supplies. Given the political polarization of their communities at that time, these were high-risk activities. It was because of the groups' history with the guerrillas, and ANTA's own links with the FMLN, that the organization was able to "find" the La Victoria and La Joya del Lago peasants when it began mobilizing people for the *excedentes* struggle in the spring of 1995.

Few members of the La Filadelfia encampment had experiences similar to those of La Victoria and La Joya del Lago. Only five of the twenty-eight members who were interviewed reported having participated in any kind of organization before the land struggle. One woman had been a guerrilla combatant. Don Miguel, the group's secretary, had been involved in clandestine political work organized by a Jesuit priest in the late 1970s and had been imprisoned for three weeks as a result. No one else in the group had been involved in political activities, though several had lost close relatives in the armed conflict. Another member had been in the army for four years during the civil war but had deserted for personal reasons.

As a result of their prior experiences, La Victoria and La Joya del Lago members had a greater appreciation for social movement struggle as a means of obtaining land. This helps explain why La Joya del Lago returned to ANTA and to the movement after the group's demoralizing experience of corruption, while La Filadelfia fell apart. La Joya del Lago members were deeply embarrassed by the French Embassy affair, probably because their conscious attempt to fraud the system had backfired on them. When they realized they had been swindled, several members stated they had given up all hope in the peasant movement. But compared to La

Filadelfia, they had a longer relationship with ANTA, which they knew was still closely linked to the former guerrillas. In contrast, La Filadelfia members had less reason to trust ANTA, even if they were aware of its political links.

Another important influence on peasant attitudes was the liberation theology teachings of the progressive Catholic Church. Prior to the advent of liberation theology in El Salvador in the early 1970s, the traditional church encouraged the poor to view inequality and poverty as the will of God. By bringing about new notions of individual morality and social justice, the pastoral mission of the progressive priests and lay clergy encouraged peasants to perceive their material condition as an outcome of social relations. A crucial component of this message was that God championed the poor and favored collective efforts to end their oppression. This was also conveyed through the archdiocesan radio station and news bulletin.[25]

Immersion in liberation theology distinguishes La Victoria from La Joya del Lago. Prior to their participation in clandestine struggle, La Victoria members were initially politicized through the progressive church. Don Alejandro, the president of the cooperative, and his sister Estela, acquired and studied the Latin American Bible (a liberation theologian version of the Old and New Testaments) on their own in the 1970s. They were among the thousands who regularly tuned in to the broadcast of the weekly mass held by Archbishop Romero, whose homilies interpreted scripture readings in light of events and conditions in El Salvador. Eventually they approached a priest to inquire how they could get involved in the Christian Base Communities (CEBs). He put them in touch with Grupo Maíz, a national organization that created and supported CEBs.

Through Equipo Maíz, Alejandro and his brother-in-law, Francisco, who would become the treasurer of La Victoria, became "Catechists of the Word" in 1980. They created a Bible study group in their community, and used comedic theater to dramatize the liberation theology message among peasants in neighboring communities as well in other departments. Through Equipo Maiz they obtained popular education critiques of the government that they used in their CEB activities. They also participated in CEB events in Nicaragua and Colombia.

Through the CEB La Victoria members began to participate in the popular movement during the 1980s. They took part in numerous demonstrations in the capital city during the latter half of the 1980s to demand economic reforms, peace, the cessation of military repression, and so on. Their religious beliefs are also consonant with the sense of responsibility for the collective good that they displayed in their civic activism, described earlier. La Victoria members also became avid campaigners for the FMLN in the 1994 and 1997 elections in the rural areas of various Santa Ana municipalities. In recognition of their contributions, the FMLN held a victory celebration in their hamlet in the wake of its dramatic success in the 1997 municipal and legislative races. (The party had done particularly well in Santa Ana and the other western departments).

La Joya del Lago did not share the CEB experience or the religious convictions of the peasants in La Victoria. Three members were Seventh Day Adventists, which, like other Pentecostal denominations in El Salvador, did not encourage social or political activism.[26] In general, the group had a less ideologically informed, more pragmatic outlook on the *excedentes* movement and the popular struggle than was found in La Victoria. At some point during their involvement in struggle, their own material improvement had become their main concern. This is evident in the nature of their approach to the FMLN after the Peace Accords. This consisted mainly of efforts to obtain material assistance to which they felt entitled as a reward for their support to the insurgents during the war. In addition to their attempt to benefit from the PTT, they also signed up for and received vocational training courses through a program for former combatants and supporters. Although they voted FMLN, they did not take on any campaign responsibilities.

La Joya del Lago members were not unique in regarding the *excedentes* movement as a means of improving their own situation. Most members of La Victoria also stated that they wanted to provide a better life for their children. But this was not the only basis of their participation. As Don Alejandro pointed out in reference to the core members of the cooperative, "We are not just in this for land." Indeed, they were involved in a range of social movement activities not directly related to this goal.

La Victoria members were not uncritical of ANTA. For example, they complained that some of the promoters' reports on the land investigation process were unclear. They felt let down when the organization repeatedly promised and then failed to provide transportation to a property they wanted to inspect. But unlike members of La Joya del Lago, the La Victoria activists did not seriously consider abandoning the organization or the struggle. This is in keeping with their ideological commitment to social change. A conversation between several of the cooperative's founding members and an additional member who was planning to quit was revealing in this respect. It took place after a third consecutive instance in which ANTA staff had left them waiting in downtown Santa Ana without picking them up. Don Roberto, the member who planned to quit, expressed his conviction that ANTA had been co-opted. "They've sold out to the government," he said. "I know this strategy well. They're hiding something. Why don't they have us doing continual pressure on the government for the *excedentes?* It's because they don't want us to get the land." Emilio, who at twenty-four was one of the youngest members, disagreed: "It's not that they sold out. They didn't have a car that day. The land is there; the problem is that a lot of us don't want to be bothered. We want land that's close by and easy."

Don Roberto went on, "I've decided to leave this struggle. . . . If a lousy bit of land comes out, I've been thinking I'm not going to leave the land I have now, which cost me a lot of effort, to go and work some place far away." Don Edilberto, a member in his fifties, countered, "I've thought of the same thing, but I've concluded yes I *can* leave it. It's just a matter of having to move around a lot more, to work a few days here in my coffee and a few days there, growing *maicillo* [sorghum]."

Emilio added, "This is all a process. Obviously the rich aren't just going to give up their land easily. It may not be us directly who get the property that we invaded. It could be other people."

Historically rooted structural and ideological factors influenced the strength and cohesion of the land struggle at the grassroots level. Social networks, access to land, and established political beliefs and values shaped the actions and fate of the four groups of peasants. The crucial factor distinguishing the groups that disintegrated from those that remained together is the presence or absence of a core residential network. The groups with a residential movement center were better able to coordinate actions and share interpretations of ongoing events. As seen in the contrasting fates of La Joya del Lago on the one hand and La Santaneca and La Filadelfia on the other, having this residential focus enabled them to withstand the disintegrative impact of rural corruption.

Material resources, particularly access to land but other sources of income as well, distinguished the leaders from the other members in most of the base groups. These resources also set La Victoria apart from the other groups. La Victoria's core members could afford to act on their political values and were less likely to pursue desperate measures as occurred in La Joya del Lago.

If land ownership were the only factor shaping peasant politics, all the Agrarian Reform beneficiaries in the cantón of Santo Tomás would have supported the FMLN and joined the land struggle. In fact, several *finateros* in the community did neither. Clearly, ideologies were also important and to some degree were independent of one's position in the agrarian structure. Whether people approached the struggle solely as a means of obtaining land for their own families or whether there was a deeper ideological component to their participation made a difference in their expectations of the peasant organizations. The more immediate and circumscribed their objectives, the more they were drawn to the dangerous promise of a quick and easy reward, and the less involved they were in the movement overall.

In some ways the *excedentes* struggle displayed continuity with peasant collective action of earlier decades. Like the members of the radical peasant organizations of the 1970s, many participants in the land struggle first became involved in social movements through contact with the insurgent forces. Others were politicized through the progressive church. But a number of new phenomena also affected the cohesion of the movement. At the level of the peasant organizations, old alliances shifted after the Peace Accords. Former friends, like the ADC and ATAES, became bitter enemies, perhaps because they no longer had the imperatives of war and a formidable foe to keep them united. Some peasant leaders abandoned the basic ethics they at one time espoused, abusing their positions to exploit the grassroots affiliates. Other astute and articulate individuals took advantage of the land struggle to organize and then rob unwary peasants, leaving them bewildered and demoralized.

Various social and historical features of the Salvadoran countryside provided these individuals with rich opportunities for deception and fraud. Perhaps the most obvious factor is the low level of formal education. According to a Salvadoran government survey in 1991, rural illiteracy stood at 43 percent, compared to 27 percent for the country as a whole. The fact that five of the peasants who complained of being coerced by ATAES's top leaders could not sign their own names (they "signed" their formal grievance with thumbprints) testifies to the vulnerability of the uneducated. Added to the lack of schooling was several generations of authoritarian government, which resulted in a limited awareness of rights and how to defend them. As well, the enormous surge in the presence of donor agencies and nongovernmental organizations since the early 1990s provided unscrupulous individuals with a handy ruse. The idea of access to foreign funding (such as the French Embassy project) could serve as a pretext for exploiting the unwary.

The possibility cannot be dismissed that corruption reflects the sabotage efforts of movement opponents. Among ADC leaders and cadre, Sánchez was believed to have been co-opted by the government. He did possess unusually detailed information on several properties that ATAES base groups were pursuing, including maps of properties and photocopies of public land registry entries. Commenting on the fact that none of the other ADC organizations had acquired information of such exactitude, he stated, mysteriously, "We got the help of some friends." Corruption and fraud in the peasant movement warrant greater attention from scholars and peasant leaders themselves. As state violence against social movements has declined, future research should examine the impact of other means used to control and discredit popular struggle.

Section Three

Culture and Ideology in Contemporary El Salvador

The chapters in this section address three themes of great interest to Latin
American social scientists: migration, violence, and ethnicity. Postwar El Salvador
leads Latin America in international migration and violent deaths, and it has become an important comparative case for many researchers interested in these
phenomena elsewhere. Its contribution to ethnicity studies is more subtle due to
its location on the periphery of Mesoamerican "high cultures" and a common
but erroneous belief outside the country that its postindependence indigenous
population was either acculturated to the national, mestizo culture or physically
eradicated during the 1932 *Matanza* (mass killing).

At any one time approximately 20 percent of the Salvadoran population resides outside the country—overwhelmingly in the United States, remitting home
upwards of $1 billion annually. The foreign exchange obtained from migrant re-
mittances is more than twice that generated by the export of coffee, and it has
played a key role in sustaining relative parity between an overvalued *colón* and
the U.S. dollar. Remittances to El Salvador account for more than 10 percent of
gross national income, the highest percentage in Latin America and among the
highest relative contributions in the world.

David Pedersen's discussion of the formation of a cultural space that links El
Salvador and the United States employs the case of Intipucá in southeastern El
Salvador to investigate the limits of dominant views about transnational migra-

tion between these two countries. Pedersen argues that the Salvadoran state, international financial institutions, and the press portray migration as the movement of persons and goods between relatively fixed social spaces, enabling them to represent remittances from Salvadorans in the United States as part of national economic development. But the experiences of Intipucaños in Washington, D.C., and other areas, as well as in Intipucá, illustrate that such abstracted accounts fail to come to grips with the multiple, interlocking, and extremely unequal relationships that make migrant value flows possible. In particular, the story of Marvin Chávez links 1980s remittances from Intipucaños to Ronald Reagan's Strategic Defense Initiative, Washington high finance, and even (in one case, at least) recreational drug use and the countries in the developing world involved in the production, processing, and commercialization of cocaine and other substances.

Lamentably, El Salvador also has the dubious distinction of leading Latin America in homicides and other forms of violent crime, variously estimated at between 100 and 150 annually per 100,000 people. During most of the "peaceful" postwar 1990s, more people were killed annually—some 6,000–7,000—than during all but the worst years of the civil war. All regions and all social strata are affected, giving rise to public outcries and a vigorous debate over whom to blame and how to alleviate the situation. In "El Capitán Cinchazo: Blood and Meaning in Postwar El Salvador," Ellen Moodie compares a variety of discursive approaches to urban violence by moving between two events that took place on the same day in 1994: a highly publicized assault on a San Salvador bank and the attempted robbery of a local banker. The bank robbery, or "Cinchazo" of the chapter's title, received an enormous amount of media coverage when examination of an accidental videotape of the event implicated members of the National Police, then in the process of replacement by the National Civilian Police. The late afternoon attempted robbery of the banker received little media coverage, despite the fact that two assailants died and the victim, shot four times, barely survived. Rather than effect a single, overarching explanation of postwar violence, Moodie opts to show how institutional discourses disseminated by the press, government authorities, the United Nations, and others offer little solace to at least some victims, who find comfort in transcendental explanations based on religious beliefs. Without offering a final reason for the violence or suggesting a resolution, Moodie investigates the complex, slippery field of postwar discourse and poses an important challenge to researchers seeking pat explanations of complex phenomena.

Finally, ethnicity has less *caché* in El Salvador than in Guatemala or southern Mexico for the reasons mentioned here. However, self-identified indigenous Salvadorans do exist and have adopted a more public persona as a consequence of the recent spread of global ethnodiscourses, as Henrik Ronsbo points out in "'This Is Not Culture!': The Effects of Ethnodiscourse and Ethnopolitics in El Salvador." Ronsbo discusses how "ethnodiscourse" has taken root among the villagers of Santo Domingo de Guzmán (department of Sonsonate), who exhibit few of the standard anthropological markers (dress, language, house type, productive technology) of Indianness. While they consider themselves to be Indians—and are so taken by residents of surrounding mestizo-dominated towns—globalized ethnodiscourse relegates them to what Ronsbo calls the "discursive borderlands." They are, as one informant argued, "Indio Indígena"—Indians locally and regionally but non-Indians to outside observers. Ronsbo makes the point that ethnodiscourse, which has generally been treated as a discourse of empowerment, is actually a double-edged sword, particularly for those who fail the stereotypical "Indian" test.

All three chapters compare individual, household, and community (transnational or otherwise) discourses with those "projected" by government, media, international financial institutions, and others as means of containing and thereby domesticating local beliefs and practices that strain institutional comprehension. In the process the authors, each in his or her own way, highlight social and ideological dimensions that have been historically marginalized in social science writing on El Salvador. Without doubt, the approaches employed in these chapters—influenced by deconstruction and postmodernism without necessarily being postmodern—represent one among various trends in contemporary anthropology. But they are approaches that, importantly, take seriously anthropological subjects, whose everyday views and practices frequently challenge institutional claims to speak on their behalf. Since the 1992 Peace Accords ended the civil war, El Salvador has undergone a top-down transformation, without thereby having become either more peaceful or more egalitarian. If progressive social change—change that improves both the life chances and the life conditions of the majority—is to be achieved, its seeds are likely to be found, for those patient enough to look, in the interstices of everyday life, precisely where these scholars have centered their investigations.[1] These articles and others in this book make it clear that detailed knowledge of local-level phenomena is required if we are to avoid in the future the simplistic, overgeneralized, and frequently teleological discussions of Salvadoran society that were far too common in the past.

Henrik Ronsbo

"This Is Not Culture!"

The Effects of Ethnodiscourse and Ethnopolitics in El Salvador

How many indigenous people live in El Salvador? This question was posed fifty years ago by the demographer Barón Castro.[1] It was posed forty years ago by the anthropologist Richard Adams and twenty years ago by sociologist Alejandro Marroquín.[2] In the present postconflict situation with its attendant focus on individual and collective human rights, the question has returned again.[3] According to present estimates, the indigenous population of El Salvador has fallen during the last fifty years from 20 percent of the total population to somewhere between 5 and 10 percent.[4] The last Salvadoran census based on ethnic categories (1930) found that 5–6 percent of the population was indigenous; this contradicts figures recently extracted from birth records for the same period.[5] All these counts, however, were made while modernist notions of *indigenismo* and *mestizaje* prevailed. Since then we have witnessed the emergence of local, regional, national, and transnational ethnopolitics carried forward by northern and southern nongovernmental organizations (NGOs) with support from international organizations.[6] We may legitimately ask how the advance of these movements has influenced the self-definition of indigenous peoples in El Salvador and in what ways if any it has enabled these movements to advance a political project based on indigenous identity.

One analyst has suggested that "if [indigenous peoples] are to have any power at all, they must have a traditional culture."[7] The observation that Amerindian cultural heritage in the form of tradition at the present conjuncture is empowering is shared by most observers of Latin American identity politics.[8] The observation that tradition empowers raises an important issue, however; that is, what happens to those Amerindian communities that for a variety of reasons appear not to possess tradition, and who is authorized to make such evaluations?

One of the well-documented effects of ethnopolitics is that anthropologists can no longer pass judgment on the traditionality of particular social groups or individuals, nor can they without contestations evaluate the inherent cultural value of particular traits or customs. The times when anthropologists were only held accountable by other anthropologists are gone. Today, subject populations claim and assert ownership over the circulation of information about them, whether in the form of population data, images, symbols, or objects collected in their midst. Seen from this perspective, ethnopolitics is the politics of empowerment, and ethnodiscourse is its vehicle. I seek to draw attention to a far less studied effect of ethnodiscourse: its disempowering consequences. At the margins of Central American nation-states (notably El Salvador, Honduras, and Nicaragua), a plethora of ethnic groups exist who locally, regionally, and sometimes nationally are recognized as indigenous, although they do not display the characteristics that ethnodiscourse posits as prerequisites. Thus, behind the recent emergence of ethnopolitics lurks a dimension of continuity in the ways cultural difference is conceptualized. Difference between indigenous and nonindigenous populations is still defined by the observable traditional culture indigenous groups possess.

Although some NGOs have made considerable effort to ensure that the definition of indigeneity is based on self-identification—in particular, the IWGIA (International Working Group for Indigenous Affairs) and Cultural Survival—the dominant notion among multilateral donors such as the World Bank, Inter American Development Bank, and state apparatuses, as well as the concerned public, is still that indigenous peoples are outside national society, control a separate space, use different productive techniques based on different knowledge and world views, work communally, and dress and speak in ways different from the national majority. This chapter concerns the ways in which this dominant definition of tradition is making its way into constructions of difference and indigeneity in the small village of Santo Domingo de Guzmán in western El Salvador and thus creates an emergent ethnopolitics.

An Ethnography of Identities in Discursive Borderlands

During the last two decades or so, social scientists have been deconstructing knowledge complexes such as the ethnodiscourse. We have learned that the reproduction of knowledge is linked to the reproduction of power, and scholars have asserted that such power/knowledge complexes are related to the creation of new subjectivities. How these supposedly new subjectivities are created remains an open question. The ethnographic record of such processes of "subject creation" is thin, although a certain body of literature emerges from discussions of state-formation processes as well as studies of encounters between the development apparatus and target populations in the postcolonial world, yet little of this has the fine-grained ethnographic detail that the field of anthropology calls for.[9] I consider here how members of the community of Santo Domingo de Guzmán inhabit, reproach, or flee ethnodiscourse, and what conditions and possibilities this creates for the emergence of an ethnopolitics. I contend that the end of the civil war and the widespread focus on human rights has opened up spaces that can be used for a politics of identity, that the penetration of ethnodiscourse has taken place through gatekeepers,[10] and that this discourse is presently reorganizing the notion about what it means to be indigenous in Santo Domingo.

As mentioned earlier, we have little ethnography of such meetings, and what we do have tends to represent them as a rather effortless process, whereby subjectivities are "created" by discourses. Here I am thinking particularly about the transformation from target population to politicized subjectivity posited by Escobar, as well as the apparently unproblematic creation of western subjectivities in equally effortless ways by colonial and postcolonial discourses.[11] Common to these studies, known as the power/culture approach, is that they give little attention to the ways in which subject populations actively engage in the construction and destruction of the "common discursive frameworks" through which they are objectified and governed.[12] Escobar argues that development discourse reorganizes subjectivities in a unidirectional process of social change. It appears as if Escobar equates subject position with subjectivity, the former referring to the clearing opened by a discourse, the latter to the ways in which this clearing is traversed or inhabited by particular subjects. In a study on the central northwestern Amazon (the southeast corner of Columbia) Jackson analyzes the meanings of culture, Indianness, language, and kinship among the Tukaroans as these factors change under the influence of an emergent politics of Indianness.[13] The Tukaroans inhabit an integrated social universe, with the descent group as the fundamental unit, but characterized by language exogamy. This social universe consists of sixteen different groups each with its own language, but the groups share a common creation myth, productive practices, and settlement patterns. They belong to the same social universe and share models for structuring and interpreting the world.[14] Within this social universe, the advent of ethnopolitics is leading the different language groups to conceptualize themselves as ethnic groups. This change is largely the outcome of what I have termed the *ethnodiscourse*. The notion that an ethnic group has a language as its barrier has produced descriptions "that heighten the distinctions separating them, while failing to mention certain crucial similarities."[15]

Most Tukaroans now take the concept of culture to denote a savage with a loincloth, a picture most people consider suspect. On the other hand, cultural brokers in the area use the concept in the sense of something positive the group possesses; this creates a cleavage between leadership and rank-and-file members. What Jackson provides us with is a careful description of the ways in which the notion of Indianness has changed during the last twenty years. She shows that ethnodiscourse filters into the everyday life of people and restructures their knowledge about themselves and the ways in which they conceptualize relationships between language groups and between these and nonindigenous outsiders. Jackson concludes, however, that if Tukaroans are to have any power at all, they must have a traditional culture. Winning the battle for self-determination increasingly involves acting and speaking with an authority that arises from an "Indian way."[16]

So far, the discussion has focused on people who move into discursive clearings. If we explore the metaphor of the clearing a little further, we see groups materialize that are relegated to its edges. Little attention has been given to these groups. They are the ones who, for a variety of reasons, are marginal to but influenced in powerful ways by the social effects of ethnodiscourse and ethnopolitics. I suggest that we think of these groups as residents in the discursive borderlands. From the outset, we can identify two types of borderland residents. One would be the refugees of discourse, those who try to evade particular categories and thus escape their practical implications. A historical example would be the *forasteros* in sixteenth-century Latin America. The second residential type would be the deportee, one who realizes that with changes in the semantics of power he or she has been left in a limbo without an authorized identity. A classical historical example would be the *Indian casta* (caste) in the liberal republics of early independent Central America, who during the nineteenth century revolted on various occasions in order to regain their status as indigenous. Initially, Ambrosius (a local informant) taught me the importance of these issues. During a regular Sunday meeting in the development association of the upper moiety of Santo Domingo, we were discussing what it meant to be *indígena*. To explain it he lifted his baseball cap and said, "This is not culture!" Then he pointed at Don Con's straw hat and said, "That's culture!" Such a distinction between what is and what is not culture is important to Ambrosius, to Don Con, and to the rest of the members of the organization, the moiety, and the community. More than anything else, this incident compelled me to consider the ways in which the increasingly strong ethnodiscourse simultaneously empowers and redefines the meanings ascribed to objects, practices, and institutions in village life, that is, the interpretation of the straw hat as an icon of Indianness.

Although I disagreed with Ambrosius and tried to argue that wearing a baseball cap with the logo of a Los Angeles utility company was a cultural statement, it was of little importance. He was not discussing cultural anthropology but instead was engaged in the everyday negotiation of the meanings ascribed to artifacts and valued in particular ways by the ethnodiscourse. It is a process whereby relations between particular signs and embodied practices are being reworked while accommodated to the emerging ethnodiscourse.

Being indigenous in Santo Domingo is, therefore, not a static identity based on cultural homogeneity and essence; instead, "indigenousness" is part of an ongoing argument over what marks the borders of the community within particular contexts. A similar argument has been raised by Ruth Phillips, who asks the very relevant question of museum representations of Native American culture, "Why not tourist art?" What is it about these creolized forms of cultural production that appears to be destructive of the discursive framework established and maintained by ethnodiscourse? What is it about Native American tourist art that makes it noncultural? Phillips proposes that it is the defiance of the colonial script, the demonstration of creativity and change capabilities and trajectories that colonial discourse has denied to these peoples.[17]

Communal Identity in Santo Domingo de Guzmán

Today Santo Domingo de Guzmán is a small, primarily indigenous village of about 1,700 people. It is surrounded by four rural subdivisions known as *cantones* (villages) populated by people who arrived in the municipality from 1880 to 1920, a population referred to in the Mesoamerican ethnography as *ladinos* or *mestizos*. This pattern is in itself a deviation from the typical Guatemalan pattern in which a ladino center is surrounded by an indigenous periphery. This spatial structure represents a palimpsest of the region's social history and can only be explained thus.

In the late sixteenth and early seventeenth centuries western El Salvador was the center of commercial cocoa production in the Americas, spurring a substantial immigration to villages around the town of Sonsonate, thereby maintaining village communities in the face of genocidal population losses that ran as high as 90–95 percent in the coastal regions of Mesoamerica. Immigration could, however, only postpone the collapse of a commercial village economy, and by the end of the sixteenth century the lack of available labor brought the export boom to an end.[18] From the early seventeenth century, Sonsonate, like the rest of the Audiencía de Guatemala, was characterized by a severe labor shortage. Agricultural outputs fell, trade with Spain contracted, and the Spanish colonizers moved from their small towns and into the countryside, where they established agricultural units based on the labor-extensive production of livestock.[19]

By the early eighteenth century, changes took place in the livestock-based production system. The population had grown, and the industrialization of European textile production created an increased demand for indigo, a natural dye produced in central and eastern El Salvador.[20] The growth of the population combined with the increased production of indigo by large as well as smaller farmers generated a new group of immigrants in Sonsonate from the areas of eastern and central El Salvador, which lead to a substantial rise in the population of the region.[21]

The emergence of western El Salvador as an indigenous zone was therefore a process very different from those that shaped the mountainous regions such as Cuchumatenes and Quiché.[22] It was the outcome of successive waves of immigration into a region characterized by village settlements and commercial agriculture, very unlike the peripheral regions of Highland Guatemala and Mexico. Near the end of the eighteenth century Sonsonate was nevertheless described in a discourse similar to that which framed indigenous populations in these other regions of Mesoamerica.[23]

During the early postindependence period, the political development of western El Salvador was influenced by the region's proximity to the Guatemalan border. Indigenous males were important for the formation of armies fielded in the numerous battles between various Central American caudillos, and networks of patronage developed between elites and the political leadership of indigenous villages.[24]

As coffee production expanded in western El Salvador it was originally based on the participation of indigenous as well as nonindigenous growers, who often formed interethnic alliances within municipal councils against nongrowers. This increased the already existing levels of socioeconomic differentiation within indigenous communities and led to high levels of intracommunal conflict.[25] This situation was unlike that in Guatemala, where the expansion of commercial agriculture, rural trade networks, and the state apparatuses led to the reorganization of the colonial category, the ladino. This development never touched Santo Domingo. The village lands lie below the minimum altitude for growing coffee, so the indigenous community remained in control of municipal politics until the imposition of a ladino mayor after the *Matanza* of 1932. It is therefore difficult to sustain the argument that Salvadoran state formation took place on the ground of a nationalized racial structure, nor did it give rise to such a structure.

Categories of race and ethnicity in western El Salvador grew out of the region's high levels of creolization during the colonial period, and they remained in use well into the twentieth century. Sporadically, the ladino-*Indio* duality was used in Santo Domingo's municipal records but never consistently. Categories tended to change with the coming and going of secretaries, and by the late 1930s they fell out of use. In this sense Santo Domingo represents one of a number of cases in western El Salvador in which linguistic and racial modes of distinction were reworked, on the one hand, by socioeconomic differentiation within the community and, on the other, by the location of any given village within the regional political economy of coffee and sugar production. In this political economy the indigenous population of Santo Domingo became a migrant labor force, which for two months a year worked in the coffee, sugar, and later cotton harvests on the region's large estates.

The maintenance of Santo Domingo as an indigenous village community with communal land seems to be an anomaly in western El Salvador and represents a historical continuity valued by villagers. This continuity can also be observed in the usage of the term *Mulatuh*. This is the Nahuatl word of Spanish origin for nonindigenous individuals and was used in Santo Domingo de Guzmán as late as the 1980s. The Spanish term used today among Mingüino community members is *gente de afuera* (people from outside). With this they name migrants that arrived during the coffee boom in the late nineteenth and early twentieth centuries. It is interesting to note that the term points not only to a colonial mode of distinction made on the basis of locality—also expressed in the category *originario* (original)—but also to the possibility for a nonracialized mode of distinction, a denial of racial distinction also represented by the expression *todos somos Indios* (we are all indigenous). This is an often-used remark expressing the view that on phenotypic grounds no distinctions can be made within the village population. The group referred to as *gente de afuera,* which maintains that a clear phenotypic distinction can be upheld, denies this nonracialized view of difference. As will be clear later in the chapter, particular individuals use the term *ladino,* a term also used by some indigenous organizations in the region. This no doubt represents a strategy for the introduction of the Guatemalan system of distinction, a strategy far from shared by everybody.

The arena of communal or indigenous sentiments in Santo Domingo is constructed within a field of alliances between households and migrating individuals, as well as between different households located within the village and the nearby vicinity. These alliances are built and maintained through the sharing or pooling of labor, capital, and other productive resources such as clay for the production of *comales* (pans) or land for the cultivation of *milpas* (subsistence crops).

This practice of sharing and pooling is organized through the kinship system, which works toward the inclusion of lateral paternal as well as maternal kin of multiple generations of men as well as women. In this manner multigenerational, same-gender groups spanning several households are maintained through working on pooled resources. Through this set of gendered livelihood practices a shared social world is sustained in which kinship and generation organize and structure social relations stretching from Seattle to Santo Domingo de Guzmán to the suburbs of San Salvador. Since the resident ladino population does not undertake the same livelihood practices nor gender them in similar ways, livelihood practice—understood as practices of exchange and reciprocity between individuals belonging to different households and between entire households—in effect marks the boundary of a separate indigenous sociality. Community as a positive emotion and experience is created by members of this social field through participation in public performances carried out in the space of the village, often but not always pitting ladinos against the indigenous community and producing a reflexive discourse that centers on the constitutive norms and values of community membership.[26]

It is to these forms of lived and experienced community that ethnodiscourse must relate. To be indigenous in this discourse means to use different artifacts, to live in distinct houses, and to undertake a particular set of productive practices based on indigenous knowledge of the environment. This definition is based on categories and features different from the ones that are central in Santo Domingo de Guzmán.

To most outsiders *Mingüinos* (residents of Santo Domingo) appear similar to all other rural Salvadorans, and Ambrosius is painfully aware of this. By failing to display the straw hat, he and his fellow villagers fail to display the signs of Indianness and to acquire the symbolic power that enables them to claim rights, secure funds from NGOs, and thus "improve their lives" *(mejorar la vida)*, as they say. Groups that are scattered through the southern parts of Mesoamerica and that for a variety of contingent historical reasons have evaded or ceased to use such visual distinctiveness are forgotten in the semiotic conquest of otherness but equally so in the struggle for rights.[27]

Practicing Ethnodiscourse

Most people who have visited El Salvador would opt for the lowest of the population estimates mentioned in the introduction. Even in the countryside one rarely sees an Indian—a person who is dressed, speaks, and acts differently from the mestizo majority. When considering the multiple and context-dependent definitions of what it means to be indigenous, however, it should be clear that we are dealing with at least three different kinds of distinction: an everyday one articulated in livelihood strategies, a performative one articulated as discursive community, and the politico-administrative one derived from an ethnodiscourse based on notions of "cultural distinctiveness."

Several times while I was living in Santo Domingo I had a chance to observe these distinctions as practiced by social scientists. At the beginning of my fieldwork, for example, I made a survey together with a North American anthropologist. Over the course of a week, we visited a variety of small villages in western El Salvador. Both of us were interested in identifying an indigenous element in western El Salvador, so our conversations were naturally made up of continual references and comparisons to other regions such as Guatemala, Bolivia, and Peru. Most often we structured the comparison around the gendered construction of indigeneity, where women through dress and hair style express indigeneity, yet men dress similarly across different ethnic groups. The basis for our distinctions was almost exclusively their visibility. We both agreed that the village of Santo Domingo was probably the most indigenous village in the region, and she supported me in the choice of field site for the study I was going to carry out.

Three months into my fieldwork an American political scientist visited the village. Having only recently arrived myself, I found his visit to be an important watershed in my work. During our discussions I readily assumed the position of inside informant and he the outside observer, and with this positionality in place, I slowly realized that what constituted indigeneity inside the village was not what the dominant discourse required. Later we went to a meeting with the leaders from Ambrosius' organization. Here the particularity of the Salvadoran case was brought out by a question he asked; toward the end of the interview, in which I only participated with some translation between Spanish and English, the political scientist asked, "What was the indigenous nation?"

What he intended to explore was the relationship between the past and the present, an imagined cultural unity stretching from the pre-Columbian period to the present, thereby laying the groundwork for a political project directed toward the future recognition of the political and cultural rights of the indigenous nation, the form that ethnopolitics has taken in Guatemala recently. In Guatemala it has emerged in the form of the Maya nation, the historical imagination of an antecedent cultural unity to be remade in the present and future and thus representing a voice different from the one emanating from the Guatemalan ladino nation.[28] The question, however, failed to make any sense to the members of the association. The political scientist did what I had done—that is, he implicitly assumed a structural similarity in the construction of difference in El Salvador and

Guatemala, his particular point of departure being that Salvadoran indigenous people were supposed to imagine themselves as belonging to a nation constituted outside the Salvadoran nation.

Later I realized that the phrase used by *Mingüinos* when referring to themselves as an indigenous community is, "we are Salvadoran Indians" *(somos indígenas Salvadoreños)*. The names of two Salvadoran organizations reinforce this sense of national incorporation: the National Coordination Council of Indigenous Salvadorans and the older National Association of Indigenous Salvadorans, both of whose members are those individual Salvadorans who are also indigenous. In both cases we have a group of individuals inside the political and cultural nation and not a distinct culture and nation outside.

Like me, the political scientist had failed to recognize the particularity of the Salvadoran case of cultured acculturation. This was not because we were inherently stupid; rather, it is an artifact of the abstractness of the ethnodiscourse and the generic quality of the concepts used in the study of indigenous peoples. What this discourse assumes is that indigenous peoples occupy a position of opposition vis-à-vis the state and of symbiosis with nature. It is exactly these two aspects that create indigenous peoples as a species of subjects in the south, install compassion in the north, and facilitate the emergence of transnational governance in the form of development assistance. I suggest that these two movements in the constitution of indigenous peoples are fundamental.

The opposition to the state creates them as the internal others of the underdeveloped societies. In a certain sense, they are not underdeveloped but rather non-developed. Indigenous peoples are not part of the civilizational historicity; instead, they have been placed with nature and are part of a new natural historicity constructed by development practice as the space of its other, a space in which people accumulate techniques and knowledge as a mirror image of the nature they live in. In the World Bank, for example, indigenous peoples are handled by the Environment Department: "Implementation . . . [of the World Bank Operational Directive 4.20 Indigenous Peoples] . . . seems to depend largely on those few bank staff in the Environment Department and regional technical departments that are interested in and concerned about indigenous peoples."[29] What are the implications of these policies, sensibilities, and modes of distinction? Consider the following quote from an International Workgroup of Indigenous Affairs publication: "Exact figures on the diversity of cultures are hard to come by, but anthropologists at Bergen University Norway estimate that there are as many as 5,000 different indigenous cultures in the world. . . . If we compare the number of national state cultures and national minorities in the world, we would find that indigenous peoples constitute 90–95% of the cultural diversity of the world."[30]

Indigenous peoples thus form a family of cultural species that, although outnumbered by the national family of cultural species, constitute the diversity of the world. The relationship between indigenous peoples and nature is therefore of a dual character. In the epistemological realm, biology provides the metaphors through which indigenous peoples are conceptualized, and at the level of ontology, biology provides the matter conceptualized by the indigenous people; hence, indigenous knowledge constitutes a separate realm for investigation and a potential field of knowledge extraction. These groups are therefore most logically protected as a part of the environmental protection strategy. Brysk sees this in rather instrumental terms—that is, environmental rights have proved to be the most powerful vehicle of indigenous rights, and the argument appears to be that, although this practice of equating indigenous groups with nature is patronizing, it is nevertheless necessary.[31]

One might ask what the consequences of this are. During my fieldwork, the association in the upper moiety received a loan to buy a tract of land in order to make a new settlement outside the old perimeter of the village. It also managed to secure funds for the future construction of houses. These funds are earmarked for an indigenous settlement, and consequently concrete blocks and duralite roofs are forbidden, even though they are the preferred construction materials in Santo Domingo because their low weight makes them easy to transport, they consume less labor, and they are considered more hygienic. Instead, the settlement must reflect its indigenous character by using adobe bricks and clay tiles as construction materials. This may seem like a reasonable way to preserve indigenous knowledge and techniques. But building with adobe and clay tiles was introduced by ladino settlers who arrived at the end of the nineteenth century, and only forty to fifty years ago did this style of housing become dominant among members of the indigenous community. Before this, houses were made of cane with thatched roofs, of which there is now only one left in the village.

Indigenous subjectivity is thus interpolated through a discourse that establishes an identity between nature and indigenous culture, thereby putting in motion a process of knowledge formation where the identification of the indigenous group takes place through the presence of nature. It is this process of identification that subsequently led to the formulation of a settlement project for a part of the indigenous community by the European Union, which envisioned a clustered settlement, a shared style of housing, and a communal form of governance, the latter enforced through a shared debt with the funding agency.

Thus, under the influence of ethnodiscourse, the change in the relations between different styles has recreated the meaning of the adobe house as the indigenous house and the concrete house as national and developed. In this way artifacts and the whole material framework for life are continually being reworked so that what in the synchronic perspective appears as an icon of Indianness, in a diachronic perspective becomes but a transitory symbol. The irony of this was not lost on the leadership of the upper moiety's development association, which after having acquired the lands turned it into agricultural plots and subsequently transferred the remaining funds to other activities.

Indios, Indios Indijenas, and the Discourse of Culture

On the walls of the village's *Casa de Cultura* (the local cultural center, a government–supported multi-use facility found in every municipality in the country), there is a continuous display of short essays on a wall—*el periódico mural.* The themes range from moral lessons about mothering to the more political ones. In March 1996 two of these essays caught my eye. One was titled *"Pobreza y Trabajo Pesado"* (poverty and heavy work), the other *"Que es un Indio?"* (what is an Indian?). Both texts were written by the director of the *Casa de Cultura,* Don Genaro, who is in his early sixties. In the early 1970s he was an active lay catechist, and as such he was actively engaged in the CEB in the village. He became director of the *Casa de Cultura* because of his good knowledge of Nahuatl. In this function, he is an important cultural gatekeeper for the community. Through his participation in Latin American congresses for the salvage of indigenous languages, he has been exposed to ethnodiscourse. Within the community Don Genaro tries to assert his authority on language vis-à-vis the other community members, but with little effect. Most Nahuatl speakers in the village distrust him because of his government employment, and they repeatedly criticize him for "making up words." The extent to which there is any substance to these allegations is unclear, but it is clear that in his explanation of the worldview of the Nahuatl speakers Don Genaro repeatedly includes references to Quetzalcoatl and Tlaloc figures in the classic Nahuatl pantheon. In this way, Don Genaro is looking for ways in which the quite legitimate claim that the village is indigenous can be authorized. The same takes place within the realm of public performance. In this field Don Genaro is the main inspiration for the younger generations in reawakening traditional village performances that were discontinued during the period of religious modernization followed by the civil war.[32]

I analyze how Don Genaro in his textual strategies tries to accommodate the bridge between global ethnodiscourse and the indigenous identity as it is lived and experienced in Santo Domingo. By looking at his narratives in this way they become global travel stories, stories that by moving back and forth between different political locations simultaneously produce these.[33]

In the first narrative, it is through the concept of work that the category of *Indio* is produced. The *Indio* works, the Ladino dresses, eats, and sleeps. The *Indio* is a working animal, the Ladino is proud. The only positive value related to the *Indio* is his force, the same force referred to by young men when talking about their military service, in which case they say, *"El Indio es resio."* In this text, the *Indio* is the opposite of all markers of civilization and progress. These are concentrated on the Ladino who sleeps, dresses, eats, works in an office, is rich, lives in the shadows, and, most of all, is greedy.

Pobreza y trabajo Pesado

> Los Indios somos pobres, los Ladinos ricos, y el Ladino, aunque no tenga dinero—tiene orgullo. El Indio es animal de carga que hace todo el trabajo afuera del sol, el Ladino no tiene fuerza . . . nos dicen Indios por que pasamos la vida trabajando . . . el Ladino trabaja en buena oficina come bien, se viste bien, duerme bien . . . el Ladino no puede trabajar en el campo; termina en el hospital . . . el Ladino es avaro.

Poverty and Heavy Work

> The Indians we are poor, the Ladinos rich, and although the Ladino doesn't have money—he has pride. The Indian is a beast of burden that does all the work outside in the sun, the Ladino doesn't have force . . . they call us Indians because we spend life working . . . the Ladino works in a nice office, eats well, sleeps well . . . the Ladino cannot work in the field; he ends in the hospital . . . the Ladino is greedy.

These aspects of the *Indio* as a social category are drawn, not from some distant pre-Columbian time, nor from colonial experiences, but from personal experiences of work in the coffee farms El Centenario and El Quelite, or the cutting of sugarcane and the picking of cotton on the coastal plain. It is not a notion of *Indio* derived from ethnodiscourse as culturally distinct, with a different world view, but a notion that reflects on the experiences of generations of agro-industrial migrant workers. It is personal experience uttered within the framework of the *mestizaje* ideology; that is, *Indios* are defined by their lack of civilization, in this case in the form of clothing and pride.

The concept of the *Indio* as a culturally distinct subject is not entirely absent but under considerable reorganization. How this is worked out can be seen in the second text, from *el periódico mural,* titled *"Que es un Indio?"*

Que es un Indio?

> Como se identifica un Indio en El Salvador hoy en día?
> Que separa a un Indio de un Ladino?

> *En el aspecto físico, es difícil destinguir a los Indios de El Salvador de las demas personas que les rodean. Los rasgos étnicos tradicionales come lo son el idioma Nahuatl el tipico físico y el vestido no existe en forma tan marcada come en el caso de los grupos indíjenas.*
>
> *Casi todos los Indios indíjenas de esta comunidad hablaban el Nahuatl y hoy en día solo quedan más que un puñado de ancianos con conocimientos de la lengua indíjena.*
>
> *A comienzos del año 70 a 1996, Santo Domingo tiene hablantes nativos a 50 a 70 todos son adultos. Los niños demuestran poco interes en aprendera hablar el idioma.*

What Is an Indian?

> How does one identify an Indian in El Salvador today?
>
> What separates an Indian from a Ladino?
>
> In the physical aspect it is difficult to distinguish the Indians of El Salvador from the rest of the persons who surround them. The traditional ethnic traits such as the Nahuatl language, the physical type, and the dress don't exist in that marked a form as in the case of the indigenous groups.
>
> Almost all the indigenous Indians from the community spoke Nahuatl and today there is only a little handful of elders with the knowledge of the indigenous language.
>
> From the beginning of the 1970s to 1996, Santo Domingo had from 50 to 70 native speakers, all of them adults. The kids show little interest in learning to speak the language.

What strikes one in this text is that the author fails to distinguish between the *Indio* and the ladino in today's El Salvador. Taking into consideration the other text hanging next to this one on the wall, in which the distinction is absolute, this is, of course, surprising. But before moving to the intertextual level of interpretation, we should dwell on the text in itself.

Given that there is no difference between *Indios* and ladinos in today's El Salvador, Don Genaro introduces a new identity, the *Indio-Indíjena,* of which he concludes that only fifty to seventy exist. They live scattered in the two *barrios* and in the valley above the village; they all belong to the older generation and will be dead in ten to twenty years. The deployment of the hyphenated identity of *Indio-Indíjena* is important because it draws our attention to the negotiations taking place between global ethnodiscourse and local constructions of indigenous identity. By deploying the notion of *Indio-Indíjena,* Don Genaro tries to establish a discursive framework that incorporates the politicized identities authorized by ethnodiscourse without subsuming the local notion of what an *Indio* is. The hyphenated identity of *Indio-Indíjena* thus poses a question to those who are *Indios* but not *Indíjenas,* the villagers who are almost indistinguishable from ladinos. Who are they?

The group is made up of those individuals who are not *Indíjenas*, a substantial part are not even *comaleros* in the sense that female kin produce *comales*. They are nevertheless considered *Indios*. The definition of this group is particularly difficult for outside observers looking for the visual ethnographic difference, and their definition as *Indios* hinges on their being *naturales del pueblo* (natives of the town). In short, this identity as *Indio* is linked to the formation and maintenance of alliances as these are expressed in livelihood strategies, village politics, and performances.

Although ethnodiscourse does empower a variety of different Amerindian groups through the global circulation of objects, pictures, and texts, this globalization of indigenous culture also gives rise to concern. In places such as western El Salvador, very few people assert their cultural identity through clothes and language. Yet a considerable group of people consider themselves *Indios* and are defined as such. The same holds for communities in Nicaragua and Honduras. The self-definition of *Indio* is related not to the pre-Columbian or colonial categories stressing primordial culture but rather to the labor in the *milpas* and *fincas* undertaken in associations and alliances within a large group of kin. More than anything else, it is field work that forms the core of the *Indio* identity, and this identity is thus linked to the search for livelihoods. The same applies to the notion of *Indio comalero*, a notion directly related to the livelihood strategies of indigenous women. Such an identity does not open itself up for incorporation by ethnodiscourse.

Indigenous groups are left in the borderlands of this concept's common use. They are hardly indigenous to the outside observer, but they are definitely *Indios* to the local ladinos. They have suffered the same repression as most other indigenous groups of southern Mesoamerica, but in their rightful quest for vindication they cannot base their claims on cultural primordialism, nor on a distinct cultural nation, and even less on a body of indigenous knowledge. They are, therefore, according to the ethnodiscourse, not part of diversity but part of sameness, they are not part of nature's historicity but part of their nation's. Yet they also fail to be just Salvadorans, and they are, therefore, what I have termed the deportees of the ethnodiscourse, left in a limbo without authorized subjectivities.

Ellen Moodie

"El Capitán Cinchazo"

Blood and Meaning in Postwar San Salvador

Four years later, her brother's blood had splashed so many times into the overflow on the Calle Rubén Darío's rumpled sidewalk that she could no longer tell red from red. The way Doña Nohemí remembered it, the same green blur of police uniforms filmed firing M-16s at a corpse-strewn corner in front of a bank on the morning of June 22, 1994, would later aim eighteen bullets at Renato as he crouched in his Toyota 4Runner.[1]

The air is fragrant with flowering maquilishuát, El Salvador's national tree. The maid carries in a tray with glasses of fresh pineapple juice. I savor the juice's sugary tang and listen as Nohemí Trabanino de Bernal, a soft-spoken, middle-aged mother, recounts crime stories for my shirring Sony tape recorder. Nohemí herself has never been robbed. She doesn't go out much, just to church and a part-time job nearby at the Central American University (UCA). Now, her oldest son, yes, he got his watch stolen as he was leaving his exclusive private school a few years ago. The mugger pushed a pistol into his forehead. And her husband, his car taken (1980—the guerrillas told him where to find it). Then, a brother, in 1982, abducted in his car. "They made him drive around for an hour and a bit until they found another vehicle they liked more and decided to steal it—he got away, they shot at him as he floored the accelerator. Thank God he was okay, but that was what made him decide to leave the country."

Then there are the break-ins. Just a few days ago a strange man was lingering out front. It looked as if he was scoping out the site, as if he wanted to rob it. He left after the maid called the limping German shepherd over to bark. And just last week a friend was "imprudent" enough to go out with her wedding ring on her finger, to dare to wear gold in *the street. They grabbed it, and everything else. "Just over here, just over here." Nohemí gestures out toward the midday cacophony, muffled by thick brick walls.*

Labeling as Excess

"Violence is an event in which there is a certain excess: an excess of passion, an excess of evil," anthropologist E. Valentine Daniel tells us. "The very attempt to label this excess (as indeed I have done) is condemned to fail; it employs what Georges Bataille called *mots glissants* (slippery words). Everything can be narrated, but what is narrated is no longer what happened."[2]

Yet only through the (mis)labeling of excess (indeed, the labeling as excess) does the "postwar" come into being. Named, made intelligible, made into a public text, it can circulate. As a text, it is about the world, bearing meaning. It is also in the world, "thing-like," performed and circulated in repeatable texts, that, transient, can never be determinate yet are always already situated in a social, political, and historical moment. These "slippery words" come from all points, each competing for legitimacy and power as they attempt to impose meanings on the world. Each offers some version of the unexpected peace surplus: postwar violence. These possibilities are contested and reimagined, replicated, and mutated in everyday talk and gossip about episodes of intrigue and conspiracy and strange-yet-strangely-expected coincidence shared among neighbors, cousins, and old school chums during chance encounters over German beer at La Ventana or ice cream cones at POPS Metrocentro. Each instance, discharged from its moment of mute sensibility, flows (or, failing to conform, dissipates) into circulating narratives, theories, and discourses that co-construct shared understandings of the postwar.

By 1995, one postwar narrative seemed to carry special truth value: the Attorney General's Office reported an intentional homicide rate of 136.5 per 100,000 population—more murders per capita than during the war.[3] This statistic placed El Salvador among the most dangerous countries in the world. (In the mid-1990s, according to the Pan-American Health Organization, Costa Rica's rate was 3.9 per 100,000; the United States', 8.5; Mexico's, 19.4, and urban Colombia's, 110.4.)[4] The murder rate, now considered inaccurate,[5] was widely publicized, girded by headline after headline about the crime wave, the crime increase, the crime surge. All the numbers, all the headlines, all the talk I heard in the 1990s belied El Salvador's world image as a war-to-peace success story.

In this chapter I ponder two briefly overlapping instances of narrative production of postwar "peace" during the early 1990s. I explore how different forces maneuver to control meaning, to fix labels; I inquire into the ways "entextualization" of embodied experience both rubs up against and balks at such national and institutional metanarratives.[6] I begin by recalling the historical conjuncture sparked by a spectacular and particularly bloody bank robbery caught by TV cameras in June 1994. I follow the ensuing public discussion of postwar violence, words haunted by ghosts of past narrative constructs and residual cultural formations. Finally, I contrast official stories of the bank heist with accounts of a near-fatal assault on San Salvador banker Luis Renato Trabanino Aguilar.[7]

Renato's version of his experience provides a singular, flesh-and-blood encounter that exemplifies the Salvadoran crime and violence that government officials, international experts, and university scholars have failed to explain. Rather than following any kind of national metanarrative on postwar chaos, Renato's search for meaning, or semiosis, resists detachment from its context, from physical pain, from the body itself. In contrast, public semiosis spirals out and out, lurching toward abstract concepts of democracy, security, and peace that circulate in political gatherings, newspapers, academic conferences, and United Nations assemblies. Rather than setting these different semiotic flows against each other, I am observing them, recording their divergence and convergence. Renato's is not an "oppositional" voice as commonly defined through theories of counterhegemony. A well-connected businessman from moneyed origins, he lives a comfortable (if not secure) life. He supports the dominant Nationalist Republican Alliance (ARENA) political party. Yet he hardly adheres to a "dominant" ideological perspective. His story, as told to me in 1998, weaves a combination of what Raymond Williams might call dominant, residual, and emergent strands of cultural practices, just as the loosely linked mass-mediated narratives on the bank robbery constructed in 1994 do as they try to fix hard labels on amorphous, unfolding events.[8]

Modes of domination, Williams argues, "select from and consequently exclude the full range of human practice," exiling most experience to the realm of the "personal or private."[9] That someone like Renato turns to spiritual and personal terms rather than social and public ones to confront his encounter with violence suggests that El Salvador's official "peace," that state and institutional discourses, did very little to help him (nor, I would argue, most Salvadorans) confront the task of daily living, to strategize survival in unpredictable times. In the 1990s the powerless majority, as well as many comfortable Salvadorans from the business and professional classes, believed that the state continued to operate largely in its own circles of meaning. Whether this view was a residual one, history holding down the postwar emergence of more hopeful ways of experiencing and acting on the world, remains to be seen.

"It's True, He Was Really Flashy"

"Oh, and my brother," Nohemí exclaims, interrupting her own musing, "my brother almost got killed. Four years ago, it's going to be in June, on June 22, 1994. In fact, that same day, there was that assault on the Banco de Comercio over by the Calle Rubén Darío, when they killed all those people there."

"Oh—that famous case, the armored truck—"

"That case of Lieutenant Coreas—"

"Yes, I remember—"

"The Coreas case. In the morning, that had happened. At 6:15 in the evening, close to the old former American embassy, that's where my brother was working. So he came out—it's true, he had a flashy car, a 4Runner, and he went around with a really flashy watch, a big gold one. It's true, he was really flashy, because I don't think there's any reason to go around being more, or less, than others."

Videotape of a Midmorning Massacre

It still haunts San Salvador. Back during the drought of 1994, the Coreas case played and replayed across San Salvador's small screens. It pushed to the back pages news like the latest death threats against Salvadoran celebrities, from ARENA maven Milena Calderón de Escalón to Archbishop Arturo Rivera y Damas. It "disappeared" the fallout from the defamation trial of gabby ex-guerrilla commander Joaquín Villalobos (before his retreat to Oxford, England) for calling Orlando de Sola, a far-right coffee and cooking-oil king, a death-squad financier. It even detoured the prolonged partisan debate over which new Supreme Court justices would replace a corrupt group so notorious that the UN Truth Commission had urged its members to resign immediately, to much elite umbrage.[10] By August, the story had morphed into a comic strip, "El Capitán Cinchazo" (a twice-removed corruption of Lieutenant Coreas—both names derive from words Salvadorans use for "belt," *correa* and *cincho*), about the adventures of a greedy, bumbling ex-army captain and his goony gang of thugs (including ex-National Guard and ex-FMLN).[11]

On that hot June morning in 1994 a crew from the Channel 6 news program *El Noticiero* happened to be driving a few blocks west of the sagging, earthquake-shuttered National Cathedral at 8:50 A.M. They heard shots, dashed in their direction, cameras on, and recorded the most dramatic ten minutes of footage since the war. At noon thousands of Salvadorans were watching videotaped images of the event that had already been reported in urgent, rat-a-tat updates over the radio.

The film shows blurs of four or five men in bullet-proof vests wielding M-16 and G-3 rifles,[12] running, shooting, ducking, shouting, *"Dale!" "Ahuevalo!" "Tené cuidado, vieja!" "Andate a la esquina!" "Hey men!"*[13] One man caught on film was seen scrambling through the smoke with a bag grabbed off an armored truck parked outside a branch of the Banco de Comercio, at the corner of Rubén Darío Street and South 21st Avenue. At least two of the men were wearing the familiar green National Police uniforms.

Within two days, the beady-eyed, beak-nosed second-in-command of the National Police's investigative division—Lieutenant José Rafael Coreas Orellana—would be pulled from his Ahuachapán home and arrested for the midmorning massacre that left at least four dead and pierced a wilting state stance on public security. Cinchazo, as I will refer to the bank heist in this chapter, briefly became a locus of debate in the struggle to define "peace" while the news was issuing daily reports of violence. It also catapulted the debate over the role in a new democracy of a state apparatus with a history of fierce repression.

In 1994 the National Police (Policía Nacional, PN) was slowly being dismantled, as demanded by the Peace Accords, and replaced by the National Civilian Police (Policía Nacional Civil, PNC). The famously corrupt PN had been tied to numerous human rights abuses. The PN was a paramilitary unit under the Salvadoran Defense Ministry, commanded by army officers. It had overseen "law and order" in urban areas and investigated crime throughout the country. Its investigative division was the national intelligence unit, investigating both criminal and political cases.[14] With the Peace Accords, the old military PN uniform was, in effect, being cast out of the complex of signs that iconized the law, indexed order, and symbolized the state,[15] though this expulsion was resisted by certain powerful sectors of the society. Just before Cinchazo, then-president Alfredo Cristiani had extended PN's life, pointing to rising crime rates. As chroniclers of El Salvador's much-watched peace process would soon pronounce, Cinchazo forced the recalcitrant government to move. "After a bloody bank heist in June, a police lieutenant in charge of the old National Police criminal investigative division was identified in a videotape of the crime and arrested as a suspect," Margaret Popkin of the Lawyers Committee for Human Rights would write. "This official confirmation of high-level police involvement in organized crime led the president to speed up the [long-delayed] demobilization of the National Police."[16] The term "bloody bank heist" would recur in a number of versions of this incident.

Flows and Fragments: Tracing a Narrative

"It was about 6:15 that evening." Nohemí's voice is suddenly animated after her oblig-atory recitation of run-of-the-mill watch- and ring-snatchings, house break-ins, and car-jackings. "So. So they held a gun to his head and told him to get into his car, into the back, and they started it up. There was one of them in front and one in back. My brother, he was always armed. He still is. And so when he gave—when they told him to get in the car, he said to them, 'Well, if you want my car, here are the keys, take the car.' . . . But they said no, that they wanted him. 'No you're coming with us.' So he got the idea that these people, that they were going to kill him.

"And he shot both of them and he—really he killed them.

"But . . . there were more [men], there—and so they shot him—and my brother is alive, miraculously, I mean, they shot him, he was hit by at least four shots, and they shot even more. He was really in bad condition, critical. No one can explain how—"

For Nohemí de Bernal, this family story became linked to national intrigue through clues left by the corpses stiffening in the seats of Renato Trabanino Aguilar's still-running SUV. For her, her brother's thwarted kidnapping outside the old U.S. embassy in the evening has become infused with the dramatic hap-penings downtown that morning—with Cinchazo. "And the wallets of the thieves that died," Nohemí says, in a conspiratorial tone, "they were full of money, full of money."

"Wow."

"Totally, right." Renato's bank colleague, who rushed him to the hospital, had told her this. "He saw . . . that some of them had dollars, and others, [Guatemalan] quetzales and more than anything colones, but they were completely full. Also another thing, . . . the ones who shot him were [not the ones he killed]. The dead ones, the dead ones, the paraffin tests on the guns came out positive. They had shot at someone, someone else, that day, at someone. And also one of them had, eh, eh, marijuana, the tests showed that one had drugs in him.

"And both of their wallets were full of money. And then it came out they had used guns that only had been ordered for the army. No one knows how they got them. . . . But a very sophisticated gun that had been delivered not long before to the army."

"But is there some kind of theory that it's related to the bank robbery?"

"It could be true," Nohemí says. The links [military guns-money-drugs] were clear to any Salvadoran—it was obviously something bigger than a little carjacking. "Because they had so much money. But we didn't find out anything more."

"Voice Interference": Crime and Peace?

M. M. Bakhtin might call it "voice interference."[17] There it is, still present, Cinchazo's recorded and replayed gunfire, the urgent news commentary, and the loud, angry public debate that followed, shooting through Nohemí's memory. It must be absorbed into the text of the telling, transforming its shape, its very taste. The public news form, a secondary genre, absorbing primary utterances of witnesses before reporters' notebooks and microphones, is reabsorbed, recontextualized again into conversation and gossip. The bank robbery made the air waves within minutes of its 8:50 A.M. commencement and had already distended news dispatches for hours before Renato's attack. The Trabanino-Bernal household was saturated with the loud struggle of national dialogue, with four newspapers delivered daily and the news always on. The family would fit the incident into the heteroglot, intertextual Salvadoran genealogy: recitations of daily experiences with violence and crime, paralleling and crossing into the dense, intense daily banter circulating in San Salvador's radio call-in shows, morning interview marathons, evening news carnivals, and daily newspaper columns. And on June 22, 1994, that replicating and mutating stream of meaning swirled around Cinchazo.

Cinchazo could not have happened without the post–Peace Accords opening of a mass mediated public sphere. And, though this space may seem overlain with the elites' hegemony, daily news journalism by its nature is a space that cannot be fully manipulated. Too many fugitive facts fall in the way. In the first months of the transition hundreds of uncredited news items appeared in El Salvador's dailies, inserted into corners and between advertisements, told a different story of violence than conveyed in the summaries prepared by the UN, which was primarily concerned with "political" crime. Those newspaper items were the articles most Salvadorans read. In February 1993 the UCA's Public Opinion Institute carried out its first poll focused on crime.[18] A total of 73.2 percent of the urban respondents said "crime, thievery, lack of authority, robbery, violations, and gangs" were the country's principal problems; 88.6 percent said crime had increased since 1992. Problems related to the carrying out of Peace Accords and the conflicts of postwar politics, which dominated the front pages, were identified as problems by only 10.6 percent of the respondents.

The survey revealed how intimate people were with everyday violence one year into the transition—and how distant the dominant media discourse was. One-third of the respondents said a close friend or relative had been assaulted within four months of the survey. Of those assaults, only 22.4 percent of the victims said they had reported the crimes to the authorities, whether for fear (31.9 percent) or because "it wouldn't have made any difference" (39 percent).

Simulating the State

On the day of Cinchazo and of Renato's attack, June 22, 1994, the first paper to hit the street was the thin left-leaning tabloid *Diario Latino*. The headline trips down the left-hand side of the front page, blurting the basics in black and white: "Five Dead and the Theft of Two and a Half Million Colones [about US$286,697] in Assault Today in the Capital."[19] The headline has no "subject," and assigns no responsibility for the violence splayed across the spaces of news and city. Both the customary curtness of headlinese and the very grammar of Spanish conspire to erase agents. This gap becomes the crux of the case.

The caption below photos of prone corpses on the stained sidewalk whispers of traces that structure the photo-sign: "Millionaire Assault Today. Two employees of Salvadoran Protection Services stand guard soon after several individuals *disguised as* agents of the National Police with high-caliber arms and bullet-proof vests today assaulted an armored truck [emphasis added]." Such "anchoring" of meaning tries to limit interpretation. What we see, the newspaper tells us, is a simulation of an icon of the state. This uniform apparently representing the state must be a mask. But then the *Diario Latino* article concludes suggestively, "It is believed that, because of the precision of the robbery, it was planned in advance and executed by experts in the use of high-caliber arms used exclusively by the armed forces, who previously must have studied the movements of the security agency responsible for transporting the money." Suddenly the uniform is no mere costume, no disguise. Other details—expertise in specific arms, precise planning—dissemble the dissimulation. This description, detailing precise acts of will and force and knowing, is becoming more and more common in Salvadorans' personal accounts of postwar crime. It marshals a narrative linking past war experience with present chaos. It offers several possibly merging interpretants: organized crime, ex-combatants, and corrupt police.

On that same day the newspaper *El Mundo*'s report was also synthesized speedily. In this version two of the (at least ten) assailants are *wearing* the PN uniform and others wear blue bulletproof vests. The thieves throw a grenade. The exchange of fire lasts three minutes, and then the assailants continue to shoot—with M-16s and G-3s—at civilians in order to protect their accomplices. In a subtle turn of phrase *El Mundo* both doubts the authenticity of the uniforms and suggests that they may be real. These men are not, as in the *El Latino* account, disguised—they *are wearing* the uniforms. Bodies wearing PN uniforms could be PN. But at the same time, real PN are not usually described as merely dressed as PN. Other "facts"—signs—chosen for this article may lead a reader to think about who might throw grenades, use high-caliber weapons, and shoot to protect their accomplices' maneuvers. In the days following the heist the word first used to describe the criminals seen in PN uniforms—*disguised*—slips and stretches in various TV, radio, and print dispatches.

The next day, June 23, the nation's two fat, dominant newspapers, *La Prensa Gráfica* and *El Diario de Hoy,* illustrate their catch-up coverage with gritty color film stills from Channel 6's videotape. A figure in green is seen running through gun smoke, bag in hand. A man in official attire stands at the bank door, pointing or throwing something. Another man hides behind a car, shooting. Both newspapers have issued smooth narrative accounts. *La Prensa,* right-wing but moderating after the war, describes the suspects as "some fifteen heavily armed individuals, twelve of them *with* PN uniforms."[20] The reporter reconstructs the moments before the attack from witness accounts: "The only noticeable thing was the presence of a lot of supposed police officers, who were carrying arms of war." Later, a PN official confirms that "twelve men with uniforms of the National Police, olive-green bullet-proof vests and heavy arms—M-16, AK-47, AR-15, and rifles[21]—participated in the assault."

For *El Diario de Hoy,* nationalistic, fiercely anti-Communist, the fallout of this incident is immediately clear, leaping beyond the vagueness of fear and the specificity of one event.[22] The headline: "Citizenry Demands Security." These words define the event as a story of the nation-state. In a sidebar, "Thank God I'm Alive," a security agent who survived ended with an apocalyptic interpretant: "The time we are living in is very difficult. There isn't control over the PN, and the PNC isn't ready and maybe it won't be like the people want, but it's necessary to reinforce the security of the country. Maybe it's time for the Armed Forces to return to the streets to combat these crimes like that of yesterday, which left three families abandoned because they took the lives of my three friends."

The newspapers point to indexes of state security officials: the uniforms, the arms, the precision in the execution of the crime, the boots. These, together, make up the uniform of the PN, an arm of the state. But the newspapers hedge: these criminals are *disguised,* or *are dressed as* PN, or are *wearing uniforms,* or are *with* them. The uniform, the mark of the state, is thus loosened from the body. The state as an institution is still safe, as symbolized by the security institutions (interpretants of order). Whether or not these figures turn out to be "real" PN, they will only be bodies borrowing the costume.

Hiding the Gun Pouch

Renato and I sit under the wide glass window at the air-conditioned Mr. Donut, a Salvadoranized version of the defunct U.S. franchise. A jovial lunch crowd buzzes in the background. He is smaller than I expect, younger, his voice higher pitched. But he is not hesitant about talking, not at all, in a certain elite slang that echoes an upbringing among campesino servants, or perhaps a lot of time among workers on his family's coffee farms. (I have condensed his version, but the words—as I have translated them—are all his.)

"It was a Wednesday, June 22, 1994." His precision continues throughout his narrative, as if I am really an insurance investigator looking into a claim. "I left the office like at 6:10 in the evening. When I was going out—I had my truck, an SUV, a Toyota 4Runner, parked. And when I went out, I saw a car, a Nissan Sentra, with dark tinted windows—you couldn't see inside, but it was like three or four meters from my truck, kind of weird, halfway up the sidewalk. I saw it, but I didn't pay any attention to it.

"I had my attaché case, with things from work, in my right hand, and in my left, my mariconera [a pouch, usually used for arms, carried by men]. I've carried guns, in my pouch, ever since 1980 when I got authorized to carry arms. So at that time I carried my pouch, carried my pistol, a 9mm-caliber Beretta. I carried it under my arm. I used to think, I hope to God I never need to use it. But I always thought it would be to protect my children, or my wife. . . . When I was putting the attaché on the back seat, I don't know what it was but I saw, in the corner of my eye, that these two guys—armed—were getting out of that car that was parked nearby. . . . My reaction was to grab my pouch. I put it beneath the attaché so they couldn't see it.

"Then they came and one of them said, 'Get in,' he said, 'Get in.' Then he shoved me, like this, in the shoulder. 'Get in.' Well when he did that I moved calmly and what I did was . . . push the attaché with everything, and the pouch, to the back of the seat. And I got in, I sat in the back seat and one of them sat next to me and the other got in the driver's side. They didn't say anything, I told them, 'Here are the keys, take them,' and I gave them to the driver.

"He grabbed them, but the other one, the one next to me said, 'The truck doesn't go alone. . . . No,' he told me. 'We're taking you with us.' In this half-second . . . what I thought was, these guys are going to take me to some isolated place and they're going to kill me and . . . I would be found, an unidentified corpse, who knows where. That's what I thought, I thought, I better defend myself. . . . I was calm. But I had thought what to do. 'My God, help me, but I have to defend myself, I'm just going to have one chance and I'm just going to have a second to do it,' that's what I thought."

Breaking Old Habits and Uncovering New Mutations

Over the next days, editorial-page articles proliferate, seeking to fix meaning on Cinchazo ever more concretely. *La Prensa* editorializes about organized crime taking over the country. The paper suggests that the new "unemployed," the ex-military and ex-FMLN combatants, are easily recruited for these groups. "The authorities should demonstrate," *La Prensa* urges, "that they are not incapable of controlling this type of organized crime."[23] *Diario Latino,* too, writes of the threat of organized crime, specifically that linked with state security forces. It invokes powerful images: the eight uniformed soldiers—some of whom were later convicted, then pardoned—seen entering the home of the six Jesuit priests they murdered on the campus of the UCA.

Then, on June 25, body, state, and uniform converge. The media reveal that the second-in-command of investigations for the National Police, Lieutenant José Rafael Coreas Orellana, has been arrested. He is not described as *dressed as* or *wearing the uniform of* the PN. He is certainly not *disguised as* PN. He *is* PN. Indeed, as a lead investigator, he is an icon of a PN officer, and as such an icon of the state. The key evidence indexing his guilt comes from the Channel 6 videotape.

In El Salvador, the imposition of the label of peace could not instantly change conventions of interpretation. The news media's hesitancy and the use of the term *disguises* both testify to old habits. But, as most journalists (and many Salvadorans) tell me, Coreas *would never have been arrested in the 1980s.* The videotape would never have appeared (indeed, the PN had tried to ensure its erasure the first day when agents tried to confiscate the tape from Channel 6.[24] Further, after the robbery, PN agents, accustomed to impunity, returned to the bank to pick up guns they had forgotten.[25] Now *La Prensa Gráfica* writes, "old structures of public security have rotted, and the citizens won't be satisfied this time if this is blamed on isolated personal misconduct, as has happened in the past. . . . [The police] isn't an organ of public control, after all, but an organ of protection."[26]

Stumbling against Impunity

The June 29, 1994, edition of UCA's newsweekly *El Salvador Proceso* stressed "surprise" that an active-duty lieutenant had actually been arrested. "The surprise comes from the fact that this is the first time the government has tried seriously to investigate a crime, and because the identity of the chief suspect appears to confirm involvement by top army and police officials in this type of crime. . . . The link between crime and impunity has been starkly revealed."[27] Not all Salvadorans would concede such clarity: "If there weren't a videotape of these scenes, this bank heist wouldn't have even been investigated. They would have reached the conclusion that a group of glue sniffers had robbed the bank and it would be left at that," as anti-drug activist Carlos Avilés told newsman Mauricio Funes on Channel 12.[28]

President Cristiani's successor, Armando Calderón Sol, would soon announce that the National Police would be investigated and finally disbanded. The new president, from right-wing ARENA (proclaiming, "We will not permit abuse of authority. . . . There will be no more impunity") and the ever-left-leaning Monsignor Gregorio Rosa Chávez ("It's necessary that we now look inside the beast!") would be quoted in the same articles, supporting the same actions.[29] It seemed as if real reconciliation could take place. Both agreed that organized crime, with links to the nation's power structures, was becoming a major problem.

On July 28, 1994, the UN-initiated Joint Group for the Investigation of Politically Motivated Illegal Armed Groups released its delayed report.[30] Its members pointed to a "mutation" or "metamorphosis" in old death squad structures. "The broad network of organized crime that flails the country, in which, the evidence shows, there is active participation of the members of the armed forces of El Salvador and the National Police, cannot be divorced from many acts of politically motivated violence," they wrote. "To be sure, political motives do not seem to constitute the sole or even the essential driving force behind these structures, which engage predominantly in acts coming under the label of 'common crime,' but with a high degree of organization and infrastructure." The Joint Group concluded, "It is absolutely essential to provide [the PNC] with the necessary resources for carrying out the job of criminal investigation in such a way as to offer the citizens the certainty that political violence and organized crime in the country will be definitively extirpated."[31]

The UN Observer Mission in El Salvador (ONUSAL) later deemed Cinchazo "a turning point . . . in the area of public security." Ever since it began issuing reports, ONUSAL had been bending the events toward the "Salvadoran success story." UN report writers blamed "the intransigence of fringe elements"—a stubborn excess—for thwarting the "unanimous rejection . . . [by] all national sectors, institutions, churches, and political forces . . . of any form of violence." Then, referring obliquely to Cinchazo, ONUSAL reported, "After recent events revealed the involvement of criminal activities of individuals or groups within the public security apparatus, the Government promptly denounced the existence of organized crime and expressed its determination to take decisive actions against all those involved regardless of their origin, thus squarely confronting an issue that had not hitherto been openly addressed."[32]

Indeed, within a few days of the bank robbery, certain determined interpreters of El Salvador's story, of the narrative of peace negotiation, had swept this event into a grand narrative of "success." A year later, in June 1995, as most UN observers left El Salvador, then-secretary-general Boutros Boutros-Ghali would say in a widely publicized speech that the country had taken "giant strides away from a violent and closed society toward a democratic order."[33]

"I Never Even Saw Them"

"So I went and grabbed my gun, because I had it right there in the pouch under the attaché, I grabbed it and when I felt like I had it good—he didn't see me because I was covering myself with the rest of my body. I got right in front of his chest and shot him twice and I got him in a moment of his carelessness. He died without knowing it. Then I leaned over to the front and put my gun between the two seats and the headrest on the back of the seat and shot the guy in front, two more shots. Thank God, if I had held back—one second more—the guy in front would have killed me . . . because he was caught with his arm reaching over the back of the seat. And his gun was a Jericho, 9 mm. It landed on my feet. But I didn't realize it, it all went so fast that I didn't realize that his gun was there.

"My idea was that after defending myself I would get out of the right door and shoot at that car (the Nissan Sentra I had seen). Because I knew that in the car there was at least one more, the one who was driving. But the, the, the frequency of the shots, more or less, the speed of the shots, I still can feel it now, it was more or less like this, see, pac-pác, pac-pác, the four shots. But the fourth shot, I shot it, and pulled really fast. So the movement made my pistol jam. When I was bringing the gun down I saw the bronze color of the car door in movement, it hadn't finished closing.

"And in that moment, it's like, desperation. I heard steps. The sound of steps. I thought, 'Ah, another one of them is coming.' So in that moment what I did was play dead. I closed my eyes. I stayed still. I didn't breathe. And I just pleaded for protection from God. Just thinking, 'God, help me.' Because I said, 'If he shoots me in the head I'll die without knowing it. God help me, God help me.'

"When I didn't hear any sounds— it sounded like he was going away—I didn't hear anything, I opened my eyes slowly and saw that there wasn't anyone, because the door was still open, . . . then I looked back. And—I am looking at this guy, a person, a man—in this position. With his gun. Pointing. . . . He was a type who looked calm, serene, not nervous at all, like they say, it wasn't the first time that he had done that. And he began to shoot, through the truck window. So when I saw this I was mortified, just mortified, like they say. And my reaction was to stay still in the seat, just thinking of God. There were two of them. One in back and one at the side—and they began a shootout between the two of them. They shot like eighteen times.

"I never felt pain. When their shootout ended, I didn't feel pain, but I knew I'd been hurt. Thank God, I didn't see a drop of blood, because that really gets to me. But when I turned to look down, I saw my shirt ripped. But no blood. So I said, 'Well, there's a bullet there,' and I began to feel like sleepy, weak. [Then], a friend, I worked with him, we were friends since before, he came out and then he said, 'Chino'—that's my nickname, they call me 'Chino,' all my brothers are 'Chinos'—'Chino,' he said—I said to him, 'Paco, I'm screwed.' Then he said, 'I'm getting you to the hospital.'"

Terror between Kidnappings

Renato only made page four in sensationalist newspaper *La Noticia.* The tabloid slipped his terror between two kidnappings. Above him, "Businessman Escapes His Kidnappers"; below, "Kidnappers of Supposed Relatives of Defense Minister Captured." Embedded in the daily medley of disconnected events that merge as media commodity, Renato's episode shrinks into trite daily journalism, fill-in-the-blanks formula: "Two Deaths and Two Injured Men in Frustrated Assault." The story's life as a commodity ends there. That Renato in his fine tailored suit and his shiny SUV managed to escape and kill his assailants could have elevated the event to a point of more enduring interest if the forces of the moment had so converged. By 1999, more than half the San Salvadorans responding to surveys said they believed "people have the right to take justice into their own hands" (while more than 90 percent demanded "more rigid laws").[34] Vigilante justice was publicly heralded. But in mid-1994 this was no Bernhard Goetz story. The story was "buried" as Cinchazo filled the front pages.

"All the Sins of Your Life Are Forgiven"

"Sometimes they say it's coincidence. But, no, for me, thank God, God did me the favor, the miracle, of granting me life. They took me to the hospital at like 6:20 in the evening. The surgeon on call, who was very good, had a clinic in front of the hospital, or at least a block away. Normally he went home at 6. This day at this hour, 6:20, thank God he hadn't left. For me, all these things aren't just coincidences.

"I had five bullets. This scar I have here, the bullet went in here. It passed four millimeters above the aorta, the artery. If it hits the aorta, there, I die right away. It punctured the gland that we have in back of the sternum and it punctured my right lung. I had four broken ribs, they cut out a little piece of rib, because it could have punctured the lung more. And they cut out the gall bladder and part of my liver and, well, two bones were destroyed, the tibia and the fibula, and the bones, you could see them, it was an exposed fracture, that's what they call it.

"So they operated on me, and at 2:30 A.M. they came out and talked with my family, with my wife, my brothers. And they told them my situation was critical. Very critical. 'Look, the most optimistic is 10 percent, that he'll live.' When [my wife] heard that, she went and told my brother: 'Go and get a father, a priest, to give extreme unction.' And he went to get a priest, a friend who had in fact given first communion to my daughter.

"He arrived and he said to me—it had been years since I'd seen or heard from him. And he said to me, 'Chino,' he said. 'I'm such-and-such,' he said. When he said his name, I knew who it was, even though we hadn't seen each other for years. Then he told me, 'I'm

going to give you a special blessing of the Pope.' What, I remember was that he made a sign of the cross. After that I stayed calm. Because he said to me, 'All the sins of your life are forgiven,' he said. And so I, in that moment, what I thought of was those two men that I'd gotten. So I felt at peace, I was calm, I remained serene, content, and he left.

"There's no explanation . . . like I say, it wasn't coincidence, these weren't coincidences, but miracles of God. Right. . . . I was in the hospital almost a month. To make a long story short, I had four operations, and I had to go to the United States, and there they operated on me twice. In other words they operated on my leg six times. But thank God I'm fine. Thank God I'm fine."

Simulation of Justice

To many Salvadorans, Cinchazo proved to be just another simulation of justice, temporary, slippery. Ex-Lieutenant Coreas, after seven and a half months in jail, was freed in February 1995. By then the twenty-three-year army veteran had starred in countless editorial cartoons and had even been named one of *Primera Plana's* 1994 "personalities of the year."[35] He continued to insist that a so-called double, *El Chele Papaya* (the pale papaya, a nickname), appeared in the videotape, not him. Even after two Keystone Kops–style PN arrests of different, apparently innocent *Cheles Papayas* in Usulután and Guazapa, Coreas' lawyer Manuel Chacón would not give up the call for the sinister look-alike who had simulated the honorable lieutenant's image on screen. Then the investigative judge decided the infamous videotape, even after FBI analysis, was not definitive. "The society will never completely trust the system of justice with these kinds of rulings," the frustrated prosecutors said. "Impunity continues."[36]

Meanwhile, Coreas, who had converted to evangelical Christianity, held up a Bible and thanked God for divine justice. At least publicly, for him, the Cinchazo narrative was finally about redemption. "It was God who illuminated the mind of my lawyer and gave me the strength to survive this great slander," he told reporters as he left his cell on February 1, 1995.[37] Later news reports would say he was studying law in his native Ahuachapán.

Circulation of Impunity: Cinchazo Lives

Named, made intelligible, a public text, an ephemeral event can move beyond its moment and circulate. The story of the bank robbery and the four bodies, and the videotape that caught the "big deal suspect," became the "bloody bank heist" that rescued the hopeful tale of Salvadoran democratization, for the academics, for the international officials. The recontextualized story ended there, apparently, for their purposes. It nestled into articles and reports and books as part of the narrative of peace and progress, or relative peace and progress. But the story of the living Coreas himself is the one that I continued to hear about among Salvadorans for years. The robbery incident and its aftermath, with its vivid imagery, with the intense, swirling search for meaning, is both about the world and in the world, entextualized as something repeatable—and alive. Its meaning continues to mutate, if more slowly. But versions of the peace surplus—violence—continue to circulate.

It is not Coreas' name that returns to my friend Caro Portillo de Mejía, a Soyapango church volunteer and mother of three, in the middle of our recorded conversation in August 1998.[38] It is the videotape, and Coreas' own story of defiant redemption. I ask her why I hear so many people say, "It's worse than the war now." She answers first by bringing up a discussion she and members of her church reading group have been having, about failed state responsibilities. The Peace Accords haven't delivered all they promised, she says.

> *"Just yesterday they were saying that I don't know how many of the demobilized combatants went [to protest], but they said they were ready to go again to the mountains [to fight], that's what they threatened, if they didn't get any pensions."*
>
> *"They said that?" I ask.*
>
> *"They said it on the [radio station] KL, that's what I heard was happening. These people still, after the Peace Accords, they haven't given them anything. . . . So they came and are getting together; they've been getting together all this time, and you know they've been getting together criminal groups, really well planned, well organized, because they have experience in this, so—*
>
> *"That robbery—the first one, that was already some years ago; in fact a military man, now he's become a lawyer, because—It was the Banco de Comercio, even by coincidence they filmed it. And there was the face of this military man. They even put him in prison, but now he's a lawyer, to defend cases like his because [he claims] they unjustly put him in prison—even though in the video . . . you could really see his face.*
>
> *"All these big robberies, with all these organized people, you need a good mind because it's all coldly calculated, so that's how they have come together, because they're used to using arms and all that, and lead, and make plans. . . . They're all organized gangs, they're the demobilized combatants, the ones that end up without any training or land."*

To Caro, Cinchazo stands out today as the first bank robbery, the one that began all the postwar organized crime. She sees Coreas' continuing denial (and freedom) only as proof of the cleverness of these criminals.

Months later, office worker Teófilo Turcios Lara does remember Coreas' name.[39] They are both from Ahuachapán. He brings up Cinchazo after I ask him if he thinks the police have improved since 1992. "They've improved, they've improved a little, in the sense that they used to grab anyone to be in the PN, and they were practically illiterate, they didn't know anything. . . . They all thought they were 'supermen' and they could do anything they wanted, they raped and killed, you know the case of the nuns, the case of the North American nuns. . . . Now in the PNC there's been police abuse too."

> *"In the PN, before, there was even a robbery that was never proved, but there was a video that showed that really they were police. It was the case of Coreas Orellana. Now they let him free."*
>
> *"Do you think it was him?" I ask.*
>
> *"In the video it came out that it was him. I know him, you know, I know him because he's from Ahuachapán."*
>
> *"What do people think in Ahuachapán?"*
>
> *"That he's corrupt, right, that's he's a bad person, that afterwards he began to build more on his house, and that, he began to make more money."*
>
> *"But how did he get out of it?"*
>
> *"He had his lawyer, and it came out he was innocent. They said a video isn't sufficient evidence for the judicial system."*
>
> *"But they did get some of the group . . ."*
>
> *"Yeah, they got some, but they didn't say anything about him. I think they're still in jail, but Coreas got out, right."*

On Saturday, June 5, 1999, five years after that "bloody bank heist," the two remaining Cinchazo suspects were absolved.[40] "Who attacked the armored truck?" *La Prensa Gráfica* asked, once again.[41] By then it was a rhetorical question. The UN's famous "turning point"—the case that finally booted the big bad National Police—"would remain in the long list of impunity," *La Prensa* proclaimed.[42]

"This Was His Profession"

> *"And, well, there are people who tell me about those guys—those guys: One worked as a security guard, in a hotel. Four months ago I found out, through a friend. Because this guy was from Chalatenango, where my friend was from. And he told me, 'I was going to go to the hospital but I couldn't see you.' 'Yes,' I said. So he said, 'Well, I'm going to tell you,' he said. 'This guy, there in my hometown, in Chalatenango, once, like a month before what happened to you,' he said, 'like a month before . . . he saw an old man, about sixty years old, [at a market selling an ox]. And since he knew where he lived, he went to wait for him in a ravine, in a gorge, where he knew the old man had to pass by. So he waited there, to rob him, to assault him. The man came by and he put a bullet here in the stomach. And he took the money. The thief thought he had killed him. But the man didn't die. He survived. He lived. But he's paralyzed. He was left paraplegic.'*
>
> *"And my friend told me, 'If back there,' he said, 'everyone knew that this guy was a*

criminal and that he killed, raped, he was the worst. But everyone was afraid of him. Everyone was afraid. And no one denounced him. . . . When they found out he had been killed, everyone thanked God.' I mean, this guy, this was his profession. His job was to rob, to kill."

Indexical Relations

Nohemí de Bernal most remembers her brother's attack for its contiguity, and somehow continuity, with Cinchazo. To her the indexical relation is clear, something she has reiterated so many times that there is little doubt today of the link. Cinchazo represents out-of-control, corrupt greed, organized criminals with links to the military, just as the criminals who attacked her brother appeared to be (with their military weapons and wallets full of money). There is no need for contextualization until I ask her. The fluid movement between a bleeding personal crisis and a bloody national climax becomes part of the chain of signs flowing to and from daily conversations and corporate-national mass-mediated narratives. Perhaps Cinchazo adds value to Nohemí's anguish. But these stories hardly penetrate Renato Trabanino's own account of his corporeal suffering.

These struggles over meaning and value told on the air and in print in the days and weeks after 8:50 A.M. on June 22, 1994, did not reach Renato while he was recuperating in the hospital, while he submitted his shattered body to multiple surgeries, while he learned to walk again. His genre is not a political tract or a conversational crime story or even a family near-tragedy told in hushed tones. The voices he heard, the prayers, the priests, the thoughts that passed through his mind, the narrative later constructed, and the meanings derived focus on the miracle of survival, of salvation, of redemption (or perhaps of divine justice, of the rightness of his own sins of murder). "These weren't coincidences, but miracles of God," he repeats.

Lived Experience and Divergent Trajectories

Cynthia Keppley Mahmood, writing of terror in Punjab and Kashmir, proposes that a key feature of the lived experience of state violence is its "nonstrategic and nonpolitical quality." The language used in the analysis of such conflicts, of strategy and politics—the genre—she tells us, does not come close to the meaning of "actual personal engagement of individuals in the violence that enmeshes them."[43] While the discourse surrounding Salvadoran postwar violence in those early years could not fully detach from the old labels—the links to powerful political names, whether state or subversive violence, the rumors of death-squad mutations—the lived experience of much violence (state or not) followed divergent trajectories, different paths to significance.

If Renato Trabanino chose an alternative narrative to the end-of-history post–Cold War triumph of the mass media, of the Salvadoran state, of the UN, he did not invent his own plot. He turned to an older narrative, one Salvadorans continue to find meaningful despite its banishment from so many chronicles of their chaos. The word of God may well be as totalizing, if not more, than the discourse of conservative mass media and presidential posturing and international forums and academic books. But perhaps it is more amenable to the telling of feeling, of felt moments, than the rational logic of national metanarratives. The word of God poaches on rational structures of progress and "peace." And, indeed, by the end of the decade great chunks of the simulacra of that UN-promulgated Salvadoran success story collapsed internally. More than seven years after Cinchazo, headlines were still filled with reports of crime waves, everyday talk still told of street terror, and "big deal" suspects kept on getting off.

Shot for a Pair of Shoes

How does this narrative, so singular, so intense, fit into the larger story, that of post-war El Salvador, the peace surplus? "Has it improved, the situation?" I ask.

"In the news, there used to be more murders, assaults," Renato tells me slowly. "Now it's less." Although he has barely mentioned Cinchazo (and then only at my prompting: "That happened in the morning. This happened to me in the afternoon"), he does bring up another incident from the media. It says something much more troubling to him than the political uproar over a spectacular bank heist. Perhaps he is not fully convinced of the meaning of his own story. Alone, attached to his living, breathing body, his story of survival and recovery is miraculous. It must be told with proper gratitude, placed in the context of God and community and family and friends (conspicuously absent are the police, the law, the state). But placing the story in the larger context of postwar El Salvador, he cannot reconcile it to any explanatory theory of postwar excess. He cannot incorporate his narrative into the larger UN metanarrative of peace and progress. He cannot offer me satisfying closure, a clean conclusion for a social-science chapter. The bloody bank heist, the bleeding assault, the five bullets he shot to kill two men, the other five bullets that pierced his still-breathing body: what does it mean?

Renato turns from his body and his life to the mass media: "Back then, in 1994, an article came out: 'Shot for a Pair of Shoes.' A twenty-year-old kid was on the bus. He mustn't have had much [money], right, if he went by bus. When he got off, he was mugged. They shot him, put a bullet in his lung. Two or three days later, he died. But he was conscious for one day.

"I had five bullets in me. And I survived."

David Pedersen

In the Stream of Money

Contradictions of Migration, Remittances,
and Development in El Salvador

Migration . . . . is the oldest action against poverty. . . . It is good for the country to which they go;
it helps break the equilibrium of poverty in the country from which they come.

—*John Kenneth Galbraith,* The Nature of Mass Poverty

With the end of the Salvadoran civil war in 1992 and the reduction in official U.S. aid for the government and military under the Bush presidency, a decade-long transformation of the country and its relations with the United States appeared in stark relief. Well-known Salvadoran social scientist Mario Lungo stressed the new centrality of remittances at this juncture by drawing on research conducted by Segundo Montes.

According to Montes' calculations, remittances total about $1.4 billion a year, equal to U.S. aid and the country's total export income combined. The remittances are more than double its export income and almost double its annual national budget. Nothing in Salvadoran history can match this stream of money.[1] Thus, in the final years of the twentieth century the postwar Salvadoran government and a host of associated organizations were confronted with how to make sense of this changed reality and craft a compelling future-oriented project of rule for the country. Montes had staked out a dominant line of research, identifying the town of Intipucá as a "case study," and much subsequent research and interpretation of the new "money stream"—no matter what its vision for the future of El Salvador—drew on his evidence explicitly. This centrality of Montes' evidence together with a confluence of other events has helped to congeal the town of Intipucá and its history of ties with Washington, D.C., into an exemplary model of the country as a whole.

In this chapter I explore the emergence of Intipucá as an emblem of the future of El Salvador and its relations with the United States by first considering the discursive emergence of the *pueblo* (town) in a growing body of research directly concerned with governmental policy and "development." I then modulate the focus of the analysis in order to illuminate some of the less perceivable yet important and highly contradictory determinants of this formal presentation of the town.

Family Remittances

In January 1995 the neoliberal Salvadoran policy research organization Salvadoran Foundation for Economic and Social Development (La Fundación Salvadoreña para el Desarrollo Económico y Social, FUSADES) published a research paper by noted Salvadoran economist Gabriel Siri and his colleagues Pedro Abelardo Delgado and Vilma Calderon.[2] The report, "Uso Productivo de las Remesas Familiares en El Salvador" (productive use of family remittances in El Salvador), briefly surveyed the phenomenon of remittance transfers worldwide and compared the Salvadoran experience with the experiences of countries in southern Europe, especially Portugal. The authors' concern was that Salvadoran remittance flows should be regularized and formalized as a kind of capital transfer, according to the neoclassical definition of the term. In that regard the authors offered eleven policy recommendations designed to draw remittances into the Salvadoran financial system more effectively, potentially at their source in the United States as savings, which could be held as U.S. dollars rather than converted to *colones* in a Salvadoran bank. The development of more widespread use of private banks across Salvadoran society and the setting up of affiliated transfer agencies in the United States coincided with broader policies of financial liberalization supported in El Salvador by the World Bank since the early 1980s. More subtly, the report took part in a slight alteration in the language of money transfers. Throughout the 1980s, remittances were referred to popularly as *ayuda* (help) in El Salvador and in Intipucá as "Washington money." The FUSADES report, like Salvadoran politicians at the time, adopted a new kind of technical term: "family remittances." The deft addition of family to the category employed by economists identified the money, its source, and its purpose in a particular way.

Though FUSADES was a well-funded and powerful policy-research organization, supported in part by the U.S. Agency for International Development, other development organizations also formed in the aftermath of the conflict to offer policy options and development strategies for the country. They recruited scholars and activists from El Salvador and abroad, including the United States, obtaining some of their financial support from a host of European social democratic public and private institutions. Like FUSADES, another private organization, the National Foundation for Development (Fundacion Nacional para el Desarrollo, FUNDE), founded in 1991, sponsored several research projects designed to assess the use of remittances in Salvadoran society and more precisely identify their influence and impact on Salvadoran social life.[3] FUNDE also sought new ways to concentrate and channel these funds. However, it was more oriented toward developing smaller-scale "grass-roots" projects of cooperative savings and community reinvestment in certain kinds of productive activity rather than encouraging the immediate recirculation of the dollars through the major banks in El Salvador. To substantiate this orientation FUNDE drew on a variety of research materials, including a host of interviews conducted throughout the eastern part of the country that were designed to identify successful models and cases of small-scale remittance-led investment and development.[4]

Among the people interviewed in this research was a young man originally from Intipucá who had lived and worked in Washington, D.C., during the 1980s and had returned in 1994 to start several businesses with his saved earnings. He purchased two large buses, named them *Caballo de Troya* (trojan horse), written in large green letters on the sides, and paid drivers to operate them on the route between San Miguel and La Union. He also purchased portable well-digging equipment and began a lucrative business digging wells for new homes under construction throughout the region.

Researchers interviewed this young man and included his story as an exemplary case of successful and productive investment of money earned in the United States. The research report argued for policies that would facilitate and encourage such "productive use of remittances." Like FUSADES, FUNDE cautioned against the tendency for remittances to go into so-called nonproductive end-use consumption of imported domestic goods like refrigerators, TVs, and VCRs.

In 1996 I spoke with this businessman; he invited me to share lunch with him and his cousin, who still lived in Intipucá. He repeatedly asked why I was living in the pueblo and seemed unsatisfied with my description of myself as an anthropologist interested in writing the history of the town. Eventually he stopped questioning me directly and we began to speak more informally about his life: "It is not hard to live like a king here with a little money. Most people here are not experienced with how to run a good business. I have been very successful. You should just get some money and come back here and start a business. You will do very well."

By the standards of both neoliberal and alternative development agencies, this fellow appeared to be a living example of someone who had acquired wealth and investment savvy in the United States and returned both to El Salvador, contributing to desirable change in the country. Indeed, people from Intipucá had played this role in journalistic accounts of the pueblo since the late 1970s. In 1989 a member of the town appeared in a famous photograph that circulated widely in the United States.

A Life as Brief as Photos

In 1984, after great public debate in the United States that surrounded Salvadoran president Duarte's letter to U.S. president Reagan acknowledging the significance to the Salvadoran economy of remittances and the widespread circulation after 1987 of Montes' research on Intipucá (published both in Spanish and English), the town of Intipucá became increasingly well known to journalists in Washington and also throughout El Salvador. Reporters from both countries regularly ventured to the pueblo since it was in an area relatively free of military conflict and it provided a fresh angle for writing stories that dealt with issues connected to the large-scale Salvadoran migration to the United States. Like the identification of transnational networks, communities, and circuits in academic scholarship at the time, the journalists presented Intipucá as an important anomaly that disrupted assumptions about national identity and people's orientations toward single places based on the assumed boundaries of citizenship, territory, and sovereignty. In contrast to the more scholarly work of academics, however, U.S. journalists especially tended to recuperate and refashion assumptions about the nation, participating in the discursive normalization and moralization of the present in El Salvador.

On July 18, 1989, the *New York Times* published a short account of Intipucá written by Lindsey Gruson under the headline "Intipucá Journal" and with the subtitle "Emigrants Feather Their Old Nests with Dollars." Immediately below the title was a picture of a young man astride a Kawasaki Ninja motorcycle, taken by Robin Lubbock, a freelance photographer and journalist who had been in El Salvador covering the war. The caption under the picture read "Marvin Chávez on his motorcycle in Intipucá, El Salvador, a rural town made wealthy by millions of dollars sent home by residents who emigrated to Washington, D.C. Mr. Chávez's father was among the first emigrants."

Lubbock had taken a series of photographs of the town and had come to know Marvin during his stay in the pueblo.[5] When Gruson later wrote the article, Lubbock's photograph was chosen to accompany it. Together the picture and the article set out a powerful discursive framing of Intipucá and its history of ties with Washington that circulated widely. At the time the photograph was published, Marvin was visiting Intipucá, and his brother in Washington, D.C., called him with great excitement to tell him that he had seen it.

The vocabulary and rhetorical logic deployed by Gruson in the short article (about 1,200 words) show a particular conceptualization of Intipucá, its people, and their relationship to Washington and the pueblo. In contrast to several *Washington Post* articles published a decade earlier, the short essay interpreted changes in Intipucá as directly related to the Salvadoran war. Gruson's narrative draws on dominant understandings of several important categories and concepts, including violence, emigration, work, money, and wealth, and it establishes a series of causal relations among them that unfold according to the following logic: (1) Although the first Intipuqueños moved to Washington in the late 1960s, wartime violence caused hundreds of people to leave the pueblo and find work in Washington, where they were able to save money and send it home to those who did not leave; (2) these U.S. dollars have allowed people to purchase a host of consumer items never before available in the pueblo, nor elsewhere in this generally poor agricultural region of El Salvador; (3) as a result, the town appears to be wealthy and heavily influenced by "U.S. culture" as it is borne by the dollars and the commercial items that people purchase; (4) in turn, this has sown unease among some town residents who fear that the money and products as well as the allure to migrate to Washington are changing patterns of Salvadoran life in negative and potentially irreversible ways.

In the title and throughout the article, Gruson uses the words *emigrate* and *emigrant* rather than *migrate* and *migrant*. He also refers to Intipucá metaphorically as the "old nest" that people now "feather" with their U.S. dollars. This language corresponds with the dominant U.S. understanding of migration as a one-way movement from one situation or country (usually understood as undesirable and unworkable, as in "the old country") to a new one that might promise upward social and economic mobility, that is, the "American dream." It also suggests another dominant account of migration as a process containing "birds of passage," or people who temporarily live and work abroad only to later return home with accumulated wealth. As Roger Rouse has noted in his study of Mexican migration to the United States during the 1980s (written at about the same time the Gruson article appeared), these two conceptualizations of human movement, the emigrant and the "bird of passage" suggest a "bipolar" understanding of the migration process, where people in their life course are assumed to wholly orient themselves around a single unified place either in the sending or the receiving zone.[6] Thus the logic Gruson employed conformed to the foundational myth of the United States as a sovereign and territorially delimited "nation of immigrants."

According to Gruson, as emigrants find work in "the restaurants of Washington and on its construction sites," they are able to earn a wage adequate to enable them to save money and send a portion of it home on a regular basis, which has in turn altered the conditions of life for many people in the pueblo. According to the article, Maximiliano Arias, a resident of the town and "director of a committee that decides how to spend money raised for the town, estimates that Intipuqueños working in Washington send their families here [in Intipucá] $100,000 a month." The visible record of this transfer of wealth is the appearance of Intipucá as "probably the country's richest town." This definition of wealth, like that formulated by nineteenth-century classical political economists and interrogated by their critics, is the "immense collection of commodities" that fill Intipucá: TVs and sky-high antennas, VCRs, a town radio station, freshly painted concrete houses and church, gardens, and paved roads with four-inch high curbstones. Intipucá is contrasted with its surrounding region and the apparent absence of these items beyond the pueblo. In a meaningful opening sentence, Gruson claims that Intipucá is "a pastel oasis of plenty with more in common with an exclusive United States suburb than a destitute and devastated land."

If we explore the geo-history of social relations that not only brought those commodities into being but also brought them to Intipucá so as to yield the appearance of town wealth, we find a story vastly more complex than that suggested by the logic of one-way exchange in Gruson's article. Indeed, Gruson's opening sentence is doubly meaningful because Intipucá is directly connected to the Washington suburbs of Maryland and Virginia in ways that can be seen better by following in detail the story of Marvin Chávez and his motorcycle.

Her Beautiful Nose

At the time of the photograph, Marvin had traveled from Washington, D.C., to Intipucá and shipped his motorcycle from Washington via ground transport. When it arrived, he picked it up at the customs office in Cutuco, once a busy port out of which almost half of El Salvador's coffee production was shipped. In the late 1980s Marvin was likely the only person in eastern El Salvador with a high-powered Japanese-built *grand prix*–style motorcycle, and he relished the messages it sent to all onlookers about his wealth and status. In the weeks before Lubbock arrived in the pueblo and snapped the photograph, Marvin had ridden the bike through the hills to the beach called Cuco to visit the Fuentes family.

Marvin especially enjoyed gunning the motorcycle up and down the beach, forcing chickens, cows, dogs, and people to scatter out of his way. The many people who lived along the shore and made their living by fishing and caring for the beach houses of wealthy San Miguel families watched in amazement as he barreled through. After racing up and down the beach, he would return to the more concentrated urban areas of Cuco, where the Fuentes, owned several buildings. "I went out onto the street and did those things that you call 'donuts' in the U.S. You know, the thing that everyone with a car did in high school. I had always wanted to do that, so I tried it there in Cuco on my motorcycle."

After a while, a group of government soldiers surrounded him and ordered him to stop his bike. They had their rifles pointed at him, and he obeyed. They took the motorcycle and led him to the National Guard office in the town (a three-story building Joaquin Fuentes had constructed before the war) where they interrogated him for a time. "'Where did you get that motorcycle?,' they asked me," said Marvin later. "'Where did you get the money? You have too much money! You come down here and show off your motorcycle—next time you do that we're going to lock you up and take that motorcycle!'" After several hours, the officials released Marvin and returned his motorcycle to him—after several of them had taken a turn riding it up and down the beach.

In Intipucá, Marvin was a celebrity. During his visits to the pueblo in the late 1980s, like most people who returned for periods of time, he brought with him a variety of new consumer items. For Marvin these included expensive clothing, new televisions and VCRs, and several pure-bred dogs. Several times he donated sports equipment to the local school. And he always had cash that he was willing to spend. One year he shipped a seventeen-foot motorboat with a large outboard engine to Cutuco. On its maiden journey in the Pacific, the swells were so high that it took on water, swamping the engine and ultimately sinking the craft, and Marvin and his friends had to be rescued by nearby fishers. "Too bad that happened. We were going too fast I think," Marvin reflected.

Marvin graduated from high school in 1982 and was offered the chance to enlist in the U.S. army. "On that paper in front of me I had two boxes. One said *yes* and the other said *no*. I checked *no*. Maybe that was a mistake," he said, again looking back on his experiences with some regret. "After graduating high school I began to work in different restaurants. *Intipuqueños* were everywhere and it was easy to get a job. My cousins owned a restaurant in Adams Morgan, and all our parents and friends who had come up from Intipucá worked in restaurants. One guy would get a job and then help the rest of us to work there. The money was okay and it was fun. The only problem was going home at night. We were always afraid that we would get robbed by a black in the neighborhood."

When I spoke with Marvin in 1996 about the motorcycle, the boat, and other items and activities, he frequently recalled aspects of his life during the 1980s with a sense of having made significant errors in judgment that began at a particular moment. "It all happened when I met Billy," Marvin once sighed.

Billy Banner was the child of wealthy parents and lived in the Potomac area in Maryland, a popular and affluent neighborhood constructed after World War II and known for its solid tax base and excellent public schools. The Salvadoran government owned a house there that was usually used by the ambassador and his family during their stay in Washington. Billy's father ran a successful business in the area and his mother was part owner of a large high-rise office building on Connecticut Avenue in the District. Below the building was a commercial parking garage operated by a private family-owned company that maintained garages and lots throughout the Washington area. In the years after high school Marvin took up employment there, eventually becoming a manager. Among his responsibilities was to close the garage late at night on weekends. One Friday night he noticed on his closed-circuit video security camera a BMW parked in the lot, but he had no record of the driver having purchased a parking ticket. "I could zoom the camera to three different levels of magnification and see people inside," Marvin later explained.

After observing the car and its occupants over several consecutive weekends, Marvin cautiously walked down to the level where it was parked while his security guard friend watched on the camera. As he approached the car he saw two young women inside together with a young man. Marvin knocked on the rolled-up window, and the young people looked at him with surprise. The young man in the driver's seat quickly jumped out and ran around the car to confront Marvin. "Who are you?!" demanded Marvin as the young man approached him. Speaking rapidly and with a quality of fear, the man explained that he was just parked there to talk and listen to music with two of his friends and that he had access to the lot because his mother was part owner of the building. He seemed especially concerned that Marvin, as an employee of the garage, might in some way be able to reach his mother and tell of her son's trespassing. "Please don't tell my mom you saw me here," he begged Marvin. "That is not a problem," replied Marvin, who thought that the fellow must be about his age and seemed nice enough, although very nervous. Over the following weeks, the BMW would pull in late at night, often filled with people who remained in the car listening to loud music and drinking beer and wine late into the night. After more than a month of watching on the camera, Marvin ventured down again to visit the car. "These were rich, beautiful white people. I didn't know people like this! I was curious about their life," Marvin said, "so I walked down again and they invited me to stay."

After that, the weekend car crowd regularly included Marvin. And one day Billy asked Marvin if he would like to snort some cocaine with them. "I had never done this, ever in my life. I didn't even drink when I was in high school." Billy shared several lines of cocaine with Marvin. "After I tried it I said to myself, this is *good!* I *like* this!" Marvin recalled.

After several more cocaine parties in Billy's car at the parking garage, Billy asked Marvin if he could obtain cocaine for him. "'Can you get this stuff? You live with all the Hispanics. You must be able to get it,'" Marvin remembered him asking. Marvin explained this important exchange to me: *"Shit!* I lived in Mount Pleasant, I could get anything! I talked to the people I knew and then I began to sell to Billy. He bought a lot and kept asking for more. I could buy a kilo for $16,000 and I would sell it to Billy for $17,500."

After several months Billy began to invite Marvin to join him at parties in Potomac and at popular bars like Third Edition and Spy Club in the wealthy Georgetown neighborhood. According to Marvin, Billy lived much of the time in what appeared to be his own house in Potomac and frequently threw parties there. The events were extraordinary affairs for Marvin. "Once I met 'Miss Canada' at a party. Her nose was so beautiful when she snorted coke," Marvin reported. Gradually Marvin was accepted into this group and became well known to many of Billy's friends

"Every time that I would go to the bathroom two guys would follow me and ask me if I would sell them coke. They said that Billy was selling them one kilo for $24,000. I couldn't believe that. He was making over $8,000 in profit! I confronted Billy and he told me that he was sorry, but that was just how he did business. Gradually I got many of Billy's customers and began to make over $40,000 a week. Can you believe that?"

Marvin and Billy remained friends, and Billy continued to buy quantities of cocaine from Marvin and resell them to his acquaintances in the suburbs. He and Marvin fancied themselves as outlaws of sorts. Periodically they would spend the weekend at Billy's house, apparently given to him by his parents, and take cocaine. One day they piled Billy's bed full of money and kilos of cocaine and laid out all the small arms they had acquired. Using a camera placed on an opposite shelf, they took a picture of themselves reclining on all these goods. Years later Marvin showed me the picture, "We were gangsters back then! Just like in the movies."

According to Marvin, Billy was becoming increasingly unstable. He would smoke cocaine and then become convinced that his house was being assaulted by military troops or attacked by bands of robbers. Billy would climb under his bed and remain there for hours, paralyzed by fear. Eventually Marvin began to spend less time with Billy, and within several months they were completely estranged. Marvin's share of the distribution business continued to expand. He later heard that Billy had "gone crazy." Apparently after smoking cocaine and hiding under his bed he emerged with all his firearms and began to shoot wildly in the house. "He destroyed that house from the inside out, just shooting and shooting all afternoon," Marvin explained to me later with a quality of amazement. Eventually the police arrived. Marvin did not know what happened to Billy after this episode, but he heard from several of Billy's friends that he eventually spent time in a private detoxification center, paid for by his parents, to help him overcome his cocaine habit. "We never really spoke again; he became crazy," said Marvin.

Bound by Chains

Gradually Marvin began to sell ever larger amounts of cocaine directly to several of Billy's wealthiest friends, who in turn passed his name to others involved in Washington's fast-lane, suburban coke scene. During the heyday of his lucrative middleman business, transferring cocaine from a Dominican supplier to wealthy Anglo European children in the suburbs who had large amounts of discretionary income, Marvin was able to live out some of the fantasies inspired by the examples of suburban wealth that he was exposed to at parties and elsewhere. In one instance a young man introduced his father to Marvin: "I think that he was a U.S. senator or someone important in the government. He wanted to have some cocaine for a big party, so I sold him a kilo. He paid me all in cash with very small bills. It was just like in those movies where the guy brings a briefcase with the money. We met in this parking lot downtown and he opened the case, just like in those movies."

Nevertheless, Marvin imposed limits on his own consumption habits: "I always wanted a red sports car. But what do you think the police do when they see a short Hispanic driving an expensive sports car? Forget it. That's why I had to settle for the motorcycle."

Cocaine served as a powerful social lubricant during the 1980s in Washington, D.C., as well as in other U.S. cities and fit well with the pumped-up aggression of corporate take-overs and the rapid dismantling and reselling of companies for profit. Wealthy, white suburban residents were a significant part of the Washington regional drug trade; 42 percent of the people arrested on possession charges between 1985 and 1987 were from outside the District and a third of them were white. Among sellers who were arrested, over 20 percent came from outside the District and at least 10 percent were white.[7]

The speculative growth in the Washington suburbs linked government decision-makers in the defense establishment specialized contractors, regional banks and savings-and-loan companies, real estate developers, and construction companies. The region became the target of investors looking for lucrative opportunities to merge with or acquire area firms.

In 1987 David Rubenstein, a former policy assistant in the Carter administration and member of the Washington law firm Shaw, Pittman, Potts, and Trowbridge founded Carlyle Group, a merchant banking organization. Among pundits and journalists, Carlyle is often and mistakenly referred to as a military defense contractor because it made its reputation by aggressively buying and selling defense companies throughout the late 1980s and 1990s. These activities were facilitated especially by former CIA deputy director and Reagan administration defense secretary Frank Carlucci, who joined the firm as vice chairman and managing director in 1989. Carlyle's first attempted acquisition, however, was not a defense firm but the popular "Tex-Mex" restaurant chain known as "Chi Chi's," based in Louisville, Kentucky.[8]

Much like the Carlyle Group, which expanded its holdings by acquiring firms in the region, Marvin found that as his network of buyers grew, he could not keep up with business; hence, he recruited one of his closest friends, whom I shall call Carlos, from Intipucá who had also moved to Washington after 1983 in order to avoid fighting in the war. Carlos and Marvin had known each other well in Intipucá, and they remained close friends in Washington. "He was like a brother," Marvin later recalled.

A central problem for Marvin was that he had growing amounts of cash he needed to keep safe and available for other transactions. At first he laid out the money flat, under a rug in his small apartment bedroom. Then he asked Carlos to look after several boxes of money. Marvin was happy that Carlos would do this for him; in time they had built up a deep level of mutual trust.

Marvin also drew on other friends and acquaintances from Intipucá to help with distribution. One colleague became a trusted carrier who transported large quantities of cocaine to the growing network of suburban buyers. The eldest son of a man who became Intipucá's mayor in the early 1990s, also became involved, but more as a periodic buyer from Marvin. Marvin assumed that he was consuming the cocaine personally and possibly selling some on the side as well. Marvin and Carlos remained at the center of the business and had direct contact with a young man whom I shall call Richard. Richard was originally from the Dominican Republic and was Marvin's main supplier.

Billy's friends who bought cocaine from Marvin were people whose parents and relatives occupied some of the most powerful positions in a regional economy that during the 1980s was growing in part because of the expansion of federal spending in high-tech military technologies, most notably the Strategic Defense Initiative, introduced by President Reagan in 1983. During the 1980s most Intipuqueños found work in the expanding service sector tied to these expenditures. Marvin had inserted himself into this service sector as a commercial middleman, selling a popular though illicit good that played an integral role in the leisure and recreational activities of many wealthy young adults. It was a risky job since it involved transferring large amounts of money on a regular basis to relative strangers in exchange for a valuable commodity. The transactions were conducted under hurried and insecure conditions since no central authority wielded the power to enforce the terms of the exchange, especially the property rights that undergirded them.

Although cocaine is a fiercely addictive drug that, like alcohol and nicotine, can produce potentially deadly physiological changes in the human body if absorbed rapidly in highly concentrated amounts, it is derived from a complex process of agricultural production, processing, and export much like coffee beans or cotton fiber. The cocaine that Marvin sold to Miss Canada and dozens of others came to him from several native-born Dominicans who resided in the Washington area. They obtained the cocaine from regional distributors who were connected to the consortia of processors, shippers, and merchants concentrated in Colombia, dominated during the 1980s by a cartel founded in the city of Medellín and run by its infamous "godfather" Pablo Escobar. During the decade of the 1980s, between five hundred and seven hundred tons of prepared cocaine were shipped out of Columbia annually.[9]

Colombian merchants bought coca paste from processors and shippers in the Santa Cruz and Beni regions of Bolivia, who traded with the proprietors of the many small and medium-sized farms concentrated in the central lowland area of Chapare. Like remittances in El Salvador, during the second half of the 1980s, the sale of coca paste became the single largest source of foreign exchange for Bolivia, easily outstripping its traditional exports, tin and natural gas. Colombian processors also obtained coca paste from Peruvian growers concentrated in the 150 square mile Upper Huallaga Valley on the eastern slopes of the Andes Mountains. As in Bolivia, raw coca became Peru's most important export during the 1980s, generating about $1 billion annually, equal to about a third of the foreign exchange earned from all legal exports combined.[10] In these coca-growing areas, people lived through a mixture of commercial and subsistence farming, much like people in Intipucá before their migration to Washington. Also similar to El Salvador in the later 1980s, Peru's generation of U.S. dollars from the new export flooded the financial and commercial sectors and cushioned the effects of restructuring plans dictated by the International Monetary Fund.

Although one could trace such chains of commodities through their production and consumption phases backward through time and across space, mapping out how money and products traveled and transmogrified relationally at each moment, such boundless representation that almost mirrors the reality it proposes to stand for is unnecessary for the purposes of this chapter. Nevertheless, the exercise suggests a structured world that combines different people and experiences, objects, and places in a violently uneven way. In the small segment considered so far, Billy and his friends dealt and snorted relatively free from police inquiry, and Marvin played the role of the trustworthy middleman who maintained more dangerous commercial relations that were invisible from the parlors of Potomac mansions.

The wealth in the form of money used to buy the cocaine had been accumulated through the highly abstracted buying, selling, and renting of rights to land, money, and shares of future production of other goods and services that Billy's and his friends' parents were involved with in the Washington area. In the form of trust funds (where money appeared to make money) or as generous allowances that yielded the power to buy and sell from a position of power, this wealth was based on past and future accumulation and the basic human capacity to imagine, invent, and make and do things. The low-waged Salvadorans living alongside Marvin in Mount Pleasant who built the buildings and provided many of the services (in restaurants, for example) that were bought and sold in the booming region provided much of this harnessed capacity (and will continue to, hope the speculators). In an indirect and highly abstracted way, Gruson's narrative of remittances from hard work in the United States flowing back to El Salvador as U.S. dollars is correct. But the circuitous conditions through which value is produced and out of which particular forms of wealth circulate are highly uneven and partially invisible.

State against the Nation's Capital

On April 11, 1989, President George H. W. Bush's newly appointed "drug czar," William Bennett of Boston, Massachusetts, spoke at a national press conference and announced that Washington, D.C., was to become an exemplary case of the new U.S. "war on drugs." He stated that $80 million would be spent primarily on enforcement activities in the District, especially on the hiring of federal prosecutors, drug agents, and military analysts. Bennett blamed the city government for its failure to stop the drug trade in the nation's capital (city government officials were not invited to attend the press conference).

The intensified enforcement strategy in the District was led by the U.S. Drug

Enforcement Agency (DEA), which placed undercover agents throughout the city to try to infiltrate the distribution businesses. The agency went after small-time, street-corner dealers, many of whom were juveniles selling small amounts of drugs to local consumers. In Mount Pleasant this took place on Park Road, where buyers would drive along a one-way section and make quick curbside deals. The DEA also attempted to work its way up the chain of supply by threatening or playing apprehended dealers off one another in an attempt to get them to snitch.

In 1990, one of Marvin's colleagues, whom I will call Jorge, called to say that he had a trusted friend who was interested in buying a large amount of cocaine. To Marvin this appeared to be a good opportunity and through Jorge he sold the fellow a kilo. After several deals like this, Jorge called to say that the client wanted to purchase an especially large amount and would like the chance to meet with Marvin's supplier. Marvin consulted with Richard and they agreed to meet Jorge and the prospective client at the Ramada Inn on Connecticut Avenue in Bethesda, Maryland. The hotel was located adjacent to the sprawling grounds of the National Institute of Health's Library of Medicine and across the street from a popular restaurant called O'Donnell's.

On the day of the meeting, Marvin was delayed in traffic and arrived at the hotel fifteen minutes late. As he headed north on Connecticut Avenue and turned left across traffic into the parking lot, he saw Jorge and Richard being escorted out of the building in handcuffs surrounded by DEA agents. Marvin kept driving and quickly returned to Mount Pleasant. "I was freaking out," he explained later. "That fucking Jorge, I kept thinking!" Over the following week, Marvin went to visit his friend Richard in jail. When he arrived he encountered all of Jorge's family from Intipucá who had flown up to stay with him through the ensuing trial. "They looked at me with such anger like they blamed me for everything," said Marvin. "Jorge was the coke-head and had been stupid, but of course they didn't believe that because he was their son!"

Eventually Richard was released because the police had insufficient evidence to charge him with a crime. Several months later Marvin was driving in the area, heading to a party, when he was pulled over by an unmarked police vehicle. DEA agents jumped out, questioned him, and searched his car. They found a moderate amount of cocaine and he was arrested for narcotics possession with intent to distribute. "In jail that night they put a gun to my head and said that they would kill me if I didn't tell them who my suppliers were. They also tried to be nice and promise me things if I became a witness for them." The next day Marvin consulted with a lawyer who was able to get him out on bail for eight days before his upcoming court hearing. The lawyer spoke with the prosecuting attorney and agents and informed Marvin that the least severe punishment he could expect would be five years in prison with the possibility of up to forty years. Marvin described the moment when he learned of these terms: "I said no way, so on the seventh day I woke up, put on a wig and walked out the back door of my apartment. The agents were sitting in a garbage truck watching the building, but they didn't recognize me. My friend picked me up and we drove to Wheaton, picked up some things and just drove straight back here to Intipucá! At nine o'clock the next morning when I didn't arrive at court, they stormed the building and then went straight to my mother's house and broke down her door. I had never spoken about my mother to them. She eventually got a lawyer and sued them for damages and for wire-tapping her phone and won the case.

Coke

On one of his trips to Intipucá before his final return, Marvin had met a jovial fellow whom I shall call Enrique at a small restaurant and bar located at the beach called Icacal at the southern-most edge of Intipucá. Throughout the early 1980s Enrique had worked at the Coca-Cola bottling factory located at the western edge of San Salvador. During the war, the factory was attacked several times by Farabundo Martí National Liberation Front (FMLN) forces, and it became increasingly difficult for large trucks laden with Coca-Cola products to safely travel beyond the capital, lest they be robbed or destroyed by guerrilla forces. The plant executives effectively subcontracted the transportation of products to conflicted zones by offering especially low wholesale prices to anyone who would assume all the risks and deliver Coca-Cola products using their own vehicles. At the time Enrique was able to obtain a small truck, and he cautiously plied the roads between San Salvador and the eastern part of the country, distributing Coca-Cola products around Intipucá and its nearby beaches.

Enrique was attracted to the daughter of the owners of the restaurant in Icacal, and he liked to visit on his rounds delivering Coca-Cola products. It was there that he first met Marvin. Over drinks he and Marvin made a deal together. Years later Marvin explained the evolution of the arrangement: "A few months later, after I got back to Washington, I bought an old UPS delivery truck in Rockville [Maryland] for about $10,000. Then I drove it with a friend down through Mexico to Intipucá and sold it to Enrique. In San Miguel they have a place where they strip it down and build racks on the back for cases of soda and beer. Those brown [UPS] ones are good trucks—strong motors, brakes, and suspension—what we need here in El Salvador."

Enrique's business expanded dramatically with the new truck, and he eventually moved to Intipucá with his wife and two young sons, storing crates of soft drinks in the backyard of his modest house and redistributing them throughout the region with his considerably smaller first truck. Marvin periodically returned to Intipucá to visit and several times helped Enrique drive the large load of drinks lashed to the converted UPS truck between San Salvador and Intipucá. Marvin explained the challenges and also one surprise encounter on the trip: "The war was still going. Because we were Coca-Cola, we always thought that we would be targets for the guerrillas. Once when I was driving they stopped us. They were young guys, but an older guy, their commander, had a lot of money and bought our soda from us! Usually when the [Salvadoran] military stopped us they made us give out the soda to the soldiers for free!"

Marvin also explained some of the dynamics of Enrique's drink distribution business and his participation during the 1990s: "In 1992 when I moved back here to care for my grandmother, I became the main driver. It was a good business then and I made a trip almost every day. Now business is down [1996]. We have competition from people who are growing watermelons. You take your family to the beach and the kids are thirsty. What will you do, buy them each a soda and yourself a beer or one big watermelon for ten *colones?* It's not a problem; when the season is over we will go up again."

Reflections

From the vantage point of the pueblo in 1996 and his new job as a truck-driver, Marvin recalled the experiences of the "go-go 80s" in Washington, D.C. "Cocaine is powerful because it made me high and it gave me money like I had never seen in my life! I never could control [the effects of] that. When I had the chance to join the U.S. Army after high school, I should have taken it. I never would have met Billy."

In the end Marvin's life in Washington during the 1980s was extremely complex, and he worked it out to the best of his abilities. As a cocaine middleman he extracted a fee that allowed him access to people, goods, and services that were otherwise unavailable and deemed highly desirable according to his upbringing in Intipucá and Washington, D.C. But as much as he tried to make a life for himself, certain things took part in making him, especially the conditions he was thrown into, beginning at least with the growing violence in El Salvador that led to him moving to the United States. He grew up in Washington during a period of economic expansion and through chance and his own initiative came to occupy a unique position as a Salvadoran who had regular contact with wealthy cocaine buyers and users; he also knew someone who offered a reliable and relatively inexpensive supply of the drug. In many ways the saying "money makes the man" was true in his case, cocaine and the money he earned from it made him.

Through Lubbock's photograph and Gruson's text the *New York Times* article showed not how the conditions of the cocaine trade in Washington, D.C., made Marvin, but how he as the owner of the motorcycle took part in making Intipucá—"feathering the nest," as Gruson called it. In the article, Gruson vaguely described the restaurants and construction sites of Washington, D.C., prompting the reader to infer that work in Washington is yielding modern goods, like a motorcycle, that make Intipucá appear wealthy in contrast to other pueblos in the region. The article is a narrative of the empirical, that which is immediately present to the reader (and the journalist), and it compresses all the actual conditions that brought Marvin and his motorcycle to Intipucá into an abstract and highly partial account. Into this form, the complex geo-history of Marvin and his motorcycle are squeezed and the model of Intipucá as a wealthy pueblo is constructed.

The power of the discursive model of remittance flow built on the Intipucá-Washington connection is that this model simultaneously draws on and obscures the concrete experiences not only of Marvin but also of Billy, his friends, their parents, and the DEA agents who arrested Marvin, among many other people. It is accurate in its partial accounting of events—money and goods were brought to Intipucá—but it is wrong because at each moment of exchange presupposed in the model the structural inequity that forms its condition of possibility is occluded.

During the twentieth century El Salvador's geographical and historical niche in the world as a country organized around producing and exporting a small number of primary agricultural commodities to regions of the world with more diversified economies has not changed. Yet the transition from coffee and cotton to the most recent period dominated by labor-power has entailed a difficult transformation from a country oriented toward commodity production to one increasingly organized around the circulation of dollars and the new kinds of commercial and financial activities and social outlooks that this has stimulated. There remains a silent struggle within Salvadoran society to maintain this "migration money," capture it, move it into other circuits of world finance, and use it to help script a plausible story of national progress, much like coffee and cotton money in earlier decades. The emergent model as I have described its contours now participates in and is wielded in this struggle. Intipucá and the more than 15,000 people who claimed origins in the town and had moved to the Washington area while keeping close ties to the pueblo were caught up in these changes in El Salvador and in the country's relations with the United States. For people across both places, the transformation in the space of two generations has been dramatic and difficult in ways that remain invisible in dominant accounts.

Epilogue

With Marvin's clandestine return to Intipucá in 1992, Carlos was left at the center of the business, but without Marvin's other friends who had been arrested, and without the history of ties with the wealthy buyers in the suburbs. Carlos attempted to sell cocaine through various channels, but his was an operation in decline. He began to plan his exit from the business and how he would transfer what assets he could back to El Salvador. In Intipucá one day in late 1996 as the new bus pulled up to take on and let off passengers, a woman in the park, muttered out loud with a twinkle in her eye for those who cared to listen, "Ha! Nobody knows what's in a Trojan horse!" Her comment serves as a counterpoint, though less visible, to Gruson's article and Lubbock's photograph.

Notes

The following abbreviations are used in the notes for sources frequently cited.

AGN   Archivo General de la Nación, San Salvador, El Salvador
AGN-FC   AGN-Fondo Clasificádos
AGN-FG-So   AGN-Fondo Gobernaciones-Sonsonate
AGN-FI   AGN-Fondo Indiferente
AGN-FM-MG   AGN-Fondo Ministerios-Ministerio de Gobernación
AGS   Archivo de la Gobernacíon de Sonsonate
AMI   Archivo Municipal de Izalco
DES   *Diario del Salvador*
DO   *Diario Oficial*
FA   Fondo Alcaldías
FG   Fondo Gobernaciones
FI   Fondo Indiferente
FO   Foreign Office
PRO   Public Record Office
RG   Record Group
USNA   U.S. National Archives

Local History, Politics, and the State in El Salvador

1. For recent work by Jeffrey Gould on *mestizaje* in El Salvador in comparative perspective, see Jeffrey Gould, "Hacia un marco comparativo para el estudio de mestizaje en Centroamérica," in *Memorias de Mestizaje en América Central, La Política Cultural desde 1920* (Antigua Guatemala: CIRMA, forthcoming); and "Revolutionary Nationalism and Local Memories in El Salvador, in *Reclaiming "the Political" in Latin American History: The View from the North,* ed. Gilbert Joseph (Durham, N.C.: Duke University Press, 2001), 138–71.

2. Leigh Binford, *The El Mozote Massacre: Anthropology and Human Rights* (Tucson: University of Arizona Press), 236, n. 6; Ana Lilian Ramírez and América Rodríguez, "Algu-

nas reflexiones sobre el desarrollo de la antropología en el Salvador," *Cuadernos de Investi-gación* 29.

3. Tina Rosenberg, *Children of Cain: Violence and the Violent in Latin America* (New York: Penguin, 1991), 234; Thomas Anderson, *Matanza* (Willimantic, Conn.: Curbstone, 1992 [1971]), 24. Rosenberg opines that "probably nowhere is there a group of foreigners as 'American' as Salvador's oligarchy." Rosenberg, *Children of Cain*, 238.

4. See, for instance, Roque Dalton, *El Salvador,* monograph (San Salvador: UCA Edi-tores, 1989; original La Habana: Casa de las Americas, 1963); and Dalton, *Las historias prohibidas del pulgarcito* (México City: Siglo XXI, 1980). Dalton also sought to rescue the history of twentieth-century working-class organization and struggle through the testi-mony he collected from Communist Party organizer Miguel Marmol. See *Miguel Marmol* (Willimantic, Conn.: Curbstone Press, 1987).

5. Enrique Baloyra, *El Salvador in Transition* (Chapel Hill: University of North Car-olina Press, 1982); Cynthia Arnson, *El Salvador: A Revolution Confronts the United States* (Washington, D.C., and Amsterdam: Institute for Policy Studies and the Transnational In-stitute, 1982); Robert Armstrong and Janet Shenk, *El Salvador: The Face of Revolution* (Boston, Mass.: South End Press, 1982); Tommie Sue Montgomery, *Revolution in El Sal-vador: Origins and Evolution* (Boulder, Colo.: Westview Press, 1982); Robert G. Williams, *Export Agriculture and the Crisis in Central America* (Chapel Hill: University of North Car-olina Press, 1986); Anjali Sundaram and George Gelber, *A Decade of War: El Salvador Con-fronts the Future* (New York: Monthly Review, 1991); Marilyn Thompson, *Women of El Sal-vador: The Price of Freedom* (Philadelphia, Pa.: Institute for the Study of Human Issues, 1986); Raymond Bonner, *Weakness and Deceit: U.S. Policy in El Salvador* (New York: Times Books, 1984); Tom Barry, *El Salvador: A Country Guide* (Albuquerque, N.Mex.: Inter-Hemi-spheric Education Resource Center, 1990); Marvin Gettlemen et al., *El Salvador: Central America in the New Cold War* (New York: Grove Press, 1986); Joe Fish and Christina Sganga, *El Salvador: Testament of Terror* (New York: Olive Branch Press, 1988); Michael McClintock, *The American Connection,* vol. 1 of *State Terror and Popular Resistance in El Sal-vador* (London: Zed Books, 1985). We will not consider here the many local testimonies written during the revolutionary war. Despite the fact that they can be used to under-stand the history of local people and communities, they rarely provide enough under-standing of local social organization. The most problematic testimonial accounts are those that are so blinded by either a theological or political orientation that they take as a natural fact that peasants' poverty compels them to rebel, organize, protest, and so on. In doing so they assume exactly what needs to be studied and questioned. Scott Wright's *Promised Land* provides an example of this literature. Scott Wright, *Promised Land: Death and Life in El Salvador* (Maryknoll, N.Y.: Orbis Books, 1993). For a series of interesting discussions of the possibilities and limitations of testimonial literature, see Arturo Arias, ed., *The Rigoberta Menchú Controversy* (Minneapolis: University of Minnesota Press, 2001).

6. William H. Durham, *Scarcity and Survival in Central America: Ecological Origins of the Soccer War* (Palo Alto, Calif.: Stanford University Press, 1979); Segundo Montes, *El com-*

padrazgo: Una estructura de poder en El Salvador (San Salvador: UCA Editores, 1979). Prior to the civil war several anthropologists, seeking what remained of "the exotic" or non-mestizo, did publish on the western, indigenous region. See, for instance, Alejandro Dagoberto Marroquín, *Panchimalco* (San Salvador: Ministerio de Educación, 1974), and his "El problema indígena en El Salvador," *América Indígena* 35, no. 4 (1975). The western, indigenous area also served as the locus of several thesis projects carried out by students at the University of El Salvador.

7. Carlos Rafael Cabarrús, *Génesis de una revolución: Analisis del surgimiento y desarollo de la organización campesina en El Salvador* (Mexico: Ediciones de la Casa Chata, 1983); Carlos Rafael Cabarrús, "El Salvador: De Movimiento Campesino a Revolución Popular," in *Historia política de los campesinos latinoamericanos,* vol. 2, comp. Pablo González Casanova (Mexico: Siglo Veintiuno, 1985), 77–115. Though published in the early to mid-1980s, the ethnographic present of Cabarrús's work was the late 1970s, when he served as a priest to peasants and rural workers in the region.

8. Anderson, *Matanza;* David Browning, *El Salvador: Landscape and Society* (Oxford: Clarendon, 1971).

9. Jenny Pearce, *Promised Land: Peasant Rebellion in Chalatenango, El Salvador* (London: Latin America Bureau, 1986).

10. See Christian Smith, *Resisting Reagan: The U.S. Central America Peace Movement* (Chicago: University of Chicago Press, 1996).

11. Four of the books we survey were written by contributors to this volume.

12. See Aldo Lauria-Santiago and Jeffrey Gould, "'They Call Us Thieves and Steal Our Wage: Toward a Reinterpretation of the Salvadoran Rural Mobilization, 1929–1931," *Hispanic American Historical Review,* forthcoming (2004).

13. Aldo Lauria-Santiago, *An Agrarian Republic: Commercial Agriculture and the Politics of Peasant Communities in El Salvador* (Pittsburgh, Pa.: University of Pittsburgh Press, 1999); "'That a Poor Man Be Industrious:' Coffee, Community, and Agrarian Capitalism in the Transformation of El Salvador's Ladino Peasantry, 1760–1900," in *Identity and Struggle at the Margins of the Nation-State: The Laboring Peoples of Central America and the Hispanic Caribbean, 1850–1950,* ed. Aldo Lauria-Santiago and Aviva Chomsky. (Durham, N.C.: Duke University Press, 1998); "Los Indígenas de Cojutepeque, la política faccional, y el estado nacional en El Salvador, 1830–1890," in *Construcción de las identidades y del estado moderno en Centro America,* ed. Arturo Taracena (San José: UCA Editores/CEMCA/ FLACSO, 1995); Patricia Alvarenga, *Cultura y ética de la violencia: El Salvador 1880–1932* (San José: EDUCA, 1996).

14. Erik Ching, "From Clientelism to Militarism: The State, Politics, and Authoritarianism in El Salvador, 1840–1940" (Santa Barbara: University of California, 1997); Erik Ching, "La Historia de Centroamérica en los Archivos Rusos del COMINTERN: Los Documentos Salvadoreños," *Revista de Historia* 32 (July–December 1995): 217–47; Erik Ching and Virginia Tilley, "Indians, the Military, and the Rebellion of 1932 in El Salvador," *Journal of Latin American Studies* 30 (1998): 121–56.

15. Philip J. Williams and Knut Walter, *Militarization and Demilitarization in El Salvador's Transition to Democracy* (Pittsburgh, Pa.: University of Pittsburgh Press, 1997).

16. Binford, *El Mozote Massacre;* Leigh Binford, "Hegemony and Counter-Hegemony in the Interior of the Revolution: The ERP in Northern Morazán," *Journal of Latin American Anthropology* 4 (1): 3–45.

17. See Carolyn Nordstrom and Antonius C. G. M. Robben, eds., *Fieldwork under Fire: Contemporary Studies of Violence and Survival* (Berkeley: University of California Press, 1995).

18. Rodolfo Cardenal, *Historia de una Esperanza: Vida de Rutilio Grande* (San Salvador: UCA Editores, 1985).

19. Elisabeth Jean Wood, *Insurgent Collective Action and Civil War: Redrawing Boundaries of Class and Citizenship in Rural El Salvador* (Cambridge: Cambridge University Press, 2003); and Wood, *Forging Democracy from Below: Insurgent Transitions in South Africa and El Salvador* (Cambridge: Cambridge University Press, 2000).

20. Mark Pedalty, *War Stories: The Culture of Foreign Correspondents* (New York: Routledge, 1995); Serena Fogaroli and Sara Stowell, *Desarrollo rural y participación campesina: El caso de Tecoluca* (San Vicente, El Salvador: Universidad Centroamericana "José Simeón Cañas," Department of Economics, 1997); John L. Hammond, *Fighting to Learn: Popular Education and Guerrilla War in El Salvador* (New Brunswick, N.J.: Rutgers University Press, 1998); Mandy MacDonald and Mike Gatehouse, *In the Mountains of Morazán: Portrait of a Returned Refugee Community in El Salvador* (London: Latin America Bureau, 1995); Steve Cagan and Beth Cagan, *This Promised Land El Salvador* (New Brunswick, N.J.: Rutgers University Press, 1991).

21. Gil Joseph and Daniel Nugent, eds., *Everyday Forms of State Formation* (Durham, N.C.: Duke University Press, 1994).

22. For instance, see Jeffrey Gould, *To Lead as Equals: Rural Protest and Peasant Consciousness in Chinandega, Nicaragua, 1912–1979* (Chapel Hill, N.C.: University of North Carolina Press, 1990); Mark Edelman, *Peasants Against Globalization: Rural Social Movements in Costa Rica* (Palo Alto, Calif.: Stanford University Press, 1999); David Nugent, *Modernity at the Edge of Empire: State, Individual, and Nation in the Northern Peruvian Andes, 1885–1935* (Palo Alto, Calif.: Stanford University Press, 1997); Gavin Smith, *Livelihood and Resistance: Peasants and the Politics of Land in Peru* (Berkeley: University of California Press, 1989).

23. The change was not total, of course. For instance, El Salvador's economy was capitalist-dominated before, during, and after the war.

24. On the return of refugees and displaced persons, see Beatrice Edwards and Gretta Tovar Siebentritt, *Places of Origin: The Repopulation of Rural El Salvador* (Boulder, Colo.: Lynne Rienner, 1991); Martha Thompson, "Repopulated Communities in El Salvador," in *The New Politics of Survival: Grassroots Movements in Central America,* ed. Minor Sinclair (New York: Monthly Review, 1995), 109–51.

25. For instance, see José Miguel Cruz, "Los factores posibilatadores y las expresiones de la violencia en los noventa," *Estudios Centroamericanos* 588 (1997): 977–92; Philippe

Bourgois, "The Power of Violence in War and Peace: Post–Cold War Lessons from El Salvador," *Ethnography* 2, no. 1 (2001): 5–34; Leigh Binford, "Violence in El Salvador: A Rejoinder to Philippe Bourgois's 'The Power of Violence in War and Peace: Post–Cold War Lessons from El Salvador,'" *Ethnography* 3, no. 1 (2002): 177–95; Philippe Bourgois, "The Violence of Moral Binaries: Rejoinder to Leigh Binford," *Ethnography* 3, no. 1 (2002): 221–31.

26. For instance, Michael W. Foley, "Land and Peace in Postwar El Salvador: Structural Adjustment, Land Reform and Social Peace in the Salvadoran Countryside" (paper presented at the annual meeting of the Latin American Studies Association, Guadalajara, Mexico, April 1997); Share Foundation, "El Salvador Peace Accords Land Transfer Program: A Report on Its Progress, Problems, and Sustainability" (San Francisco, 1996); Jenny Pearce, "From Civil War to 'Civil Society': Has the End of the Cold War Brought Peace to Central America?" *International Affairs* 74, no. 3 (1998): 587–615; James K. Boyce, ed., *Economic Policy for Building Peace: The Lessons of El Salvador* (Boulder, Colo.: Lynne Rienner, 1996). The most detailed extant regional or community study on the postwar period probably remains Fogaroli and Stowell, *Desarrollo rural y participación campesina.*

Land, Community, and Revolt in Late Nineteenth-Century Indian Izalco

A longer version of this chapter appeared in *Hispanic American Historical Review.* It won the 2000 Criscenti Best Article Prize from the New England Council of Latin American Studies. I thank Jonathan Amith, Avi Chomsky, Jeff Gould, Lowell Gudmundson, Gil Joseph, Mark Szuchman, and especially Ingrid Vargas for their useful comments and suggestions.

1. The term *faction* is useful because it implies a degree of political self-consciousness and organization that, I believe, the documents used here justify. It is also appropriate as the contemporary El Salvadoran term used to denote a political grouping that mobilizes for power or revolt.

2. Abelardo Torres, "More from This Land," *The Americas* 14, no. 8 (1962): 9.

3. Gustav Ferdinand von Tempsky, *Mitla: A Narrative of Incidents and Personal Adventures on a Journey in Mexico, Guatemala, and Salvador in the Years 1853 to 1855,* ed. J. S. Bell (London: Longman, Brown, Green, Longmans & Roberts, 1858), 414. In 1895 Izalco had 9,100 residents; see Santiago I. Barbarena, *Monografías departamentales: departamento de Sonsonate* (San Salvador: Imprenta Nacional, 1910), 56.

4. Mrs. Foote, *Recollections of Central America and the West Coast of Africa* (London: T. Cautley Newby, 1869), 86.

5. Nicolás Barrera (alcalde of Izalco) to governor of Sonsonate, report, 12 December 1892, AGN-Fondo Gobernaciones-Sonsonate (hereinafter AGN-FG-So). El Salvador, *Memoria presentada por el Ministro de Gobernación, Guerra y Marina Doctor Domingo Jiménez a la Asamblea Nacional (1892)* (San Salvador: Imprenta Nacional, 1893), 62.

6. These farms held 200 *manzanas* (1 *manzana* equals 0.7 hectares, 1.7 acres, or 7,000

square meters) and produced 40,000 pesos worth of sugar. Nicolás Barrera (alcalde of Izalco) to governor of Sonsonate, report, 12 December 1892, AGN-FG-So.

7. On communal control of irrigation and water resources, see Cruz Shupan, "Administrador y juez de la comunidad de Asunción Izalco solicita al gobernador prevenga al señor alcalde municipal se abstenga . . . ," 26 November 1891, Archivo de la Gobernacíon de Sonsonate (hereinafter AGS). Except for a conflict in 1852, the two communities had amicable relations that included agreements on the separation of their lands; Lorenzo López, *Estadística general de la republica de El Salvador* (San Salvador: Ministerio de Educación, Dirección General de Publicaciones, 1974).

8. "Documentación de la solicitud de las comunas de Dolores y Asunción Izalco para que se les entregaran las listas de las personas que deben pagar canón," 1870, AGS.

9. "Testimonio de los títulos ejidales y comunales de Izalco," 1878, AGN-FG-So. For a revealing document on Indian attempts to exclude ladinos from participating in their local polities, see "Informe que el secretario de relaciones hace a la Nación de orden del Presidente de la República, sobre la conducta del Licenciado Nicolás Espinosa, Gefe del Estado del Salvador," Archivo Nacional de Costa Rica, Sección Federal, exp. 384.

10. "Libro de actas municipales de Izalco," 1874–1885, Archivo Municipal de Izalco (hereinafter AMI). That same year Izalco joined the many other municipalities that gave its *ejido* tenants an incentive to plant commercial crops by reducing the land rent to those who planted one-third of their lands with these crops. Revenues from these rentals were controlled and expended by community leaders and not redistributed to community members.

11. "Título de las tierras de Izalco sacado a solicitud del común de Asunción," 1866, AMI. An 1893 report indicated that the municipality of Izalco held a total of 500 *caballerías* of land; "Informe de comercio y agricultura correspondiente al distrito de Izalco," 7 February 1893, AGN-FG-So.

12. Inés Masín, who served as municipal secretary (1891) and mayor (1893–1896) and became a successful farmer of lands that he had purchased from one of the *particioneros* of Dolores, was in all likelihood an *indígena*. His father had served as community administrator during the 1870s, and he went on to write articles about the dialect of Izalco's Indians; see Inés Masín, "El pipil de Izalco," *Revista de Etnología, Arquelogía y Lingüística* (San Salvador) 1, no. 5 (1926).

13. "Libros de documentos privados de Izalco," 1880–1900, AMI.

14. Governor of Sonsonate, "Informe de la visita oficial a los pueblos del departamento," 20 September 1913, AGS.

15. See "Los señores Indalecio Chilulum y Teodoro González . . . se quejan de que el alcalde municipal . . . dá apoyo a Martín Sanches para que éste les despoje . . . ," 20 September 1898, AGS, for an example of a conflict involving support by municipal authorities for one party. See also "Varios individuos del común de indígenas de Dolores Izalco se quejan contra don Calixto Vega por haberles tapado un camino," 1892, AGN-FG-So; and "Solicitud de la municipalidad de Izalco," 1892, AGN-FG-So, for examples of conflicts between Indian peasants and a local landowner.

16. See Lauria-Santiago, *Agrarian Republic,* chap. 8, for a discussion of the class-based divisions and conflicts that erupted within Asunción during this same period.

17. "Solicitud al SPE sobre exijir al administrador Simeón Morán la partición de la extinguida comunidad de Dolores Izalco," 13 July 1885, AGN-FG-So.

18. Duke to Porter, 28 May 1885, U.S. Department of State, dispatches from U.S. consuls in San Salvador, U.S. National Archives (hereinafter USNA), record group 59; and Baltasar Estupianián, *Memoria con que el Sr. Ministro de Gobernación Doctor Don Baltasar Estupinián, dió cuenta a la Honorable Asamblea Nacional (1885–1886)* (San Salvador: Imprenta Nacional, 1887), 232. In La Paz, Zaldívar's own properties were attacked by his workers; see Julio C. Calderón, *Episodios nacionales: Anastacio Aquino y el por qué de su rebelión en 1833 en Santiago Nonualco* (San Salvador: Imprenta Moreno, 1957), 48.

19. Local ladino merchants and artisans had also supported the coming to power of Santiago González in 1871 by providing funds for the revolt against the Dueñas government; see "Lista de los individuos que voluntariamente ha emprestado dinero a esta gobernación para los gastos en la revolución," 12 May 1871, AGN-Fondo Quemados.

20. "Información de orden superior sobre perjuicios causados por las tropas del General Figueroa en la ciudad de Izalco," 1885, AGN-FG-So.

21. "Solicitud al SPE sobre exijir al administrador Simeón Morán la partición de la extinguida comunidad de Dolores Izalco," 13 July 1885, AGN-FG-So. On the division of lands by Morán in Dolores, see Eduardo Barrientos (alcalde of Izalco) to governor of Sonsonate, 1886, AGN-FG-So.

22. "Carta del alcalde de Izalco respondiendo a quejas sobre la repartición de tierras," 1 December 1886, AGN-FG-So; and Santiago Contreras, *Memoria con que el señor sub secretario de estado encargado del despacho de gobernación, Dr. D. Santiago Contreras, dió cuenta de los actos del poder ejecutivo ocurridos en 1887 a la Honorable Asamblea Nacional* (San Salvador: Imprenta Nacional, 1888), 113.

23. "Los individuos de la comunidad de indígenas de Dolores Izalco piden la remoción del administrador y juez partidor Francisco Conco [*sic*] por ciertos delitos que le han denunciado," 1887, AGN-FG-So.

24. Of 184 members of the community who attended the election, 49 had not been officially registered as *comuneros,* although the mayor recognized them as community members. The minister of the interior ruled that the votes of these additional *comuneros* should be registered, even though this would not alter the election results.

25. "Consulta que el alcalde municipal de Izalco dirije al Supremo Gobierno por conducto de la gobernación con motivo de la elección del administrador juez partidor y socio de la comunidad de Dolores," 1889, AGN-FG-So. Governor of Sonsonate to ministro de Gobernación, draft of report, 1889, AGN-FG-So.

26. Governor of Sonsonate to ministro de Gobernación, draft of report, 1889, AGN-FG-So.

27. Samuel Carrizales (local commander in Izalco) to commander general of the Department of Sonsonate, 24 September 1888, AGS; and "Información seguida sobre averiguar algunas novedades ocurridas en Izalco," 1888, AGN-FG-So.

28. "Luciano Argueta administrador y juez partidor de la comunidad de Dolores Izalco pide autorización para vender una galera de teja que corresponde a la misma comunidad," 1889, AGN-FG-SO.

29. "Varios indígenas de Izalco que haga la partición de los terrenos que pertenecieron a la extinguida comunidad de Dolores," 1903, AGN-Fondo Ministerios-Ministerio de Gobernación (hereinafter AGN-FM-MG).

30. See "Copia de la matrícula de los comuneros de Dolores Izalco," 1889, AGN-FG-So. Another registry book drawn up in 1891 lists 617 male community members. An incomplete sample of the parcels titled in the 1880s by Morán lists 123 plots, ranging in size from 1 to 66 *manzanas*, with an average of 4. The larger plots were probably those that were rented to outsiders, since this register lists only a handful of plots of more than 12 *manzanas*. Most *comuneros* received plots that would only guarantee subsistence production while allowing for minimal commercial cropping. Nevertheless, many insiders, as well as some outsiders, benefited disproportionately from the land partition. See "Libro de registro de la comunidad de Dolores Izalco," 1891, AGN-FM-MG; and "Comunidad de Dolores Izalco, comuneros titulados por Simeón Morán," 1898, AGN-FG-So. Another list from 1891 shows 164 untitled possessors in Dolores; "Libro de registro de posedores de terrenos comunales de Dolores i Asunción," 1891, AGN-FG-So.

31. The decree was published in *Diario Oficial:* "Los comuneros de Dolores Izalco solicitan al Supremo Poder Ejecutivo haga extenciba al común a que pertenecieron el decreto de 1ro de junio del año corriente," 1895, AGN-FM-MG.

32. "Luciano Argueta y varios vecinos de la ciudad de Izalco en concepto de comuneros que fueron de la extinguida comunidad de Dolores solicitan del Spmo. Gobno. se digne prorrogar por dos meses el tiempo que se designó . . . para el nombramiento del ingeniero," 1895, AGN-FG-So.

33. "El señor Luciano Argueta de Izalco denuncia a Simeón Morán porque está estendiendo títulos de terreno el punto 'Rincón del Tigre,'" 21 August 1895, AGS.

34. "Solisitud de varios vecinos y comuneros de Dolores Izalco relativa a que se nombre juez y partidor de varios terrenos que han quedado sin repartir," 1895, AGN-FG-So.

35. "Varios comuneros de Dolores Izalco se quejan de que el Sr. Luciano Argueta está despojando de sus terrenos a los poseedores que no tienen títulos mediante una contribución," 1895, AGN-FG-So.

36. "Queja presentada ante el Supremo Poder Ejecutivo por varios indígenas de Izalco contra Luciano Argueta . . . por despojo de sus terrenos," 1896, AGN-FG-So.

37. "Solicitud al gobernador de Sonsonate," 1888, AGS.

38. Castillo Morán's claim is supported by other documentation in which he presents the titles to four *caballerías* (64 *manzanas* each) purchased from four *comuneros* to whom he had given title; see "Proceso sobre ocupación ilegal de terrenos en El Volcán," 1900, AGN-FM-MG.

39. "Queja presentada ante el Supremo Poder Ejecutivo por varios indígenas de Izalco contra Luciano Argueta . . . por despojo de sus terrenos," 1896, AGN-FG-So.

40. "La señora Guillerma Arevalo vecina de la ciudad de Izalco denuncia a Simeón

Morán administrador que fue de la comunidad de Izalco," 22 August 1896, AGS.

41. "Protocolo de títulos revalidados de la comunidad de Dolores Izalco," 1897, AGN-FG-So.

42. "Los señores Simeón Morán . . . [todos] vecinos de Izalco piden se señale el día en que se comiense a realizar los títulos de la comunidad de Dolores," 1897, AGN-FG-So.

43. Ing. Carlos Zimmerman to governor of Sonsonate, leg. of letters, 1898, AGN-FG-So.

44. "Partición de los terrenos comunales de Dolores Izalco," 1890, AGN-FG-So. Unlike in previous documents, here all the *comuneros* listed were men.

45. "Varios individuos comuneros de Dolores de la ciudad de Izalco se quejan de que Juan Tino, Manuel Lue . . . y Blas Shul que encabezan una pandilla, los perturban en el ejercicio de sus derechos," 1893, AGS.

46. The Indians of Izalco's indigenous communities had a history of bitter confrontations with the Indian community of Nahuizalco over the determination of boundaries and the use of unclaimed land that lay between both towns. The conflicts dated as far back as 1849, when a survey of the border came close to precipitating a violent clash. See "Nota manifestando que las comunidades de Izalco y Nahuizalco es necesario que suspenda sus actitudes hostiles y recomienda tomar medidas convenientes para evitar una asonada," 1849, AGN-Fondo Clasificádos (hereinafter AGN-FC), M1.12, exp. 108. There is also evidence of some friction between Izalco's two Indian communities; see "Los vecinos de Asunción Izalco han presentado ante el Supremo Gobierno quejas de exesos por parte de los vecinos de Dolores," 2 April 1852, AGN-Fondo Pre-Clasificádos.

47. Governor of Sonsonate, "Carta al alcalde de Izalco sobre usurpación de terrenos cometidas por los indígenas de Nahuizalco," 23 March 1899, AGN-FG-So.

48. The Indian peasants of Izalco had also engaged in a series of border conflicts with the ladino community of El Volcán de Santa Ana; see "Solicitud al Supremo Poder Ejecutivo por los miembros de la extinguida comunidad de ladinos de El Volcán de Santa Ana sobre tierras," 1896, AGN-FM-MG.

49. Eugenio Araujo had litigated with the community of Dolores Izalco over the boundary line between his hacienda and their communal lands. According to sources cited by Zimmerman, Araujo's stone wall extended 60–80 meters into communal lands that were marked off by an older boundary stone. The hacienda of El Sunza was originally part of Los Lagartos, a colonial-era hacienda that spread over the municipalities of Izalco and Caluco; see "Expediente de remedida de los linderos de Izalco y Caluco," 1879, AGS.

50. "Partición de los terrenos comunales de Dolores Izalco," 1890, AGN-FG-So.

51. José Larreynaga, *Memoria de los actos del poder ejecutivo en el ramo de Gobernación durante el año de 1889* (San Salvador: Imprenta Nacional, 1890), 138.

52. Machado had also unsuccessfully engaged in land litigation with peasants from Cuisnahuat in 1886. In that case, the minister of the interior forced him to give up his claim; see Estupinián, *Memoria,* 229.

53. "Libro compuesto de 32 hojas útiles . . . para que el juez partidor de la comunidad

de indígenas de Asunción Izalco, señor Simeón Tensún, lleve la cuente que le corresponde," 1885, AGS.

54. "Los infraescritos alcaldes de Dolores Izalco exponen que el administrador señor Simeón Morán no ha concluido aún la partición de nuestro terrenos municipales," 1885, AGS.

55. Castillo Mora served as governor of Ahuachapán during 1882. He was also involved in a claim in Asunción Izalco, where he purchased the claim to a valuable farm that a *comunero* had developed on communal lands.

56. Castillo Mora was also speculating in lands in Ataco (Ahuachapán). The governor of the department of Ahuachapán opposed his claim against a group of "intrusos," although this same claim was later supported by the Ministerio de Gobernación; see "Proceso sobre ocupación ilegal de terrenos en El Volcán," 1900, AGN-FM-MG; and "Libro de acuerdos del Ministerio de Gobernación," 1893, AGN-FM-MG.

57. General Carlos Zepeda was governor and military commander of Sonsonate during 1894.

58. "Partición de los terrenos comunales de Dolores Izalco," 1890, AGN-FG-So.

59. "Memorandum de la memoria del Ministro de Gobernación," 1899, AGN-FM-MG.

60. "Mesura de los terrenos Los Cuilotales en Izalco y Nahuizalco," 1899, AGN-FG-So.

61. See Francisco J. Monterrey, ed., *Historia de El Salvador: anotaciones cronológicas*, 2 vols., 2d ed. (San Salvador: Editorial Universitaria, 1977–1978), 1:225; "Carta sobre confrontamiento entre los Izalqueños y las tropas de Malespín," 26 November 1846, AGN-FC, M1.12, exp. 182; and Rafael Reyes, *Nociones de historia del Salvador* (San Salvador: Imprenta del Dr. Francisco Sangrini, 1885), 502–503; *Boletín Oficial* 74 (28 September 1872); Hubert Howe Bancroft, *History of Central America,* vol. 3: *1801–1887* (San Francisco: History Company Publishers, 1887), 400. On the 1885 and 1894 mobilizations, see Duke to Porter, 28 May 1885, U.S. Department of State, dispatches from U.S. consuls in San Salvador, USNA; and Alejandro Orellana and Carlos Orellana, *Sonsonate histórico e informativo* (San Salvador: Imprenta Nacional, 1960), 51.

62. Gustave de Belot, *La Republique de Salvador* (Paris: Chez Duntu, Libraire, 1965), 33; Foote, *Recollections of Central America,* 61; and *Gaceta Oficial* 9 (24 April 1861): 3.

63. Izalqueños had been recruited into the army for decades; see de Belot, *La Republique de Salvador.*

64. Regalado was kept from the presidency by a more powerful liberal faction led by Prudencio Alfaro; see Italo López Vallecillos, *El periodismo en El Salvador* (San Salvador: UCA Editores, 1974); Patricia Andrews, "El liberalismo en El Salvador a finales del siglo XIX," *Revista del Pensamiento Centroamericano* 36 (1981): 172–73.

65. For events in Santiago Nonualco, see Piñeda Alvarado, *Reseña histórica de Santiago Nonualco,* 14–16. For La Libertad, see A. Molina Guirola (governor of La Libertad) to Ministro de Gobernación, report, 9 February 1899, AGN-FM-MG.

66. Regalado received about 600 votes in Izalco (as the only candidate) when Izalco had about 2,000 potential voters; see "Electoral Results," 1899, AGN-FM-MG.

67. José María Martínez, "História de Cojutepeque," in *Papeles históricos,* ed. José Manuel Gallardo (Santa Tecla: Ed. Léa, 1978), 296.

68. Governor of Sonsonate, "Informe de la visita oficial a los pueblos del departamento," 20 September 1913, AGN-FG-So.

69. "Los señores Pedro Bolaños, Domingo Huela, Marcelino Felilo, Obispo Mayo y Nicomedes Gómez se han quejado al Supremo Poder Ejecutivo como indígenas que pertenecieron a la comunidad de Dolores Izalco de que varios ladinos avecinados," 1900, AGN-Fondo. Tierras, leg. 3/4, doc. 2.

70. Greg Grandin discusses a similar reversal in the popular memory of struggles over land and local power in Cantel, Guatemala; see Greg Grandin, "The Strange Case of 'La Mancha Negra': Maya-State Relations in Nineteenth-Century Guatemala," HAHR 77 (1997).

71. See C. Varaona (governor of Sonsonate) to Ministro General, 22 November 1898, AGN-FG-So.

72. "Solicitud de varios vecinos de los valles de 'El Chorro,' 'Matazano,' 'Cruz Grande,' 'Teshacalate' . . . que comprendían antiguamente la comunidad de Dolores Izalco, sobre que se les remidan sus propiedades por encontrarse muy obscuros los títulos antiguos de terrenos comunales dados a los naturales por mandato real en 1582," 15 April 1901, AGN-Fondo Asamblea Legislativa; and "Varios indígenas de Izalco que haga la partición de los terrenos que pertenecieron a la extinguida comunidad de Dolores," 1904, AGN-FM-MG.

73. "Varios indígenas de Izalco que haga la partición de los terrenos que pertenecieron a la extinguida comunidad de Dolores," 1904, AGN-FM-MG.

74. Larreynaga, *Memoria;* and "Partición de los terrenos comunales de Dolores Izalco," 1890, AGN-FG-So.

75. "Varios indígenas de Izalco que haga la partición de los terrenos que pertenecieron a la extinguida comunidad de Dolores," 1904, AGN-FM-MG.

76. For a discussion of a case in which these connections are more evident, see Aldo A. Lauria-Santiago, "Los indígenas de Cojutepeque, la política faccional y el estado nacional en El Salvador, 1830–1890," in *Construcción de las identidades y del estado moderno en Centro América,* ed. Arturo Taracena (San José: UCA Editores; CEMCA; FLACSO, 1995).

77. See, for example, "Los señores Indalecio Chilulum y Teodoro González . . . se quejan de que el alcalde municipal . . . dá apoyo a Martín Sanches para que éste les despoje," 20 September 1898, AGS.

78. Thomas Anderson, *Matanza: The Communist Revolt of 1932* (Lincoln: University of Nebraska Press, 1971), 110. However, the demise of the indigenous community of Dolores and the decreasing number of individuals identified as Indians in the surviving indigenous community of Asunción did not lead to a significant decline in the number of

Izalqueños identified as Indians in official sources. Demographic data from 1914 and 1915 indicate that about 50 percent of all births were still classified as Indian; see "Libro de Actas Municipales," AMI, 1903–1917.

79. In 1924 the community of Asunción listed about 210 adult males, representing about 800 family members (the total municipal population was between 17,500 and 19,000). The community held yearly elections for *alcalde* and reported to the departmental governor; see Sotero Pasín to governor of Sonsonate, 1924, AGS.

80. In 1905 community leaders, with the support of eighty *comuneros,* had to request official permission for their fiestas; see "Solicitud de los indígenas de Izalco a que se les permita celebrar funciones religiosas y velaciones de las imágenes y patrón del pueblo," 27 May 1905, AGN-FM-MG.

The Formation of the Urban Middle Sectors in El Salvador, 1910–1944

This chapter was translated by Aldo Lauria-Santiago. I wish to thank the German BUNTSFIFT foundation for research support. My thanks also to Gabriela Villalobos and Carlos Gregorio López, who collaborated in the research. Guillermo Nañez Falcón of Tulane also assisted in the research for this project.

1. Edelberto Torres Rivas, *Interpretación del desarrollo social centroamericano* (San José: Educa 1971), 166.

2. David S. Parker, "White-collar Lima, 1910–1929: commercial employees and the rise of the Peruvian middle class," *Hispanic American Historical Review* 72, no. 1 (1992): 47–72.

3. John J. Johnson, *Political Change in Latin America. The Emergence of the Middle Sectors* (Palo Alto, Calif.: Stanford University Press, 1958). Among the best known are "La crisis de las clases medias" by Jorge Graciarena, in his book *Poder y clases sociales en el desarrollo de América Latina* (Buenos Aires: Editorial Paidós, 1972).

4. Everett A Wilson, "The crisis of National Integration in El Salvador, 1919–1935" (Ph.D. diss., Stanford University, 1970); Patricia Parkman, *Nonviolent Insurrection in El Salvador. The Fall of Maximiliano Hernández Martínez* (Tucson: University of Arizona Press, 1988).

5. The principal sources for this research are *Diario del Salvador* (hereinafter DES) between 1918 and 1932, especially the column *Gremios y Corporaciones.* I also examined the *Diario Oficial* (hereinafter DO) of El Salvador, during the 1920s. La Concordia still exists, and in its offices in the center of San Salvador I located the books of minutes of the Junta Directiva and the Asamblea General and portions of its correspondence for the years 1909–1940.

6. *Memoria de los trabajos de la Sociedad de Artesanos "El Porvenir" verificados desde el día 15 de junio de 1902 hasta la fecha* (Santa Tecla: Tipografía Católica, 1903), 10. Usually the statutes of these organizations appeared in the *Diario Oficial;* see, for example, "Estatutos de la Sociedad de Artesanos de San Miguel" DO, 15 January 1895.

7. Erik Ching, "In Search of the Party: The Communist Party, the Comintern, and the Peasant Rebellion of 1932 in El Salvador," *The Americas* 55, no. 2 (1998): 204–39.

8. Víctor Hugo Acuña Ortega, *Clase obrera, participación política e identidad nacional en El Salvador (1918–1932)* (paper presented at the National State and Political Participation in Central America seminar, Universidad de Costa Rica, February 1995).

9. Miguel Angel García, *Diccionario histórico-enciclopédico de la República de El Salvador*, vol. 2 (San Salvador: Imprenta Nacional, 1954), 44–46.

10. DO, 21 November 1899. I have also located the reformed statutes of 1884, 1907, 1918, and 1941; see DO, 29 April 1884, 18 November 1907, 31 July 1918, and 4 January 1941.

11. *Informe que la Comisión Directiva de la Escuela Nocturna de Artesanos dió a la Junta General de la Sociedad de Artesanos de San Salvador, en la sesion del 3 de enero de 1875, sobre la fundación y estado de las escuelas nocturna y diurna durante el año de 1874, 3° de la Sociedad* (San Salvador: Imprenta Nacional, 1875), 15.

12. DO 1 December 1878. Miguel Angel García, *Diccionario histórico-enciclopédico* 3: 92–93.

13. *Dr. Rafael Zaldívar. Recopilación de documentos históricos relativos a su administración*, vol. 2 (San Salvador: Ministerio de Educación, 1977), 132–33.

14. "Estatutos de la Sociedad de Artesanos 'Excelsior,'" DES, 25 July 1901.

15. AGN-Fondo Indiferente,-box 7, Document 3, 1913: *Juicio civil ordinario promovido por la Sociedad de Artesanos La Concordia contra la Sociedad de Artesanos del Salvador, a efectos de que le restituya unos bienes* (Cámara de tercera instancia, San Salvador, 12 December 1913).

16. *Album del Centenario* (San Salvador: Imprenta Nacional, 1912), 214. See also "Reglamento del Comité Central "General Francisco Menéndez", DO, 28 February 1912; and the pamphlet *Francisco Menéndez. El por qué de la estatua* (San Salvador: Imprenta y Encuadernación de José B. Cisneros, 1912), 27.

17. "La Concordia," *Actualidades. Revista mensual literaria, instructiva, humorística, noticiosa* (San Salvador), Avance al no.. 19, p. 25; and Salvador R. Merlos, "Los certámenes de la sociedad de artesanos 'La Concordia'" *Fraternidad Centroamericana. Revista Mensual* (San Salvador) 1 (1911), 12–13.

18. L. A. Ward, comp. and ed., *"Libro Azul" de El Salvador* (San Salvador: Bureau de Publicidad de la América Latina, 1916), 352. It has a photo montage with the title "Primera exhibición de la Sociedad de Artesanos 'La Concordia.'"

19. Sociedad de Artesanos del Salvador "La Concordia," *Actas de la Junta General, 1911–1915*, 189 pp.; *Correspondencia, 1909–1916*, 191 pp.; *Actas del Consejo Directivo, 1914–1928*, 299 pp.

20. In 1922 *La Concordia* was considered the "decana de las agrupaciones obreras salvadoreñas" (dean of the *obrero* associations), DES, 25 September 1922.

21. Sociedad de artesanos del Salvador "La Concordia," *Actas del Consejo Directivo, 1928–1940*, 135 pp.; and *Actas de la Junta General, 1928–1931*, 200 pp. In general, the minutes of the general assemblies have more information than those of the board of direc-

tors, but unfortunately I could not locate the minutes for most of the 1920s. This is compensated for by the data from *Diario del Salvador.*

22. Sociedad de artesanos del Salvador "La Concordia," *Actas de la Junta General, 1931–1938;* and *Actas de la Junta General, 1938–1940.*

23. L. A. Ward, *Libro Azul,* 182, 249, 265, 271, 278.

24. Alejandro Bermúdez, *El Salvador al vuelo* (San Salvador, 1917), 176–77. A photo of Ciudad-Real appears on the unnumbered page opposite p. 166.

25. Jorge Ramírez Chulo, *Tres contactos para una superación en el Coronel Salvador Ciudad Real* (Sonsonate: Imprenta y Editorial Excelsior, 1943), 22; it contains a biography of Ciudad Real written by a teacher.

26. Gerardo Barrios, *Órgano de la Sociedad Cooperativa "Gerardo Barrios 29 de agosto"* (San Salvador, 29 August 1932).

27. *Estatutos de la Sociedad Filotécnica "Los Veintiuno," de San Salvador, C.A.* (n.p. 1928). In this teacher's organization there were various members of La Concordia: Francisco R. Osegueda, Marco Tulio G. Terezón, and Napoleón D. Cañas.

28. DES, 12 and 14 March 1921.

29. L. A. Ward, *Libro Azul,* 275.

30. I have located issue 12 of this publication dated August 15, 1918.

31. For example, Meléndez Arévalo wrote the eulogy at the services offered by La Concordia for ex-President Carlos Meléndez. See *Ateneo de El Salvador. Revista de Ciencias, Letras y Artes,* VII, 72–73 (April–June 1919), 1383–84. Among other things he wrote *El 63: Episodios nacionales histórico-novelescos* (San Salvador: Imprenta Arévalo, 1916), 179.

32. Sociedad de Artesanos del Salvador "La Concordia," *Actas de la Junta General, 1938–1940,* 69.

33. DES, 7 March 1928.

34. The minutes of the association allow for small financial contributions to members in poverty.

35. DO, 9 August 1882.

36. DES, 17 September 1919. In March 1914 during an assembly of the members of *La Concordia* Meléndez Arévalo "pronunció una disertación escrita por él, en la que patentizó la actitud imperialista del gobierno yanqui y la manera de conjurar el mal. Fue muy aplaudido al concluir su lectura por la concurrencia." Esta sería una de las pocas tomas de posición política radicales de *La Concordia.* Sociedad de Artesanos del Salvador "La Concordia," *Actas de la Junta General, 1911–1915,* 95.

37. DES, 7 October and 22 December 1919.

38. *La Concordia* was not alone its struggle against communism. In 1931 the Sociedad de Zapateros Propietarios announced that it would "contrarrestar las exigencias de los asalariados y las doctrinas comunistas." DES, 30 May 1931.

39. "Observaciones sobre la vida del campesino salvadoreño de otros tiempos y la del campesino actual. Estudio leído por su autor Don Francisco R. Osegueda, en la radio difusora de esta capital, después de los sucesos comunistas del mes de enero del presente año." *Revista del Ateneo de El Salvador* 20, no. 143 (1932): 11–15.

40. En 1920 *La Concordia* participó con otras sociedades mutuales y con el respaldo del gobierno en la creación del "Comité permanente pro-moralidad pública" para combatir los vicios del alcoholismo, el juego y la prostitución; DES, 12 January 1920.

41. DES, 8 May 1918.

42. DES, 17 September 1929. En esa ocasión Romero Bosque atribuyó a *La Concordia* "el impulso que tiene el obrerismo en la actualidad."

43. Sociedad de Artesanos del Salvador "La Concordia," *Actas de la Junta General, 1928–1931*, 197–98.

44. R. J. Morris, *Class and Class Consciousness in the Industrial Revolution, 1780–1850,* Studies in Economic and Social History (London: Macmillan, 1979), 31.

45. See Erik Ching's chapter, this volume. I have discussed the subordination and differential integration of subaltern sectors in the power networks of the liberal regimes in "Autoritarismo y democracia en Centroamérica: la larga duración, siglos XIX y XX," in *Ilusiones y dilemas: la democracia en Centroamérica,* ed. Klaus D. Tangermann (San José: FLACSO, 1995), 63–97.

46. DES, 17 September 1929.

47. DES, 4 November 1919.

48. *El Aventino. Semanario Político. Órgano del Comité Central de Obreros Quiñonistas* I, no. 12 (15 August 1918).

49. DES, 21 June 1920.

50. See Pierre Bourdieu, "Espace social et pouvoir symbolique," in *Choses dites* (Paris: Les Editions de Minuit, 1987), 147–66. This article synthesizes the argument of the author of *La distinción.* See also Martine Segalen, *Rites et rituels contemporains* (Paris: Éditions Nathan, 1998).

51. This process is analyzed in detail in Carlos Gregorio López Bernal "El proyecto liberal de nación en El Salvador (1876–1932)" (master's thesis, San José: Universidad de Costa Rica, 1998).

Patronage and Politics under General Maximiliano Hernández Martínez, 1931–1939

I wish to thank Aldo Lauria-Santiago, Héctor Lindo Fuentes, Knut Walter, David Rock, Patricia Alvarenga, and Michael Schroeder for comments on my work. The research was supported by a Department of Education Fulbright Fellowship; the Graduate Division at the University of California, Santa Barbara; and the Research and Professional Growth Committee at Furman University.

1. See Williams and Walter, *Militarization and Demilitarization;* and William Stanley, *The Protection Racket State: Elite Politics, Military Extortion, and Civil War in El Salvador* (Philadelphia, Pa.: Temple University Press, 1996).

2. Martínez's full last name was Hernández Martínez, but he went by his maternal name.

3. Jeffrey Rubin, *Decentering the Regime: Ethnicity, Radicalism, and Democracy in Juchitán, Mexico* (Durham, N.C.: Duke University Press, 1997).

4. Overviews of the dialogue between social and cultural history can be found in Victoria Bonnell and Lynn Hunt, eds., *Beyond the Cultural Turn: New Directions in the Study of Society and Culture* (Berkeley: University of California Press, 1999); Terrence McDonald, ed., *The Historic Turn in the Human Sciences* (Ann Arbor: University of Michigan, 1996); Miguel Cabrera, "On Language, Culture, and Social Action," *History and Theory* 40, no. 4 (2001): 82–100; and Jay Smith, "No More Language Games: Words, Beliefs, and the Political Culture of Early Modern France," *American Historical Review* 102, no. 5 (1997): 1413–40.

5. This quote is from Cabrera, "On Language."

6. Past studies on Martínez failed to document the internal workings of the regime, assuming that the regime's authoritarian nature was stable. See David Luna, "Análisis de una dictadura fascista latinoamericana: Maximiliano Hernández-Martínez, 1931–1944," *La Universidad* (San Salvador) 94, no. 5 (1969); Patricia Parkman, *Nonviolent Insurrection in El Salvador: The Fall of Maximiliano Hernández Martínez* (Tucson: University of Arizona Press, 1988); Carmelo Astilla, "The Martínez Era: Salvadoran-American Relations, 1931–1944" (Ph.D. diss., Louisiana State University, 1976); Raúl Padilla Vela, *El fascismo en un país dependiente: la dictadura del General Maximiliano Hernández Martínez* (San Salvador: Editorial Universitaria, 1987); and Kenneth Grieb, "The United States and the Rise of Maximiliano Hernández Martínez," *Journal of Latin American Studies* 3, no. 2 (1971): 151–72. A rich interview with Martínez in the 1940s can be found in William Krehm, *Democracies and Tyrannies in the Caribbean* (Westport, Conn.: Lawrence Hill, 1984). See also Ching, "Clientelism," chaps. 7, 8.

7. Victor Bulmer-Thomas, *The Political Economy of Central America Since 1920* (Cambridge: Cambridge University Press, 1988), 326 and 328.

8. The main secondary sources on 1932 include Anderson, *Matanza;* Hector Pérez-Brignoli, "Indians, Communists, and Peasants: The 1932 Rebellion in El Salvador," in *Coffee, Society, and Power in Latin America,* ed. William Roseberry et al. (Baltimore, Md.: The Johns Hopkins University Press, 1995), 232–61; Douglas Kincaid, "Peasants into Rebels: Community and Class in Rural El Salvador," *Comparative Studies of Society and History* 29 (1987): 466–94; and Ching, "In Search of the Party."

9. I concur with Williams and Walter's assessment that the evidence is too inconclusive to determine Martínez's degree of culpability. *Militarization,* chap. 2.

10. Some of the main examples of direct military interventions include Cuba (after 1898), Nicaragua (1912–1933), Mexico (1914), Haiti (1915–1934), and the Dominican Republic (1916–1924).

11. Leon Zamosc, "The Landing that Never Was: Canadian Marines and the Salvadoran Insurrection of 1932," *Canadian Journal of Latin American and Caribbean Studies* 21 (1986): 131–47.

12. *Diario Latino* (San Salvador), 11 July 1931. This article was found in a book of press clippings in El Salvador's AGN-FG.

13. Shepherd, San Salvador, 4 December 1933, PRO, FO 371/16560, A8750/706/8.

14. From the diary of Henry Stimson, 25 January 1932, Yale University Manuscripts Collections, cited in Astilla, "The Martínez Era."

15. On the military's response to the 1932 uprising, see Ching and Tilley, "Indians."

16. See Grieb, "The United States"; and Ching and Tilley, "Indians."

17. From "listas de gobernadores políticos," 1930, in AGN-FA, box "C, no. 2"; and a list of governors in DO, 29 August 1934, reprinted in *Diario La Prensa,* 30 August 1934, 1.

18. For a good introduction to the historiography of patronage and clientelism, see Luis Roniger, "Caciquismo and Coronelismo: Contextual Dimensions of Patron Brokerage in Mexico and Brazil," *Latin American Research Review* 32, no. 2 (1987): 71–99.

19. Lauria-Santiago, *An Agrarian Republic;* and Ching, "In Search of the Party," 230–37.

20. Ching, "Clientelism," chap. 6.

21. The strong showing of the Communist candidate in San Salvador was reported in *Diario Latino,* 5 January 1932, and in *Patria,* 4 January 1932. On the municipal election of January 1932, see Ching, "In Search of the Party," 224.

22. A copy of the announcement can be found in *Diario Latino,* 12 December 1931. The copy I saw was in a collection of press clippings in AGN-FI, Capitulo 1, box 17.

23. See *Diario La Prensa,* 14 January 1932, and *Diario Latino,* 14 January 1932. Both of these are in the collection of press clippings, AGN-FI, Capitulo 1, box 17. A low approximation of eligible, albeit not necessarily registered, voters in San Salvador is 20,000. See Dirección General de Estadística, *Población de la República de El Salvador* (San Salvador: Imprenta Nacional, 1930).

24. McCafferty, San Salvador, to U.S. secretary of state, 19 January 1932, USNA, RG 59, 816.00/826.

25. *Diario Patria,* 11 January 1932. From a collection of press clippings in AGN-FI, Capitulo 1, box 17.

26. The organizational structures of Pro-Patria are found in a circular from Enecón Paredes, San Salvador, to the fourteen departmental governors, 16 August 1933, AGN-FG-So, box "Politica, 1930-39"; and also in a circular dated 1 June 1934, AGN-FG.

27. The figures for Sonsonate are from two memos from Joaquín Guzmán, secretary of the Sonsonate chapter, to president of the national chapter of Pro-Patria, San Salvador, 6 October and 31 December, 1934, respectively, AGN-FG. The population figures are from the 1930 census, *Población de la República.*

28. The survey, conducted between June and August 1940, is located in AGN-FG.

29. From a circular dated 1 June 1934, in AGN-FG.

30. The names of the municipal list are found in AGN-FG-So, box "Politica, 1930–39." The cantonal lists are in AGN-FG, box "C." The list of moneyed citizens is from a comprehensive list of the financial holdings of every "well-to-do" citizen in El Salvador. It was compiled by the government in 1943 and can be found spread out between folder 070, "Comercio"; folder 010, "Asuntos Gremiales"; and in a paquete, AGN-FG, 1943. The list of landowners in Nahuizalco is from *Directorio Comercial* (San Sal-

vador: Imprenta Nacional, 1924), 494–96. See also "principales ganaderos, Nahuizalco," 7 June 1935, AGN-FG-So, box 3; and for a list of coffee growers in Nahuizalco from 1926, see "nomina de las personas cultivadoras de café en la villa de Nahuizalco," AGN-FG, 1926, box 5.

31. Pro-Patria's membership lists for Sonsonate City are found in two boxes: AGN-FG, box "C" and another box. Herrera's properties are listed in *Directorio Comercial,* 477–80. His role as auditor is found in DES, 22 and 28 July 1932.

32. Ching and Tilley, "Indians."

33. Enecón Paredes (member of the Consejo Supremo), San Salvador, to governor of Sonsonate, 4 November 1933, AGN-FG-So, box "Politica 1930–1939."

34. Guillermo Barrientos, San Julián, to José Santos Zepeda, 6 November 1933, AGN-FG. Zepeda was on the directiva of the Pro-Patria chapter in Sonsonate City, as revealed in "nomina de las personas que forma la Directiva del Comité Pro Patria," Sonsonate, 22 July 1934, AGN-FG.

35. Gabino Mata, hijo, to Julio C. Calderón, governor of Sonsonate, 11 and 22 November 1937, AGN-FG-So, box "2.2." Mata's recommendation for alcalde of Nahuizalco was Rodolfo Brito. His victory in the December 1937 election is confirmed in "Alcaldes electos, 1938–39," AGN-FG.

36. For instance, one letter to a governor from his local agent begins, "In compliance with the verbal instructions you gave me personally, I am sending you . . . the name of the persons to be selected in the next election." Alberto Engelhard, San Julián, 29 November 1937, AGN-FG-So, box "2.2."

37. Hermogenes Alvarado, hijo, to governor of Ahuachapán Department, 2 December 1937, AGN-FG, 1937, paquete.

38. Circular telegram from governor, Sonsonate, to alcaldes, Sonsonate Department, 11 December 1937, AGN-FG-So, box "2.2."

39. Jesús Rivas, Guazapa, to minister of government, 12 December 1937, AGN-FG, 1937, paquete.

40. General Galdamez, governor of Usulután Department, to Ministerio de Gobernación, San Salvador, 5 February 1936; Flamenco, Santiago de María, to Ministerio de Gobernación, 6 February 1936; Francisco Llach, Santiago de María, to Ministerio de Gobernación, 6 February 1936. All materials relating to this case in Santiago de María are in AGN-FG, 1936, box 3.

41. José Trabanino, governor, San Salvador, to subsecretary of Gobernación, 11 December 1937, AGN-FG.

42. Telegram from Anacleto Menéndez, vice president of directorio, Nueva Concepción, to Ministro de Gobernación, 8 December 1937, AGN-FG.

43. "Cambio de Autoridades," 9 December 1937, AGN-FG.

44. As revealed in Joaquín Guzmán, Sonsonate, to president of Pro-Patria, 13 November 1934, AGN-FG; and Lisandro Larín, Sonsonate, to president of Pro-Patria, 30 December 1934, AGN-FG.

45. Telegram Circular 7, from General José Tomás Calderón, 3 January 1935, AGN-FG-So, box "Politica, 1930–9."

46. Pedro Ramos, Alcalde of Santiago de Guzmán, 11 January 1935, AGN-FG-So, box 1. The box is filled with similar reports.

47. Juan Vidal, departmental comandante, Cabañas Department, to governor of Sonsonate, 14 January 1935, AGN-FG-So, box 1.

48. Telegram from Juayúa to Sonsonate City, 14 January 1935, AGN-FG-So, box 1.

49. In Annual Report, 1935, Birch, Guatemala, to Foreign Office, 23 January 1936, PRO, FO 371/19771, A 1281/128/8.

50. The case of the teacher/spy is contained in José Cruz Peñate, to General Felipe Ibarra, 18 August 1932, AGN-FG-So, box 2. The term *oreja* is found in Colonel Julio César Calderón, governor of Sonsonate Department, to General José Tomás Calderón, 22 July 1935, AGN-FG-So, box "Politica, 1930–9."

51. These coups, both actual and plotted, occurred in January 1934, October 1935, October 1936, and January 1939. For more information, see Ching, "Clientelism," chap. 7.

52. A brief discussion of the meaning of regime change and references to appropriate literature can be found in Hagopien, *Traditional Politics.*

53. Harris, Military Attaché in San José, Costa Rica, G-2 Military Report no. 2318, 23 February 1934, USNA, RG 59, 816.00/941.

54. Rubin, *Decentering the Regime,* 14.

55. Hagopien, *Traditional Politics,* 16.

56. It could be argued that Brazil's civil society was stronger comparatively and thus more able to limit the military's initiatives. For example, see Maria Alves, *State and Military Opposition in Brazil* (Austin: University of Texas Press, 1985).

57. Williams and Walter, *Militarization.* See also Stanley, *The Protection Racket State.* For an excellent study of the military during the Peace Accords, see Knut Walter, *Las Fuerzas Armadas y el Acuerdo de Paz: la transformación necesaria del ejército salvadoreño* (San Salvador: FLACSO, 1997).

Colonels and Industrial Workers in El Salvador, 1944–1972

The Fulbright and Fulbright Garcia-Robles Programs made research and writing for this chapter possible. We thank Luis Armando González for facilitating research in El Salvador. We also thank Aaron Bobrow-Strain, Leigh Binford, Amy Carol, Erik Ching, Michael Foley, Jill Jeffrey, and Aldo Lauria-Santiago for their helpful comments.

1. Williams and Walter, *Militarization and Demilitarization.*

2. For example, Alistair White, *El Salvador* (San Salvador: UCA Editores, 1973).

3. Jean Larson Pyle, *The State and Women in the Economy: Lessons from Sex Discrimination in the Republic of Ireland* (Albany: State University of New York Press, 1990).

4. This chapter draws on *El Salvador al Día* and *Informaciones de El Salvador* 1949 and 1952; *Memorias* and *Estadísticas de trabajo* in the 1948–1968 period; Ministry of Labor reports of labor conferences; *Diario de Hoy* from 1944 to 1951; *La Prensa Gráfica* from 1949

and 1963; headlines in *La Prensa Gráfica's* summary journal, *Libro de Oro*, from 1944 to 1965; and over thirty interviews by the author with labor leaders, scholars, and state officials.

5. Victor Bulmer-Thomas, *The Political Economy of Central America since 1920* (Cambridge: Cambridge University Press, 1987), 117; James Dunkerley, *The Long War: Dictatorship and Revolution in El Salvador* (London: Junction Books, 1982), 49–50.

6. *Diario de Hoy*, May 1944–February 1945. *Diario de Hoy*, 2 March 1946; *Memoria*, 1947, Ministry of Labor; *Memoria*, 1948, Ministry of Labor, Anexo 9. For September and October strikes, see *La Prensa Gráfica*, 17 and 26 September 1946.

7. *Diario de Hoy*, June, 1944, see eight editorials entitled "La sindicalización como necesidad nacional." For evidence of how politicians appealed to labor, see 21 July 1944, "Posición de obreros y campesinos en los partidos políticos capitalistas."

8. *Memoria*, 1948, Ministry of Labor, 9–10.

9. *Diario de Hoy*, 23 August 1950, "Incorporado el Código de Trabajo a la constitución."

10. Rafael Guidos Véjar, "El movimiento sindical después de la segunda guerra mundial en El Salvador," *Estudios Centroamericanos XLV* (1990): 892.

11. See *La Prensa Gráfica*, 21 April 1949, "Celebraciones del Día del Trabajo preparan Obreros." Also see Aristides Augusto Larín, *Historia del movimiento sindical de El Salvador* (San Salvador: Editorial Universitaria, 1971), 150. The state favored some commercial unions as well but focused on industrial unions.

12. Larín, *Historia del movimiento sindical*, 151. They considered a prepared statement by labor, see Salvador, *Documentos Históricos de la Constitución Política Salvadoreña de 1950*, 222.

13. *Informaciones de El Salvador*, 14 February 1951 "Algunas de las actividades realizadas por los distintos ministerios," and *La Prensa Gráfica*, 4 November 1953, "Sindicatos envían delegados a discusiones de la asamblea."

14. James Dunkerley, *Power in the Isthmus* (London: Verso, 1988), 355, and others maintain that the form of political dominance is fairly consistent from 1950 to 1979.

15. Italo López Vallecillos, *El Periodismo en El Salvador*, 1987 ed. (San Salvador: UCA Editores, 1974), 172; and Larín, *Historia del movimiento sindical*, 154.

16. Carpio, "Las corrientes sindicales en El Salvador," *Rev. Universidad* (1969), 66.

17. *La Prensa Grafica*, 18 February 1957, "Pronto será fundada una confederación de obreros"; and Mario Lungo, *La lucha de las masas en El Salvador*, vol. 7 of Colección Debate (San Salvador: UCA Editores, 1987), 45.

18. Stephan Webre, *Jose Napoleón Duarte and the Christian Democratic Party in Salvadorean Politics 1960–1972* (Baton Rouge: Louisiana State University Press, 1979), 75.

19. Webre, *Jose Napoleon Duarte*, 69.

20. For example, *La Prensa Gráfica-Libro de Oro*, 25 May 1960, "Se inauguró la II Reunión Nacional de la Confederación General de Sindicatos"; and White, *El Salvador*, 295.

21. For labor leader and state official discussions of the labor code at CGS's II National Conference, see *La Prensa Gráfica*, 1 October 1962; See also *La Prensa Gráfica*,

5 January 1963, "Informe Esperan para discutir Código Laboral"; 8 January 1963, "Inician Lectura de Código de Trabajo"; 11 January 1963, "Sugieren reformas al Código Laboral"; 12 January 1963, "Discusión pública al Código Laboral"; "Reformas a la Ley de Fomento Industrial," *Industria,* March 1967, 36–37. In 1964 two labor representatives participated in the seven-member National Commission regarding minimum salaries; *La Prensa Gráfica,* 8 September 1964, "Consejo de Salario Mínimo."

22. Carpio, "Las Corrientes Sindicales en El Salvador," 66; White, *El Salvador,* 298; Dunkerley, *The Long War,* 58.

23. Quoted in *Diario de Hoy,* 2 June 1961, cited in Webre, *José Napoleón Duarte,* 39.

24. White, *El Salvador,* 134–35; and Montgomery, *Revolution,* 46. For information regarding state industrial training programs, see *La Prensa Gráfica,* 18–19 February 1951. For social security, see Dr. Ernesto Romero Hernández, "Historia del Régimen del Seguro Social en El Salvador 1954–1979" (San Salvador, 1979), 1–35.

25. For labor demands, see *Diario de Hoy,* 1 July 1944, "La Comisión de Legislación Obrera Pide Colaboración"; *La Prensa Gráfica,* 2 October 1944, "El Congreso Obrero no tiene miras políticas," and Rafael Guidos Véjar, "El movimiento sindical después de la segunda guerra mundial," *Estudios Centroamericanos* 45, no. 504 (1990), 885.

26. *Diario de Hoy,* 11 August 1944, Luis Mendoza "El Obrerismo Nacional espera que sea aprobado un hermoso Proyecto de Ley; Que se refiere a la creación de Departamento del Trabajo"; and *La Prensa Gráfica,* 4 September 1944, "El Departamento Nacional del Trabajo es la Esperanza de los Obreros."

27. Quoted in *Diario de Hoy,* 27 May 1944, "La Unión Nacional de Trabajadores dio a conocer ya su declaración de principios."

28. Quoted in *Diario de Hoy,* 30 June 1944, "Surge a la vida pública otra agrupación con fines obreristas: Plataforma ideológica de la 'Unión Fraternal de Trabajadores.'"

29. Quoted in *Diario de Hoy,* San Salvador, 6 May 1946, "Organización futura del obrerismo Salvadoreño." All translations are the author's. The shorthand term *labor* refers to organized or unionized urban industrial workers.

30. Quoted in *El Salvador al Día,* 25 March 1950, "Sociedad que cumplió años."

31. Quoted in *Diario de Hoy,* 9 February 1950, "Urge protección a la mujer trabajadora."

32. Quoted in Ministerio de Trabajo, *Memoria Del Primer Congreso Nacional del Trabajo y Previsión Social* (San Salvador: Ministerio del Trabajo, 1955), 196.

33. Ibid., 205.

34. Ricardo Gallardo, ed., *Las constituciones de El Salvador,* (Argentina: Edit. BID/INTAL, 1973), 263, 265–66.

35. Quoted in Ministerio de Trabajo, "Memoria," 205.

36. Ibid., 207.

37. See *La Prensa Gráfica,* 19 November 1954, "Resoluciones del Primer Congreso del Trabajo"; and *Memoria,* 1958, Ministry of Labor, 43.

38. Jorge E. Solórzano, "Adiestrar a nuestros trabajadores es fomentar la economía na-

cional," in *Industria* (San Salvador: Asociación Salvadoreña de Industriales, February 1963), 19–21.

39. Ministry of Labor officials suggest that women's union participation remained low throughout the 1950s and 1960s. Interviews by author, 20 October and 2 November 1999.

40. All of the members of the executive committee of the 1918 Workers' Congress, for instance, were men. Vallecillos, *El Periodismo en El Salvador*, 307.

41. *Diario de Hoy*, 7 January 1944, "Cambio de directiva en Federada de Obreros"; 14 January 1944, "Tomará posesión la nueva directiva de panificadores"; 24 January 1944, "Interesante y positiva labor de la Sociedad Obrera Salvadoreña"; 24 January 1944, "Magnífica fiesta ofreció la cooperativa de los Sastres"; 25 May 1944, "Directiva de los sastres"; 30 May 1944, "Quedó organizada la Unión de Trabajadores Ferrocarrileros"; 25 June 1944, "Sindicato de Zapateros se forma"; 27 June 1944, "Mensaje de la Unión Fraternal de Trabajadores"; 30 June 1944, "Actividades de la Asociación de Trabajadores de Fabricas"; 5 October 1944, "Floreciente sociedad obrera en esta ciudad"; 19 September 1944, "Protesta de unos obreros"; 10 February 1945, "Comisiones de una sociedad de obreros"; and 8 January 1946, "Los obreros electricistas de Santa Ana presentan demandas."

42. *Diario de Hoy*, 22 July 1944, "Cooperación obrera para lograr código de trabajo"; 14 October 1944, "Fue nombrada la Junta Directiva para el Tercer Congreso Nacional"; 12 May 1946, "Federación de Sociedades de Trabajadores Particulares"; and *La Prensa Gráfica*, 2 April 1949, "Celebraciones del dia del trabajo preparan obreros."

43. *Diario de Hoy*, 4 June 1944, "Se comprometerá no ir a la Huelga los Obreros." There were also no female organizers of the National Workers' Congress, held 5 November 1950. *Diario de Hoy*, 25 August 1950, "El 5 de noviembre será el Congreso Obrero Nacional."

44. For 1940s labor delegations, see *La Prensa Gráfica-Libro de Oro*, 1 November 1945, "La 'Confederación de Sociedades Gremiales de El Salvador' ha enviado un memorial al Presidente de la República"; 30 November 1945, "Ante el Ministro de Trabajo la Unión de Trabajadores Ferrocarrileros y la Corporación de Protección y Mejoramiento de ese gremio firmaron un acuerdo"; and *Diario de Hoy*, 2 March 1946, "Detalle completo de la reunión de funcionarios, trabajadores, reporteros celebrada antier en Casa Presidencial." For Labor Law Defense Committee, see *Diario de Hoy*, 6 September 1950, "Progresa Comité Pro-Derechos Laborales."

45. *Diario de Hoy*, 12 February 1946, "Costureras se unifican en pro de bienestar."

46. Elsa Moreno, *Mujeres y Política en El Salvador* (San José, Costa Rica: FLACSO, Sede Costa Rica, 1997), 27.

47. Miguel Marmol comments that "our women were selling fruit during the morning, and during the afternoon they made tamales to sell in order to endure the situation and so that the men could dedicate full time to organizing and revolutionary work," Dalton, *Miguel Mármol; los sucesos de 1932 en El Salvador*, 148.

48. Quoted in Italo López Vallecillos, *El Periodismo en El Salvador,* 1987 ed. (San Salvador: UCA Editores, 1974), 307.

49. Quoted in Larín, *Historia del movimiento sindical,* 140.

50. None of the fourteen newspapers contain reports of women workers' demands (June 1944–July 1946). *Diario de Hoy,* 23 June 1944, "Cordura y Unificación, Aconseja la Sociedad 'Obreras Salvadoreñas'. Para lograr la buena resolución de problemas de los gremios"; 15 July 1944, "Precaria es la Situación de Nuestras Costureras. Estamos a merced de patronos inhumanos, dice la señora Mejia"; 17 July 1944, "Compañeras Salvadoreñas, la Salvación es el Sindicato"; 28 July 1944, "Justo mejorar el sueldo de sufridas costureras"; 4 August 1944, "Cuales son los precios justos para la costurera que hace pantalones. Razonada opinión de un grupo de obreras residentes en esta capital"; 9 August 1944, "Los sastres se solidarizan con las costureras que piden mejor salario"; 5 September 1944, "La Huelga de Costureras. Más de sesenta obreras en Santa Ana piden mejores salarios a palestinos"; 25 September 1944, "Facilidades para el voto femenino fueron pedidas ayer al Señor Presidente de la Republica por millares de mujeres capitalinas"; 10 October 1944, "'Obreras Salvadoreñas' retira su Delegación al 20. Congreso"; *Diario de Hoy,* 12 February 1946, "Costureras se unifican en pro de bienestar"; 4 January 1946, "Voto de la mujer será objeto de Discusión en el Congreso"; 1 May 1946, "Gran Desfile Hoy 'Día del Trabajo.' Tomarán parte en el todos los gremios obreros de ambos sexos de esta ciudad"; *La Prensa Gráfica,* 23 June 1944, "Llamamiento a las obreras de fábricas 'La Sociedad Obreras Salvadoreñas'"; and *La Prensa Gráfica-Libro de Oro,* 18 June 1944, "Varias obreras han sido despedidas de fábricas de camisas por intentar, asociarse en sindicatos y otras han sido amenazadas." Reviewed *La Prensa Gráfica,* June 1944; *Diario de Hoy,* January and May–December 1944, January–March 1945, and January–March, May, and July 1946; and *La Prensa Gráfica-Libro de Oro,* January 1944–May 1965.

51. See *La Prensa Gráfica-Libro de Oro,* 18 June 1944; *Diario de Hoy,* 23 June 1944; 15 July 1944; 17 July 1944; 28 July 1944; 4 August 1944; 9 August 1944; 5 September 1944; and 12 February 1946.

52. *La Prensa Gráfica,* 23 June 1944; *La Prensa Gráfica-Libro de Oro,* 18 June 1944; *Diario de Hoy,* 10 October 1944; 12 February 1946; 1 May 1946; and 17 July 1944.

53. *Diario de Hoy,* May 1946, "Gran desfile hoy 'Día del Trabajo.' Tomarán parte en el todos los gremios obreros de ambos sexos de esta ciudad."

54. Moreno, *Mujeres y Política,* 27–28.

55. See for example, *La Prensa Gráfica,* 15 January 1949, "Manifiesto de las mujeres salvadoreñas al Consejo de Gobierno Revolucionario."

56. Moreno, *Mujeres y Política,* 24.

57. *Diario de Hoy,* 1 February 1951, "El sábado será clausurado el Seminario de Mujeres"; and *Informaciones de El Salvador,* 14 February 1951, "Exitosamente celebrose en El Salvador el Primer Seminario Interamericano de Mujeres."

58. Rafael Menjívar, *Formación y lucha del proletariado industrial salvadoreño,* 4th ed., vol. 7 of Colección Estructuras y procesos (San Salvador: UCA Editores, 1987), 42.

59. Quoted in Jorge Arias Gómez, *Farabundo Martí* (San José: EDUCA, 1972), 90.

60. Quoted in *Diario de Hoy*, 30 July 1944.

61. Quoted in *Memoria*, 1947, Ministry of Labor, 11.

62. Quoted in *La Prensa Gráfica*, 28 June 1958, "Crean Prestación Social en Beneficio de Obreras."

63. Quoted in *Diario de Hoy*, 9 May 1961, "Mensaje a las madres de Cuscatlán," cited in Stephan Webre, *Jose Napoleón Duarte and the Christian Democratic Party in Salvadorean Politics 1960–1972* (Baton Rouge: Louisiana State University Press, 1979), 64.

64. It should be noted that there were limits to the reformist nature of the state. The state was unwilling, for instance, to concede to labor's demand to mandate a shorter female work week; see Gallardo, *Las Constituciones de El Salvador*, 263, 265–66. According to Ministerio de Trabajo, "Memoria Del Primer Congreso Nacional de Trabajo y Previsión Social" (San Salvador, 1955), 206, the state's unwillingness to implement this proposal may reflect the hesitation of businessmen to support this idea.

65. For information regarding preliminary drafts of 1950 gendered labor law, see *Informaciones de El Salvador*, 14 October 1950, "Política de Amplia Protección Para Las Clases Laborantes Salvadoreñas." Martínez (1932–1944) also included limited protections for women workers in the 1939 and 1944 Constitutions, but the 1950 Constitution and further legislation significantly enhanced gendered reforms.

66. Constitution of El Salvador, 1950, Article 180.

67. *La Prensa Gráfica*, San Salvador, 5 November 1954. The conference was designed to bring together an equal number of state, labor, and business leaders.

68. Doctor Mario Héctor Salazar, minister of Labor and Social Prevision, *Diario de Hoy*, 9 November 1954, "Discurso del Ministro Salazar."

69. Quoted in *Informaciones de El Salvador*, 14 April 1951, "Importante estudio previo a la elaboración de códigos sanitarios y legislación sobre higiene industrial."

70. *Tribuna Libre*, 14 November 1954, "Temas de gran actualidad en el Congreso del Trabajo"; and Ministerio de Trabajo, "Memoria Del Primer Congreso Nacional de Trabajo y Previsión Social," 197, 199.

71. *Memoria*, 1957, Ministry of Labor, 38.

72. *Memorias*, various years, Ministry of Labor. Also, from 1956 to 1957, the Women and Minors' Division conducted maternity rights inspections. Ibid., 1957.

73. For training of women and minors' staff, see *Memoria*, 1952, Ministry of Labor, 14. For expansion of staff and program capacity, see UCA and Ford Foundation, "Historical Evolution of the Public Sector in El Salvador" (San Salvador: Ford Foundation, 1980); and Ministerio del Trabajo, *Memoria Del Primer Congreso Nacional de Trabajo y Previsión Social*, 208.

74. A home economics school was founded in 1949 according to *El Salvador al Día*, 14 January 1949, "Establecerán escuela de economía doméstica"; and in 1950 the National Institute of Young Ladies was founded, according to *Informaciones de El Salvador*, 14 September 1950, "La Revolución está en marcha!"

75. *Informaciones de El Salvador,* 14 December 1950, "Algunas de las Actividades Realizadas por los Distintos Ministerios."

76. They also did research on policies on how to use women workers, see *Memoria,* 1955, Ministry of Labor, 57.

77. *Memoria,* 1958, Ministry of Labor, 19–20.

78. Ministry of Labor officials (names withheld on request), interviews by author, San Salvador, 3 and 4 March, 20 October, and 2 and 3 November 1999.

79. *Memoria,* 1958, Ministry of Labor, 76–78. See also Juan Pablo Pérez Sáinz, *De La Finca a La Maquila: Modernización capitalista y trabajo en Centroamérica* (San José, Costa Rica: FLACSO, 1996), 60–61.

80. *Memoria,* 1956, Ministry of Labor, 39.

81. *Memoria,* 1958, Ministry of Labor, 43, 76–78.

82. For the Apprenticeship law, see DO, 193 (204), 8 November 1961; and *La Prensa Gráfica,* 30 January 1963, "Servicio de Aprendizaje Ampliará Ministerio del Trabajo."

83. DO, 201, 10 December 1963.

84. *Memoria,* 1965, Ministry of Labor, 133.

85. *La Prensa Gráfica* job announcements from the first Sunday of every month in 1964, 1966, 1968, 1970, 1972, and 1974 were reviewed. All nine announcements calling for apprentices were directed exclusively toward men.

86. Several interviews with Ministry of Labor officials confirmed that these programs were sex-segregated and that the few female apprentices benefiting from the program were "sewing apprentices." Ministry of Labor officials, interviews by author, 11 November and 20 October 1999.

87. For examples, see Mitchell Seligson, "Development, Democratization, and Decay: Central America at the Crossroads," in *Authoritarians and Democrats: Regime Transition in Latin America,* ed. James Malloy and Mitchell Seligson (Pittsburgh, Pa.: University of Pittsburgh Press, 1987), 167; Montgomery, *Revolution;* Dario Moreno, *The Struggle for Peace in Central America* (Gainesville: University Press of Florida, 1994); Robert Armstrong and Janet Shenk, *El Salvador: The Face of Revolution* (Boston, Mass.: South End Press, 1982); and Tom Barry and Deb Preusch, *The Central America Fact Book* (New York: Grove Press, 1986), 215–216.

88. For a discussion of these demands, see Kati Griffith and Leslie Gates, "A State's Gendered Response to Political Instability: Gendering Labor Policy in Semi-Authoritarian El Salvador," *Social Politics* 9, no. 3 (2002).

89. Teresa Rendon, "Evolución del Empleo en México: 1895–1980," *Estudios Demográficos y Urbanos* (1987).

90. Ministry of Labor officials, interviews by author, San Salvador, 20 October and 2 and 3 November 1999.

91. 1994 *Salvadoran Labor Code Reforms.*

92. See Table 2. Also see Encuesta de Hogares, Ministerio de Planificación, 1985, 1991–1998; *Encuesta Económica Annual,* Ministerio de Economia, 1996–1998.

93. Lic. Aracely C. Zamora Rivas, "Realidad y Desafíos de la Mujer Trabajadora," *Procuradora Adjunta para la Defensa de los Derechos Humanos de la Mujer* (July 1998).

94. Maria Patricia Fernandez-Kelly, *For We Are Sold: I and My People* (Albany, N.Y.: SUNY Press, 1983); Irene Tinker, ed. *Persistent Inequalities: Women and World Development* (Oxford: Oxford University Press, 1990); and Kathryn Ward, ed., *Women Workers and Global Restructuring* (Ithaca, N.Y.: ILR Press, 1990).

95. Leslie Sklair makes the latter argument in *Assembling for Development: The Maquila Industry in Mexico and the United States* (San Diego, Calif.: Center for U.S.-Mexico Studies, 1993). Others that have found evidence of the former include Susan Tiano, *Patriarchy on the Line: Labor, Gender, and Ideology in the Mexican Maquila Industry* (Philadelphia: Temple University Press, 1995).

The Formation of a Rural Community

This work is part of a larger study undertaken in Joya de Cerén, July 1995–June 1996, and financed by UNESCO and supported by the National Council for Art and Culture of El Salvador.

1. *Cantones* and *caseríos* are geopolitical units akin to hamlets and villages, respectively, in anglophone usage.

2. "El I.S.T.A. y la Reforma Agraria," 1.

3. Instituto de Colonización Rural, Lo Que Dice La Prensa Nacional, 69.

4. Instituto de Colonización Rural, Acta no. 44, 20 December 1951.

5. Founding member of Joya de Cerén, interview by author.

6. Regarding the pervasiveness and fundamental importance of corruption in rural cooperatives, see Lisa Kowalchuk's chapter, this volume.

7. Founding member of Colonia Joya de Cerén, interview by author.

8. Ibid.

9. Ibid.

10. Member of church board, interview by author.

11. CEPAL-FAO-OIT, *Tenencia de la tierra y desarrollo rural en centroamerica* (San José: EDUCA, 1973).

12. Michael Kearney, *Reconceptualizing The Peasantry: Anthropology in Global Perspective* (Boulder, Colo.: Westview Press, 1996).

13. Lourdes Arizpe, *Parentesco y economia en una sociedad nahua* (México: INI, 1973).

Civil War and Its Aftermath

1. For an important exception to this neglect, see Hammond, *Fighting to Learn*.

Peasants, Catechists, Revolutionaries

This chapter benefited from close, critical readings by Marcus Taylor, Nancy Chance, and Aldo Lauria-Santiago.

1. Compare Penny Lernoux, *Cry of the People* (New York: Penguin, 1982); Anony-

mous, *Rutilio Grande, mártir de la evangelización rural en El Salvador* (San Salvador: UCA Editores, 1978); Cardenal, *Historia de una esperanza;* Teresa Whitfield, *Paying the Price: Ignacio Ellacuría and the Murdered Jesuits of El Salvador* (Philadelphia: Temple University Press, 1994); Cabarrús, *Génesis;* Pearce, *Promised Land.*

2. Yvon Grenier, *The Emergence of Insurgency in El Salvador: Ideology and Political Will* (Pittsburgh, Pa.: University of Pittsburgh Press, 1999), 131–35.

3. Compare Whitfield, *Paying the Price,* 48–50.

4. Anna L. Peterson, *Martyrdom and the Politics of Reason: Progressive Catholicism in El Salvador's Civil War* (Albany, N.Y.: SUNY Press, 1997), 55–56.

5. Montgomery, *Revolution,* 103.

6. Lauria-Santiago, *An Agrarian Republic.*

7. Cabarrús, *Génesis,* 144.

8. Leigh Binford, "After the Revolution: Economic Autarky in Northern Morazán, El Salvador," submitted to a book in preparation on militarization and daily life, edited by Lesley Gill and Linda Green (forthcoming).

9. Raymond Williams, *Marxism and Literature* (Oxford: Oxford University Press, 1977); William Roseberry, "Hegemony and the Language of Contention," in *Everyday Forms of State Formation: Revolution and the Negotiation of Rule in Modern Mexico,* ed. Gilbert M. Joseph and Daniel Nugent (Durham, N.C.: Duke University Press, 1994), 355–66.

10. Centro Reina de la Paz is commonly referred to by its location in El Castaño.

11. Abraham Argueta, interview by author, Joateca, Morazán, 1 and 28 May 1995.

12. Felipe, interviews by author, Joateca, Morazán, spring 1995; Leigh Binford, "The History of Fabio: Peasant Intellectuals and the End of Testimonio?" (book manuscript), chap. 1.

13. Miguel Angel Benítez, interview by author, Jocoaitique, Morazán, 5 June 1995.

14. Compare Paul Willis, *Learning to Labour* (New York: Columbia University Press, 1977).

15. Pierre Bourdieu, *The Logic of Practice* (Palo Alto, Calif.: Stanford University Press, 1990).

16. The concentric-circle technique was discussed by Ramón Díaz and in more detail by Abraham Argueta, in interviews by author, Joateca, 5 December 1992, and Morazán, 1 and 28 May 1995. Miguel Angel Benítez described the "wall method" as follows: "They put one of us in front of a wall and the rest of the people around the edges, . . . and one had to say whatever he had the urge to say. It's like when a politician is speaking in a public plaza. One had to choose a theme—whatever one wanted—and after he spoke strongly, then the group met and began to keep track of all one's defects, you know, related to the things he said, in relation to the time he was given, etc." Benítez, interviews by author, Jocoaitique, Morazán, 5 June 1995. See also Binford, "After the Revolution."

17. Abraham Argueta, interviews by author, Joateca, Morazán, 1 and 28 May 1995.

18. Michel Foucault, *Discipline and Punish: The Birth of the Prison* (New York: Vintage, 1977).

19. Bourdieu, *Logic of Practice.*

20. Maximino Pérez, interview by author, 30 May 1995.

21. Abraham Argueta, interviews by author, Joateca, Morazán, 1 and 28 May 1995.

22. Ibid. The structure of the centers was also discussed by Fabio Argueta in Binford, "History of Fabio."

23. Cited in Binford, "History of Fabio," chap. 2.

24. Pedro Rodríguez, interview by author, Perquín, 29 November 1992.

25. Abraham Argueta, interview by author, Joateca, 5 December 1992.

26. Ibid.

27. Ibid., 19 December 1992.

28. Pablo Richard and Guillermo Melendez, *La iglesia de los pobres en América Central: un análisis socio-político y teológico de la iglesia centroamericana (1960–1982)* (San José, Costa Rica: Departamento Ecumenico de Investigaciones, 1982), 127; Miguel Ventura, interview by author San Salvador, 18 September 1992.

29. Ibid.

30. Mistalia Altimirano, interview by author, San Fernando, Morazán, 20 July 1992.

31. Miguel Ventura, interview by author, San Salvador, 22 September 1992.

32. For example, Cabarrús, *Génesis,* 145; Cardenal, *Vida.*

33. See Binford, "History of Fabio," chap. 2.

34. Table 1 should not be taken as either a complete listing or a random selection of catechists. Many former catechists were assassinated before the war or died in combat during it. The sample includes a few catechists who settled in northern Morazán after the civil war but who originated from areas to the south, such as Guatijiagua or Cacahuatique.

35. Ventura continued to teach one week of each course in El Castaño until 1977. Miguel Ventura, interview by author, San Salvador, 22 September 1992.

36. Binford, "History of Fabio," chap. 2.

37. Miguel Ventura, interview by author, San Salvador, 18 September 1992.

38. Binford, "History of Fabio," chap. 2.

39. Ibid.

40. Ibid.; Leigh Binford, "Hegemony in the Interior of the Revolution: The ERP in Northern Morazán, El Salvador," *Journal of Latin American Anthropology* 4, no. 1 (1999): 2–45; Juan Ramón Medrano and Walter Raudales, *Ni militar ni sacerdote (de seudónimo Balta)* (San Salvador: Arcoiris, 1994).

41. See Binford, "History of Fabio," chap. 4. Ventura went into exile following his release from captivity in 1977. He returned clandestinely to northern Morazán in 1981 and remained there during the remainder of the civil war.

42. Binford, "Hegemony," 103; Binford, "History of Fabio," chap. 4.

43. CEBES, "Dios en Morazán: Experiencias pastorales en las zonas liberadas de El Salvador" (mimeo, n.d.); Wright, *Promised Land,* 113–70.

44. Binford, "History of Fabio."

45. Grenier, *The Emergence*, 131; Cabarrús, *Génesis.*

46. Douglas A. Kincaid, "Peasants into Rebels: Community and Class in Rural El Salvador," *Comparative Studies in Society and History* 29 (July 1987): 466–94.

47. Miguel Ventura, interview by author, San Salvador, 18 September 1992.

48. Serena Fogaroli and Sara Stowell, *Desarrollo rural y participación campesina: El caso de Tecoluca (San Vicente, El Salvador)* (San Salvador: Universidad Centroamericana, 1997).

49. Compare Equipo Postoral de la Comunidad de Reparados, "Ignacio Martín Baro," "Historia del cantón La Joya, que comprende desde el año 1968 hasta 1993" (Sociedad, Morazán, mimeo, 1993); Lou Keune, *Sobrevivimos la guerra: La historia de los pobladores de Arcatao y de San José de las Flores* (San Salvador: Adelina Editores, 1995), 7–11.

Civil War and Reconstruction

1. Americas Watch, *Settling into Routine: Human Rights Abuses in Duarte's Second Year* (New York: Americas Watch, 1986), 79, 157.

2. See Robert Gersony, Raymond Lynch, and William Garvelink, *The Journey Home: Durable Solutions for the Displaced* (San Salvador: USAID. 1986); Segundo Montes, *Desplazados y refugiados* (San Salvador: UCA, 1985).

3. Americas Watch, *Free Fire. A Report on Human Rights in El Salvador* (New York: Americas Watch, 1984); Martin Diskin and Kenneth E. Sharpe, "El Salvador," in *Confronting Revolution,* ed. Morris J. Blachman, William M. Leogande, and Kenneth Sharpe (New York: Pantheon, 1986); Michael T. Klare and Peter Kornbluh, *Low Intensity Warfare* (New York: Pantheon, 1988).

4. Armed Forces of El Salvador, "Counterinsurgency Campaign, 'United to Rebuild'" (1986).

5. Segundo Montes, *El agro salvadoreño (1973–1980)* (San Salvador: UCA, 1986); and USAID, *Baseline Survey* (San Salvador: USAID, 1985).

6. Beatrice Edwards and Gretta Tovar Siebentritt, *Places of Origin: The Repopulation of Rural El Salvador* (Boulder, Colo.: Lynne Rienner, 1991).

7. How many returned to the countryside during this period with no organizational rubric was the subject of some dispute. A 1986 USAID study claimed that 5–10 percent of the displaced population had already returned by mid-1986. Other analysts believe the figure to be much lower. See Gersony et al., *The Journey Home.*

8. For detailed studies of the repatriations and repopulations, see Cagan and Cagan, *This Promised Land;* Petrona Josefina Siebentritt, "El Desarrollo del Pensamiento Político/ Ideológico de los Campesinos Desplazados por el conflicto armado en El Salvador" (master's thesis, University of San Salvador, 1990).

9. For a detailed discussion of the UPR projects, see Edwards and Siebentritt, *Places of Origin;* and Tom Gibb, "Salvador: Under the Shadow of Dreams" (manuscript, 2000).

10. See Edwards and Tovar Siebentritt, *Places of Origin;* A. J. Hallums, J. D. Bacevich, R. H. White, and T. F. Young, *American Military Policy in Small Wars: The Case of El Salvador* (paper presented at John F. Kennedy School of Government, Harvard University, 1988).

11. The history of violence in Tenancingo in the 1970s and early 1980s is similar to the much-better documented history of Suchitoto and Aguilares, other towns near the Guazapa Volcano. See C. Cabarrús, *Génesis;* Cardenal, *Historia de una esperanza;* Pearce, *Promised Land.*

12. William Durham, *Scarcity and Survival in Central America: The Ecological Origins of the Soccer War* (Palo Alto, Calif.: Stanford University Press, 1979), 84.

13. Ibid., 81.

14. Ibid.

15. According to Cabarrús, incentives to join ORDEN included access to agricultural inputs, health care, and education and some degree of security from the arbitrary repression of the peasants by the National Guard. Cabarrús, *Génesis.*

16. *El Mundo,* 26 July 1985.

17. Monseñor Rosa Chávez, sermon, 1 September 1985 (*El Mundo,* 2 September 1985).

18. FUNDASAL, with close ties to the Archdiocese, was founded in 1969 to help poor families displaced by flooding; its philosophy is one of community development through the construction of low-cost minimal housing. FUNDASAL, "Memoria de Labores," 1985.

19. Peter Shiras, "Tenancingo: A Seed of Hope in Land of War," *America,* 12 (July 1986): 7.

20. Joaquín Villalobos, "El Estado Actual de la Guerra," *Estudios Centroamericanos* 449 (1986): 177.

21. FMLN press release, as summarized in *Inforpress Centroamericana* 692 (5 June 1986).

22. Americas Watch, 1986; confidential interviews; FUNDASAL, "Informe Narrativo Tenancingo," 9.

23. *El Mundo,* 29 January 1986.

24. Americas Watch, *Settling into Routine,* 84.

25. Officer in charge of the brigade at the time, interview by author.

26. Americas Watch, *Settling into Routine,* 85; *Christian Science Monitor,* 9 June 1986.

27. For details, see FUNDASAL, "Informe Narrativo Tenancingo," anexo 1, p. 13.

28. For example, in March the FMLN kidnapped a resident whom they charged was collaborating with the departmental commander to facilitate guerrilla desertions by issuing safe conducts. She was released by the FMLN in the central park and publicly warned to leave town.

29. FUNDASAL, "Informe Narrativo Tenancingo," 18.

30. Americas Watch, *The Civilian Toll, 1986–1987.* Ninth supplement to the Report on Human Rights in El Salvador (New York: Americas Watch, 1987), 159; *Christian Science Monitor,* 9 June 1986.

31. Troops occupied the Villa beginning May 5 for several days and set up mortars in the plaza. *Christian Science Monitor,* 9 June 1986.

32. FUNDASAL, "Informe Narrativo Tenancingo," anexo no. 1, p. 25.

33. As quoted in a FUNDASAL press release, *El Mundo,* 19 June 1986.

34. *El Mundo,* 13 June 1986; also *La Prensa Gráfica,* 15 June 1986.

35. *Christian Science Monitor,* 3–9 September 1986.

36. *El Mundo,* 19 June 1986; versions of the press release also appeared in *La Prensa Gráfica,* 20 June 1986; and *Diario Latino,* 26 June 1986.

37. Ibid.

38. Carranza stated explicitly, in an interview with the author, that this move was in response to the vaccination photo, that the military presence was under the control of the Estado Mayor and would be permanent, and that there would be no base established.

39. Americas Watch, *The Civilian Toll,* 164.

40. *New York Times,* 29 August 1987.

41. FUNDASAL, "Informe Narrativo Tenancingo"; see also sermon by Bishop Rosa Chávez cited above, n. 17.

42. FUNDASAL, "Proyecto de repoblamiento y reconstrucción de Tenancingo" (San Salvador: FUNDASAL, 1985).

43. FUNDASAL, "Informe Narrativo Tenancingo," 2–3.

44. Edwards and Tovar Siebentritt, *Places of Origin.*

Between Clientelism and Radical Democracy

This chapter draws on fieldwork conducted during various visits to Ciudad Segundo Montes and other parts of northern Morazán from 1990 to 1999. The survey was conducted between June and August 1995, with financial support from the Tinker Foundation, made available through the University of Pittsburgh Center for Latin American Studies. I made follow-up visits in 1996 and 1999. The survey was conducted with the assistance of Ever Jesús Guzmán. I thank various residents of Ciudad Segundo Montes, the representatives of the Fundación Segundo Montes, and other agencies working in the region. Anonymity of sources has been respected where requested. Thanks also to Leigh Binford, Michael Foley, John Markoff, Mitchell Seligson, Steve Cagan, Beth Cagan, and Aldo Lauria-Santiago for helpful comments.

1. Binford, *El Mozote Massacre;* Binford, "History of Fabio."

2. UNDP, *Índices de Desarollo Humano en El Salvador* (1997), departmental human-development indexes, measured by life expectancy, income per capita, and education level.

3. Northern and southern Morazán are separated by the Torola River, which represented a military as well as a physical border between insurgent and counterinsurgent populations.

4. Ministerio de Economía, *Segundo Censo Agropecuario de 1961* (San Salvador: Ministerio de Economía, 1961); Ministerio de Economía, *Tercer Censo Agropecuario de 1971* (San Salvador: Ministerio de Economía, 1971).

5. The estimated Gini coefficient for land distribution in Morazán for 1961 was 0.67,

compared to a national land Gini of 0.83. Ministerio de Economía, *Segundo Censo,* 1961.

6. Robert G. Williams, *Export Agriculture and the Crisis in Central America* (Durham: University of North Carolina Press, 1986), 63. Barbarena reports that the migration to northern departments like Morazán began in the late seventeenth century. Peasants who settled what is now the municipality of Meanguera emigrated from the Salvadoran island of Meanguera in the Fonseca Gulf, fleeing the attacks of English pirates common along the coast of Spanish colonies. Santiago I. Barbarena, *Monografías Departamentales: Departamento de Morazán* (San Salvador: CONCULTURA, 1998 [1914]), 572.

7. Ignacio Martín-Baro, "Psicología del campesino Salvadoreño," *Estudios Centro Americanos* (ECA) 28 (297–98): 476–95; and "The Lazy Latino: The Ideological Nature of Latin American Fatalism," in *Writings for a Liberation Psychology* (Cambridge, Mass.: Harvard University Press, 1994).

8. *Compadrazgo* is both a spiritual and an economic relationship of mutual dependence between godparent and parent of a child. See Segundo Montes, *El Compadrazgo: Una Estructura de poder en El Salvador* (San Salvador: UCA Editores, 1987).

9. Binford, "History of Fabio," 18.

10. Martin Baro, "Psicología," 217.

11. Pearce, *Promised Land,* 133.

12. My historical reconstruction of Ciudad Segundo Montes relies heavily on the work of Leigh Binford, particularly, Binford, "History of Fabio."

13. The displacement of Salvadorans from northern Morazán began as early as July 1980. Many made the torturous journey to Honduras in December of that year, ultimately arriving in Colomocagua. R. Camarda et al., *Forced to Move: Salvadoran Refugees in Mexico, Solidarity Publications* (San Francisco: Bureau for the Americas and Evaluation and Policy, 1985), 12.

14. CONADES, "Cuadro Resumen de la población desplazada a nivel nacional por departmento" (CONADES, San Salvador, mimeo, 1983).

15. For the best description of life in Colomocagua, see Cagan and Cagan, *This Promised Land.* This section also draws from Mandy Macdonald and Mike Gatehouse, *In the Mountains of Morazán, Portrait of a Returned Refugee Community in El Salvador* (New York: Monthly Review Press, 1995).

16. Estimate of support is from Leigh Binford, "The State, NGOs, and Grassroots Organizations in the Transition from Wartime to Peacetime in Northern Morazán, El Salvador (paper presented at the Latin American Studies Association Congress, Washington, D.C., 1995), 4. The FMLN civilian refugee strategy is outlined in the 1987 document, *El Poder Popular de Doble Cara,* authored by ERP Commander Mercedes de Carmen Letona.

17. Cagan and Cagan, *This Promised Land,* 119.

18. Cited in Ibid., 181.

19. The choice of Meanguera as the location of the repatriation was also largely ERP's, although in consultation with civilian organizations working in the zone.

20. This vision is best described in Aquiles Montoya, *La Nueva Economía Popular* (San Salvador: UCA, 1993).

21. Anonymous, *Plan Alternativo para el Desarollo de Morazán,* 1991.

22. Ciudad Segundo Montes reports that the total amount of outside financing between 1990 and 1994 is about $6.2 million. "CSM: Proceso de Inserción," San Salvador, 1994. Other estimates go as high as $9 million. Former member of the community board of directors, interview by author, July 1995.

23. Cited in Cagan and Cagan, *This Promised Land,* 116–17.

24. I adopt Tarrow's conception of political opportunity structure as "consistent—but not necessarily formal or permanent—dimensions of the political environment that provide incentives for people to undertake collective action by affecting their expectations for success or failure." Sydney Tarrow, *Power in Movement: Social Movements, Collective Action and Politics* (Cambridge: Cambridge University Press, 1994), 85.

25. Murray, "The Salvadoran Peace Accords and Democratization: A Three Year Progress Report and Recommendations (Hemisphere Initiatives)" (Washington, D.C.: Washington Office on Latin America, 1995).

26. The reform of the Municipal Code in 1983 promoted the devolution of power to local government; however, the resources to carry out newly assigned functions did not follow until the passage of the 6 percent law in 1998, which transfers 6 percent of the national budget directly or indirectly to local governments, distributed according to poverty level and population.

27. Gloria Romero, interview by author, 8 January 1993.

28. Ministerio de Economía, *Encuesta de Hogares de Propósitos Múltiples* (EHPM) (San Salvador: Ministerio de Economía, 1997).

29. This figure represents only a fraction of the estimated economically active population in Ciudad Segundo Montes of 2,700. Fundación Segundo Montes staff and officers, interview by author, August 1995 and September 1998. Fogaroli reports permanent employment in Ciudad Segundo Montes at 80. Serena Fogaroli, "Proyecto: 'Mujer, población y medioambiente,'" final report on project ELS/97/P10 for UNFPA-APS, 1998.

30. The 1994 population is cited in IDEA (1994) "Diagnostico Situacional de Salud de la Comunidad Segundo Montes," mimeo. Current population estimates are from the 1997 FSM-ICCO study. Morazán's population grew at a rate 60 percent slower than the nation's population growth rate, the slowest of any department (Ministerio de Economía, *EHPM* 1998).

31. FSM-ICCO study (1997).

32. Mandy Macdonald and Mike Gatehouse, *In the Mountains of Morazán: Portrait of a Returned Refugee Community in El Salvador* (New York: Monthly Review Press, 1995), 15.

33. Correspondence between Jeff Colledge and author, 6 March 1996; see full article by Colledge, Philip L. Borkholder, Paul M. Damery, and Bryan Flynn in *Irish Times,* 23 March 1996. See Beth Cagan, "Salvadoran City of Hope," *Dollars and Sense,* January–February (1994): 10–13, 36, and Colledge's letter to the editor, 34, July–August 1994 edition.

34. This section is based on interviews with work coordinators at several workshops in January 1994.

35. Four women employed in the clothing workshop, interviews by author, July 1995.

36. Peter Sollis, IDB, interview by author, July 1999.

Not Revolutionary Enough?

The seventeen months of ethnographic research on which this article builds were made possible through the generous support of many institutions and grants: Tinker Research Fellowship, Fulbright-Hays, Inter-American Foundation, and Organization of American States. Writing support came from New York University's Dean's Dissertation Award and the Charlotte Newcombe Dissertation Fellowship. I thank Aldo Lauria-Santiago and Leigh Binford for their insightful comments.

1. The name of the community is a pseudonym, as are the names of community members and staff of CORDES, CCR, and other NGOs.

2. Wood, *Forging Democracy,* 3, 12.

3. Elsewhere I talk about the verticalist legacies of the FMLN in Chalatenango that impede full self-governance: Irina Carlota Silber, *A Spectral Reconciliation* (Ph.D. diss., New York University, 2000).

4. James Ferguson, *The Anti-Politics Machine: "Development," Depoliticization, and Bureaucratic Power in Lesotho* (Cambridge: Cambridge University Press, 1990).

5. FUNDE, "Diagnostico Agro-socioeconomico Microregion VI Oriente," report, 1997.

6. Florence E. Babb, *After Revolution: Mapping Gender and Cultural Politics in Neoliberal Nicaragua* (Austin: University of Texas Press, 2001), 15.

7. D. E. Leaman, "Participatory Outsides and the Reach of Representation in Post-War El Salvador: The Community of El Jicaro in Changing Political Contexts" (paper presented at the International Congress of the Latin American Studies Association, Chicago, September 1998), 1.

8. MSI, *Assistance to the Transition from War to Peace: Evaluation of USAID/El Salvador's Special Strategic Objective* (Washington, D.C.: MSI, 1996), 3.

9. Montgomery, *Revolution.*

10. Boyce, *Economic Policy for Building Peace.*

11. Kevin Murray and Ellen Coletti, *Rescuing Reconstruction: The Debate on Post-War Economic Recovery in El Salvador* (Cambridge, Mass.: Hemisphere Initiatives, 1994).

12. Tully Cornick, interview by author, November 1997.

13. See Rae Lesser Blumberg, "Risky Business: What Happens to Gender Equity and Women's Rights in Post-Conflict Societies? Insights from NGOs in El Salvador," *International Journal of Politics, Culture, and Society.* 15, no. 1 (2001): 161–73.

14. Jack Spence et al., *Chapúltepec, Five Years Later: El Salvador's Political Reality and Uncertain Future* (Cambridge, Mass.: Hemisphere Initiatives, 1997).

15. Rene Ivan Morales, interview by author, December 1997.

16. Las Vueltas was one of the areas hardest hit during the war and was one of the original sites of repopulation in 1987. In 1977 the prewar population of the municipal-

ity was 5,081. See M. Hernandez Rodriguez and K. I. Mendez, *Marco Historico-Social y Socio-Cultural de Las Vueltas.* Dept. de Chalatenango. IV. Ano de Lic. en Letras (San Salvador: Universidad Nacional de El Salvador, 1996). Las Vueltas presently consists of a municipal head and six surrounding neighborhoods with a total population of 1,486 (more women than men), a substantial decrease resulting from the war of 47.78 percent. See FUNDE, "Diagnostico Agro-socioeconomico Microregion VI Oriente," report, 1997. There are seventy-nine houses and 319 people in El Rancho (Censo Poblacional por Grupos, Unidad de Salud 4/2/97). Residents did not repopulate to their original place of origin. There are only three *originario* families. Residents are originally from nearby villages and hamlets. Others through marriage, war-ties, and refugee experiences come from such distant departments as Usulutan.

17. Representative from Plan Internacional, interview by author, December 1997.

18. Many repoblaciones have garnered sister-city relationships with cities in either the United States, Canada, or Europe, relationships that bring in international assistance for particular projects.

19. CODEM, *Plan de Acción para el Desarrollo: Municipio de Las Vueltas: Chalatenango* (El Salvador: CODEM, 1996).

20. These are very much in the tradition of war-time *poderes populares locales*—PPLs (FMLN organized community structures).

21. CORDES receives funds from international donors such as Oxfam America, Paz y Tercer Mundo, and Prochalate. The Chalatenango regional office budget for 1996 was $1,040,965.39. CORDES, *Annual Report,* 1997.

22. A branch of the FMLN that dominated in the region.

23. CORDES, "Construyendo el Desarrollo Participativo y la Autogestión Comunal," in *Memoria de Labores. enero-diciembre 1996,* VII Asamblea General Originaria (San Salvador, June 1997), 7.

24. Originally Mexican, she is a charismatic woman who joined the revolution in Chalatenango in 1979. She is a survivor of collective and personal violence.

25. M. Bergman and M. Szurmuk, "Gender, Citizenship, and Social Protest: The New Social Movements in Argentina," in *The Latin American Subaltern Studies Reader,* ed. I. Rodríguez (Durham, N.C.: Duke University Press, 2001), 383–401. They also build on Habermas and Offe's insights on globalization, capitalism, and democracy.

26. Binford, "Hegemony," 16.

27. The group was sponsored by a long-term, faith-driven, community-based "development" worker affiliated with the Central Menonite Committee (MCC).

28. Philippe Bourgois, "The Power of Violence," 20.

29. Nestor Garcia Canclini, *Consumers and Citizens: Globalization and Multicultural Conflicts,* trans. George Yúdice (Minneapolis: University of Minnesota Press, 2001).

30. Roger Schrading, *El Movimiento de Repoblación en El Salvador* (San José, Costa Rica: Instituto Interamericano de Derechos Humanos, 1991), 94.

31. See Schrading, *Exodus,* 80, where CCR identifies communities as characterized by unity over individualism.

32. Lou Keune, *Sobrevivimos la Guerra: La Historia de Los Pobladores de Arcatao y de San José Las Flores* (El Salvador: Adelina Editores, 1995), 181.

33. Mario Lungo, J. Serarols, and A. S. de Síntigo, eds., *Economía y Sostenibilidad en Las Zonas Ex-conflictivas en El Salvador* (El Salvador: FUNDASAL, 1997), 27.

34. Argueta in Keune, *Sobrevivimos* (my translation).

35. Bourgois, "The Power of Violence," 29–30.

36. Dr. Smith, interview by author, October 1997.

37. Interview by author, December 1997.

38. Interview by author, November 1997.

39. Interview by author, December 1997.

40. See, for example, A. E. Villacorte et al. *Desarrollo regional/local en El Salvador: Reto Estratégico del Siglo XXI* (El Salvador: FUNDE, 1997).

41. W. Fisher, "Doing Good? The Politics and Antipolitics of NGO Practices," *Annual Review of Anthropology* 26 (1997): 442.

42. Laura MacDonald, *Supporting Civil Society: The Political Role of Non-Governmental Organizations in Central America* (New York: St. Martin's Press, 1997).

The Salvadoran Land Struggle in the 1990s

The research for this chapter was supported by the Social Science and Humanities Research Council of Canada. I would also like to thank Leigh Binford, Neil McLaughlin, and Aldo Lauria-Santiago for their valuable comments and suggestions.

1. Michel A. Seligson, "Thirty Years of Transformation in the Agrarian Structure of El Salvador, 1961–1991," *Latin American Research Review* 3 (1995).

2. Martin Diskin, "Distilled Conclusions: The Disappearance of the Agrarian Question in El Salvador," *Latin American Research Review* 2 (1996).

3. Jeffery M. Paige, "Land Reform and Agrarian Revolution in El Salvador: Comment on Seligson and Diskin," *Latin American Research Review* 2 (1996).

4. Alfonso Goitia, "La Lucha por la Tierra en Centroamérica," documento de trabajo 13 (San Salvador: FUNDE, February 1993).

5. This observation was made in a seminar on the PTT held at FUNDE, October 1995.

6. Paige, "Land Reform," 131.

7. Mitchell A. Seligson and Vincent J. McElhinny, "Facing Up or About Face: Agrarian Inequality and the Prospects for Rural Development in Postwar El Salvador" (paper presented at the annual meeting of the Latin American Studies Association, Washington, D.C., September 2001).

8. Interview by author, 15 November 1995.

9. The peasants interviewed for this research have been given pseudonyms, as have the two cooperatives in the Lake Coatepeque region. As well, the locations of these two cooperatives have been disguised.

10. Over a five-year period Rivera collected an average of US$2,000 from several

dozen would-be cooperative members. Though this is fairly petty criminality, the fact that this was all he could obtain, and that it strained peasant finances to provide these sums, testifies to the level of rural poverty in El Salvador.

11. Doug McAdam, *Political Process and the Development of Black Insurgency 1930–1970* (Chicago: University of Chicago Press, 1982); Joel Migdal, *Peasants, Politics, and Revolution: Pressure toward Social Change in the Third World* (Princeton, N.J.: Princeton University Press, 1974); Paige, *Agrarian Revolution: Social Movements and Export Agriculture in the Underdeveloped World* (New York: Free Press, 1975); Maurice Pinard, *The Rise of a Third Party: A Study in Crisis Politics* (Montreal: McGill-Queen's University Press, 1975); Samuel Popkin, *The Rational Peasant: The Political Economy of Rural Society in Vietnam* (Berkeley: University of California Press, 1979); James C. Scott, *The Moral Economy of the Peasant: Rebellion and Subsistence in Southeast Asia* (New Haven, Conn.: Yale University Press, 1976); Theda Skocpol, *States and Social Revolutions* (Cambridge: Cambridge University Press, 1979); David A. Snow, Louis A. Zurcher, and Sheldon Eckland-Olson, "Social Networks and Social Movements: A Micro-Structural Approach to Differential Recruitment," *American Sociological Review* 45 (1980), 787–801.

12. Pinard, *The Rise.*

13. Migdal, *Peasants;* Paige, *Agrarian Revolution;* Popkin, *The Rational;* Scott, *The Moral Economy;* Skocpol, *States.*

14. Suzanne Staggenborg, "Social Movement Communities and Cycles of Protest: The Emergence and Maintenance of a Local Women's Movement," *Social Problems* 45, no. 2 (1998): 180–204.

15. Aldon Morris, *The Origins of the Civil Rights Movement: Black Communities Organizing for Change* (New York: Free Press, 1984).

16. As with the properties transferred through the Land Transfer Program of the Peace Accords, the 3 July Accord properties were held *pro-indiviso.* This meant that, although the beneficiaries invariably cultivated individual parcels, legally the property was still collectively owned.

17. In the study of social movements, this variable is central to the resource mobilization paradigm, a classical explication of which is found in John D. McCarthy and Mayer N. Zald, *The Trend of Social Movements in America: Professionalization and Resource Mobilization* (Morristown, N.J.: General Learning Press, 1973); and Charles Tilly, *From Mobilization to Revolution* (New York: Random House, 1978). Some students of social movements regard networks and ideologies as resources. In fact, virtually all phenomena that in some way help movements to mobilize and achieve their goals have been referred to as resources. But I concur with those who preserve the utility of the concept by limiting it to material assets and those nonmaterial goods that derive from possession of monetary resources, such as education and communications technology.

18. Cabarrús, *Génesis;* Eric Wolf, *Peasant Wars of the Twentieth Century* (New York: Harper and Row, 1969); Scott, *The Moral Economy;* Skocpol, *States;* Timothy Wickham-Crowley, "Winners, Losers, and Also-Rans: Toward a Comparative Sociology of Guer-

rilla Movements," in *Power and Popular Protest*, ed. Susan Eckstein (Berkeley: University of California Press, 1989), 132–81.

19. Wolf, *Peasant Wars*.

20. Cabarrús, *Génesis*.

21. Pinard, *The Rise*.

22. Charles D. Brockett, *Land, Power, and Poverty: Agrarian Transformation and Political Conflict in Central America*, 2d ed. (Boulder, Colo.: Westview Press, 1998); William Gamson, *Talking Politics* (Cambridge: Cambridge University Press, 1992); Sydney Tarrow, "Mentalities, Political Cultures, and Collective Action Frames," in *Frontiers in Social Movements*, ed. Aldon Morris and Carol McClurg Mueller (New Haven, Conn.: Yale University Press, 1992), 174–202.

23. Tarrow, "Mentalities," 177.

24. McAdam, *Political Process*.

25. Cabarrús, *Génesis;* Pearce, *Promised Land;* Anna L. Peterson, *Martyrdom and the Politics of Reason: Progressive Catholicism in El Salvador's Civil War* (Albany, N.Y.: SUNY Press, 1997); Montgomery, *Revolution;* see also Binford's chapter, this volume.

26. Evangelical Christianity does not neatly divide Salvadoran peasants into Left versus Right, or politically active versus passive.

Culture and Ideology in Contemporary El Salvador

1. Henri Lefebvre, *Everyday Life in the Modern World* (New Brunswick, N.J.: Transaction Publishers, 1971).

"This Is Not Culture!"

1. Rodolfo Baron Castro, *La Población de El Salvador* (San Salvador: UCA Editores, 1978).

2. Richard N. Adams, *Cultural Surveys of Panama-Nicaragua-Guatemala-El Salvador-Honduras* (Washington D.C.: Pan American Sanitary Bureau, 1957); Alejandro D. Marroquín, "El problema Indigena en El Salvador," *America Indígena* 35, no. 4 (1975), D.F. de Mexico.

3. Marc Chapin, "La población indígena de El Salvador," in *Mesoamérica* 21 (1991); Ching and Tilley, "Indians."

4. Both these latest estimates are probably based on Marroquín's figures from the 1960s; Marroquín, "El problema Indígena"; Baron Castro, *La población;* George Thomas Kurian, ed., *Encyclopedia of the Third World* (New York: Facts on File, 1992); James Wilkie, ed., *Statistical Abstract of Latin America* (Los Angeles: UCLA Latin American Center Publications, 1995).

5. Adams, *Cultural Surveys,* 487; Ching and Tilley, "Indians."

6. Alison Brysk. "Turning Weakness into Strength: The Internationalization of Indian Rights," in *Latin American Perspectives: A Journal on Capitalism and Socialism* 23, no. 2 (1996): 38–57; Alison Brysk, "Acting Globally: Indian Rights and International Politics in Latin America," in *Indigenous Peoples and Democracy in Latin America*, ed. Donna Lee van

Cott (Basingstoke, England: Macmillan, 1994), 29–51; Donna Lee van Cott, ed., *Indigenous peoples and Democracy in Latin America* (Basingstoke, England: Macmillan, 1994), 29–51.

7. Jean Jackson, "Culture, Genuine and Spurious: The Politics of Indianness in the Vaupés, Colombia," in *American Ethnologis* 22, no. 1 (1995), 5.

8. Brysk, "Turning"; Brysk, "Acting Globally"; Lyle Campbell, *The Pipil Language of El Salvador* (Berlin: Mouton Publishers, 1985); Charles R. Hale, *Resistance and Contradiction—Miskitu Indians and the Nicaraguan State, 1894–1987* (Stanford, Calif.: Stanford University Press, 1994); Charles R. Hale "Between Che Guevara and the Pachamama: Mestizos, Indians and Identity Politics in the Anti-Quincentenary Campaign," in *Critique of Anthropology* 14, no. 1 (1994); Diane M. Nelson, *A Finger in the Wound—Body Politics in Quincentennial Guatemala* (Berkeley: University of California Press, 1999); Kay B. Warren, *Indigenous Movements and Their Critics: Pan-Maya Activism in Guatemala* (Princeton, N.J.: Princeton University Press, 1998).

9. Escobar, *Encountering Development;* Ferguson, *Anti-Politics Machine;* Norman Long and Ann Long, eds., *Battlefields of Knowledge: The Interlocking of Theory and Practice in Social Research and Development* (London: Routledge, 1992); Ana Maria Alonso, *The Thread of Blood: Colonialism, Revolution, and Gender on Mexico's Northern Frontier* (Tucson: The University of Arizona Press, 1995); Gilbert M. Joseph and Daniel Nugent, eds., *Everyday Forms of State Formation: Revolution and the Negotiation of Rule in Modern Mexico* (Duke, N.C.: Duke University Press, 1994); David Nugent, *Modernity at the Edge of Empire: State, Individual, and Nation in the Northern Peruvian Andes, 1885–1935* (Stanford, Calif.: Stanford University Press, 1997).

10. From July 1995 to August 1996 I carried out field work in Santo Domingo de Guzmán. I have since visited the village on one occasion and carried out shorter field work with migrants living in the Seattle, Washington, area. Gerald Lumbee Sider, *Indian Histories: Race, Ethnicity, and Indian Identity in the Southern United States* (Cambridge: Cambridge University Press, 1993).

11. Escobar, *Encountering Development;* Mary Louise Pratt, *Imperial Eyes—Travel Writing and Transculturation* (London: Routledge, 1992).

12. William Roseberry, "Hegemony and the Language of Contention," in *Everyday Forms,* ed. Joseph and Nugent, 355–66.

13. Jackson, "Culture."

14. Ibid., 4.

15. Ibid., 12–13.

16. Ibid., 5.

17. Ruth B. Phillips, "Why Not Tourist Art? Significant Silences in Native American Museum Representations," in *After Colonialism—Imperial Histories and Postcolonial Displacements,* ed. Gyan Prakash (Princeton, N.J.: Princeton University Press, 1995).

18. Murdo J. Macleod, *Spanish Central America: A Socioeconomic History, 1520–1720* (Berkeley: University of California Press, 1973).

19. Miles L. Wortman, *Government and Society in Central America 1680–1840* (New York: Columbia University Press, 1980); David Browning, *El Salvador. La tierra y el hombre* (San Salvador: Dirección de Publicaciones e Impresos, CONCULTURA, 1975).

20. Browning, *El Salvador.*

21. Henrik Ronsbo, *Landscapes Full of Spanish Dreams—Indians, Land Reform, and State Formation in the Salvadoran Space* (in Danish) (master's thesis, Roskilde University, 1994).

22. George V. Lovell, *Conquest and Survival in Colonial Guatemala: A historical geography of the Cuchumatán Highlands (1520–1821)* (Toronto: McGill-Queen's Press, 1985); Robert M. Carmack, *Rebels of Highland Guatemala: The Quiché-Mayas of Momostenango* (Norman: University of Oklahoma Press, 1995).

23. Pedro Cortés y Larraz, *Descripción geográfico-moral de la Diocesis de Goathemala. Hecha por su Arzobispo, el Illmo. Sr. Don Pedro Cortés y Larraz del Consejo de S.M.,* Biblioteca "Goathemala" de la sociedad de Geografía e Historia de Guatemala, vol. 20 (Guatemala, 1958 [1770]).

24. Lauria-Santiago, *An Agrarian Republic;* Ching, "Clientelism."

25. Lauria-Santiago, *An Agrarian Republic.*

26. Henrik Ronsbo, "The Embodiment of Male Identities, Alliances, and Cleavages in Salvadoran Soccer," in *Sport, Dance, and Embodied Identities,* ed. Noel Dyck and Eduardo P. Archetti (London: Berg Publishers, 2003).

27. Escobar, *Encountering Development.*

28. Hale, "Between Che"; Nelson, *A Finger;* Warren, *Indigenous Movements.*

29. Kay Treakle, *Indigenous Peoples and Democracy in Latin America* (Basingstoke, England: Macmillan. 1994).

30. IWGIA, *The Indigenous World: International Working Group for Indigenous Affairs* (Copenhagen: IWGIA, 1995).

31. Brysk, "Acting Globally," 37.

32. Henrik Ronsbo, *Indians and Baseball Caps—Ethnicity and Everyday Life in a Salvadoran Village* (Ph.D. diss., Copenhagen University, 1999).

33. A. Gupta. and James Fergusson, eds., *Anthropological Locations—Boundaries and Grounds of a Field Science* (Berkeley: University of California Press, 1997), 35; Michel de Certau, *The Practice of Everyday Life* (Berkeley: University of California Press, 1994).

"El Capitán Cinchazo"

Thanks to Leigh Binford, Ruth Behar, Sueann Caulfield, Esra Ozyürek, and Penelope Papailias for comments on earlier versions of this chapter. I received funding for this research from the Social Science Research Council and the American Council of Learned Societies, the U.S. Institute of Peace, Fulbright-Hays Doctoral Dissertation Research Abroad Fellowship, the Organization of American States, and the University of Michigan.

1. Taped interview, San Salvador, 18 May 1998. All names have been changed. I have translated all Spanish to English unless otherwise noted.

2. E. Valentine Daniel, *Charred Lullabies: Chapters in an Anthropography of Violence.* (Princeton, N.J.: Princeton University Press, 1996), 208.

3. According to the University Institute of Public Opinion (IUDOP) of San Salvador's UCA and the Interamerican Development Bank (IBD), an average 131 intentional murders occurred for every 100,000 citizens from 1994 to 1996, compared with an estimated 130 violent deaths per 100,000 during the twelve-year war. IUDOP, "La violencia en El Salvador en los años noventa. Magnitud, costos, y factores posibilitadores," working paper R-338, Interamerican Development Bank, Washington, D.C., October 1998.

4. José Miguel Cruz, "La violencia en El Salvador," in *Estudios Centroamericanos (ECA)* 569 (March 1996): 242.

5. José Miguel Cruz (of IUDOP) points to a "lack of credibility" and "lack of political willingness" among Salvadoran state institutions to statistical rigor in collecting crime statistics, José Miguel Cruz, Alvaro Trigueros Argüello, and Francisco González, "The Social and Economic Factors Associated with Violent Crime in El Salvador" (paper presented at "Crime and Violence: Causes and Policy Responses" conference, Universidad de los Andes, Bogotá, Colombia, May 1999, part of the World Bank project *Crime and Violence in Latin America,* November 1999, 3.

6. I use the term *entextualization* in the sense of the movement of detached texts through transformations in genre, first discussed in detail by Charles Briggs and Richard Bauman, "Genre, Intertextuality, and Social Power," *Journal of Linguistic Anthropology* 2 (2): 131–72. Greg Urban further develops this idea: "Entextualization is understood as the process of rendering a given instance of discourse a text, detachable from its local context." See Greg Urban, "Entextualization, Replication, and Power," in *Natural Histories of Discourse,* ed. Michael Silverstein and Greg Urban (Chicago: University of Chicago Press, 1996), 21.

7. Taped interview by author, San Salvador, 20 May 1998.

8. Raymond Williams. *Marxism and Literature* (Oxford: Oxford University Press, 1977), 121–27.

9. Ibid, 125.

10. United Nations, *De la locura a la esperanza: La guerra de 12 años en El Salvador: Informe de la Comisión de la Verdad para El Salvador* (New York: United Nations, 1993), 213. In the words of Boutros Boutros-Ghali, the commission judged the Supreme Court to be "incapable of fairly assessing and carrying out the punishment."

11. The cartoon ran during the 1994–1995 tenure of the San Salvador newsweekly *Primera Plana.* Editor Miguel Huezo Mixco confirmed the comic strip's connection to the case, in a September 1995 interview.

12. Most adult Salvadorans know who used these: the Army, M-16, and the National Guard, G-3.

13. "Go on!" "Fuck that!" "Careful bitch!" "Get to the corner!" "Hey man!"

14. Cynthia Arnson, "Window on the Past: A Declassified History of Death Squads

in El Salvador," in *Death Squads in Global Perspective: Murder with Deniability,* ed. Bruce Campbell and Arthur D. Brenner, 85–124 (New York: St. Martin's Press, 2000).

15. In E. Valentine Daniel's interpretation of C. S. Peirce's semiotic philosophy. See E. Valentine Daniel, *Fluid Signs: Being a Person the Tamil Way* (Berkeley: University of California Press, 1984). Through the sign, one knows something about the object. The most general definition of a sign is something that stands *to* somebody (an "interpretant") *for* something (an "object") in some respect or capacity. Peirce delineated three different modes of signs: *iconic, indexical,* and *symbolic.* An object connects to an *iconic* sign through likeness (a statue); some material connection links an object to its *indexical* sign (for example, a pointing weathervane); convention adheres the object to its *symbolic* sign.

16. Margaret Popkin, Jack Spence, and George Vickers, *Justice Delayed: The Slow Pace of Judicial Reform in El Salvador* (Washington, D.C./Cambridge, Mass.: Washington Office on Latin America/Hemisphere Initiatives, December 1994), xx.

17. M. M. Bakhtin, *Problems of Dostoevsky's Poetics,* ed. and trans. Caryl Emerson (Minneapolis: University of Minnesota Press, 1984), xxxvi.

18. IUDOP, "La violencia."

19. *Diario Latino,* 22 June 1994, p. 1, "Cinco muertos y el robo de dos millones y medio de colones en asalto efectuado hoy en la capital." Later versions put the death toll at four and the take at 1.5 million *colones.*

20. *La Prensa Gráfica,* 23 June 1994, p. 3, "6 muertos en asalto a vehiculo blíndado."

21. The PN officer adds a weapon that no other witness reported: AK-47s, known weapons of the guerrillas, in the bank robbers' arsenal.

22. *El Diario de Hoy,* 23 June 1994, pp. 1–4, "Ciudadanía exige seguridad."

23. *La Prensa Gráfica,* 24 June 1994, Editorial, "Esta no es delincuencia común."

24. Wilkinson 1994. Tracy Wilkinson, "Law Enforcement: Cop's Alleged Role in Heist May Be Last Straw in El Salvador" *Los Angeles Times,* 8 July 1994.

25. Gino Costa, *La Policía Nacional Civil de El Salvador (1990–1997)* (San Salvador: UCA Editores, 1999), 167–68.

26. *La Prensa Gráfica,* 28 June 1994, editorial.

27. *El Salvador Proceso 617,* 29 June 1994, editorial, "Who Is Investigating?"

28. Indeed, only a week before, forty-four *"huelepegas,"* homeless youth who likely begin sniffing glue to stave off hunger pangs, had been arrested at the Plaza Libertad. Quote from *Entrevista Al Día,* Channel 12, 29 June 1994, transcribed by INSISTEM; cited in Flor de Izote's newsletter.

29. *Diario Latino,* 29 June 1994, editorial.

30. The Joint Group for the Investigation of Illegally Armed Groups with Political Motivation (Joint Group) was mandated to investigate political killings from January 1992 until January 1994. It found that post–Peace Accords activities of wartime death squads included such organized crime activities as car theft, kidnapping, blackmail, and narcotics trafficking. Summary from Human Rights Watch/Americas, "Darkening Horizons: Human Rights on the Eve of the March 1994 Elections" in *Human Rights Watch* 6, no. 4 (March 1994), 2.

31. Joint Group, *Informe del Grupo Conjunto para la Investigacion de Grupos Armados Ilegales con Motivación Política en El Salvador* (San Salvador: United Nations, 28 July 1994).

32. United Nations, *United Nations and El Salvador 1990–1995*, UN Blue Books Series, vol. 4 (New York: United Nations, 1996), 515, 536, 577.

33. UN, "ONUSAL: Mission Accomplished. Verification Group Set Up," in *United Nations Chronicle*, June 1995, 7.

34. José Miguel Cruz, "El autoritarianismo en la posguerra: un estudio de las actitudes de los salvadoreños," in *Estudios Centroamericanos (ECA)* 603 (January 1999): 95–106; *Primera Plana*, 23 December 1994–95 January 1995, 4–6, "Personajes hechos en El Salvador."

35. RUZ, *100 Caricaturas sin gracia* (San Salvador: CONCULTURA, 1995); *Primera Plana*, 23 December 1994–5 January 1995, 4–6 "Personajes hechos en El Salvador."

36. Two government prosecutors would protest many irregularities in the actions of the judge who freed Coreas while refusing to carry out the inquiries they had asked for—including a scientific comparison of the facial features of Coreas and the figure filmed. *La Prensa Gráfica*, 21 January 1995, "Tte. Coreas vrs. video inoportuno."

37. *La Prensa Gráfica*, 2 February 1995, "La honra y la gloria es para Jesucristo."

38. Taped interview by author, Soyapango, 21 August 1998.

39. Taped interview by author, Santa Tecla, November 1998.

40. *El Diario de Hoy*, 6 June 1999, 2, "Libres dos acusados de asaltar camión blindado."

41. *La Prensa Gráfica*, 8 June 1999, 9, "¿Quién asaltó el blindado?"

42. Cinchazo reemerged in the news in July 2003, when one of the suspects absolved in the case, Gonzalo Alberto Salmerón Villanueva, became the subject of witness testimony in another case. The witness claimed Salmerón participated in Cinchazo, as well as other crimes, including the robbery of an armored car in September 2000 in the town of Ilobasco. "It's the first possibility that Salvadoran justice has to be able to prove his participation in these kinds of illicit activities," commented prosecutor Daniel Martínez." *La Prensa Gráfica*, 28 July 2003, 14, "Testigo implica asaltante de blindado."

43. Cynthia Keppley Mahmood, "Trials by Fire: Dynamics of Terror in Punjab and Kashmir," in *Death Squad: The Anthropology of State Terror*, ed. Jeffrey A. Sluka (Philadelphia: University of Pennsylvania Press, 2000), 70–90.

In the Stream of Money

1. Mario Lungo Uncles, *El Salvador en los 80: contrainsurgencia y revolucion* (EDUCA-FLACSO, 1990), chap. 3.

2. In March 2001 I spoke with Gabriel Siri, who at that time was residing in Washington, D.C., and working for the World Bank.

3. See, for example, Mario Lungo, ed., *Migracion internacional y desarrollo*, 2 vols. (San Salvador: FUNDE, 1997).

4. Discussion with Kay Eekhoff, research director of FUNDE in 1996–1997.

5. In spring 2000 I spoke with Lubbock: "Marvin was a great guy; full of energy and enthusiasm. I really enjoyed meeting him," the photographer recalled.

6. See Roger Rouse, "Making Sense of Settlement: Class Transformation, Cultural Struggle, and Transnationalism among Mexican Migrants in the United States," in *Toward a Transnational Perspective on Migration: Race, Class, Ethnicity, and Nationalism Reconsidered,* ed. Nina Glick Schiller, Linda Basch, and Cristina Blanc-Szanton, *Annals of the New York Academy of Sciences* 645 (6 July 1992): 25–52.

7. See *Washington Post,* 19 July 1989, A1, Lynn Duke, "Drugs Are Shadowy Force in D.C. Area's Economy"; and Peter Reuter, Robert MaCoun, and Patrick Murphy, *Summary of Money from Crime: The Economics of Drug Dealing in Washington, D.C.* (Washington, D.C.: Greater Washington Research Center, 1990).

8. UPI, Kentucky News Briefs, 7 October 1987.

9. Peter R. Andreas and Kenneth E. Sharpe, "Cocaine Politics in the Andes," *Current History,* February (1992): 74–79.

10. Andreas and Sharp, "Cocaine Politics."

Bibliography

Adams, Richard N. *Cultural Surveys of Panama-Nicaragua-Guatemala-El Salvador-Honduras.* Washington D.C.: Pan American Sanitary Bureau, 1957.

Alonso, Ana Maria. *The Thread of Blood: Colonialism, Revolution, and Gender on Mexico's Northern Frontier.* Tucson: University of Arizona Press, 1995.

Alvarenga, Patricia. *Cultura y ética de la violencia: El Salvador 1880–1932.* San José: EDUCA, 1996.

———. "Los indígenas y el estado: Alianzas y estrategias políticas en la construcción del poder local (1920–1944)." In *Memorias del Mestizaje,* edited by Darío Euraque, Jeffrey L. Gould, and Charles R. Hale. Antigua, Guatemala: CIRMA, 2003.

Americas Watch. *Free Fire. A Report on Human Rights in El Salvador.* New York: Americas Watch, 1984.

———. *Settling Into Routine: Human Rights Abuses in Duarte's Second Year.* New York: Americas Watch, 1986.

———. *The Civilian Toll, 1986–1987.* Ninth supplement to the Report on Human Rights in El Salvador. New York: Americas Watch, 1987.

Anderson, Thomas. *Matanza: El Salvador's Communist Revolt of 1932.* Lincoln: University of Nebraska Press, 1971.

Anonymous. *Rutilio Grande, mártir de la evangelización rural en El Salvador.* San Salvador: UCA Editores, 1978.

Arguello Sibrian, Petrona Josefina. "El Desarrollo del Pensamiento Político/Ideológico de los Campesinos Desplazados por el conflicto armado en El Salvador." Master's thesis, University of San Salvador, 1990.

Arias Peñate, Salvador. *Los subsistemas de agroexportacion en El Salvador.* San Salvador: UCA, 1988.

Arizpe, Lourdes. *Parentesco y economia en una sociedad nahua.* México City: INI, 1973.

Armstrong, Robert, and Janet Shenk. *El Salvador The Face of Revolution.* Boston, Mass.: South End Press, 1982.

Arnson, Cynthia. *El Salvador: A Revolution Confronts the United States.* Washington, D.C.: Institute for Policy Studies and the Transnational Institute, 1982.

———. "Window on the Past: A Declassified History of Death Squads in El Salvador." In *Death Squads in Global Perspective: Murder with Deniability,* edited by Bruce Campbell and Arthur D. Brenner, 85–124. New York: St. Martin's Press, 2000.

Bacevich, A. J., J. D. Hallums, R. H. White, and T. F. Young. *American Military Policy in Small Wars: The Case of El Salvador.* Paper presented at the John F. Kennedy School of Government, Harvard University, 1988.

Baloyra, Enrique. *El Salvador in Transition.* Chapel Hill: University of North Carolina Press, 1982.

Baron Castro, Rodolfo. *La Población de El Salvador.* San Salvador: UCA Editores, 1978.

Barry, Tom. *El Salvador: A Country Guide.* Albuquerque, N.Mex.: The Inter-Hemispheric Education Resource Center, 1990.

Binford, Leigh. *The El Mozote Massacre: Anthropology and Human Rights.* Tucson: University of Arizona Press, 1996.

———. "Hegemony in the Interior of the Revolution: The ERP in Northern Morazán, El Salvador." *Journal of Latin American Anthropology* 4, no. 1 (1999): 2–45.

———. "After the Revolution: Economic Autarky in Northern Morazán, El Salvador." Manuscript, 2002.

———. "Violence in El Salvador: A Rejoinder to Philippe Bourgois's 'The Power of Violence in War and Peace: Post–Cold War Lessons from El Salvador.'" *Ethnography* 3, no. 1 (2002): 177–95.

———. "The History of Fabio: Peasant Intellectuals and the End of Testimonio?" Manuscript.

Bonner, Raymond. *Weakness and Deceit: U.S. Policy in El Salvador.* New York: Times Books, 1984.

Bourdieu, Pierre. *The Logic of Practice.* Palo Alto, Calif.: Stanford University Press, 1990.

Bourgois, Philippe. "The Power of Violence in War and Peace: Post–Cold War Lessons from El Salvador." *Ethnography* 2, no. 1 (2001): 5–34.

———. "The Violence of Moral Binaries: Rejoinder to Leigh Binford." *Ethnography* 3, no. 1 (2002): 221–31.

Briggs, Charles, and Richard Bauman. "Genre, Intertextuality, and Social Power." *Journal of Linguistic Anthropology* 2 (2): 131–72.

Brockett, Charles D. *Land, Power, and Poverty: Agrarian Transformation and Political Conflict in Central America.* 2d ed. Boulder, Colo.: Westview Press, 1998.

Browning, David. *El Salvador. La tierra y el hombre.* San Salvador: Dirección de Publicaciones e Impresos, CONCULTURA, 1975.

Brysk, Alison. "Acting Globally: Indian Rights and International Politics in Latin America." In *Indigenous Peoples and Democracy in Latin America,* edited by Donna Lee van Cott, 29–51. Basingstoke, England: Macmillan, 1994.

———. "Turning weakness into strength: the internationalization of Indian rights." In *Latin American Perspectives: A Journal on Capitalism and Socialism* 23, no. 2 (1996): 38–57.

Bulmer-Thomas, Victor. *The Political Economy of Central America since 1920.* Cambridge: Cambridge University Press, 1987.

Cabarrús, Carlos Rafael. *Génesis de una revolución. Análisis del surgimiento y desarrollo de la organización campesina en El Salvador.* México, D.F.: Ediciones de la Casa Chata, 1983.

Cagan, Steve, and Beth Cagan. *This Promised Land El Salvador: The Refugee Community of Colomoncagua and Their Return to Morazán.* Piscataway, N.J.: Rutgers University Press, 1991.

Camarda, R., et al. *Forced to Move: Salvadoran Refugees in Mexico.* San Francisco: Bureau for the Americas, Evaluation and Policy, 1985.

Campbell, Lyle. *The Pipil Language of El Salvador.* Berlin: Mouton Publishers, 1985.

Cardenal, Rodolfo. *Historia de una esperanza: vida de Rutilio Grande.* San Salvador: UCA Editores, 1985.

Carmack, Robert M. *Rebels of Highland Guatemala: The Quiché-Mayas of Momostenango.* Norman: University of Oklahoma Press, 1995.

CEPAL-FAO-OIT. *Tenencia de la tierra y desarrollo rural en centroamerica.* San José: EDUCA, 1973.

Chapin, Marc. "La población indígena de El Salvador." In *Mesoamérica* 21 (1991).

Ching, Erik. "From Clientelism to Militarism. The State, Politics, and Authoritarianism in El Salvador, 1840–1940." Ph.D. diss., University of California, Santa Barbara, 1997.

———. "In Search of the Party: The Communist Party, the Comintern, and the Peasant Rebellion of 1932 in El Salvador." *The Americas* 55, no. 2 (1998): 204–39.

Ching, Erik, and Virginia Tilley. "Indians, the Military, and the Rebellion of 1932 in El Salvador." *Journal of Latin American Studies* 30 (1998).

Cortés y Larraz, Pedro. "Descripción geografico-moral de la Diocesis de Goathemala. Hecha por su Arzobispo, el Illmo. Sr. Don Pedro Cortes y Larraz del Consejo de S.M." In *Biblioteca "Goathemala" de la sociedad de Geografía e Historia de Guatemala,* vol. 20. Guatemala: Central America, 1958 [1770].

Costa, Gino. *La Policía Nacional Civil de El Salvador (1990–1997).* San Salvador: UCA Editores, 1999.

Cruz José, Miguel, "Los factores posibilatadores y las expresiones de la violencia en los noventa." *Estudios Centroamericanos* 588 (1977): 977–92.

Cruz, José Miguel. "La violencia en El Salvador." In *Estudios Centroamericanos (ECA)* 569 (March 1996): 240–49.

Cruz, José Miguel. "El autoritarianismo en la posguerra: un estudio de las actitudes de los salvadoreños." In *Estudios Centroamericanos* 603 (January 1999): 95–106.

Cruz, José Miguel, Alvaro Trigueros Argüello, and Francisco González. "The Social and Economic Factors Associated with Violent Crime in El Salvador." Paper presented at conference "Crime and Violence: Causes and Policy Responses." Universidad de los Andes, Bogotá, May 1999, as part of the World Bank project *Crime and Violence in Latin America,* November 1999.

Dalton, Juan José. "Refundar nación con la verdad." In *La Prensa Gráfica,* 4 June 2000.

Dalton, Roque. *Miguel Marmol*. Willimantic, Conn.: Curbstone Press, 1987.

Daniel, E. Valentine. *Charred Lullabies: Chapters in an Anthropography of Violence*. Princeton, N.J.: Princeton University Press, 1996.

de Certau, Michel. *The Practice of Everyday Life*. Berkeley: University of California Press, 1994.

Diskin, Martin. "Distilled Conclusions: The Disappearance of the Agrarian Question in El Salvador." *Latin American Research Review* 31, no. 2 (1996): 111–26.

Diskin, Martin, and Kenneth E. Sharpe. "El Salvador." In *Confronting Revolution*, edited by Morris J. Blachman, William M. Leogand, and Kenneth Sharpe. New York: Pantheon, 1986.

Dunkerley, James. *The Long War: Dictatorship and Revolution in El Salvador* (London: Junction Books, 1982).

———. *Power in the Isthmus* (London: Verso, 1988).

Durham, William. *Scarcity and Survival in Central America: The Ecological Origins of the Soccer War*. Stanford, Calif.: Stanford University Press, 1979.

Edelman, Marc. "Transnational Peasant Politics in Central America." *Latin American Research Review* 33, no. 3 (1998): 49–86.

Edwards, Beatrice, and Gretta Tovar Siebentritt. *Places of Origin: The Repopulation of Rural El Salvador*. Boulder, Colo.: Lynne Rienner, 1991.

Equipo Postoral de la Comunidad de Reparados "Ignacio Martín Baro." "Historia del cantón La Joya, que comprende desde el año 1968 hasta 1993." Sociedad, Morazán, mimeo, 1993.

Escobar, Arturo. *Encountering Development: The Making and Unmaking of the Third World*. Princeton, N.J.: Princeton University Press, 1994.

Farah, Douglas. "U.N. Closing Book on Rare Success Story." *Washington Post*, 21 April 1995.

Ferguson, James. *The Anti-Politics Machine: "Development," Depoliticization, and Bureaucratic Power in Lesotho*. London: Cambridge University Press, 1990.

Fish, Joe, and Christina Sganga. *El Salvador: Testament of Terror* (New York: Olive Branch Press, 1988).

Fogaroli, Serena, and Sara Stowell. *Desarrollo rural y participación campesina: El caso de Tecoluca (San Vicente, El Salvador)*. San Salvador: Universidad Centroamericana, "José Simeón Cañas," Departamento de Economía, 1997.

Foucault, Michel. *Discipline and Punish: The Birth of the Prison*. New York: Vintage, 1977.

Fowler, James. *The Cultural Evolution of Ancient Nahua Civilizations. The Pipil-Nicarao of Central America*. Norman: University of Oklahoma Press, 1989.

———. "The Political Economy of Indian Survival in Sixteenth-Century Izalco, El Salvador." In *The Spanish Borderlands Perspective*, edited by David Hurst Thomas. Washington, D.C.: Smithsonian Institution Press, 1991.

FUNDE. "Diagnostico Agro-socioeconomico Microregion VI Oriente." Unpublished report. San Salvador: 1997.

Gamson, William. *Talking Politics*. Cambridge: Cambridge University Press, 1992.

Geertz, Clifford. *Conocimiento local. Ensayos sobre la nterpretacion de las culturas.* Barcelona: PAIDOS, 1994.

————. *La interpretación de las culturas.* México City: GEDISA, 1987.

Gersony, Robert, Raymond Lynch, and William Garvelink. *The Journey Home: Durable Solutions for the Displaced.* San Salvador: USAID, 1986.

Gettlemen, Marvin et al. *El Salvador: Central America in the New Cold War.* New York: Grove Press, 1986.

Gibb, Tom. "Salvador: Under the Shadow of Dreams." Manuscript, 2000.

Goitia, Alfonso. "La Lucha por la Tierra en Centroamérica." Documento de trabajo, no. 13. San Salvador: FUNDE, February 1993.

Goitia, Alfonso, and Ernesto Galdámez. "El Salvador: Movimiento Campesino." In *Modernización en el Agro y Movimiento Campesino en Centroamérica,* edited by Klaus D. Tangermann and Ivana Ríos Valdés, 133–58. Managua: Latino Editores, 1994.

Gould, Jeffrey L. "Revolutionary Nationalism and Local Memories in El Salvador." In *Reclaiming "the Political" in Latin American History: The View from the North,* edited by Gilbert Joseph. Durham, N.C.: Duke University Press, 2001.

Grenier, Yvon. *The Emergence of Insurgency in El Salvador: Ideology and Political Will.* Pittsburgh, University of Pittsburgh Press, 1999.

Gupta, A., and Fergusson, James, eds. *Anthropological Locations—Boundaries and Grounds of a Field Science.* Berkeley: University of California Press, 1997.

Hale, Charles R. "Between Che Guevara and the Pachamama: Mestizos, Indians, and Identity Politics in the Anti-Quincentenary Campaign." *Critique of Anthropology* 14, no. 1 (1994).

————. *Resistance and Contradiction—Miskitu Indians and the Nicaraguan State, 1894–1987.* Palo Alto, Calif.: Stanford University Press. 1994.

Hammond, John L. *Fighting to Learn: Popular Education and Guerrilla War in El Salvador.* Piscataway, N.J.: Rutgers University Press, 1998.

Hernández Rodriguez, M., and K. I. Mendez. *Marco Histórico-Social y Socio-Cultural de Las Vueltas.* Dept. de Chalatenango. IV. Año de Lic. en Letras. San Salvador: Universidad Nacional de El Salvador, 1996.

Human Rights Watch/Americas. "Darkening Horizons: Human Rights on the Eve of the March 1994 Elections." *Human Rights Watch* 6, no. 4 (March 1994).

IUDOP. "La violencia en El Salvador en los años noventa. Magnitud, costos, y factores posibilitadores." Working paper R-338, Interamerican Development Bank, Washington, D.C., October 1998.

IWGIA. "The Indigenous World." International Working Group for Indigenous Affairs. Copenhagen: IWGIA, 1995.

Jackson, Jean. "Culture, Genuine and Spurious: The Politics of Indianness in the Vaupés, Colombia." *American Ethnologist* 22, no. 1 (1995).

Joint Group. *Informe del Grupo Conjunto para la Investigacion de Grupos Armados Ilegales con Motivación Política en El Salvador.* San Salvador: United Nations, 28 July 1994.

Joseph, Gilbert M., and Daniel Nugent, eds. *Everyday Forms of State Formation: Revolution and the Negotiation of Rule in Modern Mexico.* Durham, N.C.: Duke University Press, 1994.

Kearney, Michael. *Reconceptualizing the Peasantry. Anthropology in Global Perspective.* Boulder, Colo.: Westview Press, 1996.

Keune, Lou. *Sobrevivimos la guerra: La historia de los pobladores de Arcatao y de San José de las Flores.* San Salvador: Adelina Editores, 1995.

Kincaid, Douglas A. "Peasants into Rebels: Community and Class in Rural El Salvador." *Comparative Studies in Society and History* 29, no. 3 (1987): 466–94.

Kincaid, Douglas. *Agrarian Development, Peasant Mobilization, and Social Change in Central America: A Comparative Study.* Ph.D. diss., Johns Hopkins University, 1987.

Klare, Michael T., and Peter Kornbluh. *Low Intensity Warfare.* New York: Pantheon, 1988.

Lara Martínez, Carlos Benjamín. *Joya de ceren. La dinamica sociocultural de una comunidad semi-campesina de el salvador.* San Salvador: UNESCO-CONCULTURA, en prensa, 1997.

Larín, Aristides Augusto. *Historia del movimiento sindical de El Salvador.* San Salvador: Editorial Universitaria, 1971.

Lauria-Santiago, Aldo A. "Los Indígenas de Cojutepeque, la politica faccional, y el estado nacional en El Salvador, 1830–1890." In *Construcción de las identidades y del estado moderno en Centro América,* edited by Arturo Taracena. San José: UCA Editores/CEMCA/FLACSO, 1995.

————. "'That a Poor Man Be Industrious': Coffee, Community, and Agrarian Capitalism in the Transformation of El Salvador's Ladino Peasantry, 1760–1900." In *Identity and Struggle at the Margins of the Nation-State: The Laboring Peoples of Central America and the Hispanic Caribbean, 1850–1950,* edited by Aldo A. Lauria-Santiago and Aviva Chomsky. Durham, N.C.: Duke University Press, 1998.

————. *An Agrarian Republic: Commercial Agriculture and the Politics of Peasant Communities in El Salvador, 1823–1914.* Pittsburgh, Pa.: University of Pittsburgh Press, 1999.

Lauria-Santiago, Aldo A., and Jeffrey Gould. "'They Call Us Thieves and Steal Our Wage': Toward a Reinterpretation of the Salvadoran Rural Mobilization, 1929–1931." *Hispanic American Historical Review,* (May 2004).

Lernoux, Penny. *Cry of the People.* New York: Penguin, 1982.

Long, Norman, and Ann Long, eds. *Battlefields of Knowledge: The Interlocking of Theory and Practice in Social Research and Development.* London: Routledge 1992.

López Bernal, Carlos Gregorio. *El proyecto liberal de nación en El Salvador (1876–1932).* Master's thesis, Universidad de Costa Rica, 1998.

López Vigil, María. *Muerte y vida en Morazán: Testimonio de un sacerdote.* San Salvador: Universidad de Centroamérica, José Simeón Cañas, 1987.

Lovell, George V. *Conquest and Survival in Colonial Guatemala. A Historical Geography of the Cuchumatán Highlands (1520–1821).* Toronto: McGill-Queen's Press, 1985.

Macdonald, Mandy, and Mike Gatehouse. *In the Mountains of Morazán, Portrait of a Returned Refugee Community in El Salvador.* New York: Monthly Review Press, 1995.

Macleod, Murdo J. *Spanish Central America: A Socioeconomic History, 1520–1720.* Berkeley: University of California Press, 1973.

Mahmood, Cynthia Keppley. "Trials by Fire: Dynamics of Terror in Punjab and Kashmir." In *Death Squad: The Anthropology of State Terror,* edited by Jeffrey A. Sluka, 70–90. Philadelphia: University of Pennsylvania Press, 2000.

Marroquín, Alejandro D. "El problema Indígena en El Salvador." *America Indígena* 35, no. 4 (1975), D.F. de Mexico.

Martín-Baro, Ignacio. "Psicología del campesino Salvadoreño." *Estudios Centro Americanos* 28 (297–298): 476–95.

———. "The Lazy Latino: The Ideological Nature of Latin American Fatalism." In *Writings for a Liberation Psychology.* Cambridge, Mass.: Harvard University Press, 1994.

McAdam, Doug. *Political Process and the Development of Black Insurgency, 1930–1970.* Chicago: University of Chicago Press, 1982.

McCarthy, John D., and Mayer N. Zald. *The Trend of Social Movements in America: Professionalization and Resource Mobilization.* Morristown, N.J.: General Learning Press, 1973.

McClintock, Michael. *State Terror and Popular Resistance in El Salvador.* Vol. 1 of *The American Connection.* London: Zed Books, 1985.

Medrano, Juan Ramón, and Walter Raudales. *Ni militar ni sacerdote (de seudónimo Balta).* San Salvador: Arcoiris, 1994.

Menjívar, Rafael. *Formación y lucha del proletariado industrial salvadoreño.* 4th ed. Vol. 7 of *Colección Estructuras y procesos.* San Salvador: UCA Editores, 1987.

Migdal, Joel. *Peasants, Politics, and Revolution: Pressure toward Social Change in the Third World.* Princeton, N.J.: Princeton University Press, 1974.

Montes, Segundo. *Desplazados y refugiados.* San Salvador: UCA, 1985.

———. *El agro salvadoreño (1973–1980).* San Salvador: UCA, 1986.

———. *En busca de soluciones para los desplazados.* San Salvador: UCA, 1986.

———. *El Compadrazgo: Una Estructura de poder en El Salvador.* San Salvador: UCA Editores, 1987.

Montgomery, Tommie Sue. *Revolution in El Salvador: From Civil Strife to Civil Peace.* 2nd ed. Boulder, Colo.: Westview Press, 1995.

Montoya, Aquiles. *La Nueva Economía Popular.* San Salvador: UCA, 1993.

———. "La Realidad Agraria en El Salvador de Fines del Siglo." In *El Salvador a Fin de Siglo,* edited by Guido Béjar, Rafael Roggenbuck, and Stefan Roggenbuck, 89–136. San Salvador: Fundación Konrad Adenauer/UCA, 1995.

Morris, Aldon. *The Origins of the Civil Rights Movement: Black Communities Organizing for Change.* New York: Free Press, 1984.

Nelson, Diane M. *A Finger in the Wound—Body Politics in Quincentennial Guatemala.* Berkeley: University of California Press, 1999.

Nugent, David. *Modernity at the Edge of Empire: State, Individual, and Nation in the Northern Peruvian Andes, 1885–1935.* Palo Alto, Calif.: Stanford University Press, 1997.

Paige, Jeffrey. *Agrarian Revolution: Social Movements and Export Agriculture in the Underdeveloped World*. New York: Free Press, 1975.

———. "Land Reform and Agrarian Revolution in El Salvador: Comment on Seligson and Diskin," *Latin American Research Review* 31, no. 2 (1996): 127–39.

Palerm, Angel. *Antropología y marxismo*. México City: Nueva Imagen, 1980.

Parkman, Patricia. *Nonviolent Insurrection in El Salvador. The Fall of Maximiliano Hernández Martínez*. Tucson: University of Arizona Press, 1988.

Pearce, Jenny. *Promised Land: Peasant Rebellion in Chalatenango, El Salvador*. London: Latin American Bureau, 1986.

Pérez-Brignoli, Hector. "Indians, Communist, and Peasants: The 1932 Rebellion in El Salvador." In *Coffee, Society, and Power in Latin America*, edited by William Roseberry et. al., 232–61. Baltimore, Md.: Johns Hopkins University Press, 1995.

Peterson, Anna L. *Martyrdom and the Politics of Reason: Progressive Catholicism in El Salvador's Civil War*. Albany, N.Y.: SUNY Press, 1997.

Popkin, Margaret, Jack Spence, and George Vickers. *Justice Delayed: The Slow Pace of Judicial Reform in El Salvador*. Washington, D.C.: Washington Office on Latin America, December 1994; Cambridge, Mass.: Hemisphere Initiatives, December 1994.

Popkin, Samuel. *The Rational Peasant: The Political Economy of Rural Society in Vietnam*. Berkeley: University of California Press, 1979.

Portes, Alejandro. "Social Capital: Its Origins and Applications in Modern Sociology." *Annual Review of Sociology* 24 (1998): 1–24.

Pratt, Mary Louise. *Imperial Eyes: Travel Writing and Transculturation*. London: Routledge, 1992.

Richard, Pablo, and Guillermo Melendez. *La iglesia de los pobres en América Central: un análisis socio-político y teológico de la iglesia centroamericana (1960–1982)*. San José, Costa Rica: Departamento Ecumenico de Investigaciones, 1982.

Ronsbo, Henrik. *Landscapes Full of Spanish Dreams—Indians, Land Reform, and State Formation in the Salvadoran Space* (in Danish). Master's thesis, Roskilde University, 1994.

———. *Indians and Baseball Caps—Ethnicity and Everyday Life in a Salvadoran Village*. Ph.D. diss., Copenhagen, Copenhagen University, 1999.

———. "The Embodiment of Male Identities, Alliances, and Cleavages in Salvadoran Soccer." In *Performing Bodies: Sport, Dance, and Identity*. Oxford: Berg Publishers, forthcoming.

Roseberry, William. "Hegemony and the Language of Contention." In *Everyday Forms of State Formation: Revolution and the Negotiation of Rule in Modern Mexico*, edited by Gilbert M. Joseph and Daniel Nugent, 355–66. Durham, N.C.: Duke University Press, 1994.

Rubin, Jeffrey. *Decentering the Regime: Ethnicity, Radicalism, and Democracy in Juchitán, Mexico*. Durham, N.C.: Duke University Press, 1997.

RUZ. *100 Caricaturas sin gracia*. San Salvador: CONCULTURA, 1995.

Scott, James C. *The Moral Economy of the Peasant: Rebellion and Subsistence in Southeast Asia*. New Haven, Conn.: Yale University Press, 1976.

Seligson, Mitchell A. "Thirty Years of Transformation in the Agrarian Structure of El Salvador, 1961–1991." *Latin American Research Review* 30, no. 3 (1995): 43–74.

Seligson, Mitchell A., and Vincent J. McElhinny. "Facing Up or About Face: Agrarian Inequality and the Prospects for Rural Development in Post-War El Salvador." Paper presented at the annual meeting of the Latin American Studies Association, Washington, D.C., September 2001.

Sider, Gerald Lumbee. *Indian Histories: Race, Ethnicity, and Indian Identity in the Southern United States.* Cambridge: Cambridge University Press, 1993.

Silverstein, Michael, and Greg Urban. "The Natural History of Discourse." In *Natural Histories of Discourse*, 1–17. Chicago: University of Chicago Press, 1996.

Skocpol, Theda. *States and Social Revolutions.* Cambridge: Cambridge University Press, 1979.

Snow, David A., Louis A. Zurcher, and Sheldon Eckland-Olson. "Social Networks and Social Movements: A Micro-Structural Approach to Differential Recruitment." *American Sociological Review* 45 (1980): 787–801.

Staggenborg, Suzanne. "Social Movement Communities and Cycles of Protest: The Emergence and Maintenance of a Local Women's Movement." *Social Problems* 45, no. 2 (1998): 180–204.

Stanley, William. *The Protection Racket State: Elite Politics, Military Extortion, and Civil War in El Salvador.* Philadelphia, Pa.: Temple University Press, 1996.

Sundaram, Anjali, and George Gelber. *A Decade of War: El Salvador Confronts the Future.* New York: Monthly Review, 1991.

Tarrow, Sydney. "Mentalities, Political Cultures, and Collective Action Frames." In *Frontiers in Social Movements*, edited by Aldon Morris and Carol McClurg Mueller, 174–202. New Haven, Conn.: Yale University Press, 1992.

Thompson, Marilyn. *Women of El Salvador: The Price of Freedom.* Philadelphia, Pa.: Institute for the Study of Human Issues, 1986.

Thompson, Martha. "Repopulated Communities in El Salvador." In *The New Politics of Survival: Grassroots Movements in Central America*, edited by Minor Sinclair, 109–51. New York: Monthly Review, 1995.

Tilly, Charles. *From Mobilization to Revolution.* New York: Random House, 1978.

Torres Rivas, Edelberto. *Interpretación del desarrollo social centroamericano.* San José: Educa 1971.

Treakle, Kay. *Indigenous Peoples and Democracy in Latin America.* Basingstoke, England: Macmillan, 1994.

———. "Report on Indigenous Movements." *NACLA Report* 29, no. 5. New York: North American Congress on Latin America.

Turcios, Roberto. *Autoritarismo y modernizacion. El Salvador 1950–1960.* San Salvador: Tendencias, 1993.

United Nations. "ONUSAL: Mission Accomplished. Verification Group Set Up." In *United Nations Chronicle*, June. New York: United Nations, 1995.

————. *De la locura a la esperanza: La guerra de 12 años en El Salvador: Informe de la Comisión de la Verdad para El Salvador.* S/25500. New York: United Nations, 1993.

————. *United Nations and El Salvador 1990–1995. United Nations Blue Books Series,* vol. 4. New York: United Nations, 1996.

Urban, Greg. "Entextualization, Replication, and Power." In *Natural Histories of Discourse,* edited by Michael Silverstein and Greg Urban. Chicago: University of Chicago Press, 1996.

USAID. *Baseline Survey.* San Salvador: USAID, 1985.

Vejar, Rafael Guidos. *El Ascenso del Militarismo en El Salvador.* San Salvador: UCA Editores, 1980.

Villalobos, Joaquín. "El Estado Actual de la Guerra." *Estudios Centroamericanos* 449 (1986): 169–204.

Warman, Arturo. *Y venimos a contradecir. Los campesinos de morelos y el estado nacional.* México City: SEP/CIESAS, 1976.

Warren, Kay B. *Indigenous Movements and Their Critics: Pan-Maya Activism in Guatemala.* Princeton, N.J.: Princeton University Press, 1998.

Webre, Stephen. *Jose Napoleon Duarte and the Christian Democratic Party in Salvadorean Politics 1960–1972.* Baton Rouge: Louisiana State University Press, 1979.

White, Alistair. *El Salvador.* San Salvador: UCA Editores, 1973.

Whitfield, Teresa. *Paying the Price: Ignacio Ellacuría and the Murdered Jesuits of El Salvador.* Philadelphia, Pa.: Temple University Press, 1994.

Wickham-Crowley, Timothy. "Winners, Losers, and Also-Rans: Toward a Comparative Sociology of Guerrilla Movements." In *Power and Popular Protest,* edited by Susan Eckstein, 132–81. Berkeley: University of California Press, 1989.

Wickham-Crowley, Timothy. *Exploring Revolution: Essays on Latin American Insurgency and Revolutionary Theory.* New York: M.E. Sharpe, 1992.

Wood, Elisabeth. *Insurgent Collective and Civil War in El Salvador.* Cambridge, England: Cambridge University Press, 2003.

Williams, Philip, and Knut Walter, *Militarization and Demilitarization in El Salvador's Transition to Democracy.* Pittsburgh, Pa.: University of Pittsburgh Press, 1997.

Williams, Raymond. *Marxism and Literature.* Oxford: Oxford University Press, 1977.

Williams, Robert G. *Export Agriculture and the Crisis in Central America.* Durham, N.C.: University of North Carolina Press, 1986.

Willis, Paul. *Learning to Labour.* New York: Columbia University Press, 1977.

Wilson, Everett A. *The Crisis of National Integration in El Salvador, 1919–1935.* Ph.D. diss., Stanford University, 1970.

Wolf, Eric. *Peasant Wars of the Twentieth Century.* New York: Harper and Row, 1969.

————. *Los campesinos.* Barcelona: Labor, 1971.

————. *Europa y la gente sin historia.* México: FCE, 1994.

Wortman, Miles L. *Government and Society in Central America 1680–1840.* New York: Columbia University Press, 1980.

Wright, Scott. 1994. *Promised Land: Death and Life in El Salvador.* Maryknoll, N.Y.: Orbis Books, 1994.

Contributors

Victor Hugo Acuña Ortega is a Costa Rican historian who works at the University of Costa Rica. He has published many works on the economic and social history of Central America and Costa Rica during the nineteenth and twentieth centuries, and has served as director of the Central American History Institute at the University of Costa Rica.

Leigh Binford is an anthropologist with extensive research on Mexico and El Salvador. Among his books is *The El Mozote Massacre: Anthropology and Human Rights*. After working at the University of Connecticut for thirteen years, he became senior researcher at the Instituto de Ciencias Sociales y Humanidades, Benemérita Universidad Autónoma, in Puebla, Mexico. He currently carries out research on Mexican migration to the United States and Canada.

Erik Ching is a historian with a Ph.D. from the University of California, Santa Barbara. He has worked as assistant professor of history at Furman University since 1998 and currently holds the Herman Hipp Chair. He has authored numerous articles about politics in El Salvador during the 1920s and 1930s, including "Indians, the Military, and the Rebellion of 1932 in El Salvador" with Virginia Tilley.

Leslie Gates is an assistant professor of Sociology at SUNY Binghamton. She received her Ph.D. from the University of Arizona. Her work focuses on gender, workers, and neoliberalism in Mexico.

Kati Griffith is a graduate of College of the Holy Cross. She spent two years carrying out research on gender, workers, and the state in Mexico and El Salvador as a Fulbright Scholar and Rotary Scholar. She is now a law student at NYU and a recipient of the Truman Fellowship.

Lisa Kowalchuk is an assistant professor in the department of sociology and criminology at St. Mary's University in Halifax, where she also teaches courses in the women's studies and international development studies programs. She continues to do field research in El Salvador.

Carlos Benjamín Lara Martínez is a Salvadoran anthropologist who has carried out extensive ethnographic work in El Salvador. He holds a master's degree from the University of Calgary in Canada. He now works in the anthropology program at the University of El Salvador.

Aldo Lauria-Santiago is a historian who has done work on the social and political history of El Salvador from the 1830s to the 1930s. In 1999 he published *An Agrarian Republic: Commercial Agriculture and the Politics of Peasant Communities in El Salvador, 1823–1914*. He is an associate professor at the College of the Holy Cross and director of the Latin American and Latino studies program. He is currently working on a book with Jeffrey Gould on the 1932 revolt and massacre in El Salvador.

Vincent J. McElhinny is a political scientist with a Ph.D. from the University of Pittsburgh. He works at the American Council for Voluntary International Action.

Ellen Moodie, a postdoctoral scholar at the University of Illinois Urbana-Champaign, reported for a daily newspaper for seven years before earning her Ph.D. in anthropology from the University of Michigan in 2002. She is working on a book, *"It's Worse Than the War": Telling Everyday Violence in Postwar El Salvador*. Her current research focuses on the changing ways of seeing "others" and images of criminals in twentieth-century El Salvador.

David Pedersen is an anthropologist with a Ph.D. from the University of Michigan. He teaches at Central Michigan University.

Henrik Ronsbo is an anthropologist with a Ph.D. from the New School for Social Research. He currently works as a researcher at the Rehabilitation and Research Center for Torture Victims in Copenhagen.

Irina Carlota Silber holds a Ph.D. in anthropology from New York University. She is currently a Rockefeller Fellow at the Virginia Foundation for the Humanities.

Elisabeth J. Wood is a political scientist who works as an associate professor at New York University. She has recently published two books: *Forging Democracy from Below: Insurgent Transitions in South Africa and El Salvador* and *Insurgent Collective Action and Civil War in El Salvador*.

Index